WILLIAM PITT
EARL OF CHATHAM

William Pitt, Earl of Chatham,
portrait by William Hoare

WILLIAM PITT
EARL OF CHATHAM
The Great Commoner

Peter Douglas Brown

London
George Allen & Unwin Ltd
Ruskin House   Museum Street

First published in 1978

© George Allen & Unwin (Publishers) Ltd 1978

ISBN 0 04 942145 X

Printed in Great Britain
in 11 point Baskerville type
by W & J Mackay Limited
Chatham

To My Mother

PREFACE

I must firstly express my gratitude to the Master of Balliol College for the sympathy and interest he has consistently taken in my work. I am grateful, too, for valuable advice from many other friends, and in particular Sir R. J. Southern, President of St John's College Oxford, Sir Edgar Williams, Warden of Rhodes House and Fellow of Balliol College, and J. Steven Watson, Vice-Chancellor of the University of St Andrew's.

I would like to thank owners of private collections for granting me access to their muniments, in particular The Duke of Devonshire and the Trustees of the Chatsworth Settlement, The Duke of Marlborough, Earl Spencer and Earl Fitzwilliam. I am most grateful to Lieut-Colonel T. Wragg MBE, Curator of the Chatsworth Collections, for his advice.

I have received every help from the staff of the Public Records Office, The British Museum, The London Library and the Library of the University of Sheffield.

Finally, all my efforts have depended upon Mrs Maura Shaw, Mrs Anthea Ridett and most especially Mrs Margaret Harrison, who have typed this work so many times over without loss of interest or patience, and have so frequently come forward with the most helpful suggestions.

CONTENTS

CONTENTS

CHAPTER 1

Pitt's Early Life

'Temple sprang from a family which, though ancient and
honourable, had, before his time, been scarcely mentioned in
our history, but which, long after his death, produced so many
eminent men, and formed such distinguished alliances, that
it exercised, in a regular and constitutional manner, an
influence in the state scarcely inferior to that which, in widely
different times, and by widely different arts, the house of
Neville attained in England, and that of Douglas in Scotland.
During the latter years of George the Second, and through the
whole reign of George the Third, members of that widely
spread and powerful connection were almost constantly at the
head either of the Government or of the Opposition. There
were times when the cousinhood, as it was once nicknamed,
would of itself have furnished almost all the materials necessary
for the construction of an efficient Cabinet. Within the space
of fifty years, three First Lords of the Treasury, three Secretaries
of State, two Keepers of the Privy Seal, and four First Lords of
the Admiralty, were appointed from among the sons and
grandsons of the Countess Temple.'[1]

Lord Macaulay, 'Sir William Temple, Restoration statesman
and Charles II's Ambassador at The Hague.'

William Pitt, the Great Commoner, together with his son
William the Younger, stand commanding over the canvas of
British history during the second half of the eighteenth century.
They were the architects and consolidators of the glories in war

and peace which made Britain the most wealthy and resilient nation in Europe. Pitt the Elder, by reason of his personification with victory in the Seven Years War, won the hearts of his countrymen irrespective of party or creed. He has been described as the greatest English statesman who ever was, a title bestowed upon none other over the three and a half centuries which elapsed between Elizabeth the Great and Sir Winston Churchill. William Pitt the Younger beat all records by becoming Prime Minister at the age of twenty-four and heading for seventeen years without interruption one of the most effective ministries known since the Glorious Revolution of 1688. He, by his example of resistance without qualification to revolutionary France and Napoleon, set the precedent in the memory of the nation for the rejection of compromise with the Germany of Adolf Hitler.

That this happy combination of talents in father and son should have come to light was due to the instinct for adventure and acquisition in Thomas Pitt, grandfather to the first William. He was born in 1653 when Oliver Cromwell ruled, the third son of the Reverend John Pitt, Rector of Blandford St Mary in Dorset, of the cadet branch of the Pitts of Strathfieldsaye, Hampshire. Landowners in Dorset with a seat at Encombe since Elizabeth I's day, they subsequently acquired by purchase the larger estate and substantial colliery interests in Durham in addition. Young Thomas Pitt was seven at the Restoration, when good King Charles embarked on his days, golden indeed for the squire and parson after the austerities of the Commonwealth. He was of a generation to remember how the losing side in political conflict might suffer material penalties.

To his turbulent spirit the cloth made no appeal and in 1673 he sailed to India. At Madras he married Jane Innes, of an ancient Morayshire family, whose two uncles were in business there. Three sons, Robert, Thomas and John, were born of the marriage and two surviving daughters, Lucy and Essex, the latter a curious name for a girl and lacking explanation. Endowed with the violent and domineering temperament necessary for survival in the uncertain life of the East, far from the control of the authorities at home, Thomas Pitt made a fortune by illegal trading in breach of the East India Company's monopoly. With good health and moral self-assurance, and completely free from sensual inclinations, he would tolerate no obstacle in the government of men or the accumulation of material possessions. His temper ran to extremes of friendship and enmity, of parsimony and ostentation.

Thomas Pitt returned home in 1683 and bought land in Dorset and Wiltshire, his native country, and also in Berkshire, with two places, Mawarden Court near Salisbury and Swallow-field Place near Reading. He also had a town house in Pall Mall with forty-five acres of grounds and pastures under leasehold from the Crown. From the Cecil Earl of Salisbury he purchased the pocket borough of Old Sarum in Wiltshire, with the right to return two members to the House of Commons. His intention was to found a political dynasty and vie with the magnificence of the senior Pitt cousins.

The Glorious Revolution bundled James II off his throne for breaking his Coronation Oath to uphold the rights of the Church of England. Almost the entire country, Tory and Whig, favoured the accession of his son-in-law and daughter William III and Mary II. Nevertheless, the Glorious Revolution was without doubt the making of the Whig party and to them Thomas Pitt firmly attached himself. He was member of Parliament for Salisbury in the first Parliament of the new reign and in 1695 returned himself for Old Sarum. George Pitt of Strathfieldsaye, the young head of the family, first entered the House of Commons in 1694 for his pocket borough of Wareham in Dorset. There was never any question of animosity between him and the Governor and the two were always friends.

Three years later Thomas Pitt, perhaps weary of a country gentleman's existence, and very likely keen to make still more money, decided to return to India. This time he was the friend of the East India Company, which was in trouble and gladly appointed him Governor of Madras. He took with him his eldest son Robert and appointed George Pitt guardian of his affairs and remaining family. In the course of his proconsulship Thomas Pitt gained a universal fame by his acquisition of one of the few historically memorable jewels, named after him The Pitt Diamond. Estimates of how many thousands over the hundred he risked in this perilous transaction have varied widely. The gem, carried to London in the heel of his son Robert's shoe, might not be easy to sell. Safe-keeping and cutting were entrusted to George Pitt's supervision.

Arrived home, Robert Pitt had himself returned for his father's borough of Old Sarum at the general election of 1702 for the first Parliament of Queen Anne. From India the Governor sent his son excellent advice on his parliamentary conduct:[2]

'If you are in Parliament show youselves on all occasions a good Englishman, and a faithful servant to your country. If you aspire to fame in the House, you must make yourself master of its precedents and orders. Avoid faction, and never enter the House pre-posessed; but attend diligently to the end whatever. I had rather see any child of mine want than he get his bread by voting in the House of Commons.'

Robert Pitt's next step was to marry Harriet, daughter of the late Edward Villiers, eldest son of the 4th Viscount Grandison, and Katherine Fitzgerald, a great Irish heiress. Katherine, but for her husband's premature death, would have become a peeress and in compensation was created Viscountess Grandison in her own right, for life only. Subsequently she had married General William Stewart. In announcing his marriage by letter to his father, Robert Pitt made the point that he connected himself with a great house. The Villiers, 1st and 2nd Dukes of Buckingham, had been favourites in turn of James I and Charles I, and of Charles II, and besides the Grandison title the family held the earldom of Jersey. Robert and Harriet Pitt brought forth their first child Thomas II, the future head of the family, in 1704. Three daughters followed, Harriet, Catherine and Ann. Harriet Pitt was a sensible woman, which was fortunate, for she must soon have surmised her husband to be a fool.

These were stirring times, when John Churchill, the great Duke of Marlborough, was frustrating the designs of Louis XIV. *Le Grand Monarque* had in 1700 accepted for his junior grandson Philip the legacy under the will of Charles II, last Hapsburg King of Spain, of his Crown. The inheritance included the Spanish Low Countries, now known as Belgium, and in Italy, Lombardy, Naples, Sicily and Sardinia, which with the Balearic

Islands and fortified ports on the coast of Morocco made the western Mediterranean something of a Spanish lake. These formidable possessions, together with an American empire extending from San Francisco to Cape Horn, replete with gold and silver bullion, yet constituted Spain a great power. The Spanish people welcomed their new sovereign, Philip V, and English public opinion was not disposed at first to support by war-like preparations the claims of the heir male of the House of Hapsburg, the Holy Roman Emperor, which might well present the greater menace. Provided the King of Spain enjoyed a proper independence of French influence, the Bourbon solution, by upholding the existing balance, appeared best for Europe. The control of the Spanish Low Countries was relevant to the security of England and Holland. British commercial interests demanded that the integrity of the Spanish monarchy be upheld. Because of a favourable trade treaty of 1667 Spain had become the best customer for English fish and wool. Under an agreement termed the Asiento, Negroes could be transported in English ships from Africa to Latin America, by way of Jamaica as entrepôt. But Louis XIV embarked upon policies the most alarming conceivable. He placed his regiments into the fortresses of the Low Countries. There appeared a real danger that the lucrative trade with Spain might be curtailed in the interests of France. Finally, on the death of James II, the French court continued their hospitality to his son and recognised him as James III. Queen Anne was provoked into declaring war in the interests of what became the claims of the Emperor's brother to be King of Spain. Thus the alliance between England, Austria and the Dutch, founded by William III, was continued into the eighteenth century. Marlborough's triumphs at Blenheim in 1704, Ramillies in 1706 and Oudenarde in 1708 destroyed all danger of a French hegemony in Europe.

Robert Pitt in no way appreciated the patriotic mood of his countrymen. A weak man, he tried to acquire stature against his domineering father by flittering in Tory circles. From India Thomas Pitt sent a reprimand: '. . . it is said you are taken up with facticious cabals and trying to put a French kikshaw upon the throne again.'[3] On 15 November 1708, a few days after Marlborough, carrying the war into enemy territory, had

captured Lille, Robert Pitt's second son and fifth child was born
at his town house in Golden Square, Soho. The infant was
christened William at St James's Piccadilly on 14 December and
the godparents were George Pitt and the grandmother's husband
William Stewart, after whom he was named. Two more
daughters, Elizabeth and Mary, were to complete the family.

In 1710 Governor Pitt returned home to find great changes.
The throne had been entailed by Act of Parliament upon the
House of Hanover as a guarantee against Roman Catholic and
French influence. England and Scotland had by the Act of
Union become the Kingdom of Great Britain. The Governor
set about supervising the careers of his children, with whom his
relations were insecure. Like many self-made men, he perhaps
over-valued the importance of success and did little to bolster
their personalities with his harsh reminders of their natural
inferiority. At the general election of 1710 the Governor
returned himself for Old Sarum whilst Robert was chosen at
Salisbury. Two years later the second son, Thomas, who had
bought the colonelcy of a troop of dragoons, joined them as
member for Wilton. The third son, John, was still an Eton
schoolboy.[4] In February 1713 the Governor's eldest daughter
Lucy entered a highly important marriage with General James
Stanhope, just returned home from commanding the British
army in Spain. A member of Parliament since 1702, Stanhope's
military record, though unfortunate, had been gallant enough
and he was certain to enter the leading counsels of the Whigs.

Governor Pitt was representative of a new force in British
political life, the power of the moneyed entrepreneur who
controlled the great joint-stock companies that traded across the
oceans. The landed gentry were bitterly resentful at the opulence
of men such as he, which, justly or no, they coupled with the
perpetuation of Marlborough's war, although every requirement
of British interest had been met. Certainly the City men had
amassed without precedent cash in hundreds of thousands not
accessible to land tax, and then bought broad acres cheap. The
general election of 1710 returned a large Tory majority. Marlborough and his friends were ousted. The new administration was
led by Robert Harley, shortly created Lord Treasurer and Earl
of Oxford and Mortimer. Despite these resounding titles he was

a great expert on national finance, though hampered with his party by Presbyterian and Whiggish antecedents. Soon he found himself eclipsed by the shining though unscrupulous talents of the secretary of state, Henry St John, of a notable Cavalier family, who took a peerage as Viscount Bolingbroke. At this distinction his gallant old father exclaimed: 'Ah, Harry, I ever said you would be hanged, but now I find you will be beheaded.' Bolingbroke reorientated British objectives away from the Continent towards a maritime and colonial – or 'blue-water' – war. An expedition was sent against Quebec but without success. In the Low Countries the army was ordered to stay put whilst their Dutch and Austrian friends were worsted. The Elector, George of Hanover, was serving with the Emperor's army and scorned this treachery.

There was, however, no question of the importance and effectiveness of Bolingbroke in foreign affairs. Peace was brought about by the Treaty of Utrecht, which ranks with the Treaty of Westphalia of 1648 and the Vienna Treaties of 1814–15 among the great settlements of the European polity. Philip V was recognised as King of Spain, provided he renounced his rights of succession in France, and he retained his American empire intact. In addition to confirming the Asiento, he had to agree to what was known as the Permission Ship, which was that one British vessel a year could visit South America for the purpose of trade. In Europe he had to make painful sacrifices. By the cession of Gibraltar and Minorca to Britain, control of the western Mediterranean was lost to Spain. The Low Countries, Lombardy, Naples and Sardinia were to be handed to the Emperor, and Sicily, with the title of King, to the Duke of Savoy. Spain was not likely to accept as final the loss of a hegemony in Italy which had been hers since the days of Ferdinand and Isabella and Charles V. The submission of Gibraltar and Minorca to heretic rule was impossible to forgive. For all his enormous expenditure of men and treasure Louis XIV's European frontiers remained almost exactly as they had been in 1678 and in North America he had to recognise Nova Scotia and Newfoundland as British, though the French retained the right to participate in the valuable fisheries. The Whigs considered Britain poorly rewarded for Marlborough's triumphs and criticised the abandonment of the Emperor's claims to the Spanish Crown. The Governor voted against the treaties and looked forward to the Hanoverian succession. But not so his son Robert, whose obstinacy was noted by John Ward, a Tory member of Parliament: '. . . there is among them in the eldest son the greatest instance I know of a son voting agst his father.'⁵

Oxford and Bolingbroke felt very uncertain of the attitude of the prince who might one day become George I. Although the Tories still had a large parliamentary majority, the party was now to be wrecked by the recklessness of its leaders. Bolingbroke, yet in his thirties, set the exemplar of how swiftly precocious talents can degenerate into blindness of judgement together with immaturity of deportment. Here was the leader of the High Church Tories, himself a mere sceptic who disported his leisure round the whore-houses of the metropolis. Bolingbroke played with the idea of a coup in favour of the Stuarts so as to guarantee the permanence of the Tory ascendancy and Oxford lacked the character to thwart him. When in 1713 the Pretender James III publicly announced that he would never abandon the Roman Catholic religion, the peaceful accession of George I was assured. Many an honest heart wavered between allegiances and would gladly have been spared the obligation to choose. The German who had never set foot in England was just preferable to the Stuart who could only have plunged the country into civil war.

The accession of a foreign ruler with his own responsibilities in Germany was bound to bring disagreeable complications. As Elector of Hanover, George I was entitled to join with the other Electors in choosing a Holy Roman Emperor. In his homeland an absolute ruler, he appointed his ministers and generals according to his ideas of their merit and was in no way accustomed to the British parliamentary system where the King's choice was conditioned by considerations of party and family. To him the idea of popular influence over foreign policy, that peculiar department of rulers, was an absurdity. Upon the free city of Bremen, a Naboth's vineyard almost surrounded by Hanoverian territory, George I cast a greedy eye and saw no reason why his British fleet should not give point to his covetousness.

At first George I prudently intended employing Tories as well as Whigs in his government – though not of course Oxford or Bolingbroke. But even those Tories inclined towards the House of Hanover were too bemused by the divided counsels of their leaders to take the chance. The Treasury was placed in commission with a First Lord, a permanent change for there has never since been a Lord Treasurer. But the power of the old office devolved upon the new First Lord, the direct ancestor of the modern Prime Minister, and he could be a member of the House of Commons. As Secretaries of State the King appointed the 2nd Viscount Townshend, a rich Norfolk landowner, together with none other than Stanhope, who took the lead in the House of Commons. Robert Walpole, also a Norfolk man who had been Secretary at War while Stanhope had been campaigning in Spain, became Paymaster-General. Shortly Townshend would marry Walpole's favourite sister Dorothy.

Governor Pitt had hastened to be among the notables to greet the new king, though an attempt to sell him the diamond proved unrewarding. His unimpeachable Whiggery and power in the west country enabled him to push the interests of his children. Robert Pitt's Tory professions in no wise prevented his acceptance of the household post of Clerk of the Green Cloth to the Prince of Wales, the future George II. Stanhope welcomed his brother-in-law into office and Thomas Pitt proudly assured his son that this promotion was an earnest of better things to come. It was a time of confused loyalties, for that July the Governor saw his daughter Essex married to Charles Cholmondeley of Vale Royal, Cheshire, a prominent Jacobite. But the head of an ancient family, member of Parliament for his county, could no doubt make himself acceptable to an ambitious father-in-law. The grandson of the marriage was the 1st Lord Delamere.

At the general election of 1715 Stanhope and Townshend employed every pressure to ensure the large Whig majority which they brought about. When Parliament met Walpole moved the Address, in which was promised the punishment of those in whom the Pretender had rested his hopes. Craven Bolingbroke fled to France, though to prosecute him would have been awkward for he knew too much and there were few Whigs who had not themselves secretly corresponded with the Stuart.

In June, on Stanhope's motion, Bolingbroke and Oxford were impeached. Oxford went to the Tower and next month Bolingbroke entered the service of the Pretender. That August the traitor was attainted, his property forfeit and, too, his life if ever he returned home.

The King's longing for Bremen set Stanhope and Townshend some ticklish problems. Anxious to keep the King's favour without causing apprehension in Parliament, they authorised the entry of the fleet into the Baltic on a plea of protecting British shipping. Bremen was secured but that September the Pretender's standard was raised in Scotland. Governor Pitt took a most gloomy view of events, writing to Robert:

'For my part I see nothing attending us but ruine and confusion, and this is the consequence of the last cursed reigne, and what France is now doeing is the bargaine for which the fruits of our victory were given up, that villainous cessation set afoot, that cursed peace made and our commerce sacrificed, 'tis shocking to the last degree to consider seriously to what conditions we are reduced.'

But Robert Pitt, with the greatest indiscretion and a total lack of appreciation of his father's position, blabbered his Tory sympathies around London society, to receive a thoroughly merited rebuke from his wise old father; victory for the Pretender would mean the end of the family wealth and power, possibly even worse amidst the bloody proscription of the Whigs which must surely follow.[6] At least the Governor had the satisfaction of seeing his second son Thomas serving against the rebels at the head of his Regiment of Horse.

At this point Walpole became First Lord of the Treasury and his friend William Pulteney became Secretary at War. Stanhope took the lead in organising victory over the rebels. The death of Louis XIV at this juncture was adventitious. As his great-grandson and successor Louis XV was only five years of age, the Duke of Orleans became Regent. Subject to the renunciation by Philip V of Spain, Orleans was heir to the French throne and had no wish to see a Stuart King in London with Bolingbroke minister. The French did not send help to Scotland and in

February 1716 the Pretender sailed back to France. He next foolishly dismissed Bolingbroke from his service. As Stanhope was anxious to contain Tory sentiment, which he recognised to be very powerful, the punishment of the rebels was not excessive. Sir William Wyndham 3rd Bart, member of Parliament for Somerset, who had been frustrated in his design to raise rebellion in the south-west, was left unpunished and free to lead the Tories in the House of Commons. Bolingbroke, smarting at his treatment from the Stuart, was very ready to come to terms with London. Stanhope gave him every encouragement to work his passage by a consistent advertisement of loyalty to the House of Hanover. But the temptation to brand all Tories as Jacobite and to identify civil peace with a Whig monopoly of power could not be resisted. By the Septennial Act of May 1716 the life of the existing and future Parliaments was extended from three to seven years, subject to the royal power to dissolve and the requirement of a general election on the death of the Sovereign. The Act worked well, so well that it became understood that generally speaking seven years was the proper life of a Parliament. The Septennial Act was disliked by the Tories, and with reason, for there is no doubt that the stability of political life which lengthy Parliaments provided contributed to the entrenchment of Whig rule.

The crushing of the '15 made plain to the world that George I was here to stay. In February 1716 the Dutch renewed their treaty of alliance with Britain whilst Spain, hoping to engage British sympathy with her pretensions in Italy, was revising her commercial codes very favourably. Stanhope, anxious to maintain the Triple Alliance which had won the War of the Spanish Succession, travelled to Vienna and in June 1716 secured a defensive alliance. He accompanied the King to Hanover, a most enviable situation because constitutionally the King, with the counter-signature of a Secretary of State, could enter into foreign treaties, though parliamentary confirmation was necessary for any agreement involving finance. Orleans secretly asked Stanhope for a British alliance and a treaty was drawn up which the Dutch were invited to join. The King and Stanhope sent to London urging Townshend to hurry matters along. But to the King's annoyance Townshend dallied and was in consequence relegated to the Lord Lieutenancy of Ireland. Walpole was rendered most uneasy, and when in April 1717 Townshend was finally dismissed, he resigned and Pulteney followed. To Walpole's vexation and disgust Stanhope agreed to become First Lord of the Treasury. Governor Pitt's son-in-law had become the greatest man in the country. Young William's eighth birthday had fallen the preceding November, so he was quite old enough to understand that his uncle Stanhope was a most important person and doing the King's foreign business.

Though Robert Pitt was a dismal creature, the Governor found plenty for congratulation in the successes of his second son Thomas, who in March 1717 married Lady Frances Ridgeway, the eldest daughter and co-heir of the 4th and last Earl of Londonderry of the first creation, an Irish peerage dating from 1622. Thomas was on 3 June 1717 ennobled as Baron of Londonderry, it was said in return for a substantial sum of money. But he was the first member of either branch of the Pitt family to be a peer, albeit Irish, so a delighted Governor proceeded to lavish many thousands upon him. Finally in 1726 the Earldom of Londonderry was revived for him. The third son, John, had become a Lieutenant-Colonel in the Foot Guards and in 1720 entered Parliament for Hindon. Two years later he became an ADC to the King and a great favourite. His wife was Mary Belasyse, daughter of the 3rd Viscount Fauconberg. But he would disappoint his father by his wayward and dishonest conduct and was cut out of the Governor's will.[7]

Out of office, Walpole joined the Tories in a factious opposition. The Prince of Wales set the precedent for every heir of the House of Hanover by extending his patronage to the enemies of his father. The Whigs had become top-heavy with power, for the schism in their ranks could be afforded without giving the Tories any encouragement remotely serious. Walpole made himself dangerous by using his influence to secure Oxford's acquittal. Stanhope, unhappy in the House of Commons, retreated to his former position as Secretary of State and took a peerage as Earl Stanhope. His successor as First Lord of the Treasury was the 3rd Earl of Sunderland, a great favourite with George I.

Back at foreign affairs, which he loved and understood, Stanhope put forward a compromise over the rival claims of

Austria and Spain in Italy; Charles, younger son of Philip V, would become Duke of Parma, to which through his mother he had a claim, but the Emperor would be given a reversion to Tuscany, swap Sardinia for Sicily, and at the same time renounce his claim to the Spanish throne. Philip V would therefore have an absolutely secure title in Spain and the Emperor would be the most powerful ruler in Italy. But the Spaniards struck first by seizing Sicily. The British fleet destroyed their ships and by his tireless gift for negotiation Stanhope got the Emperor, Holland and even France to agree that, unless Spain accepted a compromise, force would be used against her. Next year a French army crossed the Pyrenees and in February 1720 Philip V accepted the terms of the Quadruple Alliance. Stanhope had upheld the principles of the Utrecht settlement and by common consent was acknowledged one of the great foreign ministers of Europe.

At home the ministry ran into trouble largely because Sunderland relied essentially upon the support of the King and neither sufficiently appreciated the ascendancy of the House of Commons. When in December 1719 Walpole secured the rejection of a government bill to limit peerage creations, he had to be taken back into office as Paymaster-General with Townshend Lord President of the Council. Pulteney was passed over and never forgave Walpole this desertion. Then disaster struck: in August and September 1720 the South Sea Company, which the Government had sponsored, collapsed and enormous fortunes disappeared overnight. The King, his mistresses and Sunderland were deeply implicated, though Stanhope was free from guilt. Governor Pitt and his son Londonderry, who had speculated unwisely, fervently demanded the punishment of the directors.[8] By luck Walpole escaped without burnt fingers and, because he had returned to office only after the links between the Government and the Company had been formed, commanded confidence. Stanhope was so hurt at the unjust aspersions cast upon his honour that he died of an apoplexy and in April Sunderland resigned to be succeeded by Walpole. A new era had begun.

Two years before his uncle Stanhope's death William Pitt, aged eleven, had been sent to join his brother Thomas at Eton.

In those times school and university were undisciplined places. William hated Eton and always recalled his school-days with distaste; in old age he would pass the remark, 'that he scarcely observed a boy that was not cowed for life at Eton; that a public school might suit a boy of turbulent disposition but would not do where there was any gentleness'. [9] A man's education constituted his introduction to that intimate, discerning, and very small world of polite society, politics and literature, where his talents and foibles were scrutinised from the start. William and Thomas must have been of special interest for Governor Pitt was famous and, besides, there was their uncle Stanhope.

William's abilities gained attention, and his elder brother's instability was noticed. But in fact William was an interesting rather than a brilliant boy and a delicate constitution hampered his self-confidence. He underwent his first encounter with his life-long enemy gout, which, like consumption, was a term attached to a multitude of ailments. Pitt's illness, whatever its real nature, was always accompanied by depressions so abject as to paralyse him for days and weeks together. As his complaint became manifest so early, it has been assumed to stem from heredity and through all Governor Pitt's descendants there certainly ran a streak of frenzy. They all had his defects of passion and self-will, but without that utter integrity and exalted intelligence which were transmitted only to those great men William the elder and the younger. When the world crashed with the South Sea Bubble, many of the school parents lost a lot and the Pitt lads, with their family association with the government, may have met with ragging or worse. On Stanhope's death the Governor became guardian to the boy 2nd Earl, whom he thought of sending to join his elder grandsons at Eton, but the plan was not proceeded with. [10]

Pitt's melancholy found some relief in his visits to his grandfather. 'Tomorrow morning I sett out for Swallowfield,' wrote the Governor to Robert, 'and shall call at Eaton to take your two boys with me, and some of their comrogues; and will sett them down again on Monday.' Who the 'comrogues' were we do not know and no certain evidence of Pitt's schoolboy friendships has come down. The shrewd old man discerned the younger boy's promise. William must have heard many an absorbing tale of Eastern adventure, but the object was not merely to entertain a boyish imagination: all important was the certainty that as the result of the grandfather's tough ambition, the lad would, as light follows darkness, enter Parliament at the first opportunity after his coming of age.

By this time, after much anxiety, Governor Pitt had profitably disposed of his diamond to the Duke of Orleans for £125,000 or thereabouts. Equivalent sums laid out in conventional cargoes would have brought as much if not more profit, but none of the fame that attaches to the unique. Out of the diamond money the Governor paid £53,000 for the Boconnoc estate in Cornwall, with a mansion considered the finest in the county, where he installed a portrait of himself wearing the gem. A remoteness from everyday life entered this transaction also, for the vendor was Lady Mohun, widow of the wicked Lord whose mutually fatal duel with the 4th Duke of Hamilton provided the climax to Thackeray's *Henry Esmond*. Boconnoc became the principal seat of the Pitt family and included the right to return one member of Parliament for Okehampton, Devon. The Governor extended his tentacles to Camelford in Cornwall, too, of which his attorney was several times Mayor. The old man had made himself one of the most important parliamentary proprietors in the country.[11]

In January 1726 Governor Thomas Pitt died at the good age of seventy-three, shortly before William was due to leave Eton for Trinity College Oxford. His had been a 'success story', but his achievements, though formidable, must not be exaggerated. Although the Pitt borough patronage was considerable, they were nowhere as rich and powerful as the renowned Cavendish Dukes of Devonshire, the Russell Dukes of Bedford or Thomas Pelham-Holles, the great eighteenth-century Duke of Newcastle. These families had founded their wealth upon the distribution of the monastic estates by Henry VIII, by far the greatest revolution in the ownership of land between the Norman Conquest and the taxation of wealth in the twentieth century. The Pitts of Boconnoc could not conduce the election of a member of parliament for a county; no direct descendant of Governor Pitt would serve as a knight of the shire. They would always find difficulty in nursing their parliamentary interest, which was greater than their rent-rolls could comfortably support.

The Governor had left personalty a little under £200,000, less than the fashionable world expected. After the habit of rich men his affairs were in confusion and, after the custom too of rich men's children, his sons Robert, Londonderry and John fell out. The Governor had unwisely appointed as his executors Londonderry and his son-in-law Cholmondely and by the summer of 1726 a family war was in full swing. Robert was now life tenant of the Pitt landed property and as residuary legatee came into a fortune placed at £100,000, but this figure depended upon the success of his claim that Londonderry owed the estate £95,000. This his brother not only denied but put in a demand for £10,000, which he alleged the estate owed him. Robert showed some of his father's style when he wrote to his elder son Thomas: 'The untoward behaviour of your uncles, with whom I forbid you all manner of correspondence upon pain of my highest displeasure, has obliged me to come to town to assert my rights to several things which they were attempting unfairly to invade.'

Robert Pitt's mood was not improved by what was probably not the first indication of an extravagant disposition in Thomas, who had not proceeded to Oxford or Cambridge after Eton. Now he was at Utrecht opening the Grand Tour obligatory for a gentleman's son. Robert Pitt had originally promised Thomas an annual allowance of £200 until he was twenty-five and then £500, and on his father's death, supposing himself a rich man, undertook £700. Thomas, who banked with Messrs Benjamin and Henry Hoare, 'att the Golden Bottle in Fleet Street', airily told his father that £700 might meet his needs and received a proper telling-off: 'If you cannot proceed on your travels upon these terms, you have nothing more to do than to draw for fifty pounds to bear your charges home, and so knock off all thought of travelling: for I will not starve myself and the rest of my family to support your extravagance.'

By the end of the year Robert Pitt had presented a petition in the Court of Chancery against his father's executors. Young Thomas was still no comfort and in January his father wrote to him ordering his travels to be ended. The upshot was a despairing letter; Thomas could not set out at once because he owed £180, '. . . and although it may seem extravagant to you, I can show it is what I could not avoid, for I have not spent it in any sort of raking or debaucheries, but in bare necessities . . .'.[12] Probably Robert Pitt had to send out a remittance to get his tiresome son home. It was unfortunate that the future head of the family was an uncultivated man, without the background of university or travel.

While Thomas was sowing his wild oats, William had gone up to Trinity College Oxford, the college of his uncle Stanhope. He entered for a university prize with a panegyric upon the death of George I, but the award went to William Murray, that brilliant Scot up at Christ Church. Murray was the third son of the 5th Viscount Stormont, an impecunious Scots peer whose second son was at the Jacobite court of St Germain as titular Earl of Dunbar. After completing a tough education at Perth Grammar School, where the boys lived on porridge and the whip, Murray rode on a lame horse over the border to see what fortune Christ Church might offer. Amply gifted with the supple intellectual powers that have always won acclaim at Oxford, he attracted the attention of Alexander Pope and 'drank champagne with the wits'. During his second year, while on a vacation visit to Paris to see his brother Dunbar, Murray committed the most dangerous indiscretion. He wrote to his brother-in-law John Hay, Jacobite Earl of Inverness and Secretary of State to the Pretender, declaring his loyalty to 'the King' and enclosing a small present: 'The chief end I would propose from my studies and education, and the greatest glory I can aim at is to be able to serve his Majesty in any way that he pleases to command me.'[13] But nothing came of this and he passed from Oxford to the Bar with his reputation unblemished. That incriminating letter of which the publication must have spelt his disgrace lay undiscovered in the Stuart archives to torture his conscience for many a year.

Pitt left Oxford after only one year without taking his degree, possibly because of the completely unexpected death of his father in May 1727. Today his portrait hangs in the Hall of his College. Thomas succeeded to the entail on the Pitt estates and laid his hands on everything else, so the family lawsuits were cut short. Three months later there was a general election, occasioned by the death of George I, and Thomas revelled in his parliamentary interest. He had himself returned for both Old Sarum and Okehampton and elected to represent the latter – in those days a man could be returned simultaneously for more than one constituency. At Old Sarum Thomas put in his uncle Londonderry – which may have helped to smooth over family troubles. At Camelford he put in his 'good-for-nothing' uncle Colonel John – again, no doubt, in the interests of peace. In Parliament Thomas Pitt took the conventional line of supporting Walpole.[14] The Pitt inheritance, soundly based upon broad acres, could have been freed from embarrassment by prudent management, but Thomas was unsuited to his complicated responsibilities.

William Pitt completed his years of study with a period at Utrecht University, renowned for its law school. Returned home, he lived in idleness for some eighteen months on the family estates. Only a small part of the time at his disposal would have sufficed to equip him with a tolerable fund of knowledge. He spoke and wrote excellent French, but his real taste lay in military history, the one science which he ever claimed to have studied systematically. Though never an erudite man, he had a gentleman's acquaintance with the classics and at some time acquired that mastery of phrase which for over thirty years fascinated the House of Commons. Pitt had inherited from his father a miserable rent-charge of £100 p.a., to be doubled on his mother's death. His circumstances, together with his health, prescribed a frugal regimen. Pitt had in common with his grandfather a freedom from the fashionable vices, a pleasure in governing men and the lonely ambition that soars above the humdrum preoccupations of the average. Though his appetites were sober, he nursed a love of the grand manner, fine houses, ornate terraces, landscaped prospects and splendid equipages, with servants in full livery. On the verge of active life Pitt, though above all petty meanness, must have found difficulty in not harbouring a jealousy of his elder brother, so well endowed with the things of this world yet of a personality so inadequate as to be unable truly to enjoy his good fortune.

In 1731 Thomas Pitt fulfilled his first duty as head of the

family by his marriage to Christian, daughter of Sir Thomas Lyttleton 4th Bart of Hagley Hall, Worcestershire. Her brother George, delighted at the match, would have liked his next sister, Molly, to marry William but for his poor expectations; there is no reason to think that Pitt was interested in her or contemplating an early marriage. His brother's match was important to him however because it drew him into the circle of George Lyttleton's uncle, 1st Viscount Cobham. He, the owner of that great mansion Stowe, together with much of the borough of Buckingham and the right to return one of the two members to Parliament, was a very grand person indeed.

As Sir Richard Temple 4th Bart, Cobham had fought with distinction in Marlborough's wars and in 1714 received a barony, one of the eleven peerages created to mark the accession of the new dynasty. Then in 1718 he became a viscount and as his marriage was barren this title was entailed upon his two sisters and their issue: it was the younger who had just become mother-in-law to Thomas Pitt. The elder Hester, Cobham's heir, had married Richard Grenville of Wotton, another great Buckinghamshire estate, and had five boys. The eldest, Richard, heir to Stowe and Wotton, had been born in 1711 and so was only slightly younger than the Pitt brothers. The other boys were George, James (Jemmy), Henry and Thomas and they had one sister Hester. The father of these children died while they were still at Eton, and Cobham had without hesitation undertaken their supervision. Richard he sent on the Grand Tour to Switzerland, Italy and France. George was reading for the Bar at the Inner Temple; James and Henry were still at Eton, the first also destined for the law; Thomas was already at sea as midshipman. The Lyttleton and Grenville cousinage were of the ideal age to become companions to the Pitt brethren, who thus became the intimates of Hagley and Stowe.

Cobham, a blunt old soldier with a fund of bawdy jokes, entertained the wits, poets and politicians, and foremost among these was Pope, whose first visit to Stowe was around July 1725. August found him writing to a friend: 'I have been above a Month strolling about in *Buckinghamshire* and *Oxfordshire*, from Garden to Garden, but still returning to Lord *Cobham's* with fond satisfaction.'[15] Thereafter the visit became an annual affair, Pope and Cobham finding in one another an attraction of opposites. Cobham in his friendly way offered Pitt a cornetcy in his regiment, the King's Own Regiment of Horse, known as Cobham's Own (and after 1747 as the 1st Dragoon Guards). Horace Walpole the memoirist was to be a prejudiced witness about anything concerning his father or Pitt. But as Thomas Pitt was an administration supporter his account that Walpole advanced £1,000 from the Treasury to pay for Pitt's commission could be true.[16] Pitt's meagre pay was more than absorbed by the expense of serving in a fashionable regiment but he had a position among the *jeunesse dorée*.

The consideration that Pitt was bound to enter Parliament at the next general election made him interesting to rich and influential people: a young man of expectations may always attract the generous sympathy of the older generation. Although rather stiff when dealing with his own generation, his old-world courtesy and honest qualities eased his relations with men and women who might further his career. He became acquainted with the 3rd Earl of Peterborough, who together with his uncle Stanhope had soldiered in Spain, and with the 2nd Earl of Tyrawley, Marlborough's aide-de-camp at Malplaquet. Sarah Duchess of Marlborough, a close friend of his grandmother Lady Grandison, was another useful connection. It would however be a mistake to make too much of these contacts with the grand old world. Unlike some great men, he was not recognised in early manhood as possessing talents out of the ordinary.

Although Pitt was of an age when most men find the company of the opposite sex indispensable, he experienced no serious encounter. Like some shy bachelors he kept his heart for a sister, Ann, who kept house for him at his London lodgings in Cork Street. His sister Mary at this time married Robert Nedham, a rich landowner in Oxfordshire and Ireland. The easy life of a fancy regiment allowed Pitt time to undertake a tour of France and Switzerland late in 1733. His frequent letters to Ann – 'My Dearest Nanny' – in excellent French describe his travels and showed the deep domestic affection of which this awkward man was capable. After a few days in Paris he spent two months at Besançon. There he wrote to Ann of his infatuation for a French lady, though he remarked that her lack of social station precluded thought of marriage. That any flirtation took place at all depends entirely on Pitt's account and he may have been trying to liven up the tale of a rather dull stay. In August he travelled south, apparently heart-free, to Marseilles and Montpellier and then northwards up the Rhône to Lyons and Geneva. After a stay at Lunéville he was home early in 1734, for later that year a general election was due under the requirements of the Septennial Act. As the tour had not included Italy he was not a travelled man by the standards of the time.

Pitt had reached the age of twenty-six and never again showed an interest in travel. His direct experience even of his own country was limited to London and a few of the great houses of the southern counties. Pitt, the future architect of war, never heard a shot fired in anger in the course of his career as soldier. Although he was one day to raise Highland regiments for service in North America, he never went near the border. He was to show a transient sympathy with Irish problems but never visited that country. The man who would one day despatch fleets of warships and transports laden with thousands of soldiers to North America, the West Indies and the Indian Ocean, himself travelled by ship on four occasions only, across the narrow seas between England and the Continent. Yet during the Seven Years War he issued expert directives upon nautical and military strategy and equipment. How he obtained this knowledge will never be known.

At the general election Thomas Pitt was duly returned by the complacent electors of Old Sarum and Okehampton, and decided to sit for Okehampton. Walpole put pressure upon him to place his family interest at the disposal of the Government with the suggestion that Thomas Harrison, already sitting member for Old Sarum, be returned and William Pitt be compensated with a money payment. Pitt, not to be thwarted of the chance to embark on his real career, indignantly rejected this proposal. Thomas Pitt could not decently refuse him and he became member for Old Sarum in company with his brother-in-law Nedham.[17]

CHAPTER 2

Member for Old Sarum

'He [Sir Robert Walpole] may be considered as the first . . . who threw the house of commons into the form of a regular debating society. He seems to have spoken constantly on the spur of the occasion; without pretending to exhaust his subject, he often put it in a striking point of view; and the arguments into which he was led in following the doublings and windings of a question, were such as do not appear to have occurred to himself before nor to have been made use of by others. When he had to obviate any objection, he did not do it so much by ambiguity or evasion, as by immediately stating some other difficulty on the opposite side of the question, which blunted the edge of the former, and staggered the opinion of his hearers.'[1]

William Hazlitt, *The Eloquence of the British Senate.*

When Pitt entered Parliament Sir Robert Walpole had been First Lord of the Treasury and Chancellor of the Exchequer since 1721 without a break. By virtue of his ability to manage Parliament he had convinced George I and George II that his services were indispensable. Though a sincerely clubable man, Walpole's urbanity was equivocal, for he never scrupled to use the royal confidence to outwit a rival or oust disagreement. The dimensions of his power found delineation in the symmetrical splendours of Colin Campbell's masterpiece Houghton Hall, where he housed the finest collection of pictures known to England since Charles I's superb accumulation had been marketed by Cromwell. Grasping and self-centred but a patriot at heart, Walpole's endowment to British political evolution lay in his understanding that the Glorious Revolution had made the House of Commons the keystone of the Constitution. Whereas Oxford and Bolingbroke had taken peerages as a mark of authority, Walpole discerned that to remain in the House of Commons was the surest safeguard of his primacy. The Treasury was by far the most important department, employing the largest staff, and Walpole set the precedent that the First Lord should preside, too, over that estate which by his time had wrested control of national finance to the exclusion of the House of Lords. A man of Walpole's deftness must always be uncommon and he may appear to have created the office of Prime Minister. That term was frequently employed informally, especially by his enemies. Though a minister of outstanding character must always establish a personal ascendancy, the idea of a 'sole' or 'prime' minister was abhorrent to the preconceptions of the age and Walpole was every bit a man of his time.

The settlement of the dynastic question by George I's peaceful accession left the King with wide powers which remained his until the nineteenth century. His right to appoint and dismiss his ministers and to dissolve Parliament went unquestioned. The King maintained a broad supervision of appointments over the wide fields of the armed forces, the diplomatic service and the Church. On his accession in 1727 George II had tried to replace his father's minister with Sir Spencer Compton – 'the King's favourite nonentity' – but found himself unable to dispense with Walpole. Fortified by the confidence of the King's intelligent consort Caroline of Ansbach, Walpole went from strength to strength. Yet although George II had to accept that he could not make Compton rule Britain, he none the less made him Lord Wilmington and, much against Walpole's wishes, placed him in the Cabinet as Lord President of the Council.

There was a small Cabinet of six to eight ministers, of whom the most important were the two Secretaries of State, one for the Northern, the other for the Southern Department, and the Lord Chancellor. In the House of Commons the two hundred holders of government offices, termed placemen, gave the administration a firm core of supporters but not a majority. The countenance of the independent members and in particular of the knights of the shire was essential. The importance of the House of Lords was still considerable and Walpole's Cabinets were made up entirely of peers with himself the only commoner. Although the King could not maintain a minister obnoxious to the Commons, an effective opposition was after 1721 unknown except as arising from the crisis of an unsuccessful war. The stability which this state of things implied was largely attributable to Walpole's political genius.

The Tories, though utterly broken and divided, were possessed of important residuary assets, great agricultural wealth and a prestige surely based upon the integration between squire and parson. Walpole was well aware that he could not govern as though no Tories existed, for their tacit acquiescence was necessary to the security of the dynasty, his main concern. The most voluminous content of his correspondence was directed to the counteraction of Jacobite intrigue. Walpole pursued Tory policies with the purpose of sweetening the country gentry. The nonconformists who had enthusiastically welcomed the Hanoverians were disappointed of their hope of securing civil equality with members of the Church of England. In financial affairs Walpole successfully met the most fond expectations of the squirearchy. He reorganised the national debt and established a sinking fund for its redemption. The land tax was kept down to 2s in the £. Indirect taxation Walpole rearranged so effectively that, although the rates were reduced, revenue was augmented. Given peace and prosperity the Pretender would the sooner be forgotten. So as to complete the ruin of Jacobite hopes, Walpole in May 1725 secured Bolingbroke's pardon, in respect of life and property only: he would never be allowed to take his seat in the House of Lords. Walpole saw that whereas the man's treacheries must forfeit him respect for ever, he might none the less act as a useful catalyst to split the Tories further between Hanover and Stuart.

The population of Britain, excluding Ireland, was six million. By the middle of the century two million Englishmen, a figure rapidly increasing, were settled in the mainland colonies of North America. A fair proportion of the English-speaking peoples was therefore engaged in agriculture, manufacture and trade on the other side of the Atlantic. In the Caribbean Britain held the rich sugar islands of Jamaica, Barbados, Antigua and St Kitts-Nevis. Each colony had a royal governor and sometimes a Legislative Council which he appointed. Control of local taxation rested with the Assembly, elected on a property qualification. The government of the colonies thus mirrored the home Constitution. In the Far East Bombay was held in sovereignty and the East India Company, established at Madras and Calcutta, doubled its turnover in the first half of the century. The Empire was bound together by the Acts of Trade; commerce was the monopoly of British shipping manned by British crews, so that a reservoir of trained seamen was ready for service in time of war. The colonies of Britain were forbidden intercourse with the Continent or with the possessions of another power, subject to exceptions of which the Asiento concession was the most noteworthy. An empire devoid of the philosophy of mercantilism had no meaning to men of the early eighteenth century. None the less Walpole, wisely recognising the incipient strength of the colonies with their free traditions, interpreted the Navigation System as liberally as was consistent with maintaining the whole.

Ireland was shackled by a subordination which in the case of the American colonies was precluded by considerations of distance. No Act of the Irish Houses of Parliament could become law without the assent of the British Privy Council and by the Declaratory Act of 1720 the right of the British Parliament to legislate for Ireland had been affirmed. The Irish House of Commons was returned by a franchise confined to members of the Anglican Church of Ireland with the property qualification, a small minority of a minority. Ireland was therefore peculiarly susceptible to 'management'. The Civil List was plundered for British pensioners; troops paid for by the Dublin Parliament fought overseas in British wars. Since the Union of 1707 Scotland had been an equal trading partner with Britain. Ireland was not only forbidden to trade direct with North America or the West Indies but her natural exports to Britain of agricultural produce were penalised to protect the British landed interest.

Walpole above all prided himself as a man of peace. The

first consideration of any British statesman between 1660 and 1815 was that across the Channel lay France, the most populous, wealthy and efficiently governed state in Europe. Louis XIV, although baulked of his wider ambitions, had left Louis XV a magnificent inheritance and the junior branch of his family securely upon the throne of Spain. The French King ruled some twenty-five million subjects – almost as many as Peter the Great of Russia – whilst their commerce, agriculture and manufactures were transcendent. French leadership in language, literature and the visual arts went unquestioned. The position of France could be compared to that of Germany between 1870 and 1945 but with the difference that there were in the eighteenth century no outside counterweights such as the United States and Russia later provided.

Although in America and India there was ample room for the British and French for many years, conflict arising from jealousy was inevitable. The position of Britain was incomparably more powerful. French Canada contained a mere 50,000 settlers, organised in seigneuries, ruled by a Governor and a Bishop appointed by their King. The French held Haiti, Guadeloupe and Martinique in the Caribbean and in India they too had their East India Company. Where the British colonies were independent in finance and therefore defence, the French had the advantage of a centralised system. But their colonial administrators were seldom given proper support from home. Walpole has been criticised retrospectively for making but little attempt to persuade the North American colonies to combine. Long after he was dead taxation for defence became the proximate cause of the break-up of the First British Empire. But whether the Assemblies could ever have been induced to come together at the instance of a home government they never saw and which never saw them is debatable, and Walpole saw full well the impolicy of dictation. To Britain her American possessions were a primary interest. Compared with the affairs of Europe, imperial questions never assumed great significance at Versailles.

The policy of the Court of Madrid was bound to be influenced by the loss of Gibraltar and Minorca and of those cherished Italian possessions. The commercial interests of Britain required peace with Spain. The Iberian peninsula was her best customer and without Spanish bullion the trades of the East India Company in silks, spices and tea, and of the Muscovy Company in Baltic naval stores, could not be financed. The much-vaunted Permission Ship to South America proved far less valuable than the direct trade. Under Walpole British merchants conspired to prise open the Latin American markets further than the allowance by treaty. Spanish pride and British expectations of El Dorado might operate as magnets in the direction of war.

As it was the policy of Cardinal Fleury, the great minister of Louis XV's minority, to maintain friendship, Walpole was able to keep Britain in isolation from Europe, here again following a Tory policy. A consistent diplomacy demanded complete loyalty in the Secretaries of State and in 1724 the brilliant and versatile 2nd Lord Carteret was relegated to the Lord Lieutenancy of Ireland as the prelude to his ultimate dismissal. Rich and able men, notably Townshend and the 4th Earl of Chesterfield, forfeited their careers to Walpole's insistence upon deciding the King's affairs. Carteret was succeeded by Thomas Pelham-Holles, Duke of Newcastle-upon-Tyne, only thirty-one, worth £30,000 p.a. from his vast acreages in Sussex, Nottinghamshire and Yorkshire. Newcastle's compliant disposition made unlikely any repetition of the trouble with Carteret. But he was in no way tempted to a life of ease and had a limitless capacity for work. His social life revolved round politics and he made himself a master of electioneering techniques. Although highly-strung and a hypochondriac he took part in the hustings with gusto and once exclaimed: 'I love a mob.' Newcastle's brother, Henry Pelham, member of Parliament for Sussex, became Secretary at War and in 1730 Paymaster-General. As Walpole became older Pelham's assistance became more valuable and he too learned the game.

Townshend retired to agricultural pursuits but Carteret and Chesterfield were not so complaisant. They found a ready familiar in Pulteney, whom Walpole had kept out of office from jealousy of his powers as orator. From his seat, Battersea Park, Bolingbroke spun his web and inveigled the old Tories, led by Wyndham, and dissident Whigs into forming something like a concerted opposition. They termed themselves 'The Patriots' and took up the parliamentary principles of the old Tories, adapted to conditions under the Hanoverians; the reduction of the standing army and in foreign affairs an accent upon maritime and colonial interests; a Place Act to cut down the number of government supporters and the limitation of the life of a parliament to three years. All faction should end and the King choose his ministers for the good of the country rather than at the whim of one too-powerful minister. In 1729 Frederick Prince of Wales arrived in England from Hanover; on bad terms with his father and worse with his mother, he rapidly became the figure-head for opposition. The Prince of Wales' connection was described as the Leicester House party, after his official residence on the north side of Leicester Square.

When in 1733 Walpole brought forward a novel scheme for the further reform of indirect taxation by an extended use of the hated excise, all the forces of discontent old and new broke out. His proposal was not properly understood and his enemies enjoyed a temporary popularity without appearing merely factious. Walpole prudently dropped the measure but punished severely those of his adherents who had deserted his flag, and among these was Cobham, who was deprived of his regiment. Sir Robert was unperturbed at the additions to the ranks of his already formidable enemies. Owing largely to the superb electioneering of Newcastle and Pelham, he triumphed at the 1734 general election as though no excise controversy had ever been. Bolingbroke was so disgusted at this turn of events that he withdrew to France and pretended to study philosophy. Walpole was now at the summit of his powers and there was no apparent reason why he should not govern Britain for the rest of his life.

Cobham in a pique joined forces with Chesterfield, Carteret and Pulteney and took his young friends. His eldest nephew Richard Grenville had just entered Parliament for Buckingham. Thomas Pitt, though a mediocre performer in the House of Commons, had importance as head of a connection. Besides putting William and Nedham in for Old Sarum he gave Lyttleton, who had no pocket borough, accommodation at his second seat for Okehampton. Of the Strathfieldsaye branch George Pitt, the Governor's friend, had recently died and his younger son Jack of Encombe was the new member for Wareham.

Henry Fox, too, was entering Parliament for the first time. Where Pitt's background was socially acceptable, that of Fox and his elder brother Stephen was parvenu. Their father Sir Stephen Fox had started life as a footman and after service to a series of noblemen had ended up in the household of the Prince of Wales. He accompanied Charles II on 'his travels', so that to secure the lucrative office of Paymaster-General after the Restoration followed in a fairly easy way. Fox became a very rich man and the loss of his son and heir with the absence of grandchildren prompted him to embark in his seventy-seventh year on a second adventure in matrimony. In his younger son Henry, and still more his grandson Charles James, he presented to the world of the eighteenth century two men of great mark. Initially Henry Fox did not improve his unpromising origins by the complication of scandal. Having dissipated his patrimony he fell light into the opulent bed of Mrs Strangways Horner, who kept him handsomely and clandestinely married her thirteen-year-old daughter to his brother Stephen. Shortly Fox showed earnest of a pushing nature by obtaining minor government office, whilst his brother secured a peerage as Lord Ilchester.[2]

The Parliament of George II met during only four months of the year, from November till March, with a handsome recess for Christmas. The Address, which at the opening of each session was presented in answer to the King's Speech, with the budget containing the army and navy estimates, gave opportunity for the opposition to criticise. Controversial legislation was unusual and the proceedings of Parliament were secret because it was held a free Constitution would suffer under a popular influence. Therefore a private member could establish a reputation 'out-doors' only with great difficulty. But Pitt was set upon winning his spurs. A tall and lanky young man, without being what might be called handsome, his flashing black eyes, hawk-like nose and well-formed mouth gave him an impressive appearance. The mixture of assurance and reserve in his character made his manner cold yet self-confident. So far as the records go, he is first reported as having spoken on 22 April 1735 in support of a Place bill and next on 5 April 1736 against the Mortmain bill designed to increase the number of livings which Oxford and Cambridge colleges might acquire or accept in gift.[3]

The occasion which brought Pitt to public notice was Pulteney's motion of congratulation of 29 April 1736 to the King on the marriage of the Prince of Wales to Princess Augusta of Saxe-Gotha. Pitt's speech of unctuous congratulation, punctuated by veiled and sarcastic allusions to the endemic disharmony in the royal family, delighted his friends but infuriated Walpole, whose position was already delicate enough. Lyttleton's speech attracted a similar attention but Pitt, who held the King's commission, was vulnerable. Walpole promptly had him dismissed from his regiment and jovially exclaimed: 'We must muzzle this terrible cornet of horse!'

Pitt's dismissal was the talk of London. Lord Hervey commented in his memoirs: 'At the end of the session Cornet Pitt was broke for this, which was a measure at least ill-timed, if not ill-taken. . . .'[4] To advertise his tragic circumstances, Pitt travelled around the country in a one-horse chaise, unattended by a manservant. There was always a theatrical streak in Pitt; his isolated social habits belied a deep wish to attract attention. As he explained to one of his opposition friends George Berkeley: 'I had often been told, I was obliged to Sir Robert honouring me with so distinguished a mark of his resentment.'[5] When Pitt spoke on the opposition motion of 18 February 1737 to reduce the standing army from 17,000 to 12,000 men, Walpole took occasion to defend his action: 'If an officer, of whatever rank and merit, wished to meddle with affairs of state . . . which are outside his sphere, or even show aversion to a minister, then that minister would be the meanest of creatures if he did not cashier him. . . .'[6] The principle upon which Walpole had acted would be maintained for many years, and indeed if the Treasury had advanced Pitt £1,000 towards his commission his conduct was very understandable.

Pitt and Lyttleton, the firebrands, earned the derisory nicknames of 'Cobham's Cubs' and 'The Boy Patriots'. Pitt joined those whose cry was that Walpole's régime had no foundation but votes in the House of Commons bought by pensions and places, a gross caricature of political reality. That Pitt was embarking upon his career in the ranks of Walpole's enemies was merely the consequence of connection but he believed his cause a true one. Chesterfield and Pope were ready to extend their confidence to Lyttleton, a mark of distinction not solely due to his position as heir to a great family estate. Pope enjoyed Lyttleton's company because at Hagley he found a joyous and affectionate family milieu. Moreover, Lyttleton had genuine intellectual interests, with the laudable design of writing a biography of Henry II. During the early 1730s Lyttleton began to move freely in top opposition circles, could risk teasing Pope for gluttony and appraise the mind of Bolingbroke, considerable achievements in a man not yet thirty. In their letters to Lyttleton, Pope and Chesterfield frequently dwelt upon the thorough distrust nursed by them, Wyndham and Bolingbroke towards Pulteney and Carteret, who they surmised would at a crunch barter their ideals with Walpole to their personal advantage.

Pitt was part and parcel of the households at Stowe and Hagley but the letters of Pope and Chesterfield contain no appreciative notice of him.[7] To the great he was a likeable boy, in Parliament for family reasons and of no further merit. Though never one to hide his light under a bushel, Pitt's mental development was gradual and his tub-thumping House of Commons manner gave little indication of originality, let alone power of thought. His underlying firmness of character lacked the illumination of that supple brilliance the wits so readily fell for. Pitt, though his enthusiasm and manliness could not be gainsaid, was as yet but an echo of his betters. Lyttleton, the cynosure of the opposition Court, held the stage. But like many a clever young man he would under the anvil of maturity prove a failure.

Walpole survived unshaken the death in 1737 of his best friend and counsellor, Queen Caroline. Indeed, at this time he encountered a very considerable acquisition in the appointment as Lord Chancellor of Philip Yorke, 1st Baron and subsequently Earl of Hardwicke. His rise in his profession had been meteoric and greatly aided by Newcastle who had in 1719 placed him in the House of Commons for one of his Sussex boroughs. Little by little Hardwicke's relations with Newcastle became reversed, the great patron coming to depend upon the lawyer who combined a truly great mind with a strength of character second to none. The autumn of 1736 had found Newcastle writing to his friend: 'Dear Hardwicke, without you we are nothing.'

Within days of his elevation Hardwicke was consulted by
Walpole about a crisis concerning the income of the Prince of
Wales. The Prince was entitled as of right only to the Duchy of
Cornwall revenues of £10,000, to which his father added an
allowance of £50,000. Yet George II had before his accession
enjoyed double that sum and as King was receiving greater
provision than had his father. At the instigation of Pulteney the
Prince decided to seek parliamentary intervention. Lyttleton
addressed to him a long letter pointing out the danger to his
popularity if he used political means to secure an increase of
income.[8] But Prince Frederick was set upon a course of making
trouble. Walpole was taken aback at such temerity and Hardwicke advised him to offer a settlement of £50,000 p.a. secured
upon the Civil List. When on 20 February this offer was conveyed, the Prince of Wales replied that 'the affair was now out
of his hands and therefore he could not give an answer to it'.
Two days later, Pulteney in the House of Commons moved for
an Address to the King that his heir might be endowed with a
permanent establishment. Despite his letter, Lyttleton supported the motion, followed by Pitt. But for the abstention of
forty-three Tories Walpole would have been beaten over a
financial vote for the only time in his career as minister and his
majority fell to thirty.[9]

That September Prince Frederick fled from Hampton Court
Palace with his wife who was expecting her first child. Despite
this heedlessly impetuous act of impertinence, a daughter,
named Augusta, was safely delivered. The Prince took Norfolk
House in St James's Square and rented Clifden, or Cliveden,
on the Thames. He appointed Pitt a groom of his bedchamber
at a salary of £400 p.a. and Lyttleton his private secretary. In
May 1738 Thomas Pitt joined William in the princely ménage,
becoming Assay Master of the Stannaries of the Duchy of
Cornwall, a useful position for a west country magnate.

Prince Frederick was aptly nicknamed 'Poor Fred' and has
left an unattractive reputation as a weakling and a liar, though
his memory has suffered from the contempt he inspired in his
parents and in the pen of Lord Hervey. His true contribution
to his adopted country was as a collector of pictures and he
commissioned the finest pieces from the great Huguenot silver-

smiths in London. He was apt to attend the theatre every evening of the week. Whether or not Pitt liked him, business about his household gave him a position in life. Perhaps he sometimes sat in that gorgeous, gilded barge which now stands in the maritime museum at Greenwich. The Court of the young people was pleasant compared with Kensington Palace and Hampton Court, sergeant-majored by a widower King, and in May 1738 was enlivened by the birth of a son, the future George III. Pitt accompanied his master on a state visit to Bath and received the Freedom of the borough. Here he became acquainted with that remarkable man Ralph Allen, the Man of Bath, who made a fortune out of the quarries used in the construction of the eighteenth-century city and built himself Prior Park on the outskirts.

Frederick was at one absolute and irremovable disadvantage: he could never appoint a ministry until his father was dead. With Walpole in power the Pitts, the Grenvilles and Lyttletons had no hope of political advancement. Even in the event of the minister's downfall or death, the King would appoint his successor. Pitt and his brother Thomas were building themselves a reversion for a future which, with the King a robust man in his fifties, might well prove distant. There was an unhealthy atmosphere about Leicester House similar to that of a king in exile: the adherents had nothing to do but gossip about the King of reality and speculate upon the distribution of spoils that would follow his greedily awaited demise.

Walpole finally fell into difficulties not over domestic affairs but over the situation in Europe. He had kept Britain out of the War of the Polish Succession in the mid-thirties, but his Whig opponents questioned the wisdom of isolation. France was victorious and won the reversion to Lorraine, while Philip V of Spain succeeded in installing his younger son Charles on the throne of the Two Sicilies. Public opinion in Britain was not happy at Bourbon aggrandisement and friction with Spain over the trade with South America was at bursting point. The Spanish authorities searched ships for contraband, even outside territorial waters, and if they were high-handed the British were provocative. In the course of 1737–8 petitions to Parliament from leading ports and industrial towns protesting against atrocities by Spanish officials flowed in. Walpole's enemies gladly took up the cry for revenge, although at the same time they were pressing for military economies; they rebuffed the accusation of inconsistency with the argument that, true to the national interest, they were asking for naval, not military action. Pitt supported the motion of 4 February 1738 for the reduction of the standing army from 17,700 to 12,000 men. He solemnly rebuked a government member who had joked about the opposition: 'Remove the army or but a considerable part of it and the discontents complained of will cease. . . . The loading of our people with an additional expense of £200,000 or £300,000 is in my opinion an affair of too affecting a nature to be treated in a ludicrous manner.'

Newcastle was prepared to consider the possibility of war; 7 March found him reporting to his life-long friend, the 3rd Duke of Devonshire, Lord Lieutenant of Ireland: 'There is great and just resentment against Spain.' He thought it very probable that Parliament might force Walpole's hand.[10] A Captain Jenkins stood forth before the House of Commons and produced his ear, allegedly cut off by Spanish *guarda costas*. On 28 March no less than 468 members of Parliament attended what was said to have been the largest House since the passing of the Act of Union between England and Scotland. Walpole carried his moderate resolution by forty-seven votes. With some acerbity Pitt pointed out that a similar retort over grievances against Spain eight years before had had no effect whatsoever.[11] Walpole's enemies were united only in their hatred for the minister and 1 November 1738 found Pope describing their divisions to Lyttleton, following a conference with Wyndham.[12] Pulteney and Carteret were feared by the men who conceived themselves to be the honest opposition with a bitterness as deep as any they entertained for Walpole.

Sooner than endanger the profitable trade with Spain, Walpole was ready for almost any sacrifice. By the Convention of Pardo of January 1739 the claims of British merchants were cut down to a net payment of only £27,000 and the Spanish claim to a right of search on the high seas left open to further negotiation. Nothing could have been more calculated to stir the opposition to greater efforts. Walpole's brother, Horace the elder, moved an Address of Thanks to the King on 1 March and dwelt upon the country's state of isolation. Pitt made his first serious speech upon a great issue and Sir Robert troubled to take notes on it. Although administration maintained a majority of twenty-eight (260–232), Newcastle perceived that the public was roaring for a fight and Hardwicke considered the Convention useless. Walpole's ability to control his Cabinet was ebbing fast. At a Cabinet meeting of 1 June it was decided to send a fleet to lie in wait off Cadiz and intercept the treasure galleons expected from America.[13]

That summer preparations continued and on 7 July Newcastle wrote to Devonshire: 'We are hastening the manning of our fleet.' In September a French memorandum on their ships being stopped and searched was rejected and in a further letter of 22 September Newcastle remarked: 'They are fitting out ships in all their ports but don't seem in haste to declare against us.' Pelham was worried: 'I don't like Sir Robert's looks at all, he is, I believe, fretted to death.' War was declared three days later, with Prince Frederick leading the celebrations. That Walpole should embark his country upon this hazard against his better judgement was a sure indication of loss of authority. Newcastle was well content and in no way shared Walpole's prognostications, writing to Devonshire: '. . . our foreign affairs remain much as they did, France arms in all the ports more I believe at present to amuse Spain, and alarm us, than with any real design to make a vindictive use of their armaments.'[14]

At least war had one happy consequence for Walpole in that the opposition, their point gained, withered away. When next month Parliament met, he got the supplies passed without difficulty; on 21 December he survived by a large majority a vote of censure. Eyes were already turning towards the general election due in eighteen months. To keep the 'Patriot' flag flying and still more to patch over their mutual suspicions the opposition in February brought forward a Place bill. As usual, Pitt rose to denounce the patronage system: 'It must cut up Liberty by the root and poison the Fountain of Publick Security; and who that has an English heart can ever be weary of asserting Liberty?' The bill was defeated by only sixteen (222–206), with many of Walpole's supporters abstaining.[15]

The war opened with a triumph. The axis of the Spanish empire was the Panama isthmus and there on 22 November 1739 Admiral Edward Vernon made an easy capture of Porto Bello. The country went wild with delight, but Newcastle in his bubbling optimism should have taken heed when Fleury made plain that he would not countenance successful aggression against Spanish America. When thirty French ships of the line set sail Fleury insisted this was not to be construed as belligerency, but Walpole wrote to Devonshire in despair: '. . . this great affair is come to that crisis which I always fear'd in vain. This step is not a declaration of war but in its consequences an actual war . . .'.[16] During the long peace the army, of which the commanders were Marlborough's veterans, had fallen into decay. The navy could scarcely present a line of battle. A Spanish fleet, accompanied by French warships, sailed safely to the West Indies and the Flota laden with bullion entered Cadiz unmolested. The whole year passed by with nothing achieved. Forty years of incessant activity now took their toll of Walpole and at a Council about naval dispositions he exclaimed: 'God knows, I dare not do what I think right . . . I *dare not, I will not* make any alterations . . . let them go, let them go . . .'.[17] Anson had, however, left on his three-year voyage of exploration which led him to circumnavigate the globe and made his reputation. Future commanders, including Richard Saunders and Augustus Keppel, received their first serious training on this voyage.

While the war with Spain drifted without prospect of decision, the international situation was transformed by the dramatic events of the winter of 1740. That October Charles VI, the last Hapsburg Holy Roman Emperor in direct line, died suddenly from a chill caught out hunting. His dominions had – in twentieth-century terminology – comprised the entire states of Austria, Czechoslovakia, and Hungary, Silesia, more than half Roumania, north and west Yugoslavia including the Adriatic coast, in Italy Milan and finally, from the British point of view most important, Belgium. The Imperial throne, denoting a suzerainty over Germany, was elective but for three hundred years the Electors had without interruption chosen the head of the Hapsburg family. Charles VI had sought to ensure that his dominions should pass intact to his only child Maria Theresa, with her husband Francis of Lorraine, Grand Duke of Tuscany, elected as Emperor. Unfortunately Maria Theresa's rights were not above dispute, because Charles VI's elder brother, Leopold I, had left three daughters. Therefore Charles VI had secured the consent of Britain, France and the other powers to the Pragmatic Sanction, a guarantee under international law that Maria Theresa was sole heir. The Emperor's views were not exclusively dynastic, because a disputed succession must plunge Europe into war and his peoples into misery.

Shortly before the death of the Emperor, the King of Prussia had died, to be succeeded by his son Frederick II. This kingdom ranked only twelfth in population among the states of Europe and the economy was almost wholly agricultural. Frederick II's father had taxed and conscripted his peasantry so as to build an army 80,000 strong, but was so fond of his 'toy soldiers' that he never risked them in battle. Nobody expected that his effeminate, music-loving son, so proficient at the lute, would use this formidable fighting machine to prove himself a commander inferior only to Marlborough. To Frederick the death of the Emperor appeared singularly opportune and, putting up an embroidered claim, he invaded Silesia. The gamble was not uncalculated; the Elector of Bavaria, a grandson of the Emperor Leopold I, had expectations to any plum that might fall and above all Frederick confided in arousing the ancient enmity of Bourbon to Hapsburg.

Louis XV had at his call 130,000 soldiers; his fleet of eighty of the line was manned by 60,000 sailors; his revenues of sixty million crowns were put to buying the friendship of the minor courts; as Frederick remarked: '*France était l'arbitre de l'Europe.*' But to his dismay Frederick did not find fellow-conspirators; the conscience of Europe was deeply shocked at his lawless violence and Fleury wanted to keep the peace. In London there was a strong public opinion sympathetic to Maria Theresa and Carteret, out for his own ends, promised British support to the Austrian minister. Though British interests were not touched over Silesia, at the opening of 1741 Parliament voted Maria Theresa a subsidy of £300,000 in support of the obligation to uphold the Pragmatic Sanction.

Walpole's enemies could claim with some justification that his

Continental policies had been proved as futile as the attempt to appease Spain. From his French retreat Bolingbroke continued to urge his friends in Britain to procure Walpole's downfall. Chesterfield saw that a change of government must come about. In November 1740 Pitt and Lyttleton strongly attacked Walpole on the Address of Thanks to the King's Speech. In the following January the minister made a blunder: when papers which might throw light on the failure of the Mediterranean campaign were demanded, he dismissed the motion as a waste of time and Pitt again mounted his high horse: 'On the contrary, our time cannot be more usefully employed, during a war, than in examining how it has been conducted, and settling the degree of confidence that may be reposed in those to whose care are entrusted our reputations, our fortunes, and our lives. . . .' Walpole wisely yielded to the opposition demands.

Confident of victory at last, Pulteney in the Commons and Carteret in the Lords put down motions for 13 February asking the King to dismiss Walpole from his counsels for ever. Walpole again paid Pitt the compliment of taking notes on his speech, which was not of his best, abounding in hackneyed phrases – 'the exorbitance of one man' – 'a load of debt perpetuated by destructive schemes'. The upshot was a crushing defeat for the opposition by 184 votes (290–106). Many disliked the extreme character of the motion and the savageness of some opposition speakers. The death of Wyndham in the previous year had left the Tories leaderless and, with Carteret and Pulteney distrusted as they were by many Whigs, the Tories loved them even less.

On 10 March the opposition groups again banded together to attack the ministry in a full dress debate during which Pitt, in his last speech in his first Parliament, denounced the administration's naval press-gang proposals. When he turned to his rather tedious reiteration that the ministry was maintained by a venal majority, Walpole's brother Horace tried to laugh off his high-flown sentiments as the immature gestures of a tyro. But Pitt's earnest enthusiasm recoiled upon his detractor: 'The atrocious crime of being a young man – which the hon. gentleman has with such spirit and decency charged me I shall neither attempt to palliate nor deny, but content myself with wishing that I may be one whose follies may cease with their youth, and not of that number who are ignorant in spite of experience.'[18] Pitt's words, not Horace Walpole's, have gone down in history.

In April Frederick's startling victory at Mollwitz revealed that here was a general of no mean order. At once the hotheads at Versailles, led by Marshal the Duke of Belleisle, persuaded Louis XV that he should join Prussia in the attempt to despoil Maria Theresa of the inheritance which he had solemnly sworn to defend. Given French support, the Elector of Bavaria was certain to solicit election to the Imperial Crown. Walpole, though still completely in the King's trust, was having to reap where he had not sown and knew himself unable to conduct the war he had never wanted.

That summer the country went to the polls for the general election due under the Septennial Act, but domestic and frequently local issues, not foreign policy, decided eighteenth-century elections. Walpole knew the impressive stand he had made in the House of Commons was no guarantee of a swing in his favour. To the contrary his enemies had multiplied and it was to a degree a criticism of the régime that the young 4th Duke of Bedford, of impeccably Whig antecedents, should follow the politics of his Tory father-in-law the 2nd Lord Gower.

While the country was at the hustings rumour came that Vernon had won a great victory at Carthagena on the Spanish Main, followed by news not so good. By the third week of June it was definite that Vernon had been repulsed with heavy loss. A month later Prussia and France completed their alliance against Austria and, general election or no, the King insisted upon his annual visit to Hanover. In the country as a whole Walpole held his own but the Prince of Wales, backed by Thomas Pitt, swept government men out of many Cornish boroughs. The 2nd Duke of Argyll, who had formerly 'managed' the Scots elections for Walpole but, like Cobham had fallen foul over his opposition to the excise scheme, turned against him. Given all the circumstances Walpole was lucky to suffer a net loss of only twelve seats.[19] Questions domestic or foreign could make no jot of difference to the electoral fortunes of the Pitts and Grenvilles. Thomas Pitt again elected to sit for his borough of Okehampton and for Old Sarum he of course returned William. But their brother-in-law, Nedham, had been voting with

administration and in consequence forfeited his seat at Old
Sarum, which was given to Jemmy Grenville. Richard, the
eldest of the Grenvilles, chose the dignified situation of member
for Buckingham county, thereby relinquishing the borough seat
for his brother George who like Jemmy was entering Parliament
for the first time. An interesting young man to be returned at
this election was Sir Francis Dashwood 2nd Bart – always too
clever to be really ambitious.[20]

While the general election was in progress two French armies
invaded Germany – one to attack Bohemia and the other to
occupy Westphalia and so keep a check upon Holland and
Hanover; the Netherlands as well as Britain were pledged to go
to Maria Theresa's aid. Although Parliament had promised to
allow British troops to defend Hanover in the Austrian cause,
that September George II, in a fit of cold feet, agreed with
France that his German dominions should be neutral; he then
went so far as to cast his electoral vote in favour of the ruler of
Bavaria, who became the Emperor Charles VII. For the King
to separate so markedly his duties as Sovereign of Great Britain
and ruler of Hanover must work to Walpole's disadvantage in
Parliament.

During the summer Chesterfield went abroad for his health
and Pitt wrote to him, summing up the aims of opposition: 'I
will sum up the great task, which seems to require you, in the
words of the Litany, to comfort and help the weak-hearted, to
strengthen those that stand to raise up those that fall and finally
to beat down Satan under our feet.' In semi-humorous vein Pitt
alluded to Walpole as 'The Minister of Darkness' but recognised
the danger that all the efforts of the opposition would be
frustrated under the guise of a Cabinet reshuffle, and that 'Satan'
would carry on 'only to work destruction under a new name
with a double weight of Power and Authority . . . I have already
stuffed my letter with Latin and with figures enough to pass for
a Pedant . . .'. Soon Pitt's sister Ann would join the Chesterfield
ménage in France, a prospect which gave him much pleasure:
'. . . she is in good company, which will be both agreable and
usefull to her in her designs and lastly, far from burdening her
people with extraordinary votes of credit she will be able to live
very well within her Civil List.'[21] Pitt would have been far from

happy had he foreseen that this jaunt would set his sister upon a career of travel and lead to their estrangement.

Early in October Walpole was seriously ill and his doctors urged him not to carry on, but the King would not free him. When in November the new Parliament assembled Walpole's guaranteed majority was no more than twenty. But at bay in the House of Commons, the battle-ground he knew and loved so well, he was still formidable and his health was repaired. In a letter to Lyttleton Chesterfield showed no doubt that the opposition would be betrayed: 'Those who lead it will make it their business to break and divide it; and they will succeed. I mean Carteret and Pulteney.'[22] The test of Walpole's strength came with the hearing of election petitions, which were then decided by a Committee of the House voting on party lines. On 9 December two government candidates for Bossiney, who had been defeated by the machinations of Thomas Pitt, were declared true members. Three days later Walpole just failed to carry his own candidate as Chairman of the Committee of Elections and Privileges. When on 21 December Pulteney demanded the production of papers upon negotiations pending with France, Prussia and the Netherlands, Walpole reasonably pointed out that the national interest would be prejudiced thereby and kept a majority of ten (237–227).

Newcastle among others wanted Walpole to retire gracefully but the King would not hear of it. Although George II could sympathise with the ostensible object of the opposition, to prosecute the war more thoroughly, he could not agree to his minister being deposed by the House of Commons: no sovereign since 1688 had had to face such an indignity. After the New Year Walpole persuaded the King to offer Prince Frederick an additional £50,000 p.a. and the settlement of all his debts, which was of course turned down. Even so no one was absolutely certain that Walpole could not survive the session. On 21 January Pulteney, in a surprise move, asked for an enquiry into the conduct of the war, which amounted to a 'committee of accusation'. There were some thirty-five abstentions on the part of government supporters and Walpole, despite a superb display of nerve, ended the day with a majority of only three (253–250). On 30 January abstentions on the first hearing of the

Chippenham election petition lost administration the day by one vote. Next day Walpole privately intimated to his reluctant sovereign that his moment for retirement was come. When on 2 February the final vote on the Chippenham election went against Walpole by three, one of the counsel on the opposition side was Charles Pratt, a future Lord Chancellor, who wrote to a friend: 'So I am complimented by many friends as having assisted in giving the fatal blow to this great man, – a compliment wch I don't desire the credit of, but am content with the honour of having served my clients faithfully.'[23] Walpole, as soon as his defeat was announced, declared to members sitting near him his intention to retire.

Walpole's downfall was caused primarily by his being compelled to wage a war in which he did not believe. He was out of touch with public opinion and did not understand the restlessness of a younger generation too used to the security he had given them. Walpole saw his meticulous labours on the national finances subjected to a gambler's throw. But when victory failed to materialise, the nation lost confidence and his enemies became dangerous. Walpole had created his own opposition; his masterful lust for power was in a sense his weakness, for at the end there were banded against him men of ability maybe, but quite unconnected by any spirit of loyalty or ambition other than to see his ruin. Yet Walpole's achievement had been monumental. Since the time of Elizabeth's Lord Burleigh, her principal adviser for forty years, Walpole's unbroken twenty-one years in power has been a record never equalled. Pitt, Lyttleton and the Grenvilles expected a clean sweep of the 'Old Whigs', high places for Pulteney, Carteret and Chesterfield, and offices, albeit junior, for themselves. The new Whigs and the Hanover Tories would then call the tune for reform, a detailed enquiry into Walpole's corruption followed by a Place Act and triennial Parliaments. Chesterfield who did not share these jubilant expectations would not have been surprised to learn that Walpole had already planned with the King what the new arrangements were to be.

CHAPTER 3

Pitt, Carteret and the Pelhams

'He [Dr. Johnson] said, "Pulteney was as paltry a fellow as could be. He was a Whig who pretended to be honest. He cannot hold it out." He called Pitt a meteor, Sir Robert Walpole a fixed star.'[1]

Boswell's Journal of a Tour to the Hebrides with Samuel Johnson, LL.D.

Walpole made up his mind to take a peerage and the King adjourned Parliament for a fortnight. Only the First Lord of the Treasury had resigned and, although this momentous event must involve some changes, the King was adamant that these should be limited: to a reshuffle he had to bow but guided by Walpole made sure that the old system continue. Prince Frederick gave every assurance of goodwill: faced with a real situation he had to recognise that it was not in his ultimate interests to see the royal prerogative to make and unmake ministers curtailed. As in most important transactions in life, the decisions were taken by word of mouth. Newcastle had probably got in touch with Pulteney during the last fortnight of January. It is almost certain that on 2 February, the day of Walpole's defeat, Newcastle and Hardwicke met Pulteney and Carteret. Pulteney was offered the Treasury on condition that Walpole would not be subjected to persecution but faced with the prospect of doing instead of talking lost his nerve. He could have taken the Treasury with honour, on condition that his friends receive places and the opposition programme be implemented. Instead of grasping the nettle Pulteney allowed the King to slip Wilmington in as First Lord of the Treasury, who in 1727 had unsuccessfully tried to supplant Walpole. On the evening of 2 February Walpole wrote to Devonshire announcing his own retirement and the appointment of Wilmington as though it was a thing done. As he went on to point out, the only Cabinet office vacant was the Presidency of the Council: 'so that Lord Carteret can be only President, except one of the Secretaries be removed for him. This has fallen upon the D of N if I had not prevented it, but I am of opinion that the Whig party must be kept together, which may be done with this Parliament if a Whig administration be formed.'[2] Yet Walpole cannot have visualised that middle-aged debauchee Wilmington directing affairs; he took his peerage as Earl of Orford and by virtue of the King's friendship intended to control events.

Orford was underestimating Carteret. From the King's point of view Carteret's unpopularity with Chesterfield and Bolingbroke was a strong recommendation. It is likely that on 5 February Newcastle, Hardwicke, Pulteney and Carteret met for the second time. It was agreed that Carteret become Secretary of State for the Northern Department in place of the 1st Lord Harrington, who would succeed Wilmington as Lord President. A few followers of Pulteney and Carteret were placed at the Boards of the Treasury and the Admiralty and there matters came to a halt. Bolingbroke and Chesterfield were thus proved right in their expectation of a double-cross. The reconstituted ministry had one serious weakness in that all the ministers automatically of Cabinet rank were peers. Paymaster-General Pelham took over the Leadership of the House of Commons and was summoned to Cabinet meetings, but that arrangement could not be satisfactory especially in time of war.

To his sometime friends Pulteney made the lame excuse that a general election had occurred only a year ago and new placemen would have to seek re-election. On 12 February he addressed a meeting of two hundred members of Parliament assembled at the Strand Tavern. Cobham and Argyll were particularly angry at being left out and, together with Bedford and Gower, they waited upon Pulteney, who told them that nothing more would be forthcoming: these limited changes must be taken as an earnest of future benefits. The final blow to any hope of storming the Closet came when Prince Frederick accepted from Pulteney the terms Walpole had offered him at the New Year, an extra £50,000 p.a. and minor government places for a few of his following.[3] Thomas Pitt was shortly appointed Lord Warden of the Stannaries, which greatly increased his importance locally but was not what the Cobham Cubs had been aiming at. Although Prince Frederick was committed to support his father's government, Pitt and his friends decided upon the side wind course of remaining members of his household but continuing openly to oppose.

On 9 March the 1st Viscount Limerick, an Irish peer disappointed of his hopes of office, rose in the Commons with almost five hundred members present to demand an enquiry into the conduct of government over the past twenty years. Pitt declared that to postpone would be an evasion of duty: 'According to this way of arguing a minister that has plundered and betrayed his country, and fears being called to account in Parliament, has nothing to do but to involve his country in a dangerous war or some other distress, in order to prevent an enquiry into his conduct . . .'. The motion was defeated by two votes (244–242). But the nation was not satisfied; for years the opposition had denounced Walpole's corrupt practices and yet they seemed either unwilling or unable to vindicate their accusations. Eighteen counties and twenty-seven boroughs instructed their members to seek the restoration of triennial Parliaments, a limitation on placemen and an enquiry into the late administration.[4] On 23 March Limerick rose once more, to demand an enquiry limited to ten years which was carried by seven (252–245), but as Pulteney spoke for the motion and Prince Frederick's following voted in favour there was every indication of collusion. A committee of twenty-one members of Parliament was elected, Pitt's name coming twentieth. But Pulteney and Pelham were unwilling to organise a majority in the House to compel Treasury officials to give evidence. Pension and Place bills were allowed through the Commons but defeated in the Lords and the Commons threw out a bill to repeal the Septennial Act. At the end of the session the committee of enquiry came to an ignominious end. Some more friends of Pulteney, Carteret and the Prince were given places and Cobham was made a Field-Marshal. A condition was that Pulteney should take a peerage as Earl of Bath. There was a story that he trod on his patent in the House of Lords and he was never forgiven for such base treachery, rendered all the more odious by vast wealth allied to a miserly disposition.

Walpole's alleged misdeeds were of little concern by comparison with the mounting cost of the war. With the land tax at 4s instead of Walpole's 2s, it dawned upon the House of Commons that war was not the picnic they had expected. Pitt and his friends were bent upon using every opportunity to carp and criticise. Although the defence of Maria Theresa had been forced upon Britain as a point of honour, the Continental war for the Austrian Succession was very different to the 'blue-water' war with Spain. British interests were intimately involved in preventing the Austrian Low Countries from falling to France. The Dutch, no longer the nation that had given battle to Louis XIV, sidled into neutrality. Maria Theresa failed to prevent the election of the Bavarian Elector as the Emperor Charles VII, though on 12 February, the day of his coronation at Frankfurt, her troops entered Munich. Subsidies totalling £500,000 were voted on 2 April, £300,000 for Austria and the balance in the hope of securing an ally in Charles Emmanuel, King of Sardinia and ruler of Savoy-Piedmont, the buffer state between France and Italy with its capital at Turin. Pelham was certain that without a British army in the Low Countries the Dutch would never move. Irish regiments were drafted to England for home defence, so as to release British troops. It was argued that a military presence should follow, not precede, a Dutch declaration of war on France. A motion that the Irish troops stay in Ireland was defeated by 111 (280–169); of the Prince's household only Pitt and Lyttleton voted against the Government.[5]

Carteret was the most colourful man in public life, fluent in French, German and Italian, whilst his proficiency in the classics was considered by some improper in a gentleman. Bred to the grand manner he was liked by the King and Prince Frederick, but being a peer almost from birth had no experience of the House of Commons. He once remarked: 'Give any man the King on his side and he can defy anything', but Walpole's recent experience belied this. George II was delighted to find a minister more than ready to do his Hanover business. But Carteret's exhilaration in, as he put it, 'knocking the crowned heads of Europe together', depended upon Pelham's willingness and ability to persuade the House of Commons to find the money.

By the middle of 1742 the complete break-up of the Hapsburg territories seemed possible; in Bohemia Frederick beat the Austrians at Chotusitz on 17 May while a French army occupied Prague. Carteret considered the only hope lay in inducing Maria Theresa to buy Frederick off so that she could concentrate her energies against the Bourbons. He arranged for her subsidy to be raised to £500,000 p.a., and by the Treaty of Breslau of 25 July Silesia was recognised to be part of the Kingdom of Prussia. But Maria Theresa could not be expected to accept her expropriation as final, nor would Frederick feel secure while Austria was still mobilised, no matter who the enemy. With his customary selfishness the King decided that with Austria and Prussia at peace he need no longer maintain his Hanoverian army on a war footing. Carteret and Newcastle persuaded him to allow his men to be taken into British pay. A motley army of some 40,000 British and German soldiers came into being and the King announced his intention to take command in person. The only good news was of the exploit of Commodore Martin who, stop-watch in hand, offered the Bourbon King of Naples one hour in which to choose between neutrality and the bombardment of his capital. The King complied but never forgot the insult.

During the summer recess of 1742 Pitt's life as a member of Prince Frederick's entourage continued on the same lines as before Walpole's downfall. George Grenville had to go abroad for his health; on 1 September Pitt wrote to him from Clifden, mentioning that he had been at Marble Hill and in a week would undertake a peregrination to Wotton, Stowe and Hagley,

where he expected to meet Murray. Pitt urged Grenville to
prolong his French sojourn, for the political prospect was so
bleak that there was no point in his losing this opportunity to get
well. For his own part he planned a visit to Stowe for 21 October, where he would stay until Parliament met on 16 November,
but he also went to Hagley again, where Murray was once more
of the house party.[6] Murray had by this time decided that the
time had come when he must try his hand at politics. His
practice at the Bar was so remunerative that he could well
aspire to be Lord Chancellor or Lord Chief Justice, plums
always reserved for the Law Officers who had earned the gratitude of the administration for support in the House of Commons.
For Murray therefore politics meant government favour.
Newcastle, delighted to find such a recruit, wrote to Hardwicke
on 9 September: '. . . he will beat them all, with their own
friends, I mean Pitt, Lyttleton etc. . . .'. Murray had no wish to
lose old acquaintance and what could be more delightful than
his letter to George Grenville of 3 November: '. . . Pope is at
Bath, perched upon his hill, making epigrams, and stifling them
in their birth, and Lord H — y [Hervey] (would you believe
it?) is writing libels upon the King and his ministers.' That
month Murray was returned member for Newcastle's pocket
constituency Boroughbridge in Yorkshire and on 27 November
was appointed Solicitor-General. According to a letter from
Richard Grenville to George, Pelham had recently tried to buy
Cobham with the offer of a seat in the Cabinet, which was
turned down.[7]

When Parliament met on 16 November the burdening of the
British taxpayer with the Hanoverian army exposed the
administration to easy criticism. The Cobham Cubs ignored the
Prince's threat to dismiss members of his household who failed
to support administration. Pitt took the lead in the attack on the
Address and Richard Grenville described his performance in
glowing terms: 'Pitt spoke like ten thousand angels; your
humble servant was so inflamed at their indecency that he
could not contain, but talked a good while with his usual
modesty.' The Address was carried by 259 to 150 and the
Prince of Wales remarked: 'Pitt might as well have spit in his
face as he spoke as he did against this measure.' On 1 December

Pitt spoke in favour of reviving the committee of enquiry into Walpole's misdeeds but this was easily crushed by 253–186.[8] That Prince Frederick did not rid himself of the Cobham Cubs can be explained only by a fear of annoying Thomas Pitt, the mainstay of his electoral influence in the south-west.

When on 6 December Murray made his maiden speech in support of the vote for the maintenance of the allied army, Pitt hit out at the German subsidies and Hanoverian mercenaries. Murray managed very well and Pelham and Newcastle had every reason to be pleased with him. Three days later Pitt, when Sir William Yonge the Secretary at War moved the supply for 16,000 Hanoverian troops, denounced the 'German' policy: 'It is now too apparent that this great, this powerful, this formidable kingdom is considered only a province to a despicable electorate . . . We need only look at the instances of partiality that have been shown; the yearly visits that have been made to that delightful country. . . .' Speeches in this vein, repeated session after session, however carelessly reported, carry the stamp of verisimilitude to this day and earned Pitt the lasting hatred of the King. Supply was granted by a majority of 120 and then four days later the vote for the employment of Hanoverian troops went through by 67, with Pitt, George Grenville and Lyttleton speaking contra. Then on 10 March Pitt once more rose to support a vote of censure upon the Treasury for alleged jobbery over the payment of British troops abroad. Pelham rebutted him with aplomb and won the day by 29 (211–182). When on 21 April Parliament was prorogued, Pelham could look back upon his second session as Leader of the House with satisfaction.[9] Yet, though Pitt had in no wise dented administration, his patriot line was winning him popularity 'out-doors' and the marked attentions of London journalism. His great ambition was to take charge of the War Office and tell the King and the generals how to run things. That spring a caricature depicted him declaiming: 'Am I not an Orator? Make me Secretary at War.' To proffer the King mortal insult was the last way to go about that objective.[10]

The allied army moved from the Low Countries to the Rhine to intercept a new French army of 60,000. George II, sword in hand at the head of his infantry, defeated the French at

Dettingen on 21 June, the last occasion on which the monarch has taken the field in person. John Ligonier, a gallant Huguenot soldier, was knighted by the King upon the battlefield. Also present was James Wolfe, a sixteen-year-old ensign in the Suffolk Regiment. With the French army worsted, Carteret persuaded the Emperor Charles VII to abandon his ally and promised by the Convention of Hanau the return of Bavaria and a large sum of money. But Maria Theresa was not prepared to order her army out of Bavaria, her only gain, and Pelham was not ready to ask the House of Commons for yet more money for a German prince. Frederick was alarmed at the dominant position of Maria Theresa and jealous of his uncle George II using the power of his Kingdom to interfere in Germany. In Italy Carteret scored a success by persuading Maria Theresa to make over to Charles Emmanuel of Sardinia a small part of Lombardy as a bird in hand, while by the Treaty of Worms Britain undertook a subsidy of £200,000 p.a. But the Cabinet was growing restive at these expensive commitments and as Newcastle complained in his letter to Devonshire of 20 October: 'My brother Secretary is as uncommunicative as ever & now & then sends us a bold stroke which we have some difficulty to digest.'[11]

The First Lord of the Treasury, Wilmington, died in July 1743 and the King on Orford's advice nominated Pelham his successor. Pelham was ready to negotiate with Chesterfield, who was advocating the principle of a ministry upon a 'Broadbottom', to include all parties and unite the country. Bolingbroke, since Orford's retirement and his father's death made his position personally and financially more comfortable, had returned to England. He saw his opportunity to be back at the game and have his tit-for-tat with Carteret the turncoat. Murray stressed to Bolingbroke that if Carteret was to be deposed the Whig opposition and the ministry must coalesce. Bolingbroke did all he could to restrain Pitt from upsetting the King with violent speeches about Hanover. That September Pelham and Chesterfield came to an informal understanding that the Low Countries must be defended. But Cobham was not prepared to enter a formal alliance unless Bath was expelled from Court. To gain Cobham at the expense of Bath's followers,

which must also alienate Prince Frederick, would avail Pelham
nothing and the negotiation came to an end.

November came round with the King still in Hanover and
Pelham finding his situation intolerable. He wrote to Devonshire
of his predicament on the 7th: the King was not due home for at
least a week; there was no time to prepare the business of the
session due to open a week after that; no information had been
vouchsafed about military operations next year or engagements
with foreign powers; finally, complained Pelham: 'nor indeed
do I know in the least who are to be my brethren at the Board
of Treasury.' It was at this time that Pitt was emerging un-
mistakably as a leader. On 10 November a meeting at the
Fountain Tavern resulted in a declaration against the continued employment of Hanoverian troops signed by twenty-two
members of Parliament, including Pitt, Lyttleton, George and
Jemmy Grenville. The King and Carteret did not trouble to
arrive till 16 November, and when on the 24th the Cabinet met
they refused to ratify the new treaty with Austria. That day
Devonshire's son, the Marquis of Hartington, wrote to his
father: 'I begin to wish, & so do many people that we were to
joyn with the Cobham faction but their demands are so
enormous & their leader in our House I am afraid somewhat
impracticable.' This reference to Pitt and his 'impracticability'
shows how greatly his prestige had risen and he was included in
the opposition committee of three Whigs and three Tories
elected to co-ordinate strategy.

Yet Pitt had much to learn, for when Parliament met on
1 December he overplayed his hand by proposing the rejection
of the Address, never since 1688 successfully attempted. His
vicious harangue against the whole range of government policy
even contained a reflection upon the King's conduct at
Dettingen: 'Suppose it should appear that his Majesty was
exposed to few or no dangers abroad but what he is daily
exposed to at home, such as the overturning of his coach or the
stumbling of his horse. . . .' Pitt did his cause the greatest harm
and when Dashwood imprudently insisted upon a division the
administration triumphed by 129 (278–149). Five days later
Pitt returned to the attack: '. . . unhappily for his Majesty,
unhappily for Great Britain, while he was at the army he was

hemmed in by Hanoverian generals and one infamous English minister, who seems to have renounced the name of an Englishman.' Murray answered Pitt with impeccable logic, pointing out the absurdity of dismissing the Hanoverian troops when they could not be replaced; army officers of experience rose to defend the quality and discipline of the electoral forces and Pitt's motion was defeated by fifty (181–131).

Pelham was far more alarmed at Carteret's erraticisms than by Pitt's oratory: 'I can scarce describe the behaviour and turn of that *man*, he is as much intoxicated with power as with wine.' He set about consolidating his position and this did not mean a deal with the Cobham faction: 'We have nothing to do but to keep our *Old Corps* together, and if so, I believe time will bring about all we wish, tho with great difficultys and many disagreeablenesses.' After Walpole's example Pelham annexed the Chancellorship of the Exchequer to the Treasury and gave the Paymastership to Thomas Winnington, one of Walpole's old opponents. He reorganised the Board of Treasury and there one of the new members was Fox, promoted from household to executive position. On 8 December, therefore, Gower resigned as Lord Privy Seal and Cobham gave up his regiment. That day, on a motion for the disbandment of the 16,000 Hanoverian troops in British pay, forty-three members spoke in a very full House and once more Pitt went too far, only to earn a reprimand from the Speaker. Three unexpected deaths enabled Pelham to fill some junior posts advantageously. Carteret fumed about getting Hardwicke dismissed, but gossip did not expect his reign to last.

By the end of December Pitt, Lyttleton and Chesterfield had come round to favour British troops in Flanders and still hoped to enter into a union with Pelham; Cobham and the Grenvilles, on the other hand, wished the Continental war to be abandoned and looked to overthrow the ministry on this issue. As between Pitt and Cobham the disagreement was the beginning of a personal animus. When so usually close-knit a faction as the Cobhamites were unable to agree among themselves, the chances of an effective parliamentary campaign were small and it was this which made it impossible for the King and Carteret to break Pelham. On 15 December George Grenville moved an Address praying the King not to enter into further overseas engagements without first securing the co-operation of the Dutch. Murray soon pointed out that British policy could not be thus circumscribed and although Pitt amended the actual wording, once more the administration won easily with a majority of 77 (209–132). There were complaints that the opposition committee was dictatorial: 'they have now got into a method of not telling their people what they intend to propose but only summon them upon business'. In one last effort to patch up the administration, Pelham agreed to let Carteret run the war provided the management of places and persons was his. The tensions could not be completely subdued: 'Publick affairs,' Pelham wrote to Devonshire on 9 January, 'continue in much the same way they were, Lord C — t professes and looks humbler, but his thoughts and actions, I believe, are as high as ever.'

At a general meeting at the Fountain Tavern on 10 January Pitt and Lyttleton were overruled in their wish to approve a grant of supply for the service in Flanders. When next day the House went into committee on the vote for the 23,000 British troops, Pitt and Lyttleton stayed silent rather than follow their friends. Pelham and Murray scored an easy victory (277–165) but the debate of 18 January on the Hanoverian troops gave their critics a real chance. Pitt heaped abuse upon Carteret, 'a Hanover troop minister, a flagitious taskmaster, whose only party are the 16,000 Hanoverians, the placemen by whose means he has conquered the Cabinet. . . .' When Pelham's majority fell to forty-five (271–226), it was plain that Carteret was a liability. But the ministry was held together by information at the beginning of February that the French fleet had put to sea. When towards the end of the second week of the month the enemy appeared off Torbay, there was no doubt that the object was to make Dunkirk, where was assembled an army generalled by Marshal Saxe and graced with the presence of the Young Pretender.

Pitt now showed once more that as tactician he had grave weaknesses. When on 15 February the King notified the Commons of the possibility of invasion, Pitt supported an attempt to tack a demand for an enquiry into the navy on to the Address of Thanks. He spoke with some heat, though nothing to Dashwood's comparison of King George with the tyrant James II. They were routed by 164 (287–123) and for the rest of the session such attempts to score points aroused great impatience. Pitt saw the need for caution and when on 24 February Pelham proposed increases in the army and navy, he declared that with invasion imminent confidence must be reposed in the ministers. When George Grenville attempted to oppose the suspension of the Habeas Corpus Act on 28 February, Pitt and Lyttleton left the House. Pitt might attack Carteret as 'the rash author of those measures which have produced this rash, impracticable war' but precautions for national defence had to be backed up.[12]

While the invasion scare was at its height false reports reached London that the fleet had defeated the French and Spanish off Toulon but in fact there was no battle. This disappointment was counterbalanced by the complete dispersal of the enemy fleet in the Channel by a gale so that Louis XV's formal declaration of war on 28 March fell flat. Pelham was relieved at the King's decision to stay in London that year rather than go treaty-making. As the invasion had miscarried, Saxe's army was sent into the Low Countries and this illegitimate scion of the Saxon royal house, who had distinguished himself by countless adventures in love, would now prove himself to be one of the great masters of the art of war. In view of Saxe's successes Frederick the Great once more took the field. His invasion of Bohemia proved a costly failure, but he saved Silesia in a brilliant campaign. The whole concept of Carteret's diplomacy to isolate France by Frederick being neutral had foundered.

A romantic adventure will always create an excitement that not even the most stirring public events can compete with and the London sensation of 1744 was the elopement of Fox with Lady Caroline Lennox, daughter of the 2nd Duke of Richmond. Her parents were outraged and Newcastle's horror at a marriage between the parvenu Fox and a great-grand-daughter of Charles II reflected fairly the prejudices of the time. But Lady Caroline chose well, for her life was ideally happy and soon all animosity was overcome, which meant that Fox was drawn into the orbit of the great houses.

The early winter of 1744 found Pitt seriously ill at Bath,

undergoing his worst attack of gout hitherto, and his life was not thought certain.[13] While almost at death's door he encountered a splendid turn of fortune. Sarah Duchess of Marlborough had four years before used Chesterfield as intermediary to make known her intention to make provision for Pitt in her Will, in token of his opposition to the Court. The Duchess, who had never forgiven the Hanoverians for slighting her husband, was the richest woman in England and at her death on 14 October owned property in eleven counties south of the Trent. Her senior grandson the 3rd Duke of Marlborough had not consulted her wishes over his marriage so by her twenty-seventh and last Will, dated 11 August 1744, she left her unentailed real estate to her other grandson John, or Jack, Spencer for life, and afterwards to his son, John II. It was the codicil, dated 15 August, that concerned Pitt: '*I also give* to *William Pitt* of the Parish of *St. James* within the Liberty of *Westminster* Esq; the sum of 10,000 l. upon account of his Merit in the noble *Defence* he has made for the support of the Laws of *England*, and to prevent the Ruin of his *Country*.' To Chesterfield the Duchess left 'my best and largest brilliant Diamond Ring, and the sum of 20,000 l'. Duchess Sarah provided that should the Spencer line die out her estates should pass to the secondary beneficiaries and to Pitt were apportioned lands in Buckinghamshire, Staffordshire and Northamptonshire. By Jack Spencer's death upon 19 June 1746, Pitt, together with Chesterfield, the 2nd Viscount Fane, on his mother's side a nephew of Pitt's uncle Stanhope, and Dr Stevens MD became trustees for one of the richest children in England. It was Pitt who convened their first meeting in a letter to Dr Stevens of 30 June 1746. Young John Spencer lived to become the 1st Earl Spencer and to found a family, so the landed reversion never came Pitt's way, but he had the £10,000.[14]

With the winter session of 1744–5 about to open Pelham was anxious to get rid of Carteret so as to save the Old Corps of the Whig party from defeat in the House of Commons, no matter what the attitude of the King and Prince Frederick. The opposition were ready to support Pelham because in Carteret's fall they foresaw places for themselves. George II turned to Orford for advice, to be told that Carteret must go. Recognising that the game was up, the King in a private interview with Hardwicke on 23 November announced that Carteret was prepared to resign. But Carteret's career was far from ended. About a month before his downfall he had inherited his mother's peerage, becoming the 2nd Earl Granville, and her fortune; despite the influence of the port bottle his brilliance of self-expression would never waver, to the delight of his enemies as much as his friends. When Parliament assembled on 27 November both Houses unanimously voted Addresses of Thanks for the King's Speech: Granville had been so tactless that hardly anyone except the King sympathised with him. Pelham had none the less to pacify his irate Sovereign, reorientate British foreign policy and above all find the vast sums necessary for the war. For this last object, as Hardwicke pointed out, the co-operation of the opposition was essential. To this end the Lord Chancellor proposed to distribute honours and lucrative places though not, he craftily hoped, such as would confer influence over policy.

Chesterfield forwarded to Newcastle a list of 'our necessary people' on 1 December and that month saw a series of conferences in which Cobham was included. By the Christmas recess the major changes were decided: Harrington succeeded Granville as Secretary of State for the Northern Department, Chesterfield became Lord Lieutenant of Ireland, Gower returned as Lord Privy Seal and, outside the Cabinet, Bedford became First Lord of the Admiralty. So as to prevent Granville and Bath forming an effective faction only thirteen of their followers were thrown out. Cobham secured places for his Cubs; Lyttleton became a Lord of the Treasury and there was a vacancy on Bedford's Board of Admiralty for George Grenville. Pitt was left out and his singularity became still more marked when at the New Year Jemmy Grenville was made a Lord of Trade. Horace Walpole described Pitt as 'ravenous for the place of Secretary at War', and also suggested that, not wishing to forfeit influence in the House of Commons, he deliberately asked for so senior a position knowing he would be refused.

Every day the King sat with his cronies, making and un-making Cabinets. On 5 January 1745 Hardwicke in a long audience protested against such ill usage: 'The disposition of places is not enough, if Your Majesty takes pains to show that you disapprove of your own work.' The Lord Chancellor entered a bland disclaimer to the King's allegation that he had been forced to take his ministers. The Pelhams could not, however, be expected to carry out measures contrary to their judgement of the national interest. Hardwicke gently pointed out that it was the administration which carried weight with the country: '. . . if your Majesty looks round the House of Commons, you will find no man of business or even of weight left, capable of heading or conducting an opposition.'[15] Pitt was indeed out in the cold and the Grenvilles sympathised with his plight: 'How does Pitt do?' asked Richard in a letter to George of 8 January, 'Let him know I enquired of you after him, for I am not yet resolved to forget entirely all my old friends.'[16]

As he nursed an agonising attack of gout, Pitt came to see that unless he came to terms with administration he would be completely without a future. When on 22 January 1745 Pelham proposed to increase the British contingent in Flanders Pitt appeared wrapped in blankets, a suffering patriot concerned with the good of the nation. He stoutly declared 'that a dawn of salvation to the country had broken forth . . . he should be the greatest dupe in the world if those now at the helm did not mean the honour of their master, and the good of the nation.' The vote went through with but a single negative. The Hanover troops were skilfully left out of the estimates as an independent item but Maria Theresa's subsidy was increased by £200,000 so that she could take them into her pay. Although this wangle was bound to arouse criticism, Pitt gave his support, ingenuously declaring that his real objection to the electoral troops had been to their employment in conjunction with British regiments. The enlarged Austrian subsidy was voted almost unanimously. A vote covering short pay to the Hanoverians on their leaving the British service, the Saxon subsidy and even an enormous vote of credit for half a million pounds to meet unanticipated contingencies, all went through with no trouble from Pitt. To many his conduct appeared nothing but a *volte face* calculated to win office. But it had been Pitt, Lyttleton and Grenville who early in 1744 had tried to influence the opposition into supporting the war in Flanders. With 'the Hanoverian troops minister' out of the way, the patriotic reasons for supporting the war were even stronger.

Pitt had shown Pelham how useful a recruit he might be and at the end of April resigned from Prince Frederick's household, a parting of the ways from his brother Thomas, who remained Lord Warden of the Stannaries. But if Pitt expected an immediate benefit he was due for disappointment. Pelham was in no position to forward his claims, for every day he and his brother walked in fear of dismissal. At least twice the King told them to send for Granville, who on the death of the Emperor Charles VII received the foreign envoys as though his appointment was determined. But after the prorogation of 2 May the King left for Hanover, leaving his administration as it was. The position that confronted him in Europe was far from reassuring. He had appointed his favourite son, the Duke of Cumberland, Commander-in-Chief, whom following eighteenth-century custom and the example of Horace Walpole will be referred to as the Duke with a capital. Saxe defeated the Duke at Fontenoy and shut him and his army up in Antwerp. In Italy Maria Theresa had to contend with an invasion of Lombardy. Her husband was elected Emperor as Francis I, but her attempts to wrest Silesia were defeated. By a Convention with Frederick Britain undertook to induce Austria to make a separate peace, a revival of Granville's policy which, however, George II disliked intensely without having him as minister too. The only British success was the capture of Cape Breton Island off the mouth of the St Lawrence by colonial forces on 27 July.

The landing of the Young Pretender at Glenfinnan on 25 July caught Pelham and Newcastle completely off their guard. At first the brothers believed the forces already in Scotland could contain the rebels and with great reluctance the King undertook a premature departure for London on 25 August. His real interest lay not in Bonnie Prince Charlie but in getting rid of his ministry. He refused to discuss anything except the disavowal of the Convention with Prussia and spent most of his time with Granville and Bath. Then on 17 September he offered Harrington complete direction of affairs provided he could be rid of Pelham and Newcastle. This dishonourable proposition Harrington refused to touch and it said much for

Pelham's sense of patriotism that he carried on: 'subjected to such foul language that no one gentleman could take from another.'

The Pretender's capture of Edinburgh and his victory over Sir John Cope at Prestonpans brought the King down to earth. The meeting of Parliament was put forward to 17 October. The Speech from the Throne prudently touched on the rebellion only; the mood of the Commons was one of loyalty and a Tory amendment to the King's Speech was lost without a division. Dashwood proposed tacking on to the Address of Thanks demands for shorter Parliaments and electoral reform to combat 'influence', a piece of irresponsibility which Pitt sensibly advised the House to ignore.[17] Pelham found this session of the Commons very difficult to handle; everyone knew of Granville's influence, so that attendance was very slack and few respected a minister unable to prevent the country being invaded. On 23 October Pelham had a most disagreeable audience of the King 'tho it ended', as Hartington related to his father, 'in a sort of power to settle matters as he pleased . . .'.

That afternoon Pitt mischievously produced out of the hat a motion to withdraw all British troops from Flanders. His aim was purely tactical because all but 2,000 horse had already been ordered home to fight the rebellion. Pitt had decided to teach the King a lesson in the power he could exercise if he chose, and when the ministry proposed the previous question the House gave them a majority of only 12 (148–136). This decided Pelham, who at once summoned Pitt for an interview which took place two days later. Pitt combined a request to be made Secretary at War with strong conditions: a Place Act to exclude all service officers under the rank of Lieutenant-Colonel from the House of Commons and the dismissal of Granville's friends. Pelham made no trouble about a Place Act and would no doubt have welcomed the other. But he could not yield to Pitt's demand for the limitation of the British contingent abroad to 10,000 men and the wisdom of leaving the Low Countries to Saxe's army was more than questionable.[18] Although he and Pelham parted on friendly terms, Pitt joined in a temporary alliance with a group of Whig Scots peers and members of Parliament alarmed at what the consequences of the rebellion might be for their country. Their mouthpiece was Alexander Hume-Campbell, one of the ablest practitioners at the Bar. His motion of 28 October for an enquiry into the causes of the rebellion was in reality a vote of censure upon Pelham for neglecting to foster and cherish the loyal elements north of the Border and Pitt acted as seconder. But the House of Commons had little patience with the conscience of North Britain and not even the west country Tories troubled to give Campbell and Pitt support. The motion was thrown out by a majority of eighty-two (194–112), which enabled a happy King to point out to Pelham that Pitt's standing was so poor that his services were unnecessary.[19]

In Pelham's chapter of woe Pitt's devilment was nothing to the complications Bedford was causing by his well-meant but wrong-headed proposal that noblemen should raise regiments initially at their own expense: 'once certified to be half compleat, an establishment is to be made for them, and they are to be paid by the publick.' Though none questioned the honesty of Bedford's patriotism, the executive problems were formidable. The King, who hated his army being meddled with and was in no way averse to multiplying Pelham's troubles, let it be known that he wished officers without regular commissions to have honorary rank only. When on 1 November the business came before the House the ministry was hopelessly divided. Pitt was among the administration majority of 168 (235–67) which gave approval in principle. The details took up much parliamentary time and led to embarrassing altercations among junior ministers. Pelham saw no reason why the commissions should be honorary and Pitt stood loyally by him when his majority on that question fell to only two. Then the King, a little alarmed at what he had done, changed his mind, so that on 4 November a further Address to limit commissions to regulars was defeated by twenty (153–133). Passions ran high: Fox and the Prince's followers spoke against the administration but Winnington, though he voted for the Address, was silent: 'There was high words passed between Pitt and H. Campbell. The House interposed and with some difficulty they were appeas'd.'

Pelham felt badly shaken and decided upon a further attempt to gain Pitt. Newcastle arranged a meeting for 16 November at

Gower's town house: Hardwicke, Harrington, Pelham, New-castle, Gower, Bedford, Cobham and Pitt were present. Pitt reiterated his demands of 25 October and once more Pelham would not consent to a limit on British troops in the Low Countries. Newcastle described the proceedings: 'Everything passed very civilly but Lord Cobham and Mr. Pitt were strongly of opinion against the other six that we ought to declare to the Dutch that we could not assist them with more than 12,000 men.' Pelham and Newcastle believed that this policy would merely drive Holland into making a separate peace. 'I am afraid,' Newcastle continued, 'this disposition will prevent our coming to such an agreement with Mr. Pitt as seems absolutely necessary in our present circumstances.'

In view of this impasse Pitt resolved upon a further thrust in the House of Commons. But considering that Pelham and still more Newcastle were so friendly disposed, he was most unwise to treat them as enemies and even to prevail upon Lyttleton to join in. On the morning of 21 November, as the Treasury Board was concluding a meeting, Lyttleton took Pelham aback with the intelligence of Pitt's intention later that day to put forward in the Commons an Address praying for an augmentation of the navy. This surprise proved ill-timed, for the House was thinly attended and Pelham blandly pointed out that to discuss the navy with a Jacobite army in Cumberland was very pointless. At this Pitt amended his motion to an intimation that the House would welcome an increase in supply: 'Mr. Pitt in his second speech with affected candour and great unfairness abused Mr. Pelham. . . .' Pitt got his deserts when only thirty-six members voted with him against eighty-one, who included most of the Tories there. As Fox pointed out, Bedford and Gower, all the peers lately introduced into the Government, together with the entire Board of Admiralty except George Grenville were against a war purely naval. Chesterfield, on the other hand, in a letter of 25 November advised Newcastle to make a deal with Cobham: 'The Prince and Lord Granville and company neither can nor will support you, they want the power as well as the places, whereas my friends in the opposition only want places, without being, or meaning to be, your rivals in power.'

By the first week of December the rebels had passed through Cheshire. The Commons began quietly on Thursday, 10 December, with messages from the King concerning the detention of prominent Jacobites and some slight purring from Dashwood about the suspension of Habeas Corpus. Then Pitt suddenly asked whether the order had yet been given to recall the cavalry from Flanders. When Pelham pointed out that he had three weeks ago assured the House that such was the case, Pitt jumped up and demanded that the orders and the dates be laid before the House. Pelham was furious at his good faith being queried: 'This gave me an opportunity to speak more largely than I have hitherto done upon the present posture of affairs and upon the behaviour of those gentlemen.' Pitt's impertinence was coldly received even by the Hanover Tories, many of whom walked out. When Dashwood divided the House Pitt, Lyttleton and George Grenville were joined only by the Jacobites to muster a miserable forty-one votes. Many expected the dismissal of Grenville and Lyttleton, but Pelham decided it was not worth driving the Cobham Cubs into a formed opposition. If Pitt's intention was to ease his passage into the ministry he was much in error; as Newcastle commented to Devonshire: 'My brother, I conclude, sent word of the remarkable behaviour of Mr. Pitt, the last day the House sat whereby he seems to have made all further correspondence extremely difficult.'

So as to augment the apprehensions of London at the advance of the rebels, the French assembled 14,000 troops at Dunkirk. The arrival of 6,000 Hessian soldiers sent for by the King caused general relief. But when on 19 December Parliament was informed of their arrival, Pitt spoke with great intemperance, though he knew that in the Cabinet even Cobham had been for summoning the Hessians. Fox could not comprehend why he should choose to endanger 'his own ambitious views, when he was quite sure of them. . . .' Soon the rebels would turn about and pass back over the Border. The day before Christmas the Government pulled off a coup by the signing of the Treaty of Dresden which established peace between Maria Theresa and Frederick, who kept Silesia.

Pitt came to see that his spitfire methods would not pay off and the opportunity the rebellion had offered was fast contracting. After the Christmas recess it was he who suggested through Bedford a further approach by Pelham to Cobham. Pelham met Cobham next day, but his parliamentary position was now much stronger. Policy was not mentioned: Cobham merely asked that Pitt be made Secretary at War, Lord Barrington be put on the Board of Admiralty and Jemmy Grenville be given a place worth £1,000 p.a. On 6 January Pelham and Newcastle put Cobham's proposals before the King who declared that he would never accept Pitt as Secretary at War, the rebuff they probably even hoped for. Pitt had by now alienated even such an old friend as Chesterfield, who five days later wrote to Newcastle: 'I am astonished and grieved at the unaccountable conduct of Pitt . . .'. He advised reliance upon Bedford and Gower with some sop for Lyttleton and the Grenvilles, 'which would cripple Pitt's opposition extremely'.

Pitt's tactics had indeed been utterly misjudged because Pelham himself had come round to the opinion that the Dutch must be blackmailed into meeting their full responsibilities, but George II, as always, opposed any reduction in British forces on the Continent. When on 14 January Parliament reassembled, Pelham found the Commons complaisant enough and even a vote to continue the noblemen's regiments for eight months passed by a majority of eighty-one. But with the Jacobite rebellion obviously beaten the King came out in his old colours and by the beginning of February had secretly arranged that Bath should take the Treasury with Granville in place of Newcastle at the Southern Department. He expected Harrington to bow to the storm and Winnington as Paymaster might manage the Commons. Ignorant of this intrigue, Pitt in tactful mood was offering to take, instead of the War Office, some minor place rather than force himself upon the King, but his future was now a very secondary interest. On 9 February Pelham, Newcastle and Harrington met at Hardwicke's and decided to resign; further resignations followed and finally no less than forty-five ministers and placemen either went or declared their intention of doing so. For this the King had not been ready, especially as many of the resignations were not directly solicited by Pelham but a spontaneous protest against the prospect of Granville and Bath. For four days the King hung on: Bath would have come to terms with the Tories but this the King could not stomach and sent Winnington to ask Pelham and Newcastle to come back.

Pelham took the opportunity to consolidate his position. A minute of 13 February was drawn up for the King: once and for all 'private councils' would have to end and the last henchmen of Bath and Granville must be turned out. The minute ran on to ask the King: 'That he will be graciously pleased to perfect the scheme lately humbly proposed to him for bringing Mr. Pitt into some honourable employment, and also the other persons formerly named with him.' The vacant Garters must be distributed among Pelham's friends and finally the policy of forcing the Dutch into full co-operation in the war must have full support. A number of Bath's and Granville's friends were dismissed: Barrington joined George Grenville and Henry Legge on Bedford's Admiralty Board and Jemmy Grenville became a member of the Board of Trade. But not even a crisis of this magnitude could get Pitt his coveted War Office. He could not risk alienating all his friends, so had to accept the very junior post of joint Vice-Treasurer of Ireland.

Chesterfield thought that by taking Pitt in the Pelhams had made a dangerous bargain and wrote to Newcastle on 27 February: '. . . But I promise you he will not be easy till he is Secretary at War and Dick Grenville at the Treasury.' But Pitt did not mean to make himself a nuisance for the time being. On 4 March he attended one of Pelham's 'coalition dinners', which also comprised Lyttleton, Barrington, 'Dick' and George Grenville, Yonge, Winnington, Bedford's protégé Legge and Fox. And in the House of Commons Pitt took the official line, which was a demand by Pelham for £400,000 for Austria, £300,000 for Sardinia and £310,000 for the maintenance of eighteen thousand Hanoverian troops. On the report stage he held the House in what Fox described as 'the finest speech I ever heard'. An enthusiastic Newcastle wrote to Cumberland:[20]

'Mr. Pitt spoke so well, that the *Premier* told me; he had the dignity of Sir William Wyndham; the wit of Mr. Pulteney; and the knowledge and judgement of Sir Robert Walpole. In short, he said all that was right, for the King; kind and respectful to the *Old Corps*; and resolute and contemptuous of the present Tory opposition.'

Five days later the Highlanders were massacred at Culloden.

Pelham received a shock in Winnington's death on 23 April. Yonge was in failing health and would willingly have swapped the War Office for the Paymastership. Here Pitt saw his opportunity but the King would have none of that. Pitt, realising that now or never he must press himself forward, wrote to Pelham earnestly asking to become Paymaster. To this Pelham extracted the King's concurrence and on the morning of 26 April Newcastle was given leave to inform Pitt that he was to become Paymaster-General. Two days later Newcastle wrote Bedford a word of explanation: 'His Majesty was determined not to have him at the War Office.'[21] It was a reluctant Fox who on 14 May agreed to become Secretary at War, which meant hard work for less money than Pitt would get.

At one time Pitt had seen himself, with his great reputation 'out-doors', overthrowing the administration and storming the Closet. Instead he had to bow before the unassailable strength of the eighteenth-century system of government. The truth was that the average member of Parliament did not like popular tactics and, provided the needs of the country were adequately met, found the idea of forcing the King's hand utterly distasteful. That Pitt took office in the course of an upheaval between George II and his ministers, which helped mould the eighteenth-century constitution, cannot be denied. But this aspect of things was very much played down by Pelham, Newcastle and Hardwicke. Glancing back, Hardwicke would remark: 'I remember that in 1745, when the King was pushed to make this gentleman himself Secretary at War and we were all quitting for it, he himself, the party concerned, thought fit totally to disdain force, had no thought of the resignations, and would concert in the support of the King's measures without taking any place at all, which I think he did till the Paymastership became vacant.'[22] The conditions Pitt had attempted to lay down were soon forgotten. 'Out-doors' he had lost much popularity:[23]

'He bellowed and roared at the Troops of Hanover . . .

That no man was honest who gave them a vote . . .
But nature had given him ne'er to be Harrass'd
An unfeeling heart and a front unembarrass'd.'

Pitt had no ground for disappointment, for Walpole and Pelham had both served their terms at the Pay Office after – not before – being Secretary at War. Furthermore, they had each gone straight from the Paymastership to becoming First Lord of the Treasury. Pitt, as he himself expressed it, had 'entered the stream of promotion, which by its natural current and the right of succession in the graduation of office . . . commonly bears men to fortune'. The years might well yield him a dazzling future and when his attacks upon the King were recalled, most men no doubt thought him more than fortunate. Pelham summed up the position in a letter to Ilchester: 'I don't doubt but you will be surpris'd that Mr. Pitt should be thought on for so high and lucrative an employment; but he must be had, and kept.'[24] Pitt for his part may well have reflected that, after all, Pelham was over fifty and life in the eighteenth century was a hazardous affair.

Pitt had outstripped the Cobham Cubs; his brother Thomas's abilities were merely managerial; of the Grenvilles Richard was proud, George pedestrian, Jemmy a natural subordinate and Lyttleton unimpressive away from his books. Though Pitt's qualities had taken time to emerge, there was honesty about his ambition and an imagination in his oratory which, with his evident courage, marked him for leadership. The Grenvilles were in truth jealous. Fox's promotion left a vacancy on the Treasury Board and to this George Grenville at once aspired. There was, however, a resentment at the growing power of Pitt and the Stowe set, whom Bedford described as 'the orator and his junto, who you may perceive are not easily satisfied . . .'. The post went to Legge and to Grenville it was made clear that in view of Pitt's 'great and sudden rise' his expectations must be put off.[25] In Pitt, Fox and Murray Pelham had marshalled into the service of administration the three most able, still young members of Parliament and had every reason to be satisfied. The Jacobite rebellion had enabled him to survive a constitutional crisis unscathed and left him in an unassailable situation.

CHAPTER 4

Paymaster-General

'To bring this directly to you; know that no man can make a figure in this country, but by Parliament. Your fate depends on your success there as a speaker; and, take my word for it, that success depends much more upon your manner than matter. Mr. Pitt, and Mr. Murray, the Solicitor General, are beyond comparison, the best speakers; why? Only because they are the best orators. They alone can inflame or quiet the House; they alone are so attended to, in that numerous and noisy assembly, that you might hear a pin fall while either is speaking.'

Philip Dormer Stanhope 4th Earl of Chesterfield to his illegitimate son Philip Stanhope, 11th February 1751.[1]

When Walpole had in 1714 happily accepted the Paymaster-ship, gossips commented that 'he was very lean and needed to get some fat on his bones'.[2] The job was recognised as a legitimate means of making a fortune. The splendid mansion in Whitehall and the salary of £4,000 p.a. did not compare with the perquisites. The Paymaster-General was responsible for paying the army and the Treasury handed him personally the moneys, which he could bank whilst retaining the interest together with any other profits upon the accounts. In addition he was allowed to reap a commission of one quarter per cent upon subsidies voted by Parliament to allied powers. Foreign princes keeping armies out of the British taxpayer were naturally inclined to make the Paymaster handsome presents. Pitt, as

puritan in his public dealings as in his private life, refused to
accept these plums, credited all interest to the Government and
took the residence and salary only. Although he was following
the example set by Pelham as Paymaster at the outbreak of the
Austrian war, public criticism over his acceptance of office was
disarmed. From this point Pitt enjoyed a reputation for placing
the interests of his country above paltry material ends. Pitt
appointed Jemmy Grenville deputy-paymaster. Cobham was
so incensed at one of his family being taken from his tutelage
that he cut Jemmy out of his will.[3]

So far the only British success in the war had been the
capture of Cape Breton Island, and before Culloden Bedford
had put to Newcastle that an attack upon Quebec might
follow. This 'blue-water' project had been ventured by Bolingbroke in 1711 and if effective would be a consummate riposte
to the French invasion of the Low Countries. Bedford calculated
that the expedition could be made ready by the end of April and
reach the St Lawrence by August, so that Canada might be
reduced before the onset of winter. The expectation that an
amphibious force could be organised within only a month of a
directive leaving Whitehall was far too sanguine. But Newcastle
dithered through the spring without decision. Bedford was
strongly backed by George Grenville on the Admiralty Board,
but he can hardly have relished the terms in which Pitt on
19 July assured him of his support: '. . . those great and practicable views in America, which, so far as they have gone or are to
go, we owe to your Grace alone. You are alone, however, but in
one place, for the nation is certainly with you; with such a
second, your Grace can surmount all obstacles.'

News from the Continent during the summer of 1746 was in
some respects better. Philip V of Spain died in July and his son
Ferdinand VI, convinced that the interests of his country
demanded an early peace, withdrew his troops from north Italy.
The Austrian army expelled the French from Lombardy and
even invaded Provence. But in the Low Countries Cumberland
was no match for Saxe who defeated him at Roucoux and
seized Brussels. With the approach of winter the ministry
became acutely divided over the question of peace or war;
Pelham, Harrington and Chesterfield thought peace imperative,

Newcastle and Hardwicke wanted to fight on. The King favoured war and had not forgiven Harrington his loyalty to Pelham: there ensued the type of intrigue that proved the monarch no cypher. Newcastle, although northern Europe lay in Harrington's province, had with the King's connivance been carrying on a private correspondence with the 4th Earl of Sandwich, Ambassador at The Hague. When on 28 October Harrington confronted the King with this double-dealing his resignation was relished. Chesterfield, though ostensibly of the peace party, sacrificed his principles as a bargain to win Harrington's place, a reshuffle fixed up between Newcastle and the King behind Pelham's back.[4] By this time a decision was necessary upon whether to launch an attack upon Canada during the spring of the year following. An expedition was fitted out, but Newcastle had no enthusiasm for colonial adventures which he considered of little merit compared with action on the Continent. Intelligence reports of a projected invasion gave him the excuse to divert the ships to a blockade of the naval base at L'Orient. On 24 November Bedford wrote to Grenville of his certainty that the plan for Canada was shelved.[5]

The winter of 1746 found Pitt ill at Bath, though when on 5 December he wrote to Newcastle he was hoping soon to return to London. He had ready some unpalatable advice; as the Dutch would not fight, the French could not be outmanoeuvred in the Low Countries and a firm peace depended upon Prussia's right to Silesia being recognised. In the middle of January Pitt was back in London but really no better: a further visit to Bath would, he apologetically informed Newcastle, soon be required.[6] The early summer of 1747 brought great news for the nation. Anson completely defeated the French fleet off Cape Finisterre on 3 May. Thomas, the third of the Grenville brothers, a most distinguished sailor and member of Parliament for Bridport, lost his life in the action.

Although this victory could not fail to fortify the administration, on 4 June Prince Frederick stupidly announced his intention of returning to opposition in a manifesto promising 'to abolish all distinctions of party . . .'. Faced with this challenge, the King agreed to Newcastle's request for a dissolution one year before it was due.[7] Pitt could not expect his brother

Thomas, still Lord Warden of the Stannaries, to return him for Old Sarum. Newcastle decided he should stand for Seaford; a great honour, for Sussex was Newcastle's especial domain. Pelham had sat for the county since 1722 and the other knight of the shire was the Earl of Middlesex, heir to the 1st Duke of Dorset, Lord Warden of the Cinque Ports. Dorset's friendship enabled Newcastle to nominate all four members for Hastings and Seaford. The sitting members for Seaford were William Hay of Glyndebourne and William Gage, of an old Sussex family who, being an equerry to Prince Frederick, was become an enemy. Newcastle's object was that Pitt should capture his seat. Then came an unexpected development. Middlesex, bent upon fulfilling his reputation for impetuous folly, went over to Prince Frederick, and having no chance of getting back for the county decided to raid Seaford. Newcastle sat next to the returning officer at the poll and Pitt emerged triumphant. At Stowe there was every ground for rejoicing. Richard and George Grenville won both seats at Buckingham and upon the latter Newcastle happily bestowed the seat on the Board of Treasury which Middlesex had chucked up. Jemmy Grenville, who for the same reason as Pitt could no longer sit for Old Sarum, succeeded his brother Thomas at Bridport. Lyttleton, on dangerous ground in trying to keep the seat at Okehampton that Thomas Pitt reckoned to control, won through. Thomas Pitt also failed to maintain the Prince's interest in Cornwall, where his adherents were reduced from twenty-seven to nineteen. It was small consolation that he could put Middlesex in for Old Sarum.[8]

Throughout the country Pelham triumphed. Dependable supporters of administration in the new Parliament numbered 341, leaving 216, comprising Prince Frederick with his motley Leicester House crew and members whose allegiance was uncertain. Among interesting new members were Pelham's great-nephews George and Charles Townshend, grandsons of the 2nd Viscount whom Walpole had ousted. George, heir to the title, was elected a knight of the shire for Norfolk whilst his brother Charles, just of age, sat for Great Yarmouth; his quick parts made him a man of promise. Pelham's overall position was far stronger than Walpole's even at his apogee. Whereas the one-time opposition had included men of weight, not one of Prince Frederick's band of nonentities would prove himself a statesman and where they had talent it was Pitt, now of the Government, who was the touchstone. Thomas Potter, the clever and exceedingly dissolute son of John Archbishop of Canterbury, elected for St Germans as a member of the Prince's party, put up a brilliant maiden speech of which Horace Walpole wrote, 'a young Mr. Potter, who promises very greatly; the world is already matching him against Mr. Pitt'. Immediately after the general election John Viscount Perceval, after 1748 an Irish peer as 2nd Earl of Egmont, betrayed Pelham and joined the Prince. Egmont had a vast fund of knowledge and soon established a dominating influence. He was reckoned a good speaker: 'His words are not picked out like Pitt's, but his language is useful, clear and strong.' Dr George Lee, a lawyer and experienced House of Commons man, was unique in his disinterested character.[9] The truth was that Frederick could always pick up the discontented, but with Pelham at the helm men of ability would look to administration. Pitt was far better off as Paymaster than caballing with the lightweights of the opposition court. His improved financial position enabled him to purchase South Lodge, at Enfield Chase, a mansion with some eighty-five acres. He undertook his first exercises in palladianisation and landscape gardening, besides offering a bit of rough shooting to his friends.

Pelham and Newcastle were faced with bringing some decision to the War of the Austrian Succession. British subsidies to Maria Theresa and other allies were to the tune of £1,750,000 p.a., and to no purpose, for Silesia plainly could not be recovered. That the control of North America and India were to be the issues of the century between Britain and France was not apparent to the governments, though Pitt's thinking had begun to run on these lines. In the Far East the war bore a new character; the British and French East India Companies, technically lessees, began to exploit the rivalries between the local rulers. The French, ably led by Joseph Dupleix and Baron La Bourdonnais, had captured Madras on 21 September 1746. But in the course of 1747 the tables were turned and Dupleix was beseiged in Pondicherry. That Britain was able to secure an honourable peace was due to the navy. Anson's victory in May was followed on 14 October by Hawke's beating the enemy fleet off L'Orient. The French could no longer present a line of battle on the high seas. By the spring of 1748 all parties to the war were wishing for peace; Saxe had completed the conquest of Belgium and Pelham was willing for peace on any terms that restored the Low Countries to Maria Theresa. France, her navy impotent and commerce stagnant, faced a financial crisis.

Newcastle went to Hanover with the King to undertake peace negotiations. To that end he had Chesterfield, whom he had detected in a disloyal intrigue, replaced by Bedford. The effective career of that remarkable man, whose character so ill-fitted his abilities, was ended. A general settlement was reached at Aix-la-Chapelle in November 1748; Britain, France and Spain each reverted to the *status quo ante bellum* in Europe and overseas. The French consented to evacuate the Austrian Low Countries and it was agreed that the fortifications of Dunkirk would be demolished, though less drastically than had been required by the Treaty of Utrecht. The treaties did not mention the Spanish right of search which had been the original occasion for Britain's going to war. Frederick, by his acquisition of Silesia, had almost doubled his population and won great mineral and industrial wealth. Britain handed back Cape Breton Island to France and the East India Company recovered Madras. Cape Breton might appear a small return to France for the abandonment of her conquests in the Low Countries, but without it Quebec was not secure. That the proper application of naval strategy might nullify military reverses on the Continent, where subsidies to foreign powers availed nothing, was a lesson Pitt took in. American boundary disputes were left to a demarcation commission and the colonial rivalries between Britain and France would continue unabated. Maria Theresa could never accept the loss of her territory or the leadership which Protestant Prussia had won in north Germany. To recover Silesia she required an ally able to meet Frederick on the battlefield and there maritime Britain could be of little use.

Newcastle regarded himself as the architect of peace and no sooner was the ink dry than he embarked upon a forward policy,

to be based upon the Austrian alliance and the maintenance of
a powerful navy. He believed himself to possess the makings of a
great minister and at the end of the year transferred himself
from the Southern to the Northern Department from where he
could curry favour with the courts of Germany and impress the
King. Pelham, concerned with the work of recuperation from
the war, confided in Hardwicke his utter lack of confidence in
his brother who too consciously modelled himself upon Stanhope.[10] The budget had swollen to £13 million and the national
debt had increased to £78 million. The peace brought an
upsurge of confidence and government stock rose above 100, so
that Pelham could safely reduce the interest from 4 per cent to
3 per cent. In the following year, 1749, on a reduced budget the
land tax was cut to 3s and subsequently to the peace-time rate
of 2s. Fundamentally Pelham's policy was a continuation of
Walpole's: sound finance and general prosperity were the
surest foundation for British strength.

During the winter of 1748–9 Pitt piloted through the House
of Commons a new bill providing for the punishment of mutiny
and desertion. George Grenville and Lyttleton disagreed with
some of the provisions. But Richard Grenville acknowledged
Pitt leader of the Stowe connection and followed the government
line. George Bubb Dodington, a distant relative to Cobham,
thought himself to be cleverer than Pitt or the Grenvilles. One
of the richest men, an important borough proprietor in Dorset,
with a palladian seat at Eastbury and a villa at Hammersmith
adorned with pillars in lapis lazuli, Dodington enjoyed his
position as Treasurer of the Navy. But in March 1749 he
resigned and went over to Prince Frederick, an outrageous act
of perfidy prompted solely by a desire to insure against the
death of the King. To George Grenville's disgust Dodington's
valuable place was given to Legge. He found no support for his
pretensions from his brothers or Pitt but secretly resented
having to knuckle under.[11]

When on 13 September 1749 Cobham died, Richard Grenville's mother became Viscountess Cobham in her own right. It
took him a mere ten days to ask Newcastle to persuade the King
to make her Countess of Buckingham. Pitt gave his opinion that
the application would be looked upon as reasonable. Newcastle

promised to do his best with the King but pointed out that the
county of Buckingham was already disposed of and a few
months delay out of respect for Cobham's memory might be
seemly. Richard was not concerned with trifles and rather than
wait about was ready to see his mother Countess Temple after
Cobham's family name which was accordingly conferred only
five weeks after Cobham's death.[12]*

In the course of 1749 Newcastle unfolded his foreign policy,
which was to make certain that Maria Theresa's son Joseph
would succeed as Emperor by securing his election as King of
the Romans and thus prevent a repetition of 1740. In principle
Pelham saw no objection until it became apparent that his
brother proposed buying the votes of the Electors; his just
suspicion was that they would simply pocket the money. On
31 March 1750 Newcastle, about to depart for Hanover with the
King, held a conference to settle domestic matters. Instead he
was faced with Pelham's disagreeable criticisms of his Bavarian
treaty. Newcastle retorted with a hint at resignation. Pelham
smartly told his brother he might do as he pleased, which
led Newcastle to forward to Pitt a lengthy treatise in self-
justification. Of course Newcastle had no intention of resigning
and Pitt hoped these divisions might not divert attention from
French raids into Nova Scotia. From Hanover Newcastle sent
Pitt five sheets of foolscap, both sides covered with his close
handwriting, complaining of his brother's disloyalty. What
made it so unfair, his foreign policy was turning out well, with
the votes of five Electors secured at a cost of subsidies only to
Cologne and Bavaria, though an expensive treaty with Saxony
was on the way. Pitt's answer of 13 July counselled tact: 'But
whatever it be that has raised this sort of cloud, give me leave to
prophecy, as I wish, that it cant fail to pass away and vanish of
itself: and let me most earnestly entreat your Grace, when fair
weather returns, as it instantly will do, to bid it welcome.'[13]
Newcastle, having rid himself of Harrington in 1746 and
Chesterfield in 1748, sought to turn out Bedford. He had the
excuse that Bedford neglected his desk for the rural pleasures of
Woburn – cricket in the summer and partridge shooting in the

* In 1784 Temple's nephew the 3rd Earl was created Marquis of Buckingham,
a designation taken from the borough.

winter. In February 1751 therefore Pelham with some reluctance asked Bedford's dismissal of the King who, not wishing to be completely in the hands of the two brothers, gave him a cool hearing.

Whilst Newcastle was floundering about the petty courts of Germany, Pelham brought off a diplomatic coup with a treaty of friendship with Spain. Most-favoured-nation treatment was accorded British exports and the complaints about the Spanish right of search that had occasioned war in 1739 were quietly dropped. Pitt, on 17 January 1751, defended before the House of Commons the spirit of the new arrangements. He confessed to a change of opinion with regard to the right of search, which he now admitted must be respected as a necessary attribute of sovereignty. There was, too, the important consideration that, in the event of a war with France, the King of Spain might opt for neutrality. Pelham made the mistake of taking the Spanish treaty as a pretext for naval economies. Between 1744 and 1762 two great sailors, Anson and Edward Boscawen, always sat at the Admiralty Board, the former as First Lord after 1751. Well-served though the navy was, for the year 1751 Pelham reduced the establishment to 8,000 men despite protests from Pitt. Newcastle took Pitt's side but the complement of 10,000 maintained in succeeding years was insufficient to prevent the navy becoming sadly run down.

The year 1751 saw Pelham's position finally consolidated, partly by the accident of Prince Frederick's death on the evening of Wednesday 20 March. The morning after the indomitable Dodington was full of a project 'for a union between the independent Whigs and Tories . . .'. But he was wasting his time, for the Princess had no intention of maintaining an opposition Court. She turned to Lee, who advised her to place herself unreservedly in the hands of the King. It was excellent counsel and on his side George II showed the Princess every consideration: '. . . the King continues to be perfectly satisfied with the Princess and is in raptures with the young Prince, who, he says, has taken a liking to *him*.'[14] The Duchy of Cornwall lapsed to the Crown and the Civil List provision for Prince Frederick expired. Lee arranged with Pelham for the nomination of the new household with himself as Treasurer. Those of

Prince Frederick's courtiers whom the King disliked were replaced by men of his choice.

Foremost among the Leicester House casualties was Thomas Pitt, politically and financially ruined by the loss of his position as Lord Warden of the Stannaries. Over the years his personality had deteriorated sadly; he had treated his wife abominably and she for her part despised him for the animal brute he was. When their son Thomas Pitt III, born in 1737, had been sent to school she left Boconnoc and was never allowed to see him again. In order to economise the children were kept at home to a miserable existence, for their father had no affectionate interest in their company. They now saw him crushed with humiliation, deprived of all importance in the south-west and his finances desperate.[15]

The expectation was that the King, nearing seventy, would not see his thirteen-year-old grandson come of age. A new Regency Act provided that his mother, the Princess of Wales, should be Regent, assisted by a Council with Cumberland at the head. Though he never established himself as a great general, Cumberland as Commander-in-Chief was a forceful administrator and in the event of the King's death would occupy a commanding position. In Fox, the Secretary at War, he had an ally whose abilities in the House of Commons placed him in competition with Pitt. The Princess, petty, prudish and obstinate, might be expected to clash with the Duke, and the rivalries within the royal family were bound to sharpen with the King's advancing years. Though the future possibility of conflict was evident, so long as the King lived Pelham could be confident of an ascendancy such that political life appeared suspended. Spirited divisions even upon questions of importance were practically unknown. Granville, old enmities forgotten, joined the Cabinet as Lord Privy Seal. Newcastle succeeded in ousting Bedford and replacing him by the 4th Earl of Holderness, whom he cruelly termed 'our underling'. Bedford was the only important politician outside the Government, but on his own was powerless.

When on 7 January 1752 Parliament assembled after the Christmas recess, Pelham had to put forward Newcastle's treaty with the Elector of Saxony. He was loyally supported by

Murray, Fox and Legge, but Pitt was not prepared to give his public approval to a pointless waste of money. Pelham carried without demur an expensive treaty with a German prince in time of peace, of which many knew him privately to disapprove.[16] The Empress-Queen gave no support to Newcastle's chimerical and costly project; she had far more understanding of the legal difficulties and was deeply affronted at interference in an Imperial election by a Protestant power. In 1753 Count Kaunitz, Austrian Ambassador at Versailles, became Chancellor at Vienna and his one object was to find a suitable ally for the restitution of Silesia. Frederick of Prussia, too, was angered at foreign intervention in German affairs. He despised his popinjay uncle George II, who on his side was not a man to accept contempt with indifference. Relations became so strained that Britain and Prussia ceased to exchange diplomatic representatives.

Only the absence of political strife can explain how in the course of 1752 allegations of Jacobite influence in the household of the Prince of Wales could command credence. The business was cleared up when the 2nd Earl Waldegrave, an old friend of the King who had followed Thomas Pitt as Lord Warden of the Stannaries, was appointed Governor to the Prince. Yet another storm in a teacup followed a year later. Horace Walpole, who had a grudge against Pelham, circulated an anonymous leaflet reviving the Jacobite scare and this time Murray was implicated. Gossip spread that the Solicitor-General was of a coterie in the habit of drinking the Pretender's health. The King pooh-poohed the matter and declared his complete confidence in Murray. He and Newcastle would have been severely shaken had they known that Murray's youthful activities had gone far beyond toasting the King over the water but had included that foolish letter offering his services to the Pretender. At a formal examination by the Privy Council hostile evidence was confined to trivial incidents alleged to have taken place in 1732 at latest.[17] Bedford gave notice that he would raise the matter in Parliament. Temple, as Richard Grenville had become on his mother's death, thought of joining him but was strongly dissuaded by Pitt, who on 19 March wrote to him: 'If you should entertain any thought of supporting or going with the question, give me leave, my dear Lord, to implore you to lay it aside, as I am deeply persuaded that nothing would be so fatal to me and to all our views.' Three days later, when Bedford rose in the Lords, Newcastle and Hardwicke gave the peers a full explanation and Temple said nothing. But the damage done Murray was terrible. Chesterfield wrote at the time: 'No reasonable man, I believe, thinks them Jacobites now, whatever they may have been formerly. But parties do not reason, and every Whig party man, which is nine out of ten of the Whig party, is fully convinced that they are at this time dangerous and determined Jacobites.'[18]

Pitt had been Paymaster seven years and for all he knew would continue in that way indefinitely. Pelham was only sixty, no changes were likely and the King disliked him as much as ever. As Pelham remarked to Dodington, despite the endeavours of himself and Newcastle the King could never be prevailed upon 'to be commonly civil' to his Paymaster. The man of the albeit distant future appeared to be Fox, who held all the cards; Cumberland was his patron, Bedford and Hartington his intimate friends. Newcastle and Hardwicke might mistrust him but Cumberland could be depended upon to sway the King in his favour. That Pitt must be restless at being stuck at a terminus was recognised, and the purity of his aims, 'ambition rather than avarice', acknowledged. But he had only the Grenville connection, none of whom was particularly popular, to rely upon.[19] To Pitt life already wore a dreary aspect when in the early summer he was again struck down by gout. In May he went to Tunbridge Wells and in October moved to Bath.

Pitt was therefore away when towards the end of the session of 1753 Fox blundered. Hardwicke had before Parliament his Marriage bill, which required for a valid contract the thrice reading of the banns and, in the case of minors, the consent of parents or guardians. The Lord Chancellor was justly proud of this great reform which fell peculiarly within his province as affecting the fundamental law of the kingdom. On the committee stage, through the last days of May and the first week of June, Fox attacked every clause. He accused Hardwicke of aristocratic and dictatorial motives and compared the actuations of the Lord Chancellor to those of a spider. When on 6 June the bill returned to the Lords Hardwicke struck back at 'this dark, gloomy, insidious genius, . . . an engine of personality and faction . . .'. Hardwicke for sure would always use his paramount influence with Newcastle to keep Fox away from power.[20]

That summer there was a great agitation against the Jewish Naturalisation Act which earlier that year had passed peacefully without a protest from the Bishops. Although the Jews had been allowed to live in England since Cromwell's time, there was a popular outcry of anti-semitism and the lower clergy were especially vehement. Pelham was concerned with the general election due the following year and when on 15 October Parliament met Newcastle rose in the House of Lords to propose repeal. Temple accused the administration of pandering to an ignorant electorate, conduct understandable in the House of Commons but disgraceful to the peers. Repeal passed the Lords on 22 November and five days later the Commons by 150–60. Pitt had just returned to London after a year's absence and voted with the Government. But when on 4 December the repeal of the Plantation Act of 1739 naturalising Jews in the colonies was proposed Pelham drew the line: it was one thing to repeal a recent law that had made people uneasy, but another to repeal a law of fourteen years' standing. Pitt carried the honours of the day: 'It was the Jew today, it would be the presbyterian tomorrow: we should be sure to have a septennial church clamour.' What Horace Walpole described as 'this silly effort of old prejudices' was defeated by 208–88.[21]

Shortly after Christmas Pitt made his departure for Bath, where he concerned himself with a monument to Thomas Grenville. At the New Year Potter, who had lost his post at Leicester House on Prince Frederick's death, wrote to George Grenville soliciting support for the appointment of a certain John Wilkes to be High Sheriff of Buckinghamshire. Wilkes, the companion of his debauches, was indeed made High Sheriff and, becoming an intimate of Stowe, would get to know Pitt well. His business completed Potter repaired to Bath, where he was Recorder, and thence wrote to George Grenville of Pitt's health with unbelieving jocularity:[22]

'Receive the old-fashioned wishes of an old-fashioned heart. Pitt has had a smart fit of the gout: this, I doubt not, he has told you: but perhaps he has not informed you that he is the picture of health. I hope he is not a hypocrite.'

But Potter was altogether mistaken and Pitt's inability to take effective action in face of the momentous event that would shortly take place was proof that his illness was genuine.

Pelham during the summer of 1753 had been suffering from an internal disorder producing symptoms of scurvy. A stay in Scarborough produced little benefit because he would not regulate his diet and he returned to London in worse shape. A dangerous boil subsided but on 3 March 1754 he underwent a relapse. On 6 March Pitt wrote to George Grenville of his anxiety:[23] 'The post of the day has brought a much worse account of Mr. Pelham than your letter which has given me much uneasiness. I am infinitely concerned at the state of his health. I hope, however, there is reason to think he may be safe from any present danger, as he began to mend.' Pelham had died at six o'clock that morning.

For almost twenty years Pitt had witnessed Pelham in the House of Commons. The collective resignations of 1746 had been the one controversial act of Pelham's career, but he always sought to play down the constitutional significance of that four days' drama which had taught the King where lay his true interests. Pelham was not a great man: he had been content to learn the art of government from Walpole, and having learned he led the House of Commons unchallenged. His achievements were to wind up the Austrian war and the resumption of friendly relations with Spain. In the House of Commons Pelham had enjoyed an affection deeper than Walpole's because he was less masterful; he could bow to a strong opposition without the dismissals and deprivations that had sullied the great master. By what his friends called sweet reason and his critics timid subtlety, Pelham fabricated harmony among the Whigs. The old Tories in the wilderness were of steadily diminishing number. Pedestrian and without Walpole's force or Carteret's brilliance, Pelham was above all virtuous: 'He lived without abusing his power and died poor.'[24] On learning of Pelham's death the King exclaimed: 'Now I shall have no more peace.' The remark was just for the loss opened a long period of uncertainty.

News of Pelham's death reached Bath within the day. Pitt did not receive the notification from Newcastle or Hardwicke to which he was entitled. As by nature he assumed the leadership of the Stowe connection. Next morning, 7 March, he sent a collective letter to Temple, George Grenville and Lyttleton laying down the prime objects of policy, which were to support the present administration for the King's lifetime and equally to strengthen the hand of the Princess of Wales, 'in order to maintain her power in the Government, in case of the misfortune of the King's demise'. The means Pitt considered to be the continuation of that union of all men of goodwill that had been Pelham's achievement: '. . . this might easily be effected, but it is my opinion, it will certainly not be done.' For Pitt expected great difficulties over persons: 'As to the nomination of Chancellor of the Exchequer, Mr. Fox, in point of party, seniority in the Corps, and I think ability for Treasury and House of Commons business, stands, upon the whole, first of any.' Pitt would have preferred George Grenville as Leader of the House but realised that this, in view of his own position as Paymaster, would create an unacceptable concentration of power in one family. He thought the Princess of Wales's Treasurer, Lee, also 'Papabilis' and Murray a possible Chancellor of the Exchequer. The thought must have crossed his mind how severely Murray's prospects had been damaged by slander. Pitt summed up his letter with the hope that one of the Stowe connection would be of the Cabinet – though he did not mention himself – and he did not doubt that without promotion either for them or Fox the ministry would lack foundation. A family resignation would be a great mistake and Pitt fully grasped how his enforced absence from London must clog his prospects: 'I am utterly unable to travel, nor can guess when I shall be able: this situation is most unfortunate.'

Later that day Pitt was taken aback at the tone of a joint letter from Jemmy Grenville and Lyttleton. He promptly sent Temple a private letter: 'Let me recommend to my dear Lord to preach prudence and reserve to our friend Sir George, and if he can, to inspire him with his own.' Pitt went on to give his second thoughts: that Fox would be Chancellor of the

Exchequer and Leader of the House of Commons he thought fairly certain and then Grenville could be promoted Secretary at War. Though Pitt thought Newcastle likely to take the Treasury he did not consider him comparable to Hardwicke: 'The Chancellor is the only resource; his wisdom, temper, and authority, joined to the Duke of Newcastle's ability as Secretary of State, are the dependence for Government. The Duke of Newcastle alone is feeble, not to Sir George.'[25]

Newcastle was stunned at the loss of his brother. He at once asked Hartington to assure Devonshire that nothing would be done other than in consultation with him and Hardwicke; then he shut himself away. Hardwicke went to the King who signified his wish that Fox should take the Treasury. Fox started to busy himself; firstly he called round at Pitt's house, mistakenly supposing that news of Pelham's illness had brought him to London; next he went to see Hartington. He also sent Hardwicke no less than three 'very humiliating and apologising messages'. Then he came to himself and saw that such eagerness on the day of the minister's death was unseemly, but the harm had been done. Day by day Hardwicke worked upon the mind of the King: 'He begins to find that all the world is not for Mr. Fox, as he had been told; for in truth it is a very narrow clique, and many of them of the worst sort.' Hardwicke realised that the true alternative was Pitt, but because of the King's enmity to push him forward would reopen the way to Fox, so he decided that the new First Lord of the Treasury must be a peer. Newcastle was the only choice, yet his assumption of power would not be an altogether simple matter. The last peer to occupy the Treasury had been Sunderland thirty-three years back. With Walpole and Pelham the House of Commons had been accustomed to dealing with one of their own. The septennial dissolution of Parliament was due in a matter of weeks and few members of Parliament felt a natural obligation towards Newcastle. A man capable of expounding government policy in the House of Commons and whom members would be willing to hear had to be found.[26]

By 10 March Pitt had at last been notified of Pelham's death by Hardwicke, though without any hint of what was to happen. He advised his friends in the expectation of their pretensions being altogether set aside. He wrote to Lyttleton that whatever happened they must not resign or in any way threaten to form 'a third flying squadron'; patience would find its own reward for the Court dare not alienate them: '. . . Fox is too odious to last for ever, and G. Grenville must be next nomination under any government. I am too lame to move.' On the same day Pitt sent Lyttleton a letter which he asked him to show Hardwicke after its perusal by the Grenville brothers, so the Lord Chancellor would see that eight years of office had not impaired their unity. Pitt drew attention to his own position; weight in the House of Commons had two foundations – marks from royal favour or esteem in the country, which was sometimes derived from opposition; for eight years he had abjured the latter but received none of the former: 'In this humiliating and not exaggerated view of my situation within the House, of how little weight can I flatter myself to be there?' Next day Pitt wrote to Temple, hoping this letter would receive his approval: whatever happened their connection must 'give no terrors by talking big' or 'fish in troubled waters; . . . My judgement tells me, my dear Lord, that this simple plan steadily pursued will once again, before it be long, give some weight to a connection, long depressed, and yet still not annihilated.'[27]

At a Cabinet of 12 March Newcastle was unanimously invited to take the Treasury. So as to accommodate the House of Commons Hardwicke was ready to swallow Fox's advancement, but in a form that would give him no ascendancy. Holderness was to be moved from the Southern Department to the North, with responsibility for Hanover, and Fox was to be given the vacant secretaryship. Legge, the Treasurer of the Navy, would be made Chancellor of the Exchequer and here Newcastle expected a complaisant servant. As Hardwicke explained to his friend Thomas Herring, Archbishop of Canterbury: 'If the power of the Treasury, the Secret Service and the House of Commons is once settled in safe hands, the office of Secretary of State for the Southern Province will carry very little efficient weight along with it.'[28] Once Fox had been cajoled into accepting office without authority, Pitt could safely be left nursing his gout; indeed the rumour in London was that he might be dead.

Newcastle told Hartington to sound Fox, who construed the offer to mean full Leadership of the Commons and joyfully accepted. But when on the following morning, expecting to receive his marching orders, Fox held a conference with Newcastle and Hartington he was severely disillusioned. It was made plain to him that there was no intention to place him in any special situation *vis-à-vis* members of Parliament. On 14 March Fox wrote to Newcastle refusing the proffered gift which he saw to be a ruse to fasten his services without responsibility but asked to continue as Secretary at War. Newcastle next craftily represented to the King that Fox had demanded the management of the House of Commons independently of anyone, and this, he righteously indicated, he could not have conceded. When on 16 March Fox had an audience, the King burst out at him: '*You would be above ev'ry body above the whole Council.*' The King pointed out that Sunderland had in his day shared no secrets with his Secretary of State. Evidently George II believed himself able to put the clock back a generation. Fox left his Majesty's presence still Secretary at War but wrote to Hartington of Newcastle's treachery: 'Stop here, my dear Lord & think of the shameless want of veracity in the man we have to deal with.'[29]

Pitt felt every impatience with his sorry condition and 14 March found him writing to George Grenville: 'I begin to bear it upon smooth ground without much uneasiness: my appetite returns, my pains subside and my myths are tolerable: if no relapse comes, I hope a week will go a good way towards enabling me to crawl, if not to walk.' By the 18th Lyttleton was asking George Grenville whether he ought not to write to Pitt and inform him of what was in progress. Two days later Pitt himself wrote to Lyttleton and his expectation of being left out emerged clearly. Pitt had hit the nail on the head; only he and Fox were fit to lead the Commons but Newcastle could not face giving either the power that must go with it.[30]

The King, after his years of thraldom under Walpole and Pelham, was minded not to have even a first minister. It was he who rounded off the administration. The day after he had dressed Fox down he saw Hardwicke and threw out the idea of Sir Thomas Robinson, Keeper of the Great Wardrobe, as

Secretary of State for the South. Hardwicke, taken completely by surprise, wrote to Devonshire: 'His Majesty said this suddenly & without any appearance of determination, nor do I know whether it is his way of thinking now. Your Grace will not therefore take notice of it as for me.'

Robinson had been Minister at Vienna and at the time of the Aix-la-Chapelle negotiations the King had been impressed by his knowledge. He had also been of the House of Commons ten years all told, but his tepid parliamentary record gave no indication of the stuff to carry weight. But Newcastle, desirous to please the King, pushed forward with the idea of Robinson. At an interview he gave Dodington on Thursday 21 March he summarised his situation: 'He said that by a strange fatality the direction of the House of Commons was fallen upon him, who had never thought of it; and he must expect that the great attempt would be, to show that he could not do it.' Newcastle had no intention of being beaten and Dodington's account continues: 'I said I understood the Secretary's office was design'd for Sir Thomas Robinson. – He said yes.'[31] Two days later Robinson was appointed.

Hardwicke and Newcastle, having kept Pitt and Fox out, were ready to be generous: Lyttleton became Cofferer of the King's Household and Grenville succeeded to Legge's well-paid Treasurership of the Navy – a disappointment for Dodington who had hoped to wriggle his way back. Charles Townshend took a step up the ladder, moving from the Board of Trade to that of the Admiralty. Some of Prince Frederick's old friends were taken into the fold. When Lyttleton wrote to Pitt on 23 March, describing how places had been distributed, he mentioned only the Cabinet changes and discreetly left out his own and Grenville's promotions.

Pitt's indignation at being kept out boiled over. On 24 March he penned a prolix letter of reproach to Newcastle which opened with a gentle reminder that he had heard of his decision to take the Treasury not, as would have been proper, from the Lord Chancellor, but by the way from Lyttleton. Pitt's tepid expression of satisfaction 'on this great measure so happily taken' was succeeded by this stinging apostrophe: 'Permit, my Lord, a man, whose affectionate attachment to your Grace, I believe, you don't doubt, to expose simply to your view his situation, and then let me intreat your Grace (if you can divest your mind of the great disparity between us), to transport yourself for a moment into my place.' Pitt pointed out that despite his punctilious presentation of business, especially in respect of military and foreign measures, 'an indelible negative is fix'd against my name'. To be ignored for a Fox might be one thing, but to be passed over for Legge and Robinson was more than he could bear: 'I will venture to appeal to your Grace's candour and justice whether upon such feeble pretensions, as twenty years' use of Parliament may have given me, I have not some cause to feel (as I do most deeply) so many repeated and visible humiliations. . . .'

In view of the consideration that he had not been officially notified of the government changes, Pitt saw fit to forward this protest by way of a letter addressed to Lyttleton. At the same time he wrote of his bitter disappointment to Temple and Grenville, yet had to admit: 'I am so tired I cannot hold my head down to write any longer. A fine Secretary of State I should make.'[32] Newcastle and Hardwicke each addressed long and verbose missives to Pitt dated 2 April, attempting to explain how their joint intercession with a hostile King had proved powerless.[33] Pitt knew that resignation would be construed by the general body of the Whigs as an act of pique. May found him still at Bath, where William Hoare had just completed the portrait which now hangs in the National Portrait Gallery. At this time, too, Pitt embarked upon building himself a house at Bath, No. 7 The Circus, which he embellished with his customary extravagance.

The general election that summer was a triumph for Newcastle. Only forty-two seats were contested and he commanded a greater majority than any minister since 1688. Seaford was no longer available to Pitt. Gage, whom he had unseated in 1747, having made his peace, was allowed to be returned there. Pitt had nothing to hope for from his brother Thomas, who was so hard up that he mortgaged his parliamentary interest to the Treasury, which left Old Sarum and Okehampton at Newcastle's disposal. He had to accept nomination to a seat at Aldborough, one of Newcastle's private boroughs in Yorkshire:

had he allowed resentment to goad him into resignation he would have found no easy way into Parliament.[34]

Thomas's political importance was ended and the entreaties of his creditors made his exit from England very necessary. He faced a penurious exile at the mercy of the lawyers and the bailiffs for the remainder of his days. At this time, too, he was engaged in the most disagreeable quarrel with his son, Thomas junior, who found a champion in his uncle William. Young Thomas Pitt had just entered Clare College Cambridge and his father proposed taking the lad away from his studies to join him in France. On this Pitt very rightly placed a veto, arranged for Thomas to escape from his father's lodgings and himself dictated a letter of explanation. So young Thomas remained at Cambridge and there followed a charming correspondence between him and his uncle William, a classic of parental literature.[35]

During the summer of 1754 Pitt embarked on the courtship of Temple's sister Lady Hester Grenville. Pitt was forty-six and it must have appeared unlikely that he would ever marry. Lady Hester was thirty-six and as he had known her family intimately for over twenty years it can hardly be supposed that he felt more than respect and affection for his bride. It may be hard to accept that the series of passionately styled love-letters which Pitt at this time addressed to her were mere artifice: equally the match fortified his friendship with the Grenvilles. The marriage was privately solemnised by special licence on Saturday 16 November 1754 in the bride's lodgings in Argyle Street. On the same day the couple left for a ten-day honeymoon at West Wickham, the Kentish home of Gilbert West, a cousin of the Grenvilles. The marriage was ideally happy and their first child, Hester, was born at Pitt's home at the Pay Office in November 1755.

While Pitt had been getting himself married, Newcastle had in a vague way been trying to secure Fox's loyalty. Already the team expected to lead the Commons was divided against itself, largely because Newcastle could not resist abusing Legge as 'that creature of ours'. Legge hit back by throwing aspersions at Murray – 'the Tory head of a Whig body'. At this time Pitt and Fox had come together over the affairs of Chelsea Hospital.

Cumberland was deeply concerned at the plight of the pension-ers, who were not entitled to pay until the end of their first year, so that they fell into the hands of the usurers. In August, at the Duke's command, Fox wrote to Pitt pressing for action. By the end of the month Fox had rejected Newcastle's overtures with disgust and on the 28th wrote to Hartington: 'Without rudeness in words nothing can be more contemptuous than the treatment & seems to lye chiefly on the Chancellor, the sum total being that he meant nothing nor do's any body mean anything now.' Fox called on the King's mistress, Lady Yarmouth, only to dis-cover that the King still regarded him as *'un ambitieux qui demandoit* conditions *bien fortes'*. Hartington and Cumberland sympathised with Fox but wished him not to harass the ministry.[36] When at the end of September Legge asked for the right of direct access to the King, even Hardwicke was dis-turbed and Newcastle had plaguey conjectures of some league between Pitt, Fox and Legge. Attorney-General Murray in his quiet way told Newcastle that a Leader there must be.[37]

The experiment of governing without a Leader of the House of Commons might prove viable provided no crisis in foreign affairs cropped up. During the summer a difficulty with Spain over British logwood settlements in Honduras was cleared up. Ferdinand VI, bent on keeping up good relations, appointed as his Prime Minister Richard Wall, an Irish Catholic who with the vision of a great statesman was convinced that mercantile considerations made friendship with Britain imperative. With France the situation was very different and the colonial issues at dispute of the first order. Dupleix, the Commissary-General of the French East India Company, fostered their business with an aggressive energy. The Governors of Canada, the Marquis de la Galissonière and Duquesne, never showed any intention of observing the truce. In the summer of 1754 Britain contributed £20,000 towards colonial defence, which emboldened the middle colonies to launch an expedition commanded by the Virginian squire George Washington to take Fort Duquesne. That July Washington and his men were trapped and taken prisoner.

Newcastle, Hardwicke and Holderness agreed that this reverse must be played down into a matter of incident. There was a distinction between an attack upon territory internationally recognised as French and a sally into the no-man's-land between Canada and New England. A moderate display of force might induce the French to disown the activities of their agents without loss of face. Newcastle had at his disposal a surplus of £100,000, which he could use without recourse to the House of Commons. At a Cabinet of 26 September, attended by Cumberland, it was decided to send to America General Edward Braddock with eight hundred regulars drawn from Ireland; assemblage and destination were to be a close secret. Granville, and rather surprisingly Murray, wanted, too, the augmentation of the colonial regulars, but Newcastle jibbed at that. By chance Pitt called on Newcastle on 2 October to talk over his Chelsea pensioners bill and he took Granville's part. Newcastle agreed that colonial troops should proceed from Oswego, the British base on Lake Ontario, against Niagara and up alongside Lake Champlain against Ticonderoga and Crown Point. There is no reason to suppose Pitt privy to Fox's stroke of 8 October, when the War Office *Gazette* published the order for officers appointed to command regiments in America to repair to their posts; Braddock's expedition was secret no longer but Cumberland showed no disposition to punish this insubordination.[38]

Unhappy Legge, caught betwixt Newcastle's scorn and the prospect of facing Pitt and Fox, dutifully presided over the eve of session Cockpit meeting of 15 November. Pitt briefly interrupted his honeymoon to introduce his Chelsea pensioners bill, and after his return to town joined Fox in a studied campaign to twit Robinson, for as he observed: 'The Duke might as well send his jack-boot to lead us.' Horace Walpole senior urged caution but Pitt had been nettled at a recent interview with Newcastle, who had repeated the substance of their previous conversation to the King – 'only to do you good' – the Duke mendaciously assured him. George Grenville, well satisfied as Treasurer of the Navy, hoped Pitt would not press the government too hard. Lyttleton, incapable of grasping that the failure to provide the House of Commons with a Leader had constitutional significance, refused to have anything to do with a concerted opposition.[39]

The first business before the House was always the resolution of disputed elections and on 25 November the case of Berwick-upon-Tweed came up. There a local landowner, John Delaval, had by practices venal even by eighteenth-century standards beaten Potter's chum Wilkes. Delaval defended himself with a vast jocularity, throwing the House into an uproar of mirth. At this point Pitt strode down from the gallery to express his utter astonishment at such an occasion becoming the subject of merriment: 'Was the dignity of the House of Commons on so sure a foundation that they themselves might venture to shake it?' After a flowery period in praise of the Speaker, followed by 'the strongest professions of true Whiggism', Pitt concluded with a vicious hit at Newcastle: 'All of us must assist, unless you will degenerate into a little assembly, serving no other purpose than to register the arbitrary edicts of *one* too powerful a *subject* . . . otherwise naught can stop the design of making us an appendix to – I know not what? I have no name for it.' Fox sauntered into the House and felt the atmosphere of shock and sensation. 'Displeas'd as well as pleas'd,' he observed next day, 'I allow it to be the finest speech that ever was made, & it was observed that by his first two periods he brought the House to a silence and attention that you might have heard a pin drop.' The Speaker shook Pitt by the hand, 'ready to shake it off'.

That evening Robinson, as was inevitable in one unused to active life in the House, made a mistake. Pitt was interested in the outcome of the Reading petition, where Fane, his co-trustee of the Spencer estates, had been returned by one vote. So as to secure a fair hearing, he moved for the postponement of the Colchester petition. Although there was no need for a Secretary of State to intervene in this sort of business, Robinson 'rose & with warmth asserted that it would be a short cause & on the side of the sitting member a *poor* cause'. Pitt at once interpreted Robinson's words as dictation; he then spoke of the great Whig career of Stanhope, who had once held the seals. The whole time he pointed at Robinson and stared at Murray, a constructive reminder of the Jacobite scandals. Fox put his spoke in and played upon Robinson's words '*poor* cause' and excused this 'irregular and blameable expression by his twenty years residence abroad where he had done honour to himself & his country, but which easily accounted for his total inexperience in the matter now before us'. When the committee rose members disbanded into little whispering groups of three or four. Yet if Pitt or Fox thought their conduct generally applauded they deceived themselves; rather they were blamed for creating unsettlement in order to force the hand of the King. Pitt, having only just been returned for Aldborough at Newcastle's behest, was in a specially invidious situation.

Even Newcastle could see that a minister who made a fool of himself over elementary House of Commons procedure could not manage on his own. He saw Pitt and then let fall the details of their conversation in an audience of the King. When Newcastle attempted some lame explanation Pitt snapped back: 'Fewer words, my Lord, if you please, for your words have now lost all weight with me.' Fox and Pitt talked over the situation on 27 November for two hours. On the same day Cumberland wrote to Fox: 'If Lord Hartington was well informed, Pitt will be dismissed with his whole tribe and some offer will be made you.' But the Duke warned Fox that his next decision would be his most critical since Pelham's death. That evening Pitt chose to lecture the House of Commons on the prevalent evils of Jacobitism, while gazing down at Murray, who cringed in terror; as Fox related: 'I sate next to Murray who suffer'd for an hour.' Murray had every ground for unease with that compromising letter of his young days in his memory, but his secret remained buried in the musty archives of St Germain.[40]

Fox received a summons to attend the King on 2 December and that morning wrote to his wife: 'I am to go to court where the Duke thinks I am to be offered Paymaster in Pitt's room, with Cabinet Counsellor and the direction of the H. of Commons.' But Fox was altogether wrong. George II's attitude was one of quiet contempt and he was told to state his conditions to Waldegrave. Fox naturally asked Waldegrave who was to be Leader of the House. In the course of half an hour's talk with Waldegrave on 4 December the King made clear that there was to be no Leader in the Commons and that he expected 'that his servants should act in concert and with spirit in their respective departments, and not quarrel among themselves'. Fox was asked to put his terms in writing. Next day Fox, in a letter to Pitt, tried to make out that the King's real intention was to offer him the Paymastership, not, he was bound to admit, to enable him to lead the Commons but as a bribe: 'What rascals they must be themselves, to think, as I believe they did, that I should not only accept, but be glad of it.' Fox asked to see Pitt that evening and enclosed a Paper addressed to the King. He assured Pitt that 'on no consideration will I venture on this weak scheme, unless strengthened by your acquiescence in it'. Fox's protestations were a mere ruse to win Pitt's blessing for a deal between himself and the Court.

Fox sent Waldegrave the final draft of his Paper and with it a personal note to make clear that he would not usurp Pitt's place. On 10 December Fox's surrender was delivered to the King, who handed it to Newcastle for him, Hardwicke and Granville to consider. They recommended Fox's admission to the Cabinet, but made clear in writing that Robinson's position in the House of Commons was to remain senior. It was certainly not the King's version of affairs that Newcastle was in sole command: 'You know very well there is no such thing as a first minister in England, and therefore you should not seem to be so.' The King was keen to engineer Pitt's removal and on 14 December asked of Hardwicke: 'But, my Lord, what is your opinion about turning out Pitt?' Hardwicke had to employ all his persuasive authority to save Pitt from an ignominious dismissal. Three days later the King accorded Fox a most gracious reception.[41] Fox, who in March had refused to become Secretary of State without true leadership of the Commons, capitulated on terms considerably less than he had then been offered. It was less than a month since he had been laughing at Robinson's parliamentary gaffes; now he was that man's inferior in a Cabinet which no longer feared but despised him.

CHAPTER 5

Pitt and Fox Rivals

'As to Fox, few men have been more unpopular; yet when I have asked his bitterest enemies what crimes they could alledge against him, they always confined themselves to general accusation; that he was avaricious, encouraged jobs, had profligate friends, and dangerous connections; but never could produce a particular fact of any weight or consequence. . . .

He had great parliamentary knowledge, but is rather an able debater than a complete orator; his best speeches are neither long nor premeditated; quick and concise replication is his peculiar excellence.

In business he is clear and communicative; frank and agreeable in society; and though he can pay his court on particular occasions, he has too much pride to flatter an enemy, or even a friend, where it is not necessary.

Upon the whole, he has some faults, but more good qualities, is a man of sense and judgement, notwithstanding some indiscretion; and with small allowances for ambition, parts, and politics, is a warm friend, a man of veracity, and a man of honour.'

The 2nd Earl Waldegrave, *Memoirs*.[1]

Pitt knew himself cheated by Fox who would be of the innermost councils of administration over action in North America. With some dignity he quietly piloted through his bill for the Chelsea pensioners, which passed both Houses *nem. con.* and at the New Year of 1755 received the royal assent (28 George II c. 1). This very minor though beneficial measure would be the sole legislation Pitt would propose and father to its conclusion during his career. Fox, though justly confident of his ability to manage the House of Commons, could not help but belittle himself. His mind was distempered with the consciousness of having chosen the baser part: 'Friend Pitt', he wrote, 'is as warm as I am, he is a much better speaker than I – that is the truth of it, I assure you. But tickling the palm, not the ear, is the business now, and he that can do the first is the best orator, let him speak ever so ill.' Where Fox chose, albeit in jest, to talk the language of places, sinecures and pensions, Pitt chose the theme of liberty. His opportunity came that February in the debates upon the Scots Justices bill. Since the '45 rebellion the sheriffs depute of Scotland had been nominated by the Crown at pleasure, which a government-sponsored bill now sought to continue. A group of Scots members wished their judges to be appointed for life as formerly, prominent among whom was that brilliant young advocate Gilbert Elliot of Minto, who sat for Selkirkshire. He persuaded Pitt to take their part and Horace Walpole described the debate of 26 February: '. . . Pitt, with great fire, in one of his best worded and most spirited declamations for liberty . . .'. Even Fox was brought to admit: 'That he reverenced liberty and Pitt, because nobody could speak so well on its behalf.' When at the end of the month the debate was resumed Pitt once more held the House and the bill was withdrawn. He had added greatly to his parliamentary reputation and made a disciple of Elliot.[2]

The proceedings of Parliament that winter and spring were of little moment beside the evident approach of a state of belligerency between Britain and France, despite the consideration that both governments wished to keep the peace. George II knew a great deal about the formal matter of diplomacy but was esentially a man of action. Newcastle's ignorance of the stuff of foreign affairs had long been evident. Although Louis XV was in no way bent upon aggression, his foreign minister Antoine Rouillé was allowed little authority and power lay with the Pompadour and her favourite cleric, Pierre de Bernis. From weak leadership unforeseen consequences must result.

That January the French had ordered to Quebec 3,000 of their finest regular troops escorted by eighteen ships of the line, far more than was necessary to meet Braddock. It can be taken as certain that Pitt, though still Paymaster, was not consulted over the counter-measures determined by the Cabinet. During the third week of January the fateful decision was taken to order the interception of the French expedition – but in American, not European waters. The King and Newcastle were taking the risk of starting a war with Britain plainly the aggressor. Two further regiments were got ready for America and the 4th Earl of Loudoun was appointed Lieutenant-General 'with every power civil and military that can legally be given him'. Loudoun was to be not only commander of all British naval and military forces in North America but responsible, too, for co-ordinating the efforts of each colonial government. Hawke, though in poor health, was called out of retirement to the command at Portsmouth. On 27 April Boscawen sailed for Halifax, Nova Scotia, whilst a week later the Brest fleet, commanded by Admiral de Bois de la Motte, set out for Canada. Accordingly Boscawen was sent a further six of the line under Admiral Francis Holburne.

Early that May George II, accompanied by Holderness, arrived in Germany bent upon high diplomacy. The King's great anxiety was that the obvious course for the French to adopt was simply to send an army into Hanover. Newcastle and the administration were agreed that the electorate could not be abandoned in the cause of a British colonial squabble with France. The neutralisation of Germany must be attempted and Kaunitz had made clear that he was no longer interested in maintaining the old Austrian alliance with Britain. George II chiefly feared Frederick of Prussia, still bound to France by a treaty which, however, was due for renewal. At this stage Frederick, although his tergiversations during the Austrian war had caused deep resentment at Versailles, thought he could depend upon Louis XV's friendship: 'Do you know, sir', he exclaimed to the French Ambassador, 'what I would do under the circumstances if I were King of France? As soon as the English declared war or committed any act of hostility against France, I would march a large body of troops into Westphalia to carry it at once into the Electorate of Hanover. It is the surest way to get a twist on that bugger.' But Frederick, content with his acquisition of Silesia, had no serious wish to see war in

Germany and there he and George II ultimately had a common interest to which their mutual suspicion blinded them. Kaunitz was the only statesman anxious to start a conflagration and already his mind was moving towards the revolutionary idea of an alliance with France.

For the protection of Hanover George II sought firstly subsidy treaties with his son-in-law the Landgrave of Hesse-Cassel and other German princes. His trump card was the prospect of an alliance with Czarina Elizabeth of Russia, who had good cause to resent Frederick's impertinent witticisms about her lovers. This policy of costly Continental alliances must divert British energies from North America and might lead to the stagnant stalemate of the War of the Austrian Succession. Pitt, during the course of the spring, made up his mind that here lay a suitable platform of opposition in the House of Commons. When Fox received a place on the Regency Council appointed to cover the King's absence in Hanover, he felt himself outwitted by an unscrupulous rival who would always sacrifice his honour for ambition.

Pitt's next move calls for some account of events in the household of the Prince of Wales. Prince George was seventeen and some time around the New Year had fallen under the domination of the 3rd Earl of Bute, a friend of his late father. Bute was descended from Sir John Stuart, natural son of King Robert II of Scotland, who had been given the Isle of Bute as an appanage. The rent-roll was far from glamorous, a situation this Bute had not improved by his elopement with Mary, daughter of Edward Wortley Montagu. Bute sired a large family so that employment in the Prince's household was not unwelcome and, good-looking with a lucky hand at the card-table, he fitted the part. He also mouthed exalted principles in sundry matters and that the Prince, deprived of a father at thirteen, should look up to him with deep affection was very understandable. Prince George, brought up in seclusion, suffered under a sore feeling of inferiority and felt the call for a guide through a world too full of wickedness for his own humble powers to fathom. Upon Bute this prim young man flung the responsibility for his moral and intellectual well-being. Bute took no dishonourable advantage, but soon he became reverenced as the man of the future reign and his vanity was flattered. And the wagging tongue of malice

was quick to infer a liaison between Bute and the Prince's
mother, which no one cognisant of her character could sensibly
have entertained.

At Leicester House there was great alarm at the prospect of a
Continental war. The Prince of Wales would not be eighteen
and of age until May 1756, a year off. If in this short interval
the King were to die, Cumberland would become President of
the Regency Council, Commander-in-Chief of an army swollen
to the requirements of belligerency and with his henchman Fox
of the Cabinet. Bute and the Princess indulged their fancies even
to the extent of supposing that the Duke might model himself
after the wicked uncle Richard III. In fact no base scheme
entered Cumberland's head; authoritarian and domineering he
certainly was but never dishonourable. Bute put no faith in
Newcastle, whom he nicknamed 'The Cardinal', and an understanding between him and Cumberland to cover the event of the
King's death to their mutual advantage seemed likely. Bute
discerned a useful ally in Pitt, who might welcome a chance to
shift his political ambience. Elliot of Minto, who rather wore
his admiration for Pitt on his sleeve, was the obvious intermediary and to him Bute on 27 April addressed his cogitations:
'Next session brings the Prince to age; I think 'tis likely a strong
party will be formed that will set both Fox and the Cardinal at
defiance, if Pitt can be induced to join, a point I have much to
heart; the prospect will be pleasing, though I cannot say in the
midst of such corruption my hopes can ever be sanguine.'

Having satisfied himself that Pitt was in no way connected
with Cumberland, Bute arranged a meeting; 'as both sides were
well disposed a treaty was soon arranged'. Pitt was received by
the Princess at Bute's house and was given an assurance of
support for his resistance to waging war by means of subsidies.
Lady Hester joined Lady Bute in selling tickets for the opening
night of the tragedy *Douglas*, the author John Home being a
friend of Elliot.[3]

At this time Pitt was moving into Hayes Place in Kent,
recently purchased in place of South Lodge, Enfield. Hayes
became the apple of his eye and Pitt was well known for his
perceptive taste in the fashionable hobby of landscape gardening. As Thomas Gray remarked to his friend Thomas Wharton,

himself no mean improver: '. . . the prophetic eye of *Taste* (as Mr. Pitt called it) sees all the beauties, that a Place is susceptible of, long before they are born; & when it plants a seedling, already sits under the shadow of it, & enjoys the effect it will have from every point of view, that lies in prospect'.[4] As yet Hayes was, by Pitt's standards, a poor-looking affair, but he had every intention of producing great changes, and without much regard to his bankers.

On his return to London Pitt, his world less uncosy, took occasion to indulge a public quarrel with Fox. On 9 May the rivals were guests of the 1st Earl of Hillsborough, a great Irish landowner and member of Parliament for Warwick, recently appointed Comptroller of the Royal Household. As Pitt was announced, Fox slithered off into another room. Pitt declared to Hillsborough that all connection between him and Fox was over, 'that the *ground* was alter'd, . . .'. Fox rejoined the company and Pitt, quite beside himself, turned upon him. When Fox asked what would put them on equal ground he snapped back 'a winter in the Cabinet and a summer's Regency'. Six days later they met again and though Pitt was calmer there was no reconciliation.[5] The 2 June found Pitt writing to Bute seeking an appointment that afternoon at the Privy Garden and describing himself as 'your lordship's very anxious and totally devoted friend'.[6]

Away in Hanover George II completed his treaty with Hesse-Cassel on 18 June for the hiring of 12,000 men at a cost of £300,000 p.a.; similar arrangements with Brunswick and Saxony would follow. These would be trifles compared with securing the alliance of Elizabeth of Russia, at a price. Whether or not Newcastle knew of Pitt's understanding with Bute and the Princess Dowager, he was anxious to secure his Paymaster's support for the subsidy treaties. Newcastle sent firstly old Horace Walpole to sound Pitt who asked for the Leadership of the Commons and a promise of the next vacancy in the Cabinet. Then on the evening of 6 July Hardwicke's younger son Charles Yorke saw Pitt and got the impression that he would not insist on being a Secretary of State. This influenced Newcastle into writing five days later to Holderness, urging that Pitt be included in the Cabinet, to receive the reply: 'Notwithstanding the just reasons His Majesty has to be offended with Mr. Pitt, the King will graciously accept of his services and countenance him accordingly.'[7] Newcastle trod warily and for the present had no intention of seeing Pitt, which would 'raise his vanity and his terms and make a ridiculous éclat'. His preference was that Hardwicke should deal with him and, as he sarcastically observed: 'He knows, and everybody does, that your Lordship had, and very rightly, the principal hand in preventing his being turned out.'

This precept Hardwicke acted on in the most distant manner, with a letter in the third person addressed to Peregrine Fury, a Pay Office clerk, summoning Pitt to Powis House, his London residence, at any time 'before Wednesday next, when his Lordship goes to Wimple'. Pitt had been spending a few days at Stowe and returned on the evening of 8 August to find this communication. Early next morning he informed Bute and went to see Hardwicke, who was out riding. He called again at noon, was received and stayed one hour and a half.[8] Hardwicke opened with a solemn warning to Pitt that the King was so angry at his conduct the previous session that there was no question of his becoming a Secretary of State. Pitt disclaimed all thought of promotion without the King's agreement, though he suggested the nation might be well served if Newcastle would advise it. But he stressed his inability to take a leading part without being informed as to policy. Hardwicke replied that the intention was to engage in a colonial war and to fight on the Continent in defence of Hanover only. Pitt would have been prepared to see Hanover occupied and buy it back after the war – on which Hardwicke commented: 'I have endeavoured to make him see the absurdity of that notion.' None the less Hardwicke was left with the feeling that some purpose might be served if Pitt saw Newcastle, who replied: 'I neither can nor will proceed one step without you.'[9]

Pitt went to stay a week in Hampshire with Legge and established a confederate. On his return to London in the second week of August Legge informed Newcastle that he would not as Chancellor of the Exchequer endorse any payments under the Hessian treaty until parliamentary ratification had been obtained. Bedford, out of the scene since his dismissal at

Newcastle's instance, was watching the approach of a ministerial crisis with keen interest. By this time he had adopted as his man of affairs and political adviser Richard Rigby, whom he had put into his pocket borough of Tavistock. Rigby, something of a rogue and one of the greatest spendthrifts and drunkards of the century, was none the less warm-hearted and shrewd. On 21 August he wrote to Bedford expressing the hope that Legge 'might carry his resentment a little further and speak against the Hessian subsidy in the House of Commons'.[10] When on the last day of August Pitt received advice from Bute to return to London, he at once arranged to see him: 'I had determined not to fix an interview with Lord Egmont, nor on any account to see the D of Newcastle till I cou'd have an ample conversation with your Lordship, and learn from you that final will and pleasure which shall entirely dispose of me and all my actions.'[11] Pitt introduced Legge to Bute and praised him as the most proper Chancellor of the Exchequer when the new reign arrived, which aroused George Grenville's bitter jealousy.[12]

Newcastle, dreading the prospect of seeing Pitt himself, persuaded Hardwicke to try once more. The Lord Chancellor opened their conversation of 1 September on a friendly, almost paternal note, with the hope that Pitt would 'assist them cordially in their business'. Every effort was being made to remove the King's personal prejudices; though the King was very fond of Holderness and Robinson there was the possibility that in return for a sincere assistance Pitt might secure the position of Secretary of State he so coveted. At this Pitt bridled and cutting the cackle asked what work he was being asked to assist in: 'Why', Hardwicke exclaimed, 'to carry on the war they were engag'd in.' Pitt promised that there was no doubt of 'his concurrence in carrying on the war, as it was a national one; and he thought that regard ought to be had to Hanover, if it was attack'd, upon our account'. Hardwicke expressed pleasure at his willingness to see Hanover defended but Pitt kept to his word: 'That regard was to be had to Hanover' – for Britain to maintain a defence of an open country was an impossibility whilst the method of paying subsidies meant the high road to bankruptcy. Hardwicke gently pointed out that last session the House of Commons had agreed to subsidies in principle, and there was now the treaty in usual form for Hessian mercenaries 'and there was also a treaty for a body of Russians'. Pitt retorted that subsidies, once embarked upon, would have no limit and end in good money chasing bad. In reasoning the Lord Chancellor found himself floored: 'To be sure, those things *should have their bounds*: ... *he was afraid they would not be very popular.*' Pitt pressed home and urged that Hanover be left 'to the system and constitution of the Empire' – either the Electorate should be declared neutral or depend upon the inevitable resentment throughout Germany at a French invasion. To this Hardwicke seemed to concur, 'but told him he must be sensible that talking in that manner would not make way with the King'.[13]

Newcastle steeled himself to the painful necessity of granting Pitt an audience, which was arranged for seven o'clock on the evening of 2 September and then put back an hour, 'his Grace being to dine late'. Earlier that day Pitt called upon Dodington, to whom he rehearsed his predeliberations; the Hessian subsidy must be the last and to a Russian treaty he would never subscribe. Pitt confided that he expected to find powerful allies; Devonshire might oppose subsidies even in the House of Lords and he himself had canvassed Bedford, 'who talk'd warmly and sensibly about it'. Pitt went away well pleased and penned a note to Bute – 'Mr. Dodington who holds a very good language' – evidently under the impression that he had made a convert.[14]

He did not expect his conference with Newcastle to be protracted but was kept two and a half hours. He began by deprecating the ruin that must follow from the King's sojourn in Hanover, with Holderness at his bidding, 'which they should have prevented; *with their bodies.* – A King abroad, at this time, without one man about him that has one English sentiment, and brings home a whole set of subsidies!' Newcastle switched the subject to the possibility of Pitt's being promoted. Pitt disclaimed any desire for office; the present conduct of business in the House of Commons would not do – 'while he had life, and breath to utter, he would oppose it'. What was needed was 'men of efficiency' – a Secretary or a Chancellor of the Exchequer able to convey to the King the feeling of members. Pitt 'supposed something was wanting, or why was he sent for?' Newcastle

tried to play down the subsidies; two, the Russian and the
Hessian, did not make a system and, after all, the King's honour
was engaged. Pitt was blunt to the point of rudeness; the subsidies might be approved, provided there was a public declaration that the sole purpose was to save the honour of the King,
'who had enter'd into a rash engagement: but for two, it was the
same as twenty, and no persuasion should make him for it'. But
then surely not only had the Hessian treaty to be ratified; what
of the Saxon and Bavarian treaties needing renewal? At this
Newcastle could only mumble that the Bavarian and Saxon
treaties were not to be pressed and the Russian treaty was not
absolutely concluded. Pitt and Newcastle parted with an understanding that they would meet again in ten days.[15]

Next day Pitt gave Dodington an account of what he and
Newcastle had had to say. Treating Dodington as a confidant,
Pitt talked over what support they might engage for an opposition. Dodington asked Pitt whether he was in touch with Fox.
Pitt exclaimed that, without wishing to complain, the last
session of Parliament had proved Fox to be in the same tent as
Granville and Murray. Dodington, momentarily seduced by
the prospect of an opposition to Newcastle, raised the subject
ever uppermost in his mind, of who would get what office if an
effect were attained. Pitt was rather shocked; such proceedings
smelt of faction though he would be perfectly happy to agree to
any terms Dodington might demand for himself. From some
strange impulse Pitt went on to flatter Dodington quite sense-
lessly: 'no man in this country would be more listen'd to, both
in, and out of the House, &c. &c.'. He expressed himself
desirous of connecting himself with Dodington as closely as
possible and reminded him of their relationship by marriage.
But if Pitt thought he had found a friend he was mistaken.[16]

The King, having rounded off his European business including an understanding with Russia, said good-bye to his
homeland for the last time and during the second week of
September sailed to England. Friday, 12 September, was the
day for Pitt's further audience of Newcastle and on the Thursday
morning he wrote to Bute asking him 'to give me an hour'
between eleven and lunch on the following day.[17] No doubt
they counted the heads of their supporters, Legge and the

Grenvilles for sure and possibly Devonshire and Bedford. When that evening Pitt waited upon Newcastle he found Hardwicke also present. They realised that here was a decisive occasion. As Legge's loyalty and Robinson's phlegm could neither be depended upon, without Pitt their only hope would be to give Fox the formal Leadership of the House of Commons. Pitt with some impertinence indicated that his countenance must depend upon a complete reshuffle of places in administration and the abandonment of the subsidy treaties. Of course, he knew Newcastle and Hardwicke would never bow to such effrontery.[18]

During the summer the news from America had gone from bad to worse. At the approaches to the St Lawrence Boscawen had taken two French ships of the line but the bulk of the enemy fleet eluded him. On 20 July the French Ambassador asked for his passport. Newcastle's strategy had gone badly awry, for here was a *casus belli* with Britain the aggressor, but Quebec had been reinforced. The capture of Beauséjour on the frontier of Nova Scotia in June by Colonel Robert Monckton and Captain John Rous was paltry compensation. The Cabinet ordered Hawke to intercept the Brest squadron on its return from North America and on 6 August he received further instructions to seize French merchant shipping. Shortly came the terrible news that on 9 July Braddock's little army had been cut to pieces in the forests around the Monongahela river by the Red Indian allies of the French. When Loudoun, who had been badly held up by administrative inefficiencies in London, at last arrived in New York on 17 July he took up his command confronted with a disaster bound to prejudice his chances of enlisting the co-operation of the colonial Assemblies. The Brest squadron eluded Hawke, who on 29 September returned to port, leaving John Byng to carry on the work. Newcastle and Hardwicke may have thought these miscarriages counterbalanced by the conclusion of the Russian treaty on the last day of September; the Czarina would receive a subsidy of £100,000 p.a. towards an army on the border of East Prussia, to be raised to £500,000 p.a. in the event of war with Frederick. But Newcastle and Hardwicke knew very well that Pitt would fight with every subtle device of formidable oratory which Murray could never withstand.

It was no surprise when at the opening of October Fox was

made Secretary of State for the Southern Department and Leader of the House of Commons. Robinson was returned to the Keepership of the Great Wardrobe with a pension of £2,000 p.a. upon the Irish establishment. Fox's successor at the War Office was the one-time Cobhamite Barrington, whom Newcastle judged to be one of his best supporters 'of good second rank'. Newcastle rounded off his team by enlisting none other than Hume-Campbell, who had worked with Pitt against the administration during the '45 rebellion. Campbell's terms were steep; he asked to be Chancellor of the Duchy of Lancaster with the salary augmented to £2,000 p.a. and Pitt got hold of a rumour that he would be met. But the King would not hear of it. Campbell had to be content with becoming Lord Clerk Registrar for Scotland for life with the salary made up.

Yet in important respects Newcastle was due for disappointment. He attempted to enlist Bedford's support for the treaties with an offer of the post of Lord Privy Seal. Bedford's opinion was that the treaties were more calculated to cause than avoid war and was resolved never again to serve in an administration headed by Newcastle.[19] Newcastle hoped to secure Lord George Sackville, Dorset's talented soldier son, so unlike his silly brother Middlesex. Sackville had been wounded at Fontenoy and attracted Cumberland's good mark; as intelligent as courageous he had discerned the promise of Wolfe whose career he furthered. Since 1741 Sackville had represented Dover and his ability to master and present a subject convinced many that his soldiering and politics would march together. But his judgement was distorted by an ambition too open and apropos of Fox being Secretary of State 'he complained that he was left out of everything, knew nothing, and in short must have some military distinction'. On 18 October Newcastle wrote to Hardwicke: 'He will be immediately appointed on the staff.'[20] Newcastle had a further reverse when Charles Townshend refused promotion from the Board of Admiralty to the Treasury because his elder brother disapproved of Fox.[21] None the less Newcastle hoped that his ministry had strength to withstand any onslaught from Pitt and Legge.

The coming session of Parliament was eagerly awaited and Elliot wrote to his wife: '. . . the ferment of the people is very high.'[22] The Commons assembled on 13 November, a full gathering of over four hundred members to hear the King's Speech. Sackville, though just promoted Major-General, declined the honour of seconding the Address of Thanks. When at two o'clock in the afternoon the debate opened Samuel Martin, appointed Secretary to the Treasury by Legge in 1754, moved to omit approbation of the Hessian treaty. Murray opened the case for the administration; if the King by firmness towards France in North America exposed his Electorate to danger, Britain was in honour bound to afford protection which could best be secured by the neutralisation of Germany through subsidy treaties. Pitt got up after midnight and trounced Murray for supposing that the King's true interests could be guaranteed by 'un-British' measures; these treaties with Russia and the German princes would 'hang like a mill-stone about the neck of any minister and sink him along with the nation'. He wound up his speech with his famous and brutally sarcastic comparison between ponderous Newcastle and vivacious Fox: 'I remember at Lyons to have been carried to see the conflux of the Rhône and the Saône: this a gentle, feeble, languid stream, and, though languid, of no depth – the other a boisterous and over-bearing torrent – but they meet at last; and long may they continue united, to the comfort of each other, and to the glory, honour, and happiness of this nation.'

That night sixteen spoke for the Opposition against thirteen for the Government. From the ministerial benches George Grenville, Legge, Jack Pitt of Encombe and Charles Townshend declared against the subsidies. Elliot persuaded Bute's brother James Stuart Mackenzie to support Pitt. When at five o'clock in the morning of 14 November the House divided, the administration had 311 supporters to 105: Pitt's eloquence had in no way shaken Newcastle's position, nor had he a strong following; of the opposition votes 76 were cast by Tory members motivated more by hereditary enmity to everything Whig than by admiration for him.[23] Newcastle had nothing to fear from Bedford who spoke for the Address and allowed his brother-in-law, since 1754 the 2nd Earl Gower, to step in as Lord Privy Seal. On 20 November Pitt, his cousin Jack, Legge, Martin and Grenville were informed of their dismissals in letters from Holderness.

Charles Townshend, being Newcastle's great-nephew, was left alone for the time being.

Pitt had for once in his life adopted the correct tactic by breaking with Newcastle over a clear-cut issue which everyone could grasp – the old Tory principle of the 'blue-water' school versus the Whig doctrine of a Continental war. On the day of his dismissal Pitt declared his intention to undo the disastrous policies of Newcastle; he urged the House of Commons to grant money without stint for the navy, 'an *English* object'. Murray had spoken proudly of the 140,000 European soldiers placed by British subsidies at His Majesty's disposal; Pitt retorted: 'Who boasts of the number prepared for England? – for America? Compare the countries and compare the forces that are destined for the defence of each! Two miserable battalions of Irish, who scarce ever saw one another, have been sent to America, have been sent under Braddock to be sacrificed!' Murray's praise of Russia as a 'newly risen Northern star' aroused Pitt's irony: 'Come let us consider this northern star that will not shine with any light of its own – Great Britain must be the sun of all this solar system: could Russia, without our assistance, support her own troops?' His day's work done, Pitt sent a line to Bute ending with these words: 'Good-night my dear Lord: I believe I shall sleep very quietly and wake as happy as any Minister now in England. Heaven defend and prosper the great cause we have the glory to serve.'[24]

The loss of his Paymaster's salary placed Pitt in a predicament; he had drawn his £4,000 p.a. for nine years yet was £1,000 overdrawn at his banker's, in marked contrast to George Grenville's practice of living off his small patrimony and saving the fruits of office. Temple promptly informed Lady Hester that he would be happy if Pitt would accept from him £1,000 a year to tide over his difficulties and so earned his lasting gratitude. At this time more than any other in his life Pitt enjoyed the warm hospitality of Stowe. Here, at those lavish dinner parties, he saw much of Wilkes, member for Aylesbury, one of Temple's Buckinghamshire henchmen, already prominent as a society wit; Pitt could not resist the enjoyment of his bawdy repartee.

Pitt's only regret was the breach in his friendship with Lyttleton, who declared that his opposition 'had not even the pretence of any public cause but was purely personal against the Duke of Newcastle'. Newcastle took his chance and promoted Lyttleton Chancellor of the Exchequer in place of Legge. On 22 November Newcastle announced Dodington to be Grenville's successor as Treasurer of the Navy. Four days later the land tax was raised to 4s in the £. Fox brought forward the Hessian and Russian treaties and intimated 12 December as a suitable day for debate, to which Pitt agreed. During the remainder of the session Pitt time and again lashed the Treasury bench with words which his victims knew would echo for ever not only in the minds of his hearers but in every London coffee-house. He opened one of his twenty-six speeches with an invective against Murray: 'I must now address a few words to the Attorney; they shall be few but they shall be daggers.'[25]

A month after his dismissal Pitt seconded George Townshend's motion to establish a committee of the House of Commons to draw up a bill for the formation of a militia, an institution dating from the Restoration but since become moribund. Townshend, an army officer of merit, had served in the '45 and in the Austrian war and could therefore speak to the House of Commons with authority on a military subject but was thoroughly disliked by the conservatively minded Cumberland. The militia committee upon which Pitt, together with Townshend and Sackville, served for the next few months aroused little interest. While these proceedings were under way, Pitt sat among empty benches in the House of Commons, for him a rare experience.[26]

Through the first fortnight of December Pitt continued to hit at the Government and found himself strongly supported by Charles Townshend. When on 12 December the crucial debate on the Russian and Hessian subsidies took place, Townshend saw fit to deliver a personal attack upon Newcastle and Pitt praised him in his most exaggerated manner: '. . . such abilities as had not appeared since that House was a House.'[27] Campbell got up to defend the Russian and Hessian treaties, to be crushed by Pitt's hammer: 'I apply it to him, he is the servile doctrine, he is the slave; and the shame of this doctrine will stick to him as long as his gown clings to his back.' Campbell never dared to challenge Pitt again.[28] Parliament entered the Christmas recess on 23 December and as might be expected Townshend was dismissed.

The King, completely confident that his government was safe, saw his way to a tit-for-tat with Bute and Pitt. At the end of December he proposed to Newcastle that both Houses of Parliament address the throne 'to remove from the Princess all persons who have endeavoured to create misunderstandings in the royal family . . .'. When Newcastle pointed out the complete absence of any proof for so vague an allegation, the King retorted: 'Impeachments have often been made upon *public fame* only.' Fortunately Newcastle steered his master away from a course which must lead to a false and hideous scandal.[29] The King would never have dared contemplate such vindictiveness had not he and Newcastle supposed themselves to have overcome all their difficulties in a form that must dish Pitt completely. Frederick was thoroughly alarmed at the prospect of a Russian army on his eastern frontier. Always ready to set aside his feelings for purposes of state, he offered to guarantee the neutrality of Hanover, a proposal George II embraced with relief and joy. On 16 January 1756 the first Convention of Westminster between Britain, Hanover and Prussia was signed. The European possessions of the signatories were reciprocally guaranteed, a strictly defensive arrangement not formally inconsistent with the British alliance with Russia. Frederick hoped that British influence in St Petersburg would be protection but he underestimated the Czarina's antagonism. Next Newcastle and George II hoped for a treaty with Austria in the fond hope of securing the neutrality of Europe by a series of paper guarantees. With a similar idea Louis XV and the Pompadour went behind the back of their foreign minister Rouillé and instructed de Bernis to open negotiations with Austria. Kaunitz, who realised how deeply the Convention of Westminster had disappointed the Czarina, saw his chance, welcomed the French opening and ignored the British.

In the spring of 1756 Newcastle and Hardwicke's son-in-law Anson thought they had to provide only for a colonial and naval war. Anson decided to concentrate on the protection of the Channel, writing to Hardwicke on 6 December 1755: 'I think it would be a dangerous measure to part with your naval strength from this country, which cannot be recalled if wanted, when I am strongly of the opinion that whenever the French intend anything in earnest their attack will be against this country.'[30] On 12 March 1756 Hawke once more put to sea in the Channel but foul weather enabled a new commander of the French Canadian army, the Marquis of Montcalm, to slip past with a reinforcement of 1,000 men. Anson was right in his expectation that an invasion of England would be the central theme of French strategy. Belleisle, French Minister for War, had a most daring and if successful effective master-plan to seize part of south-east England so as to halt the flow of British troops to North America and obtain peace terms on the basis of the *status quo ante bellum*. The concentration of 60,000 French troops along the Channel was sufficient to persuade Newcastle that North America should not be reinforced. Belleisle, in the vain hope of drawing the British fleet away from home, assembled an army at Toulon for a feint against Minorca. When on 25 March the House of Commons approved the Hessian subsidy without dissent, Fox was emboldened to propose that the King be requested to summon twelve battalions of his Hanoverian army to England. Pitt was stung into pointing out the humiliation of dependence upon a foreign army, but Fox carried the day by 259–22.[31]

The possibility of invasion gave Pitt and George Townshend a promising opportunity to introduce their militia bill. Their proposal was to raise a force of 60,000; a compulsory census of all able-bodied men would be followed by the drawing of lots for service; every Sunday the militia of each village would be turned out for drill and military exercises. The militia was to be paid and to be subject to the same code of martial law as the army; in each county the Lord Lieutenant would be in command with the deputy lieutenants and land tax commissioners as officers. The really important provision was that as the entire cost was to be met by parliamentary grant rather than by some county levy, the obligations under the bill could be mandatory. With much enthusiasm Pitt envisaged a nation in arms in place of Newcastle's hireling Hanoverians. The bill passed the House of Commons on 10 May. But Newcastle and the great magnates disliked the idea of arming the people and

Hardwicke had no qualms about killing the bill in the House of Lords. Murray, however, gave warning that a similar measure was bound to pass the Commons in the next year, and a further veto by the Lords would give rise to a constitutional difficulty.[32]

The concentration of the British fleet in the Channel and the arrival of Hanoverian regiments decided Belleisle that invasion was too hazardous. But Newcastle's concern for the safety of England allowed an easy capture of Minorca. John Byng was sent with but ten ships of the line to join Commodore Edgecumbe's Mediterranean squadron. Fifteen French ships of the line convoying 15,000 soldiers, commanded by the former Governor of Canada, de la Galissonière and the Duke of Richelieu, sailed from Toulon and disembarked on Minorca on 19 April 1756: Britain declared war. In the Commons debate of 7 May Pitt foretold catastrophe and 'went so far as to charge the loss of Minorca as a design to justify a bad peace'. To Newcastle's disgust Sackville backed Pitt and he found no reassurance in Fox's letter describing the debate: 'I answered as well as I could, but the loss of Minorca is a weight that it is not easy to debate under.'[33] Byng unsuccessfully attempted to draw de la Galissonière into battle on 20 May and then made his fatal blunder; instead of placing his ships between Minorca and the French mainland, he withdrew to Gibraltar. At once Newcastle and Anson ordered Hawke to Gibraltar with a commission to arrest him but too late: Port Mahon surrendered on 27 June.

While Minorca lay under siege de Bernis and Kaunitz had completed their arrangements for an alliance. The first Treaty of Versailles of 1 May 1756 between France and Austria was ostensibly defensive: under secret clauses Austria undertook not to intervene in a war between Britain and France and to guarantee the European possessions of France against attack by a third party; France therefore gave Austria a reciprocal undertaking. Frederick was dumbfounded at any treaty between Bourbon and Hapsburg, a nearly incredible inversion of international alignments. Kaunitz was not disappointed at the war preparations in Berlin which might give him an opportunity to invoke the French guarantee. A world war was under way and Britain had lost control of the Mediterranean.

Newcastle had the querulous temperament and already found

his political difficulties multiplying. The Prince of Wales on his coming of age that May became entitled to an independent establishment. The King resorted to subtlety and suggested that he and his brother Edward live at St James's or Kensington on his bounty with Waldegrave, Groom of the Stole. The Prince found the easy rejoinder that he could not be so disrespectful as to leave his mother and asked that Bute manage his household. It was at this time that Prince George heard tell of the rumours about Bute and the Princess. On 30 June he addressed a letter to Bute exhibiting all the emotional violence of an outraged eighteen-year-old; vengeance was sworn against her traducers and his friend was assured that the deeper the malice the more would their association be blazoned before the world.[34] The death of Sir Dudley Ryder, Lord Chief Justice of England, on 25 May was a further blow to Newcastle. At once Murray, exercising his right as Attorney-General, asked to succeed Ryder, which must entail the loss of his services in the House of Commons. In despair Newcastle offered him sinecures and pensions equivalent to a Lord Chief Justice's £6,000 p.a.[35] Hardwicke gave his blessing to a translation which, though unfortunate for the administration, must prove a blessing to the stewardship of justice.

Minorca held a place in the affections of the British people similar to Mary Tudor's feelings for Calais. Everywhere Newcastle was blamed. Potter wrote to George Grenville: 'This morning I heard the whole city of Westminster disturbed by the song of a hundred ballad-singers, the burthen of which was "to the dock with Newcastle, and the yard-arm with Byng".' Newcastle joined in the cry for Byng's court martial and was reported as exclaiming: 'Oh, indeed, he shall be tried immediately, he shall be hanged directly.'[36] Fortunately for him Parliament had a few days back gone into the summer recess. The ministry had become prone to mishap. When a Hanoverian soldier, convicted of stealing handkerchiefs from a shop in Maidstone, was on an order from Holderness handed over to his own authorities for trial, London was seized with a fit of xenophobia. Minorca transformed Fox from a complaisant underling into the treacherous gamester that at heart he was. On 31 July he wrote to Devonshire: 'The rage of people and of considerable people . . . increases hourly . . . when the Parliament meets the scene of action will be the House of Commons and I being the only figure of a minister there, shall of course draw all the odium on me.'

The British public knew nothing of the momentous events in far away Bengal, for news took at least six months and sometimes more than a year in coming. Suraj ud Dowlah, the young Nawab, a spoilt youth and though a Moslem given to alcohol, decided to turn the British East India Company out of their establishment in Calcutta and on 20 May the hideous crime of the massacre in the Black Hole was perpetrated. The war between the Company and the Nawab which followed was not the result of developments in Europe and North America, of which information had not yet reached India. Even had Britain and France adjusted their differences, Clive and Watson would have sought vengeance. But though the war in Bengal was in no way integrated with what happened in London or Versailles, let alone the machinations of Kaunitz in Vienna, the stage was set in India for events every bit as dramatic as might follow in North America or Europe.

At Berlin Frederick's great fear was that the French might join forces with the Austrians in central Germany. He decided to invade Bohemia by way of Saxony before the Austrian army was mobilised and in June and July 1756 informed London. Frederick knew that George II would have to accept him as an ally willy-nilly and asked for a British subsidy to help the Prussian army defend Hanover and that a naval squadron be sent to the Baltic. The Austrian government invoked the French guarantee and Louis XV accordingly broke off diplomatic relations with Prussia. Kaunitz, who knew that Russia would strike as soon as her armies were ready and that Sweden too could be counted among Frederick's enemies, had realised his dream of creating a great coalition aimed at the dismemberment of Prussia. The enlargement of the colonial squabble between Britain and France into a world conflict must be explained in terms of how Kaunitz inveigled the great powers into war against the better judgement of their rulers.

As the summer wore on the possibility of impeachment lay heavy upon Newcastle's mind. High corn prices led to rioting in Sheffield, Salop and Derbyshire and among the Cumberland miners. London, Bristol, and other cities and boroughs, not to mention the Grand Juries of several counties, presented Addresses to the Crown praying for a change of government. Fox expressed his willingness to toil on provided Pitt was included in the ministry and then on 12 August commented: 'I do not . . . think my offer with regard to Pitt in the least generous. For this Administration has, I think, lost the good will and good opinion of their country . . . and without them who can wish to be in Administration?'[37] Then on 30 September news came from North America of a further disaster. Montcalm had arrived in Canada on 12 May and at once struck at Oswego, the British naval base on Lake Ontario, which surrendered during the last week in August, with 1,700 prisoners and a vast quantity of stores. The French had won control of the Great Lakes.

Pitt spent a very relaxed summer at Hayes with his wife, who was expecting her second child, though he undertook his customary peregrination of Buckinghamshire. Potter, with whom his relations at this time drew much closer, promised to call at Hayes: 'In eight or ten days I shall be in London & will find an Hour to visit this Roman at his Plow.' Early in August Potter joined with Wilkes in inducing the Bedfordshire Grand Jury to draw up a petition for a Minorca enquiry. Potter's letters to Pit were couched in a familiarity which few dared attempt. The friendship was on the face of things ill-assorted: Potter ruined his health by his dissipations and although his admiration for Pitt was genuine he could be of little use. Pitt counselled abstinence, to receive this charmingly frank reply:

'But you have done ill to propose yourself as an example to me. It is as injudicious as to tell a sinner that he must imitate a saint . . . – you have stated with your usual Delicacy, the *fatiguing Business or exhausting Pleasures which you wish me to remit.* In this Particular it is not in my Power to gratify you for Alas! I am no longer a free Agent.'

Potter had to stay at his Bedfordshire seat Ridgmont, the prey to scurvy, gout and palsy, 'a pretty Triumvirate' he called them.

He hoped the coming baby would be a boy and on 29 September wrote to Pitt:

'Where is the little Heroe? Does the fond mother restrain him from making his entrance into a cursed world, or having the Intuition that he is born to be an Englishman, does he thro' shame of the Title, aspire to remain where he is?'

Potter was sending his son, another Thomas, to Emmanuel College Cambridge and rather pathetically commended him: 'My Son has got parts & is free from vice.' Pitt took the hint and wrote to his nephew, still up at Clare College: 'Mr. Potter is one of the best friends I have in the world.' When Potter encountered a slight rebuff from Bute, he did not hesitate to ask Pitt to clear matters up, which was done at the first opportunity.[38]

The Government which Newcastle had endeavoured to patch up over the two and a half years since his brother's death was fast crumbling to ruin. He had to accept that Murray must be Lord Chief Justice before Parliament next assembled and, after some objections from the King, he was made Lord Mansfield. Newcastle began to insure himself against impeachment by concessions to Leicester House. Robert Henley, Solicitor-General to the Prince of Wales since 1751, was appointed Attorney-General in succession to Murray.[39] On 4 October the Prince of Wales was informed that the King had waived his objection to Bute becoming his Groom of the Stole.[40] Three days later Pitt hailed Bute with the announcement of the safe delivery at Hayes of a son, John. To George Grenville he wrote: 'She had a sharp time, but not longer than two hours and a half . . . Nurse Creswell looks with satisfaction, and Nurse Long with envy, upon his quality and quantity.' Potter was thrilled: 'Such a Woman; the Sister of such Brothers, the Wife of such a Husband & may Posterity add the Mother of such children.'[41]

Fox's resignation, conveyed by Granville to the King on the morning of 15 October, was anticipated. The King was very angry and rightly accused Fox of a concern for his own skin. When on the morning of 17 October Fox was civilly received in audience he suspected a wish to leave matters open because Newcastle was awaiting Hardwicke's return to London. Then on the morning of the 18th Pitt arrived in town and he, Fox felt certain, would be offered the seals on any terms. If, however, Pitt refused, Fox had no intention of returning to office unless Cumberland asked it of him: 'I may be turned out', wrote he to Bedford, 'but whether I am or no, the Duke of Newcastle's reign is, I verily think, over.'[42] Thus was ended the brief, eighteen-months period as Leader of the House and Secretary of State of he who might have been one of the most gifted parliamentarians of all time.

CHAPTER 6

The Pitt and Devonshire Ministry

'His Royal Highness's Judgement would be equal to his parts were it not too much guided by his passions, which are often violent and ungovernable. He has abilities to perform things which are difficult, but sometimes loves an impossibility. In his military capacity, he appears greatly superior to any man in this country; and I have frequently wished that he had confined himself to that department, without entering into party disputes, or interfering in the affairs of civil government; the first of which is below his dignity, and for the latter he is not qualified.'

The 2nd Earl Waldegrave, Character of the
Duke of Cumberland. *Memoirs*.[1]

Newcastle had no intention of relinquishing power after thirty-four years in Cabinet office without a break; George II, nearing seventy-five, would not countenance an upheaval which in effect made a Prime Minister of Pitt. Newcastle's situation was not that of Walpole's in 1742, when lack of success in war had given an ascendancy to an opposition numerous, able and of long-standing. Pelham had managed things so well that the Whigs almost without exception looked to Newcastle as the pilot. But the loss of Minorca could not be glossed over and Newcastle's stratagem was to induce Pitt to join administration on terms

which left power and patronage securely with himself. Hardwicke was at Wimpole, his magnificent seat in Cambridgeshire,
and from there on Friday, 16 October, he addressed to Pitt a
summons to London for the following Tuesday. Pitt's true
appraisal of Bute came out in his deliberated preference not to
let him into the picture. Instead, in a letter to George Grenville
he rallied his connection with the proud affirmation that he was
not going to unscramble Newcastle's eggs:

'Though I expect our conference will be short and final, considering the negative I go resolved to give to any plan with the
D. of N. at the head of it, as well as to any proposal for covering
his retreat, in case he wishes to retire from being a Minister;
yet as it is impossible to be sure, in the present state of things,
how far his Majesty may be brought to open his eyes, I beg of
you, as I do of Lord Temple, to be in town Tuesday evening, at
my house in Brook Street, where I may receive your lights and
final determination as to any ulterior conversation with the
Court, should they be proposed.'[2]

Over a conversation lasting three and a half hours Pitt made
clear to Hardwicke that he would not talk business unless he
was guaranteed a parliamentary enquiry into the conduct of the
war, a militia act, a review of the case of the Hanoverian soldier
and complete freedom of access to the King. Hardwicke was
apprehensive lest Pitt's toughness had encouragement from
some secret concert with Fox.[3] Two days later Pitt called on the
unfortunate Lady Yarmouth, and to her sketched out a completely new ministry with himself Secretary of State for the
Northern Department and, surprisingly, Robinson at the South.
Pitt intended using Robinson's knowledge of diplomatic routine
while the real direction of policy would be his, and at the same
time the King would be humoured. A First Lord of the Treasury
acceptable to the Whig magnates would be the 4th Duke of
Devonshire, who had succeeded his father just over a year back.
Pitt's connection would be represented with Temple as Lord
Lieutenant of Ireland and places for the Grenvilles and Legge.
Hardwicke was relieved to learn that Fox was omitted; evi-
dently his suspicions had been misconceived. Pitt's idea of

Devonshire as figurehead was sound but his wide demands for his connection incited astonishment. On 26 October Hillsborough wrote to George Grenville discounting the exacting nature of Pitt's requirements: 'in short, to make a family administration'. Yet the rumour was true. The King was furious at Pitt's seeing Lady Yarmouth because he liked to pretend that she had no influence in state matters.[4]

Newcastle, incredulous that he was about to receive his *congé* at the hands of that bumptious upstart Pitt, manoeuvred blindly. Egmont, Prince Frederick's old courtier, was asked to become Secretary of State but he wanted a peerage of Great Britain, which was no use to Newcastle looking for someone to lead the Commons. Newcastle next turned to Granville, Lord President of the Council, with the extraordinary suggestion that they should change places. But on being informed that the consensus of the City had turned hostile, Newcastle saw the game was up and on 26 October he announced his intention to resign as soon as a new arrangement could be brought about.[5] Granville expressed his astonishment that a minister possessed of a large majority in both Houses could conceivably resign. The King was far from ready to entrust Pitt with power. Because Fox was the friend of Cumberland, Bedford and Devonshire, George II failed to grasp how deeply he was mistrusted in the House of Commons, and Pitt respected. He realised Pitt's co-operation in a scheme of coalition to be most improbable but saw no obstacle to Fox's going ahead on his own. Therefore on 27 October Fox was commanded to talk things over with Bedford and Devonshire. Fox had a pretty clear persuasion of his own unpopularity and would have welcomed an arrangement with Pitt. On 28 October the two met at the head of the staircase at Leicester House. They talked for twenty minutes but Pitt was barely civil.[6]

In the diary which at this time Devonshire began to keep he related: 'I was sent for from Derbyshire after much persuasion from the King I took the Treasury with a promise that I could be allowed to resign it at the end of the session.'[7] Devonshire was only thirty-seven and had he not been who he was this honour would never have befallen him. He was not physically strong, consented to act only as 'caretaker', and was more the friend of Fox than of Pitt, without pretending to be the natural equal of either. But he had the telling advantage of that fair-mindedness which carries weight with men of goodwill. The King expected Devonshire to form a great House of Commons ministry and many thought Pitt too should work to that end. Bedford in a letter to his Duchess stressed that Pitt's desideration for a family government must be circumvented.[8] Pitt was tormented with gout and his friend Elliot marvelled at his fortitude: 'If I were to admire one quality more than another, it was to find him thus circumstanced; without the least impatience, his thoughts perfectly free and disengaged, and as cheerful as ever I saw him.'[9] Pitt's total self-confidence blazed forth when he told Devonshire: 'I know that I can save this country and that no one else can.' He arranged to go to Devonshire House, Piccadilly, at noon on 30 October, where the Duke found him, as he put it, 'far more practicable'. Fox entirely comprehended Pitt's rejection of a coalition: 'He foresaw, I suppose, that my place would be the Treasury', wrote he to Bedford; 'I can't much blame him my Lord, for in that case what would he be but Paymaster under another Pelham, with an employment of another rank?'[10]

Bedford came to town and on the evening of 1 November he, together with Devonshire, dined by appointment with Fox at the King's Head, Pall Mall. Devonshire remarked that though personally he would prefer to see Fox Leader of the Commons, the settlement of the King's affairs must have precedence, but he was adamant against Legge at the Exchequer. Fox, anxious to allow Pitt as few pickings as possible, urged Bedford to take the Lord Lieutenancy of Ireland Devonshire would be giving up.[11] Next morning Bedford saw the King, who ranted away 'against Pitt's insolent treatment of him'. The next to be received was Granville who, as Bedford related, 'carried the King a paper drawn up by himself, which, though short, was replete with good sense, and which tended to make . . . such offers to Pitt and his family as he cannot reasonably refuse, but such as if he does . . . must put him in the wrong in the opinion of every reasonable man and enable us all to weather the storm of opposition, should they be so rash as to undertake it'. With Fox the King made one last effort, earnestly imploring him to

undertake administration. But Fox saw this to be madness for
both.[12]

That day Pitt could not leave his house because he was under
medicine. He therefore wrote to Devonshire announcing
Temple's readiness to take the Admiralty: by implication the
loss of Minorca must involve Anson in disgrace. Controversy
was indicated over the allocation of the Secretaryships; Pitt
wanted the Northern Department for himself and repeated his
suggestion that Robinson be given the South with a peerage. In
short Pitt was still affiliated to the notion of a Grenville clan
administration with Robinson as stalking horse.[13] Devonshire
was completely taken aback at such presumption. He first saw
the King and then chanced upon Bedford and Fox listening
with utter fascination to Granville's latest concoction for
Devonshire at the Treasury, Pitt Secretary of State and Fox
Chancellor of the Exchequer. Fox proposed a grand gathering
of peers and members of Parliament for the evening of 3
November, over which Devonshire would preside and his own
instalment as Chancellor be announced: '. . . the rest of Mr.
Pitt's demands, unreasonable as they are, will be complied with.
If Pitt would insist upon having Legge or any of his own people,
Chancellor of the Exchequer, that will not be complied with.'

That night Devonshire lost his nerve and said he would not
go forward at all. But next morning he veered round completely, went to the King and agreed to take the Treasury with
Legge at the Exchequer. The way was open for Pitt and Fox
acknowledged that his prospects of greatness were eclipsed for
ever: 'No system', wrote he to Bedford, 'in which I am a
minister can be carried on without great contention.' As he
could not cast himself for hero, Fox set his sights on the things
of this world and supposed the prospect of his usefulness in the
House of Commons might induce Pitt to yield easily to his
hankering to become Paymaster. He had no design of renounc-
ing the perquisites and was avid to accumulate the great fortune
the conditions of war made certain. Pitt, rejoicing in the chance
to force his one-time rival into a grovelling humiliation, asked
Fox to be Treasurer of the Navy with George Grenville given
the Pay Office. To that Fox would not submit and gave bitter
expression to the hope that Pitt by rashness and arrogance

might work his own undoing.[14] Two days later Newcastle formally resigned and Devonshire was invested with the Treasury. Hardwicke was not prepared to continue in office without his old friend and so one of the greatest Lord Chancellors of all time stepped down.

Amidst all these comings and goings Pitt came to depend a great deal upon Potter, who established contacts between him and the rump of the Old Tory members of Parliament. The representatives of families who since 1714 had shunned the Court were ready to support the man who stood for 'blue-water' principles. The adherence of William Beckford of Fonthill, Wiltshire, the millionaire proprietor of Jamaica sugar plantations, proved a milestone. Beckford, a member of Parliament for the City of London and a leading voice in Guildhall, wrote to Pitt on 5 November 1756: 'I intend to act as one of your private soldiers without commission.'[15] Pitt and Beckford, the merry begetter of a proudly acknowledged bevy of illegitimate children, may seem odd comrades. But Pitt could be charitable to the peccadilloes of his friends.

By the second week of November Devonshire had completed his ministry. Pitt suffered a bitter disappointment in having to bow to the King's objection that his views on Hanover must disqualify him for the Northern Department. On 15 November Pitt was appointed Secretary of State for the South and he had to swallow Holderness remaining at the North. Temple at the Admiralty went through without trouble and at the Exchequer Legge was expected to play an important rôle, for money had to be raised in the City for the war and Pitt had no knowledge of public finance. At Fox's pressing instance Bedford accepted the Lord Lieutenancy of Ireland.[16] The Paymastership Fox would have liked was not however bestowed upon George Grenville and here Pitt had ready a prize for none other than Potter, who was brimful with delight: 'To succeed you in your own Office, to be half a Pitt is what my ambition in its most flighty moments never aspired to.' Grenville realised that he had been put forward merely to spite Fox and great was his resentment at being returned to his vomit as Treasurer of the Navy.[17] Charles Townshend, too, had suffered for his loyalty to Pitt, but though his parts were generally commended he became merely Cofferer of the Household. Waldegrave had an explanation: 'Pitt did not choose to advance a young man to ministerial office, whose abilities were of the same kind, and so nearly equal to, his own.' Townshend had every cause to turn sour. Lyttleton, in view of his apostasy to Newcastle, was paid off with a peerage.[18]

Potter was getting a bit above himself, with his bright suggestion that he should be made a Privy Councillor, and his ebullience did not stop there. Pratt, since witnessing Walpole's defeat, had built himself a successful practice and taken silk. But in Chancery he was ignored by Hardwicke, it was thought from a jealous protection for his favourite son Charles Yorke, recently become Solicitor-General. Potter really was interfering when he suggested to Pitt that if Henley was appointed Keeper of the Great Seal Pratt might become Attorney-General. Potter was not sworn of the Privy Council and most advisedly Henley stayed Attorney. An affront to Hardwicke would have placed Devonshire in an impossible position.[19]

Pitt's prospects before Parliament must depend upon the complaisance of placemen who owed their positions to Pelham and Newcastle. Only Devonshire's presence could evoke a loyalty toward the man called upon to win the war. Where change was asked for the King could be very prickly, but by reason of his experience by no means always mistaken. His insistence upon the confirmation of Barrington at the War Office was a proper recognition of honest ability. Pitt was most concerned that Temple should have a strong Board of Admiralty, where enemies on grounds purely political could not be tolerated. Here was a niche for Elliot and also for Dr George Hay, former King's Advocate-General who had been dismissed for opposition to the subsidy treaties. Pitt insisted on his reinstatement as well as a seat on the Admiralty. The King thought this most unreasonable and Holderness told Newcastle that 'it was yielded to but with reluctance'. Shortly there arose an incident of ominous suggestion. Since 1754 Hay had been member for Stockbridge, Hampshire, and his appointment necessitated his re-election. But Fox, who controlled the borough, flatly refused to allow his return and was fully confident of the King's approval. Finally Pitt, by cunning devices, slipped in Admiral

Forbes and had secured a Board of Admiralty he could trust.[20]

Although Pitt liked to appear to the world above patronage he could show a concern worthy of Newcastle at his most zealous, and he had no scruple about invading the Duke's favourite orbit of ecclesiastical patronage. He recommended Dr Richardson, Master of Emmanuel College, to the Deanery of Ely, always held by the head of a Cambridge House. For the Deanery of Salisbury he put forward Warburton: 'the nephew by marriage of the worthiest man that lives, my true and much honoured friend Mr. Allen of Bath'. But for Pitt these opportunities might well prove limited, for the King was ready to use every underhand device to discomfort the ministry.[21]

Hardwicke apprehended how uncomfortable the King must be with a team not of his making but advised Newcastle not for the present to exploit that circumstance: 'The want of a proper person, capable of interposing in the closet, begins to be manifest, but we must not be ministers behind the curtain. The new gentlemen begin to ascribe the disagreeableness of their reception to that cause.'[22] For the first time for many years Hardwicke would not draw up the King's Speech for the opening of Parliament; this task Pitt reserved to himself and wrote to Devonshire from Hayes: 'I have drawn it captivating the People, but with regard to the King's Dignity, and have avoided any word offensive or hostile to those who no longer serve his Majesty.' The King took exception to certain passages of the Speech, which Holderness gladly passed on to Newcastle. Eight days later Pitt wrote to Devonshire: 'I am very sorry that his Majesty will have one that will spread less satisfaction. A few lines, and that is all, may be parted with.' The King's awkwardness over the Speech was nothing compared with the downright rudeness with which he treated Temple, so that Pitt already anticipated that the ministry would be shortlived. He could observe '. . . a certain unhappy difficulty of temper, but philosophy itself, in order to deserve a good name, must have its bounds; and I will own, I more than begin to fear that the King will have much vexation and plague to form a thing his Majesty will not suffer to last'.[23]

Newcastle and Hardwicke were particularly fussed about Pitt's intentions over the Minorca enquiry. On 28 November Pitt refused to see Hardwicke because he was ill, which was true, but his not suggesting a later occasion was studied rudeness. Three days later Pitt was granted an audience by the Sovereign who had hated him so cordially for so long, and late that afternoon he wrote to Bute: 'The Reception in the Closet was favourable, considering the long impressions against me; and longer than I had expected, for it lasted several minutes.'[24]

The King's Speech of 2 December was intended by Pitt as a challenge to the country for unity in a common endeavour; the Hanoverian troops imported for defence would be sent back and trust reposed in the militia. The object of the war was the battle for North America; for that service Highland Scots regiments would be raised in addition to the Black Watch founded in 1739. Above all, no British troops were to be employed upon the Elbe, 'that river of gore'; the strategy of Carteret and Pelham which Newcastle had been prepared slavishly to follow was to be completely reversed. So far all was as might have been expected, though there was surprise at Pitt's decision to honour the Hessian treaty and undertake a subsidy of £200,000 p.a. for the Hanoverian army. But without these provisions the ministry could not have continued for a day; the honour of the King, together with the prestige of the nation, were pledged not to leave Hanover to suffer in the cause of British colonial interests. And Pitt had always shown a readiness to acquiesce in the Hessian treaty, his point being that overall strategy must be biased in the direction of North America. Pitt was enraged on discovering that a sentence of gratitude to the King for the loan of his electoral soldiers was inserted in the Address of Thanks from the House of Lords. He assured Bute that Devonshire and the entire Cabinet must disapprove and he would endorse Temple's protesting in the Lords: 'What is this malignant influence? It is the Duke of Cumberland, I don't doubt.' Temple wrote to Devonshire: 'This is a very unfortunate step at the outset, and such a one as Mr. Pitt and I judge will tend to a speedy dissolution of a system of which I cannot make a part longer than I am able to prove myself consistent with myself.' Devonshire in no way relished impertinence from Temple: '. . . your lordship', he snubbingly replied, 'will forgive me if I own that I do not see any great objection to merely thanking the

King with having complied with the advice of his Parliament'.
Temple gave the peers a dressing down, but it was Devonshire's
honest opinion that the King expected a few words of thanks for
his electoral troops. Upon him fell the disagreeable business of
smoothing things over by seeing the King, Lady Yarmouth and
Bedford. On the afternoon of 3 December the entire ministry
kissed hands upon receiving their seals of office, fortunately
without incident.[25] Very properly Pitt decided that to continue
representing Newcastle's borough of Aldborough was unsuitable,
but he made no attempt to represent a London seat or any that
might be deemed popular. He chose Okehampton, the family
constituency in Devon which since 1754 had been mortgaged to
the Government.* His ancestral connection with the west
country was maintained and at the same time his position as
de facto head of the Government underlined.[26]

Pitt's formal appointment gave Hardwicke a tolerable excuse
for calling, for congratulations could surely not be unwelcome.
Hardwicke saw Pitt on the afternoon of 6 December and
described the scene to Newcastle: 'I heard last night that he had
a fresh touch of gout but decided to take my chance this afternoon. Contrary to expectation I was carried upstairs, and found
him under a thorough relapse, with one leg wrapped up in
flannel and complaining of having suffered much.' Hardwicke
gave Pitt his word that Newcastle had had nothing to do with
the Lords Address; only fear of enquiries and censures would
induce him to concert with Fox. Pitt played down the Minorca
enquiry; he thought of it only on the ground of self-consistency;
the affair of the Hanoverian soldiers was truly important. This
Hardwicke advised him to keep out of the House of Commons:
'he would bring himself under the greatest difficulty for the sake
of a bagatelle'. Pitt passed on to his alliance with the Tories and
was at some pains to convince Hardwicke that no conditions
had been imposed: 'quite free and disinterested: merely to keep
the ship from sinking'. Hardwicke smilingly asked: 'How long
do you consider it will last on that foot?' Pitt smiled back and

* Pitt remained M.P. for Aldborough until the first week in December 1756.
He was then returned for Temple's borough of Buckingham, which however he
represented for only four days, 7 to 11 December. On the latter date he was returned
for Okehampton, so that his being M.P. for Buckingham had no practical significance.

suggested, 'surely this session'. Hardwicke took his leave and to Newcastle described his interview as 'a not unfortunate beginning'.[27] Tories or no Tories, Hardwicke knew that the King would have Pitt out if he could. His Majesty did not scruple to make suggestions to Newcastle about electoral matters under cover of Holderness: 'Lord Holderness's hint was certainly from the King and I don't wonder at it,' was Hardwicke's comment in his letter to Newcastle of 12 December.[28]

That attack of gout bore grave consequence. Pitt would have to neglect much House of Commons business and on Sunday, 19 December, he informed Devonshire that he had asked Barrington to postpone the army estimates until the Wednesday: 'This will give me two days which I hope may enable me to crawl a little better.' Ill-natured speculation suggested that the infirmity had entered his head, but his friends were concealing matters. On 25 January Devonshire was able to tell Rigby – who of course passed everything on to Bedford and Fox – that Pitt was well enough to go out but not to attend Court or Parliament.[29] Newcastle gathered confidence and Granville assured him he had a majority of at least 150 in the House of Commons. Barrington noted how every Wednesday the diplomatic corps called upon Newcastle as they had for years: 'I see no alteration at Newcastle House, except that its master is more cheerful.' But for the present Newcastle decided not to court unpopularity 'out-doors' by taking responsibility for Pitt's overthrow. Fox too realised that the time to attempt a ministerial revolution was not yet. In consequence the parliamentary session following the Christmas recess was remarkably quiet. Matter for controversy would have arisen had the Minorca enquiry opened on the day announced, 21 January, but Pitt was far too ill to attend. By this time Bedford was certain the enquiry would come to nothing.[30]

To oblige the King and thereby keep life for the administration Pitt went so far as he dared, even to the point of raising the Hanover subsidy by one-third. When half-way through February he put this to the House of Commons, a conceivably embarrassing moment, he was enthusiastically seconded by Sackville, who had made up his mind that here was the man of the moment and one to further his military ambitions. The subsidy was passed without a division. Pitt received a fulsome letter of congratulation from Bute and was graciously received by a pleased Sovereign. The flowery phrases of Pitt's reply to Bute must be excused in the light of expediency: 'The perseverance my noble friend applauds so partially as mine was, in effect, his own constancy of mind and clearness of view animating and confirming wishes of mine into execution.' Pitt did not omit to pay his duty to Lady Yarmouth, to whom he spoke of Sackville in glowing terms.[31] The King's gratitude was not likely to be of duration.

Pitt, whether at Hayes or in town, organised war from the sick-room in every detail. His official residence as Secretary of State was in Cleveland Row, close to St James's Palace. He had in his department two under-secretaries, James Rivers and Robert Wood, assisted by nine clerks, and he also shared a staff with Holderness. He maintained a very strict discipline, himself correcting every despatch down to the last detail. Immediately on taking office Pitt enquired of James Abercrombie, Agent for Virginia, what the military and economic situation in North America might be. Abercrombie was a mine of information and a convinced imperialist, too. Pitt decided to keep Loudoun on as Commander-in-Chief in North America. But where Cumberland had given him every latitude, Pitt cut his powers drastically and himself undertook all correspondence with the Governors.[32]

For the naval command the choice was Rear-Admiral Francis Holburne. The first objective was the reduction of Louisbourg, the great fortress on Cape Breton Island, to be followed by an attack on Quebec. Pitt planned an initial reinforcement of seven battalions, six to be drawn from Ireland and the extra from England, and above all the army for America must be provided with an adequate siege train. In an irate letter to Devonshire of 30 January Pitt laid down the law: 'the Ruine of the Kingdom shall not be at my door, but on those, who obstruct and defeat a resource so ready on the spot, as sending another battalion and a proper, adequate train, for an expedition, on which all depends, and the success whereof depends on its not being retarded beyond the time proposed'. Devonshire was asked to impress all these points upon the King.

Devonshire's reaction was commendably prompt. Late in the

evening of the following day Pitt wrote to Bute happily announcing that Cumberland had consented to everything. Devonshire
had therefore late on Monday afternoon come round to Pitt and
in his presence wrote to Barrington, whilst Pitt undertook to
send instructions to Bedford in Ireland. As Pitt's health was so
poor the Cabinet of 1 February was at his house and he wrote to
Devonshire asking him to bring round Granville, Holderness
and the 3rd Duke of Marlborough, Master-General of the
Ordnance. Three days later he wrote to inform Bute how
efficiently all the necessary points had been disposed of: 'Our
meeting passed very well. Instructions unanimously approved,
additional train and stores, 6 engineers, and 2 more companies
of Artillery agreed to, and the sloop, I hope, to be dispatcht to
America today or tomorrow.'

The assemblage of troops, commissariat and transports at
Plymouth was a lengthy business and Holburne had to collect
his troops from Ireland. Temple was not, on his own admission,
of much use at the Admiralty: 'he found it the most uneasy
situation for a man to be in; for he was obliged to be continually
turning, first to one Admiral and then to another, to get explanations of the most common terms and forms'.[33] Pitt was eager to
risk sending troops from home, partly because George Townshend's new militia bill, in a form intended to meet the objections
of the House of Lords, passed the House of Commons easily. The
question arises how far Pitt invented a plan of war. Barrington
for one did not see any change: 'The measures, as declared and
explained by Mr. Pitt, differ in nothing from those of the last
administration.' For the present Barrington's judgement had
truth; events had swept aside Newcastle's plan for a costly
Russian alliance and Pitt had not tried to upset the programme
of modest German subsidies together with reinforcements for
North America his predecessors had left him. The difference
must lie in vigour of execution but that remained to be seen.

Public attention was fastened upon the fate of Byng, who on
27 January was found by court martial not guilty of personal
cowardice or disaffection but guilty of neglecting to do 'his
utmost to take, seize and destroy the ships of the French King'.
Neglect carried a mandatory death penalty, subject only to the
royal pardon. A letter from Byng's judges to the Board of

Admiralty, deploring the severity of an Article of War which prevented their overlooking an error of judgement, was forwarded to the King. He submitted it to the civil judges, who in their turn upheld the legality of the sentence, so Temple's request for a pardon was rejected.

The King did not want Byng spared and Hardwicke was accused of seeking his death as a means of protecting Anson. Augustus Keppel, member of Parliament for Chichester, with two of the other judges waited upon Temple and asked him to renew their application for clemency. Keppel, a shy orator, persuaded Dashwood to sponsor a bill to absolve the court martial from the oath of secrecy. In the debate of 23 February Pitt suggested that Keppel might 'break through his bashfulness and rise'. Keppel told the House that he had 'something on his mind' that he wished to disclose. Again five days later he indicated that his conscience was not clear. Fox's motion that the bill be rejected led him into severe altercations with Pitt and on the last day of February he withdrew. Then, to the amazement of all, Charles Townshend got up to declare that he would cheerfully have seconded Fox. Pitt was very angry and 'wished Townshend joy that *his conscience* was made easy'. He added an aside loud enough for half the House to hear: 'I wish you joy of him.'

The bill passed with Pitt's blessing but from the King he received the rebuke: 'Sir, you have taught me to look for the sense of my subjects in another place than in the House of Commons.' Hardwicke obtained an order for every member of the court martial to appear individually at the Bar of the House of Lords. Ten of the thirteen judges expressed no wish to be released from their oath, whilst Keppel said nothing. Hardwicke advised the peers that in passing the bill the Commons had acted from mistaken motives and Temple wrote to congratulate the King upon Byng's sentence. Byng was shot on 14 March.[34]

By this time Pitt's gout had subsided, but that circumstance had limited his seeking an audience of the King to only six occasions. These the King did not find pleasant, for where he preferred a matter-of-fact approach, Pitt bored him with rhetoric in the Closet. But though George II always treated Pitt as a gentleman, he could not bear Temple's 'pert familiarity' –

'so disagreeable a fellow there is no standing him' – 'sometimes insolent and totally ignorant of the business of his office'. That Pitt's efforts on Byng's behalf should cost him popular esteem suited the King to perfection. When Waldegrave had an audience over the routine business of resigning from the Stannaries on being given a sinecure tellership of the exchequer, the King asked him 'to hang on to it lest it go to some impertinent relation of the new minister'. He then plunged into his distaste for Pitt with 'his long speeches, which might possibly be very fine, but were greatly beyond his comprehension; . . .'. What, enquired the King, might Newcastle's position be? Waldegrave answered that Newcastle had a sound majority in both Houses of Parliament, bound to him by past gratitude and the expectation that he might come back, but that his mind was divided between fear and a love of power. The King's parting words were: 'I know he is apt to be afraid, therefore go and encourage him: tell him I do not look upon myself as King, whilst I am in the hands of these scoundrels: that I am determined to get rid of them at any rate: that I expect his assistance, and that he may depend upon my favor and protection.'[35]

Over the next week or so Waldegrave kept pressing Newcastle, who always objected that the time was not ripe. Devonshire recalled: 'In Feb[r]. King seem'd to be determined to part with his new Ministers, said ye D. of Newcastle was desirous of coming in but was for waiting till the end of the session when the enquiry w'd be over, and tho' he was fond of power he was afraid of ye danger.' Only Newcastle still believed in the Minorca enquiry and in truth he was afraid of power lest the war miscarried. The best way of getting rid of obnoxious ministers was to discredit them with the House of Commons. Hay, Advocate-General and a Lord of Admiralty, was still without a seat. Byng's execution created a vacancy at Rochester, but on 15 March the King, in a 'very *lively* conversation' with Temple, insisted that Admiral Thomas Smith was a more suitable candidate. Smith declined, but the King remained obdurate and in the event another Admiral, Isaac Townsend, was returned.[36] A ministry unable to look after its following in the House of Commons was not likely to last. Newcastle would have been yet more despondent had he known that at this time the Prince of Wales had formed the set notion that Bute should take the Treasury on his succession. Here was no apparent danger to Pitt and Bute ticked his pupil off for being too affable to Fox at a Levée. At Bute's suggestion Pitt was presented to his future sovereign on 24 February.[37]

The King felt a responsibility towards Devonshire: 'This will never do; the Duke of Devonshire has acted by me in the handsomest manner, and is in a very disagreeable situation, entirely on my account.' At the beginning of March the King had Fox sounded as to whether he would act with Newcastle. With Cumberland's blessing Fox expressed himself ready to draw up a plan of administration to be put in motion whenever opportune. That their influence was daily mounting was largely owing to Newcastle's pusillanimity, and Waldegrave tried to tell him so. Towards the end of March Fox produced a list of possible ministers, which included Egmont, Sackville, Charles Townshend and Dodington, with himself as Paymaster, which would leave open a door for Newcastle. Townshend, though offered the War Office, dared not lend himself to this plan and out of the whole bunch only Dodington was ready to gamble.[38]

Despite this harassing background of intrigue Pitt carried on with his plans for North America. Each side aimed to establish a local naval superiority, the French based upon Louisbourg and the British upon Halifax, Nova Scotia. That January the Chevalier de Bauffrémont, with five ships of the line, had slipped out of Brest with orders to proceed first to the West Indies and then north. On 5 April a further squadron under Chef d'Escadron Revest sailed from Toulon bound direct for North America, and in the following month de la Motte left Brest with nine of the line and three frigates. Four days after de la Motte got away, Holburne left Cork for Halifax with seventeen of the line, five frigates and a vast fleet of transports. Pitt hoped that Holburne might run into de la Motte at sea and destroy him. In the West Indies the first duty of the British and French commanders was to guard the departures of their respective sugar convoys, which might amount to anything up to three hundred sail. Pitt doubled the Jamaica and Leewards Island squadrons, but at this early stage there was no question of either side attacking the colonies of each other. In the Far

East the primary responsibility lay with the British and French East India Companies, whose possessions were at stake, and the support either could expect from home was meagre. The French sent Chef d'Escadron d'Aché and a new Commissary-General, the Count of Lally-Tollendal. But in view of the large forces which Pitt was sending to North America, three-quarters of the ships originally intended for d'Aché were diverted to join de la Motte's fleet. Already Pitt was dictating strategy to the enemy and he could afford no more than a small reinforcement under Charles Steevens and Richard Kempenfeldt. But at least Lally would be denied the advantage in numbers.

By this time a French army 100,000 strong – far more formidable than Frederick had bargained for – was moving across west Germany. The Prince of Soubise, a favourite of the Pompadour, took 36,000 men to join the Austrians in Saxony, leaving d'Estrées with the main body to invade Hanover. Cumberland had no wish to go campaigning unless his friend Fox controlled affairs in London. The King, confident that Fox could pull something out of the hat, agreed to force a change of ministry. On 4 April, the day Cumberland arrived in Germany, Temple was informed of his dismissal in a letter from Holderness. The intention was to goad Pitt into resignation, but as the hint was ignored, two days later Holderness wrote to Pitt appointing seven o'clock that evening 'for executing the same sort of commission His Lordship was charged with to Lord Temple'. Pitt sent a line to Bute proposing to call round upon him at eight. George II hoped that he had finished with Pitt for good. As was only to be expected Legge and George Grenville resigned but the King must have been concerted when Elliot and the entire Board of Admiralty except Boscawen threw in their hand. Charles Townshend, after dithering for over a fortnight, informed Devonshire of his resignation on 22 April.[39]

The field was open for Pitt's enemies and Newcastle at once gave a remarkable display of his latent authority. The outgoing ministers had left a matter of urgent business outstanding. That January Legge had floated a loan for three and a half millions and had promoted a lottery too. Where Pelham had always successfully raised money by negotiation, Legge, angling for popularity, opened his loan to public subscription and his lottery was really a sweepstake. As Newcastle had been advised, these methods would not raise money, and within a week of Legge's departure his old banker friends produced by closed subscription a loan of three millions at the very reasonable rate of 3 per cent.[40] Fox easily cleared up the Minorca business by moving for an enquiry by a committee of the whole House, which on 3 May exonerated the Newcastle ministry; their responsibility for the Channel had precluded sending any more ships to Byng. Finally, at the end of the session, Hardwicke and Newcastle took their chance to take the teeth out of Townshend's militia bill sent up from the Commons. Under the Militia Act (30 George II c. 25) only 32,000 men, not the 50,000 Pitt had hoped for, were to be enrolled and a mere £100,000 was allocated towards the cost.[41]

That a union between Newcastle and Fox must follow in the interests of both appeared straightforward to the King. But a popular demand 'out-doors' for Pitt became manifest and loud. He alone offered any hope of leading the nation through the crisis. On 7 May Pitt and Legge received the Freedom of the City of London. To continue with the immortal words of Horace Walpole:[42]

'Allen of Bath procured them the same honours from thence; and for some weeks it rained gold boxes: Chester, Worcester, Norwich, Bedford, Salisbury, Yarmouth, Tewkesbury, Newcastle-on-Tyne, Stirling, and other populous and chief towns following the example. Exeter, with singular affection, sent boxes of heart of oak. On the other hand, a paper was affixed to the gate of St. James's with these words, "A Secretary of State much wanted; honesty not necessary; no principles will be treated with."'

The mysterious call for Churchill in 1940 and his acceptance by a suspicious Conservative party and a repugnant opposition offers the only parallel to Pitt's situation at this hour. But whatever his popularity 'out-doors', Pitt would have to come to terms with the Whig party, which could be accomplished only by means of Newcastle.

At this point Fox held the royal commission and, the session

ended, he got down to Cabinet making. For the plank of his
proposed ministry he chose Sackville, who was offered the
Secretaryship of State from which Pitt had been dismissed. The
activities of Pitt and Newcastle during May are uncertain.
According to Horace Walpole they had a secret meeting during
the second week of the month at which Pitt asked for Legge at
the Admiralty and George Grenville at the Exchequer, an
arrangement which would leave Newcastle no power even over
the Board of Treasury. As a second meeting of 24 or 25 May, at
which Newcastle was present, had a like result, Hardwicke
broke off the negotiation. The possibility of a Fox ministry was
however completely scotched by Sackville's refusal to play ball.
Prince George commented to Bute: 'Lord George shows himself
the man of honour you have often described him to me.'[43]

At last Newcastle saw it was now or never – as Devonshire
put it: 'Ye D. of Newcastle became more couragious & desired
to know if the King ^{wd} give him leave to treat with persons in
order to form an administration, full powers given him.'[44] The
King did not expect anything reasonable from Pitt and above all
feared his meddling in his German affairs. Newcastle saw Pitt
on 4 June and found his demands so high that he knew the
King would never agree. Then Newcastle fumbled around with
the altogether impossible idea of having Lee Chancellor of the
Exchequer and Leader of the Commons. The King was ready
to try anything, but Newcastle asked for a few days to get in
touch with his friends. Bute was thoroughly alarmed lest
Newcastle was about to yield to the King's entreaties and Pitt
was upset at the thought that by childish intransigence he
might have thrown away his hand. Then the sky cleared;
Chesterfield, completely out of the limelight since his ignominious dismissal nine years back, suddenly found himself in power
for a last, brief but singularly effective moment. Bute went to
see him and begged for his intercession with Newcastle to renew
negotiations with Pitt, who he promised would be less unreasonable, whilst the Princess and her son were well disposed.
Chesterfield sent Newcastle a letter on which Waldegrave
commented: 'He wrote a very able letter to the Duke of Newcastle, the purport of which was, that his administration could
never be strong and permanent, till he was firmly united with

Pitt and Leicester House: without whose assistance he could never be safe, nor could the King be ever at ease.'[45] Legge, too, saw that only a union between Pitt and the Old Corps would do, but he went further in what he thought to be a private interview with Newcastle, when he remarked that but for Pitt's 'visionary ideas' all could well have been solved last October. The incident slipped out, as things with Newcastle were apt to do, and Pitt did not forgive this impertinence.[46]

With some reluctance the King agreed to Newcastle seeing Pitt again, though the Duke promised that if Pitt proved unreasonable he would go back to his former plan. Pitt, Bute, Newcastle and Hardwicke therefore met again on 6 June and agreed upon a scheme of things which the King rejected. Then Newcastle refused to return to the idea of Lee and so this complicated negotiation collapsed. The King, unwilling to acknowledge that he was beaten, extracted a promise from that honest courtier Waldegrave that he would form a government. Devonshire was told to make an arrangement between Waldegrave and Fox, but he recorded: 'we met and found great difficulties'.[47] Next day, to the King's great annoyance, Holderness resigned but Fox persevered. By the evening of 8 June Fox had drawn up his list. Then the situation turned to comedy. On 11 June the new ministers were gathered together at Kensington Palace to receive their appointments when Mansfield arrived to deliver up the seals of the exchequer of which he had been caretaker. He told the King bluntly that the country would never accept Fox. That evening Hardwicke was summoned: to follow Devonshire's pithy account: 'Ld. Mansfield went to ye King who bad him treat with Pitt & ye D. of Newcastle it was soon taken out of his hands and put into Ld. Hardwicke's, who at last adjusted it.'[48]

CHAPTER 7

The Pitt and Newcastle Ministry Klosterseven and Rochefort

'Dear Miller – The papers will tell you that your friend Mr. Pitt kissed the King's hand yesterday upon his being again appointed to the seals; and I believe you will wonder at the various and different interests that are now got together to form the Administration. I hope however that the superior genius of Mr. Pitt will be able to keep the various links of this chain together, or rather that, like the Jupiter of Homer, by having hold of one end of the chain he will be able to support and direct the several parts of this sublunary system. We have no news but the Duke's being obliged to pass the Weser.'

Charles Jenkinson to Sanderson Miller of Radway
30 June 1757[1]

Hardwicke summoned a conference with Pitt, Newcastle and Bute which took place a little before nine o'clock on the evening of 16 June.[2] Within three days he completed the formation of one of the most powerful ministries ever known to Parliament, expressly intended, by meeting the ambitions and prejudices of all parties, to correspond with the requirements of the country's predicament. Newcastle returned as First Lord of the Treasury and Pitt to the Secretaryship for the Southern Department, with Holderness remaining at the North. Pitt would have that political backing requisite to put teeth into the belligerent faculties suspected of him. He no longer felt any interest in Legge's advancement and saw no objection when Hardwicke persuaded the King to restore Anson as First Lord of the Admiralty. Legge was pushed back into his servile place as Chancellor of the Exchequer, much against his wishes, bitterly humiliated and despised by everyone, Pitt writing to Bute: 'I pity him with all my heart, and I leave him and all his weaknesses to Lord Bute and all his generosity.'[3] Sackville was widely tipped for the War Office, but the King, who was not having anyone in favour at Leicester House near his army, insisted upon keeping Barrington. Sackville resolved to concentrate upon active service and none doubted that if he distinguished himself his claims as politician would be vindicated.[4] Thus the allocation of places essential for the efficient conduct of the war was settled. Within the formal Cabinet the venerable experience of Granville was retained as Lord President of the Council, Bedford stayed on as Lord Lieutenant of Ireland, whilst Devonshire as Lord Chamberlain and Temple Lord Privy Seal gave the ministry a final guarantee of aristocratic patronage. To the surprise of many, Hardwicke did not seek to return as Lord Chancellor and obligingly persuaded the King to meet Pitt's request that the Great Seal remain in commission with Henley promoted from Attorney-General to Lord Keeper.

Besides the Cabinet there was a Secret Committee, an informal gathering who really directed the war, of Pitt, Newcastle, Hardwicke, Granville, Holderness, Temple, Devonshire, Mansfield and Anson, which Cumberland too could have attended but for his absence in Germany. The inclusion of Hardwicke and Mansfield preserved for each a good deal of power and also tilted the balance in Newcastle's favour. It was a government of elder statesmen; the King was in his middle seventies, Newcastle, Hardwicke, Granville and Anson had been born in the preceding century. The great men of the Augustan epoch had come together to guide the nation to glory under Pitt's leadership.

The promotion of Henley required that a new Attorney-General be appointed and this time Pitt, as Potter had first suggested, put in Pratt who at the same time entered the House of Commons as member for Downton. Hardwicke showed great forbearance in yielding to an arrangement which left his son Yorke stuck in second place as Solicitor-General, but never forgave Pratt.[5] That Fox, for so long considered Pitt's compeer, should be Paymaster was demanded of the wishes of the King, Cumberland and Bedford. But there was no question of his sharing House of Commons business and at heart he was amply satisfied at the prospect of making a fortune. Once more George Grenville's aspirations were dashed. A disgruntled man he went back to the Treasurership of the Navy and was soon put to work organising routine parliamentary agenda for which Pitt had not the time.[6] Pitt did not choose to employ the services of that clever young man, Charles Jenkinson, whose ambition it was to be his secretary. Jenkinson accordingly cultivated the acquaintance of Bute and George Grenville.

The omission to cause surprise was that of the Townshend brothers. On 18 June Pitt wrote to George asking him – though not Charles – to call next day. But both turned up and George Townshend made a note of the occasion: 'On the Friday night June the 18th 1757, I received this letter & the next morning waited on him with my Brother, & to our Astonishment heard him avow the ridiculous & dishonest arrangement of Men which is now to take place – not the least adoption of any Publick System of Measures being declared or even hinted at by him.' Both refused to have anything to do with this ministry and thereby might well have terminated their useful careers. George Townshend's resentment may have been caused by the inclusion of Fox. Charles eagerly expected high promotion but such was not on offer and they were certainly not in a position to dictate. The brothers retired to Norfolk; George threw himself into work on the militia and even in his own county found difficulty in persuading the magnates to take a sincere interest in this child of his.[7] As yet Pitt was far from trusting Newcastle and exclaimed in his letter to Bute of 28 June: 'How hard is the lot of this vile age? This is the wretch who draws the great families at his heels, and for whose elevation and power the pretended friends of the publick have so loudly passed sentence on my inflexibility.'[8] Newcastle had in fact made up his mind to leave Pitt to manage or mismanage the war, provided he had the lion's share of patronage. When on 29 June the ministers attended Kensington Palace to kiss hands Hardwicke could regard his labours with every satisfaction.

At the instance of Ralph Prior the Corporation of Bath unanimously invited Pitt to occupy the seat in Parliament Henley was obliged to vacate. The constituency was hardly popular but the thirty electors, proud of their independence and above bribery, liked to be represented by national figures. Pitt was elected on 9 July and had as his fellow member Ligonier, Lieutenant-General of the Ordnance.[9] Conscious of the pomp befitting one of His Majesty's Secretaries of State, Pitt took a town house, No. 10, St James's Square. Two Prime Ministers, the 14th Earl of Derby and W. E. Gladstone, were later occupants of the house, which during the nineteenth century was also the town residence of John, 1st Baron Tollemache of Helmingham, for over thirty years member of Parliament for Cheshire.

While between April and June 1757 Britain had been without a government, France had concluded the second Treaty of Versailles with Austria, signed on 1 May. Louis XV promised to employ an army one hundred thousand strong in Germany and to pay very large subsidies to Austria, Sweden and Saxony. There was to be no peace until Maria Theresa had recovered Silesia and in that event West Flanders would be ceded to Louis XV; meanwhile Nieuport and Ostend were occupied by the French. This treaty coincided with Frederick's victory over the Austrians at Prague, but soon the tables were turned. Frederick, hazarding the impossible, attacked Daun's strongly entrenched position at Kolin on 18 June. He was soundly beaten and the campaign wasted. News of this disaster reached London on 24 June whilst Pitt was hoping for good news from Holburne and Loudoun. On 16 July Newcastle wrote to Mitchell, the British Ambassador in Berlin: 'There has been as much business done these last ten days as there was in many months before.'[10]

Long before d'Aché and Steevens could reach Indian waters,
Clive had exacted vengeance for the Black Hole. As soon as the
dreadful news reached Madras he and Admiral Watson had
hastened to Calcutta, which they took on New Year's Day 1757.
On news of the outbreak of war in Europe they seized the French
Bengal factory of Chandernagore. Suraj ud Dowlah promptly
reinstated the British in all their privileges. Pitt received news
of these events on 8 July and at once informed Bute, with the
rider: 'This cordial, such as it is, has not power enough to quiet
my mind one moment till we hear Lord Loudoun is safe at
Halifax and the troops also with Holburne.'[11] Pitt could never
have guessed at the events, decisive for world history, being
enacted at that moment in Bengal. There the Nawab, petrified
at news of the sack of Delhi by the Afghans, became deranged
with suspicion of the powerful British East India Company. But
Suraj ud Dowlah's army of 50,000 men was crushed at the Battle
of Plassey on 23 June 1757. A week later he was murdered and
Mir Jaffir was installed as puppet ruler, Clive receiving a
personal gift of £240,000. Thus the epoch of the British raj was
begun, completely without the knowledge, still less the commendation, of either the East India Company or the King's
Government. When shortly Watson died he was succeeded in
the naval command by George Pocock, who took over the
reinforcement under Steevens and Kempenfeldt on its arrival
that autumn. The conquest of Bengal did not however affect the
French position at Pondicherry, where Lally-Tollendal soon put
things to order and in the Northern Circars between the
Carnatic and Bengal de Bussy seized Masulipatam. In south
India all must depend upon the rival seamanship of d'Aché and
Pocock, with their ships equally matched in number, for neither
Madras nor Pondicherry was viable without naval protection.

According to Pitt's original concept Louisbourg should by
this time have been taken. Long before, Loudoun had assembled
5,300 men at New York. As Holburne was so long delayed he
had risked sending them to Halifax without escort, and they
arrived safely. Pitt had wind that de la Motte, de Bauffrémont
and Revest were all destined for North America and on 7 July
sent Holburne word of a reinforcement of four of the line. In
the event of the Frenchmen attempting the return voyage he

was to return to Europe in pursuit. It was not until two days later that Holburne at last put into Halifax. Already Pitt was optimistically raising new Highland detachments to add to the battalions from England and Ireland due to arrive in North America by the following October.[12] When de Bauffrémont, after an adventurous voyage through the West Indies, arrived at Louisbourg, de la Motte, with his three contingents assembled, had a total of eighteen ships of the line and five frigates. Holburne, to his dismay, found himself outnumbered and outgunned by the French. Loudoun had to inform Pitt that there was no possibility of a British attack on Louisbourg that year and, worse still, information had just reached him that Montcalm had taken Fort William Henry on Lake Champlain. So far from Quebec being remotely endangered, the French were in a position to send raiding parties down the Hudson valley in the direction of New York.[13]

In Germany Cumberland was expected to do no more than keep up a sturdy rearguard action. On 2 July the French took by surprise Emden, the supply port for Hanover nearest to England. D'Estrées, having sent his right wing to occupy Cassel, the capital of Hesse, defeated Cumberland on the central front in a hard-fought battle at Hastenbeck on 26 July; although the French had 40,000 men to Cumberland's 35,000, they suffered more casualties. Frederick urged that British troops be sent to reinforce Cumberland. Pitt did not consider a major expedition to Hanover could be managed without interfering with the overriding interest of North America. But he eagerly adopted Frederick's suggestion of amphibious raids upon the French coast.

Nothing less than the seizure of the naval base and town of Rochefort on the Bay of Biscay became Pitt's supreme preoccupation. This suggestion originated with a man of twenty-three, Lieutenant Robert Clerk, who had in 1754 taken advantage of a holiday to inspect the fortifications, which he found very dilapidated. Clerk was promoted Lieutenant-Colonel so that he could serve as Chief Engineer. For the command Pitt's first choice was Sackville who, however, fought shy upon the flimsy but none the less plausible excuse that Cumberland would not give the expedition support.[14] This enabled the King to insist upon a favourite general of his, Sir John Mordaunt, and for second he and Pitt were agreed upon Henry Seymour Conway, a devoted professional soldier. For the naval responsibility Hawke was the only choice. On 4 August Pitt presided over a Cabinet at Holderness's London house: Mordaunt, Conway, Hawke with his second Vice-Admiral Knowles, and Clerk attended. The meeting was stormy because Newcastle, Hardwicke and Holderness pressed for the troops intended for Rochefort to be sent to Hanover. Pitt had to sit up arguing till two o'clock in the morning and later that day wrote to Bute: 'I am determin'd to meet all events in pursuit of that honest and animating cause in which it will ever be my happiness and pride to be united with the best and noblest of friends.'[15] That day Pitt signed Hawke's commission.

Two days later, in the evening, news of Holburne's reaching Halifax came to Pitt, who had spent the morning in gloomy converse with Bute, worried over the lateness of the year. Although it was ten o'clock and Bute a little poorly, Pitt could not resist sending a note which ended: 'I am infinitely happy to think the joy this news will give at Kew.'[16] The general feeling in London was in fact far from optimistic. The intervention of Spain on behalf of France was expected and on 18 August Pitt, in the course of a Cabinet meeting with Granville, Hardwicke, Newcastle and Anson even threw out the possibility of ceding Gibraltar as an inducement to Ferdinand VI to come in on the British side.[17]

How dexterous and stubborn Newcastle could be was shown by his inconvenient refusal to allow Hawke on to the Board of Admiralty, despite the recommendation of Anson which Pitt agreed with. But Newcastle had his own nominee in Hans Stanley, member of Parliament for Southampton, and declared that unless he had his way 'he would never go into the Treasury again'.[18] Despite this disappointment Hawke loyally supported the Rochefort expedition and bullied the Admiralty over the matter of transports: one ton of shipping per soldier simply was not adequate. But the generals, especially Mordaunt, disliked the enterprise; bred in the tradition of Marlborough they looked to Continental war as the proper field of distinction and Newcatle sympathised with their point of view. 3 September found him writing to Hardwicke: 'Lord Anson also told us that Dr. Hay and Mr. Elliot, who had been at Portsmouth, said that both land and sea officers *talked down* the Expedition. But Pitt is deaf . . . and I don't know who dares to take upon him to stop its going.'[19] Hay and Elliot were protégés of Pitt and he should either have countermanded the whole thing or changed his commanding officers, but this in face of the King was an impossibility.

Pitt was more disappointed than he cared to admit when, at the end of August, he received word from Loudoun that the campaign had failed. He wrote to Bute: 'I confess I find it hard to keep up my mind under this unhopeful state of things; I had my heart in America and in our windbound expedition.' No thought of rigging up a court martial crossed Pitt's mind: 'It were injurious to blame a conduct not sufficiently before us, nor must any but a military man decide upon military matters.'[20] But neither Loudoun nor Holburne was ever employed again at Pitt's instance. Barren tidings from North America were matched by disaster in Germany. There d'Estrées, despite his successful opening, had been replaced by Richelieu, the victor of Minorca. Minden, Hanover and Bremen capitulated and Cumberland had to take refuge in Stade, a supply port at the mouth of the Elbe protected by marshland.

The King ordered his son to approach Richelieu for an armistice, which was certainly premature. Richelieu, his lines of communication over-extended, was apprehensive lest the troops Pitt was gathering for Rochefort might be intended to retake Emden: these amphibious operations conferred the advantage of uncertainty. Furthermore, he had fresh instructions from Versailles to attack Magdeburg with the object of completely encircling Prussia. Both commanders welcomed the idea of negotiations, though in response to a protest from Frederick, George II countermanded his orders, but too late. On 9 September 1757 Cumberland and Richelieu signed the Convention of Klosterseven by which the Hessians and Brunswickers were to be sent home with their arms and the Hanoverian army was to withdraw behind the Elbe. News of the Convention arrived in London the day following. Two days before the signing of the Convention the Rochefort expedition had left England; with a greater show of nerve Richelieu might have taken Cumberland prisoner with his army. Equally George II, not his son, was responsible for the cease-fire at the point when the Frenchman supposed himself in a difficulty.

Bad news from North America and Germany was matched by poor morale at home. The Militia Act had never been liked by Newcastle, Devonshire and the bulk of the Whig magnates who as Lords Lieutenant were responsible for its operation. Bedford, always the exception, was a militia enthusiast and it was disconcerting that popular resentment against compulsory Sunday drilling should become manifest with riots in Bedfordshire, where he was Lord Lieutenant and Potter one of his deputies. On 1 September Bedford urgently wrote to Pitt asking for guidance about his proper course of action. The disturbances spread to Cambridgeshire, where Hardwicke's son Viscount Royston was Lord Lieutenant. Hardwicke sarcastically observed to Newcastle: 'Mr. Pitt is much mistaken in thinking that the disorders have proceeded from a want of a proper disposition in the Lord Lieutenants and Deputy Lieutenants to explain the act and enforce it.'[21] Pitt, notwithstanding all his disappointments, ordered Holburne in a despatch of 21 September to pursue de la Motte back across the Atlantic, leaving behind only eight of the line. But already, four days before Pitt wrote, Holburne's fleet had been shattered by a hurricane. There was no alternative but to settle in at Halifax to put the ships in repair.[22]

The Rochefort expedition got under way; sixteen of the line, nine frigates, numerous ancillary craft and fifty transports proceeded down the Solent; on board were 8,400 infantry, with a troop of light horse and two companies of field artillery, about one-quarter of the entire British army. Mordaunt and Hawke had orders to be back by the end of the month, leaving the port, it was hoped, a ruin and many merchant ships destroyed. On 20 September the expedition arrived off the shoals and sands known as the Basque Roads, between the islands of Rhé and Oléron opposite La Rochelle and Rochefort. Mordaunt and Hawke were agreed that the first step was to occupy Aix, an island opposite the mouth of Rochefort harbour, and this was easily achieved. Full of glorious anticipation Pitt wrote to Bute on 5 October: 'The consternation in Paris is great; the success in India and this alarm has shaken credit, so that their actions bear no price. . . .' According to Pitt's intelligence the French had only 4,000 men within easy reach: 'The Household, 6 Battalions and some detachments of guard corps and mousquetaires, march'd for Rochefort the 27th past and cannot arrive until the 14th instant.' To make things even better, news came from Germany that Richelieu had declared his intention to disarm the Hessian and Brunswicker troops and by this technical breach of the Convention Pitt saw his way clear to a complete disavowal: 'Heaven prosper our arms! Germany is saved si l'on veut.' But at two o'clock on the very next day Pitt had to address Bute with the admission of a dismal failure: 'I just receive the afflicting news that our Fleet and troops resolved the 30th past not to attempt Rochefort.'[23]

Over the next fortnight what had gone wrong became infuriatingly clear. After the taking of the Isle d'Aix consternation had reigned in the town, for the citizens knew the fortifications to be in gross disrepair. Hawke spent 23 and 24 September reconnoitring the coast and here was the first disappointment. Great reliance had been placed upon the evidence of Joseph Thierry, a Huguenot pilot, that the waters before Rochefort were deep enough for men-of-war to engage a close bombardment without entering the harbour. Hawke found this description altogether misleading, but as in the absence of French regular troops the town was practically defenceless, he saw no reason for delay and on 25 September asked for the order to land. Instead of acting Mordaunt ordered a Council, which Hawke subsequently described: 'The debates on the Council of War on the 25th ulto were so various, tedious and uncorrected that it was impossible to take Minutes.' The Generals decided that as the enemy now had five days warning, to scale the walls would be too hazardous and carried out a signed declaration to that effect. That document bore Hawke's signature, a bad error of judgement in view of his disagreement with the content. Then on 29 September Mordaunt held another Council and decided to attack. On the following day the soldiers were put in the landing craft, but then Mordaunt cancelled the whole thing and the expedition sailed home empty-handed.

Hawke and Mordaunt got to London on 10 October and, as Jenkinson wrote to Grenville next day: 'I hear that the King gave Sir Edw. Hawke a good reception, and Sir John Mordaunt an indifferent one.' An enquiry was ordered, but Hawke was not expected to attend and was sent to Portsmouth with orders to hoist his ensign. On the 21st, the day before he sailed, he took the trouble to address a long letter to Pitt exculpating himself. Unfortunately he had put his name to the negative declaration of the Generals and Pitt felt bitter about the whole business. To make appearances worse, de la Motte, homeward bound after his very successful Atlantic voyage, slipped past Hawke into Brest. The Rochefort enquiry opened on 21 October with a report highly unfavourable to Mordaunt. But despite hostile speeches by Pitt and Beckford in the House of Commons the ensuing court martial, to the King's utter disgust, found Mordaunt not guilty of any specific charge.[24]

Cumberland, following his by no means dishonourable campaign, had arrived in London on 11 October and did not at first anticipate his conduct to warrant explanation. That evening the Duke went to Fox, who expressed surprise at his peace of mind. 'You have always mistaken me Mr. Fox', Cumberland retorted, 'with respect to the King, I am perfectly easy; I have the King's orders in writing for what I have done, and I have done better for him than I thought the exigency would have allowed of.' Next day, however, when he called on his father, who was at that moment engaged at the card table, Cumberland was received with such rudeness that he at once decided to throw up all his appointments, even his Colonelcy of the Foot Guards. With real magnaminity Pitt came forward as the Duke's defender. When the King sent Gerlach Munchhausen, the Minister Resident for Hanover in London, to notify the Cabinet that Cumberland had acted against orders, Pitt observed: 'I must, as a man of honour and a gentleman, allow everywhere that H.R.H. had full powers to do what he has done.' It was widely suspected that the King, concerned with his own prestige, knowingly betrayed his son by his disavowal of his own orders. Cumberland persisted in his intention to resign and was, according to Fox, 'a little vexed . . . to be obliged, as he must own himself to be, to Mr. Pitt for his very honourable behaviour upon this occasion'.[25] If Cumberland suspected his father of duplicity his refusal to use Pitt's generosity as a means to retain his influential and lucrative appointments was very understandable.

Pitt, though scrupulously ready to defend Cumberland's reputation, was none the less swift to attempt the political harvest the Duke's downfall must bring forth. Only six days after Cumberland's arrival in London he wrote to Bute: 'The event of the Duke's retreat from all civil and military business opens a scene of vast consequence.' He went on to remark that he had given Newcastle his opinion that Ligonier was the only possible choice for a new Commander-in-Chief. Since his especial distinction at Dettingen, Ligonier as Lieutenant-General of the Ordnance had won a reputation as administrator. His advancement could bear no offence to criteria of seniority. Pitt's desire was that he become a Field-Marshal with a peerage, and be given the First Regiment of Guards as the immediate preliminary to his being placed in command of the army – 'he could not be carried too high'. Pitt was too tactful to suggest directly that Ligonier should succeed as Captain-General but the implication was plain. At the same time Pitt was solicitous to advance Sackville by making him Lieutenant-General of the Ordnance in Ligonier's place. Newcastle smelt out Pitt's designs with the nose of the hearty intriguer he was and, having no intention of having a Captain-General obligated to Pitt, countered with the unanswerable suggestion that the King should have the supreme command: though Ligonier should certainly be made Field-Marshal and have the First Regiment a peerage was not likely to be vouchsafed. Hardwicke thought Ligonier as Captain-General could not be avoided, otherwise Cumberland would have 'the whole army in his power without being responsible'. Finally, on 19 October the King agreed to Newcastle's compromise that Ligonier should be Commander-in-Chief in Europe and in America. Although at the next Cabinet meeting Pitt harked back to making Ligonier Captain-General, that office was left in abeyance.[26]

In Hanover Cumberland was succeeded by Prince Ferdinand of Brunswick, a general of Frederick's training and a cadet of the senior branch of the Hanoverian royal house. Although the

French were in possession of the Electorate, Richelieu's army was worn out. Most of his men were taken up with garrison duty and he had only 9,000 available for the march to Magdeburg. At Halberstadt he came up against Prince Ferdinand on his way to take up his command with a reinforcement of 7,000 Prussians. On 3 October Richelieu and Prince Ferdinand signed a temporary armistice and the French army withdrew into winter quarters, where it speedily went to seed through lack of discipline – Richelieu was temperamentally unsuited to formal warfare.

To Newcastle failure in North America, defeat in Germany and the repulse before Rochefort were of small moment compared with the coming opening of Parliament. Cumberland's resignation, with Fox emasculated in his Paymastership, put him into a singular sense of isolation. He was most anxious that Pitt should not draw up the King's Speech as in the previous year. Certain that only Hardwicke could prevent this, he wrote on 27 October to his old friend urging him to come to London; though he saw the need to 'manage' and 'coax' Pitt, yet he complained bitterly of 'the yoke'. Two days later he got a sharp telling off from Hardwicke who, relieved of the cares of office, was spending much time at Wimpole. Hardwicke pointed out that Newcastle could not possibly expect to control the House of Commons by himself: 'All sorts of persons there have concurred in battering down that notion. . . .' Newcastle, insisted Hardwicke, had no alternative but to co-operate with Pitt as Leader of the House of Commons in the full meaning; he must avoid 'all expostulations', especially those 'through the medium of third persons. They seldom do good . . .'. Newcastle was therefore told to get into the habit of 'confidential communications and conversation . . . I would apply this to the immediate question of *the Speech*'. Finally he firmly pointed out that it was no use Newcastle's thinking that every time Pitt had to be talked to, he could be hauled out of rustication to do it. Pitt composed the King's Speech and, Newcastle had to understand, was truly Leader of the House of Commons.[27]

Whilst winter imposed the suspension of operations in North America, the situation on the Continent could not have been worse. Following his defeat at Kolin, Frederick had to retreat out of Bohemia under terrible conditions, and when on 22 November the Austrians entered Breslau, Silesia appeared lost. A French army commanded by Soubise was moving across Germany in order to coalesce with the Austrians. The Russians had beaten a Prussian army at Gross-Jägersdorf and an Austrian expeditionary force had actually raided Berlin. At Schönbrunn Maria Theresa thought the war was won. Then Frederick dramatically reversed the situation in one of the greatest campaigns of all time. Although hopelessly out-numbered, he used his advantage of interior lines to strike decisively at his enemies in turn. Frederick first struck at the deadly combination of Soubise and the Austrians in west Saxony, whom he completely routed on 5 November at Ross-bach, of all his victories the dearest to the hearts of his soldiers. The French never again dared risk an army where Frederick was present. Then he marched his army with lightning speed 200 miles eastward and on 5 December beat Daun at Leuthen, his masterpiece. A fortnight later the Prussian army re-entered Breslau. The alliance between Britain and Prussia, a marriage of convenience forced by Frederick's impetuosity, blossomed into one of affection. Rossbach won him a deep admiration with the British public and the incongruous sobriquet of 'The Protestant Hero'. When towards the end of the year Prince Ferdinand arrived at Stade, he took advantage of the dis-avowal of the Convention of Klosterseven to keep with him the Hessians and Brunswickers. On 25 November Pitt wrote to Bute, 'God be prais'd, Prince Ferdinand is to command'.[28] Instead of confronting his new enemy, Richelieu now decided to abandon the hardships of campaigning for the pleasures of court life. The new commander of the French army in the north-west was the Count of Clermont, a cadet member of the Bourbon family.

Although on every front in Europe and America British arms had proved inglorious, news of Plassey was a pretty complement to Rossbach. The imagination of the nation was captured and on 14 December Pitt in the House of Commons met the epic note in praise of Clive – 'that man not born for a desk – that heaven-born general'. By this time Pitt had laid his plans for the coming year. On the last day of 1757 he wrote to Loudoun from

Whitehall informing him that he was to be replaced by General James Abercromby. In a despatch some three thousand words in length, entrusted to Colonel Joshua Loring, Pitt gave Abercromby his Instructions. Fourteen thousand troops were to be assigned for the taking of Louisbourg and afterwards, it was hoped, Quebec itself. The St Lawrence campaign was to be supported by attack from the landward side. Abercromby, aided by the brilliant young officer the 3rd Lord Howe, was to march northwards along the shores of Lake Champlain to Montreal with 6,000 regulars and 9,000 provincial troops. Pitt gave Abercromby little authority over the subordinate expeditions or with the colonial Governors except as negotiator. It was Pitt personally who sent Governor de Lancey of New York detailed orders to cause boats to be requisitioned or built sufficient to convey Abercromby's army up Lake Champlain. To the south, Colonel John Forbes, again acting under direct instructions from Pitt, with two regular regiments and 4,000 colonials, was detailed to attack Fort Duquesne.[29]

For the command of the expedition against Louisbourg Pitt's selection was General Jefferey Amherst, a soldier who really understood his business. Here Pitt had run up against trouble: 'The King refused Amherst flat and peremptory.' Ligonier was sent to shake the royal obstinacy and in the end the King yielded.[30] As his second Amherst was given Wolfe, as gallant an officer as Howe and probably of greater intellectual powers, if of less attractive character. After fighting in the campaigns of Dettingen and Culloden Wolfe had risen to the command of the Lancashire Fusiliers at the age of twenty-three. He had had a taste of 'combined operations' at Rochefort, where he had seen the consequences of generals and admirals holding councils of war. Although Amherst was, like Forbes, technically Abercromby's junior, he too received Pitt's orders direct and in such form and precision as to give him little scope for reference to the Commander-in-Chief. Abercromby had his orders to draw contingents from New York, Philadelphia and Boston, and his part was limited to ensuring their rendezvous with the soldiers and transports due from England. Pitt fixed the date, 12 April 1758, for the assemblage of the Louisbourg expedition at Halifax. Weather permitting Pitt anticipated that Louisbourg might be invested by 20 April.[31] The fleet was commanded by Boscawen, who with sixteen ships of the line added to the seven already at Halifax, the whole manned by 12,000 seamen, would outnumber the French at Louisbourg with twenty. Three separate sets of stores, one for each line of operations from Halifax, New York and Philadelphia, all crossed the Atlantic under the conditions of ordinary commercial convoys, a feat made possible by Hawke's blockade of the French coast. Although the interception of French ships bound for America could never be guaranteed, the enemy were never able to interfere with the British transports. The naval force assigned to North America alone for 1758 was greater than the entire British navy before the outbreak of war.

CHAPTER 8

Pitt's War: 1758

' "No, his name is James Wolfe," cried the Colonel, smiling. "He is a young fellow still, or what we call so, being thirty years old. He is the youngest lieutenant-colonel in the army, unless to be sure we except a few scores of our nobility, who take rank before us common folk."

"Of course, of course!" says the Colonel's young companion, with true colonial notions of aristocratic precedence.

"And I have seen him commanding captains, and very brave captains who were thirty years his seniors, and who had neither his merit nor his good fortune. But, lucky as he hath been, no one envies his superiority, for, indeed most of us acknowledge that he is our superior. He is beloved by every man of our old regiment, and knows every one of them. He is a good scholar as well as a consummate soldier, and a master of many languages." '

William Makepeace Thackeray: *The Virginians*.[1]

During January Pitt pressed forward with plans for the taking of Louisbourg. Charles Lawrence, Governor of Nova Scotia, was notified of the despatch of military stores from England to Halifax. Commodore Philip Durrell set off from home for New York with the transports necessary to convey the troops, battery trains and stores destined from New England to Halifax. Abercromby was reminded of the imperative necessity to rendezvous at Halifax on time. For the mainland campaign Loring was to take charge of the boats and vessels for the operation on Lake Champlain under Abercromby's immediate direction. On 11 January Pitt sent Abercromby a further despatch reiterating the need for an embargo on the use of ships for civilian purposes, so that transport could be easily requisitioned.

A fortnight later Pitt sent word to Abercromby that Amherst was the King's selection for the command against Louisbourg. Pitt could ferret out what was going on even in the junior strata of command. A certain Captain Alexander Mackintosh, former master of a Jamaican ship, who had been taken prisoner to New Orleans and subsequently released, was ordered to Halifax to give Amherst his observations concerning French settlements in Louisiana. Pitt envisaged that with Louisbourg taken, if the season were too far advanced for Quebec, then Boscawen and Amherst might make New Orleans and Mobile their winter objectives. Already Pitt was dwelling upon the possibility of extending the offensive towards the West Indies, and in complement he gave effect to the suggestion of Thomas Cumming, 'the fighting Quaker', that the French slaving settlements at Senegal and Goree on the west African coast might be attempted.

On 2 February Boscawen was ordered to join his fleet at Portsmouth. On the following day Pitt, without making any precise direction, indicated to Boscawen that the reduction of Louisbourg might be achieved most swiftly and economically by forcing the harbour. Unfortunate Loudoun, who had not as yet received notice of being superseded, on 14 February addressed to Whitehall his plan for the year which ran on exactly the lines prescribed in Pitt's despatches to Abercromby. On 19 February Boscawen reported to Pitt from his ninety-gun flag-ship *Namur* that his fleet was under sail. There were being conveyed to North America 13,600 soldiers aboard one hundred transports escorted by twenty-three of the line and eighteen men-of-war.

Clause 5 of Amherst's Instructions, dated 3 March, directed that once Louisbourg was taken Boscawen was to move on to Quebec, subject to the discretion of the military commander. This and a further despatch to Governor Lawrence were the last orders Pitt would send to North America until 10 June. By the end of April Abercromby was firmly in the saddle and in touch with all the Governors.[2] For this year the Assemblies of New England had voted to maintain over 17,400 men and those for the south over 5,000: Pitt's zeal had roused the colonies into a certain enthusiasm.[3] Already 700 of the batteaus needed for the Lake Champlain campaign had been completed. On 1 May Forbes penned his first despatch to Pitt.

On the other side of the globe d'Aché had arrived in Indian waters that January. Pocock tried to intercept him off Ceylon, but the Frenchman slipped by into Pondicherry with welcome supplies for Lally. Between the two lay that difference of disposition which can decide a campaign: Pocock's one aim was to fight a decisive battle while d'Aché, though a brave man, was concerned to keep his fleet intact and avoid risk. Lally, whose temper was the precise opposite to that of d'Aché, made Madras his aim and to that end he first laid siege to Fort St David, seventy miles to the south. D'Aché appeared on 28 April and the day following he and Pocock had their first bout, from which the Frenchman withdrew before a final settlement could be practicable. But Pocock was unable to relieve Fort St David, which shortly surrendered. The first round had gone to Lally, but his ability to take Madras must depend upon the maintenance of naval support.

Pitt knew he had months to wait for tidings from North America or India, but from the opening of the year he received ample cheer from events in Germany. Prince Ferdinand suspected how the French army had run to seed. On 18 February – six days after Boscawen's departure from home – the Prince seized his chance and broke out of winter quarters. Clermont, completely disconcerted, ordered a retreat; terrible pillage, burnings and atrocities earned the hatred of the Hanoverian peasantry towards the French soldiery. Never again could it be said that Britain had been sacrificed for a 'wretched' German electorate: the evils of fate lay completely the other way. By the beginning of April Clermont had fallen behind the Rhine, where he joined up with the Count of Broglie, who had succeeded Soubise. Broglie, though far from being the Pompadour's favourite, was a far better general and restored some order and morale to the regiments broken at Rossbach. George II had recovered possession of his native domain and was bent upon revenge for the devastation of his fairest countryside.

It may appear unjust but is none the less the case that, despite the oppressive lot of ordinary mankind inevitably occasioned by war, the statesmen responsible remain to a large degree occupied with the trivia of domestic affairs. Men die on the battlefield, sailors are pressed to the hazards of war at sea, a foreign peasantry are rooted from their villages: neither matter for political dispute nor even the jealousies of the contenders are in consequence left in abeyance. Whilst Boscawen and Prince Ferdinand were making their preparations for excursions of valour, Pitt had to ponder over Bedford's ill-starred sojourn in Dublin. The security and relative prosperity conferred by over seventy years of peace was sowing among the Protestant ascendancy a restless questioning of the justice of control from Westminster. Bedford was confronted with a series of resolutions of the Irish House of Commons complaining of financial grievances which he considered too direct for forwarding to London. Pitt ordered him to send over the resolutions without amendment and advised: 'all softening and healing arts of government, consistent with its dignity, and, as far as may be practicable, plans of comprehension and harmony'. When the Dublin House of Commons carried a motion for an enquiry into the management of the revenues for the past twenty years, Bedford in despair wrote to Pitt suggesting the appointment of a native Lord Deputy. Early in February Pitt replied rejecting all idea that the duties of an unpopular Lord Lieutenant might be conveniently delegated.[4]

Dublin politics were nothing to the sensational squabble with Newcastle and Hardwicke which Pitt conducted openly during the spring. He threw down the gauntlet over an issue tender to Hardwicke, the law: ought the rule of Habeas Corpus to apply to men pressed into the armed forces? It was an axiom that the subject had a right to a writ of Habeas Corpus under Common Law, confirmed by the Habeas Corpus Act of 1680 (31 Charles II c. 2). But the judges had made impressment cases an exception. Pratt was now Attorney-General and his opinion was that a writ of Habeas Corpus must automatically apply. To Hardwicke's great annoyance Pitt gave his support for a bill to this effect and pursued what he may have supposed to be a just cause with all the intransigence of his young days. When on the evening of 10 March Newcastle called upon Pitt in the hope of dissuading him, he was treated to a history lesson on the Petition of Right. A week later Pitt delivered before the House of Commons a half-hour dilation on the Habeas Corpus bill, punctuated by the most acrimonious asides upon the stuffiness of the judiciary. After speeches by Pratt, Beckford, Legge and George Grenville, the bill was agreed without dissent.[5]

Pitt, amidst this childish bickering, was engaged in a most delicate negotiation for a new treaty with Prussia. The talks were a long-drawn business because Frederick demanded that British troops be sent to Hanover and a fleet to the Baltic, which Pitt knew would be politically contentious and contrary to undertakings he had himself on several occasions given in the House of Commons. The British Ambassador in Berlin, Sir Andrew Mitchell, was far too much in Frederick's pocket, accompanying him wherever he went on campaign, and Pitt wrote to Newcastle: 'I do not intend for one that Andrew Mitchell shall carry me where I have resolved not to go.' A strong note of 23 February, accompanied by the threat of Mitchell's being superseded, produced a settlement.[6] By the second Convention of Westminster, signed on 11 April for one year only, Britain guaranteed Frederick a subsidy of £670,000 and to maintain a Hanoverian army of 55,000 men. Pitt also conceded that a battalion of Scots Greys should garrison Emden.

Pitt was warned by Newcastle that the combined bill for Frederick and Prince Ferdinand would come to some £1,800,000. When on 19 April he defended the treaty before the House of Commons he emphasised, as well he might, how Frederick had preserved Germany from Bourbon and Hapsburg: 'Is there an Austrian among you. . . . Let him stand forth and reveal himself.' Two days after Pitt's peroration the Scots Greys arrived at Emden. But he committed a serious error of judgement in not expounding his new diplomacy to Bute and the Prince of Wales. Still imbued with 'blue-water' principles largely of Pitt's furnishing, they were bewildered and angry at what they felt to be ingratitude for the support he had received from Leicester House when his prospects had been far from rosy.

Whilst Pitt was steadily moving in the direction of a British participation on the Hanoverian front, Bute and the Prince, instead of attempting comprehension, clung doggedly to their 'blue-water' philacteries. That his friendship with Bute should become eroded whilst he was too at loggerheads with Newcastle and Hardwicke was a misunderstanding largely of Pitt's making.

Hardwicke had no intention of being taught jurisprudence by Pitt and enlisted Mansfield's concurrence in securing the rejection of the Habeas Corpus bill by the House of Lords. He knew that in respect of the law the peers would bow to the united discretion of the Lord Chancellor and the Lord Chief Justice. Pitt, late at night on 14 April, turned up on Newcastle and read him a lecture on Mansfield's iniquities. Three weeks later Hardwicke persuaded the House of Lords that the opinions of the judges should be taken before any division on the bill. Temple maintained that the judges need not be consulted over a matter the peers could decide for themselves and then added some queries of his own. The King threw in his weight and on 16 May talked to Newcastle of dismissing Granville and Pratt, putting in Hardwicke as Lord President and appointing Charles Yorke Attorney-General. As Newcastle continued in his letter to Hardwicke: 'He expressed the greatest dissatisfaction with Mr. Pitt and I could find, though there was nothing dropped directly, that the King entertained a hope that somehow or other he should get rid of him.' To Lady Yarmouth the King talked of using Fox to get Pitt out but that, as Newcastle ruefully admitted, was out of the question. Hardwicke did his best to keep tempers down; Pitt's spleen stemmed from gout rather than malice and any thought of his dismissal must be put aside. When on 21 May Pitt saw Lady Yarmouth she thought him almost beside himself: on her gentle reminder that the opinion of the judges deserved consideration, Pitt exclaimed: 'Madam, if all the Bishops on the Bench should be of opinion that the People should not have the Bible, would the People part with their Bible?'

The Habeas Corpus bill was again due before the Lords on 2 June. On the day before Pitt saw Newcastle at Kensington Palace and changed his style to an impish familiarity. Habeas Corpus or no, the war had still to be paid for and on Newcastle

would fall the task of raising in the City the loans authorised by
Parliament. Pitt teasingly kept calling Newcastle 'my Lord
Treasurer' and the Duke, far from displeased, mused whether
Pitt's antics were just a schoolboy prank. When on the next day
the Lords rejected the Habeas Corpus bill unanimously, Pitt
remarked that it was more honourable to be an Alderman of
the City of London than a peer. Next, on 11 June Pitt opposed a
bill sent down from the Lords with Hardwicke's blessing aug-
menting the salaries of the judges, but it went through despite
him. But in respect of conducting the war the confidence of the
House of Commons in Pitt was completely unshaken and the
session ended with a truly enormous vote of credit for unforeseen
contingencies. When they had discussed the matter on 1 June
Pitt and Newcastle had talked of five to seven hundred thousand
pounds but two days later Legge had convinced 'my Lord
Treasurer' that no less than £800,000 was the figure needed and
to this the Commons agreed.[7]

While in London the politicians bickered, Louisbourg lay
under siege. Boscawen had had to battle for eleven weeks against
contrary winds and did not reach Halifax until 9 May, over
three weeks after the date for the rendezvous laid down by Pitt.
The day after weighing anchor he sent word to Pitt; Amherst
had arrived from England and the transports from Boston and
Halifax were assembled, with those from New York expected
hourly. Abercromby on the mainland wrote to Pitt of his
negotiations with the Assemblies of the northern colonies.
Forbes, whose independent responsibility lay with the governments of the south, felt compelled to remark to Pitt: 'So you
must easily see, how difficult a task it is, to keep so capricious a
people anyways steady.' The southern colonies, which were not
exposed to attack from Canada, were far less interested than
New England in giving support. By the end of May Abercromby
had some 1,500 batteaus ready to transport his men up Lake
Champlain against Ticonderoga. On 23 May a despatch left
Halifax from Governor Lawrence that the Halifax rendezvous
was practically completed. After a delay occasioned by fog,
Boscawen at last set sail for Louisbourg on the 28th.[8]

There were little more than 3,000 French soldiers to man the
greatest fortress in North America with its 400 guns. Had Louis

XV put there a fraction of the men he had in Germany, a successful defence would have been certain. At noon on 2 June Boscawen got sight of Louisbourg and that evening he and Amherst reconnoitred the shore. Next day the transports came up, but the water was so surf-ridden that disembarkation could not be contemplated. This gave the French time to prepare. The Governor, the Chevalier Drucourt, realising that the safety of Quebec that year depended on his holding out as long as possible, insisted that the Admiral, the Marquis des Gouttes, remain with his five ships of the line and seven frigates rather than try for home. Amherst and Boscawen therefore decided against forcing the harbour as Pitt had suggested. Wolfe effected a landing on 8 June and two days later the weather cleared. Amherst sat down to send Pitt a day-to-day account of progress: he had delayed writing until he was certain Louisbourg was about to be invested. On 23 June, 6 July and 23 July Amherst forwarded to Pitt his eminently practical diary of events and on the twenty-seventh day he transmitted a triumphant account of the capitulation. Over 3,000 soldiers and near as many sailors were made prisoner but at a severe price: 580 British had been killed or wounded to 350 Frenchmen.[9] And it was too late in the year to move on to Quebec: to that extent Drucourt's tactics had paid off.

Three days later Amherst received bad news: Abercromby, whom in a despatch of 10 June Pitt had praised for his energy and zeal, had failed miserably before Ticonderoga, where Howe had been killed. According to Loring's account, an army mainly colonial but well supported by regulars embarked from Fort William Henry on Lake Champlain on 5 July. They comprised 16,800 men on board about 'Eight Hundred Battoes and Sixty-Five Whail Boats'. Pitt's insistence upon strong artillery support bore fruit; four iron eighteen-pounders, six light brass twelve-pounders and six six-pounders, eight brass royals and nine eight-inch howitzers was the complement. By 9.20 on the morning of 6 July the expedition had covered the twenty-two miles to the north of the lake and disembarked four miles from Fort Ticonderoga. After this initial success prisoners were taken: 'But this piece of advantage we paid very Deer for, for here we met with a Loss that was soon felt in the most sensible

manner by the whole army. Lord Howe, who fell in the first of
the action Dead on the Spot. So far things had been properly
conducted and with Spirit. But no sooner was his Lordship Dead,
than everything took a different turne, and finally ended in confusion and disgrace.' Abercromby, instead of taking Ticonderoga by a *coup de main*, allowed his men to wander aimlessly about
the woods for a day. Then at eight o'clock on the morning of
7 July the Commander-in-Chief withdrew his troops to the
point of disembarkation. Colonel Bradstreet urgently begged to
be allowed to attack the saw-mill, a defensive position about one
and a half miles from the Fort which he took with ease. But his
request to be allowed to go on 'was not taken the Least
Notice of'.

Next day the French lines were attacked but the enemy within
their log entrenchments were more numerous than expected.
Quite inexplicably Abercromby did not bring his artillery to
play and his men wandered of their own accord back to the
saw-mill, whilst the French were far too fly to venture from their
positions. On 9 July the campaign was ended by an order from
Abercromby to take to the boats and return to Fort William
Henry. The men obeyed with the greatest reluctance and deep
was the resentment among the officers at such lack of spine. The
entire British army mourned the vain sacrifice of Howe, whom
Wolfe, not given to admiration, described as 'the noblest
Englishman who has appeared in my time and the best soldier
in the army'.[10] On 12 July Abercromby sent Pitt a lengthy
account of this costly fiasco. He could hardly expect forgiveness
for his inexcusable pusillanimity, which he tried to cover up in a
final paragraph announcing that Bradstreet was to be sent with
3,000 men to attack Fort Frontenac on Lake Ontario.[11]

Amherst had no doubt where his duty lay, and without
wasting time on correspondence with London on 28 August he
departed for New York with 6,000 men to Abercromby's
support. So as to discourage Montcalm from taking the offensive
down the River Hudson, pilots were sent up the St Lawrence to
keep him on his toes about Quebec and Wolfe went with a
raiding party to the Labrador coast. Bradstreet, burning to wipe
out the disgrace of Ticonderoga, took Fort Frontenac by
surprise, thus regaining control of the Great Lakes. Forbes, in

his despatch of 10 July, had informed Pitt of his intention to approach Fort Duquesne through the Alleghanies by a route other than Braddock's: time consumed in hacking a new road through the forest would be more than recompensed if the enemy were taken off guard.[12] Provided Forbes was as lucky as Bradstreet, there was no doubt that next year Quebec would lie at mercy from land and sea.

Information of the situation in North America as it stood could not possibly reach Pitt until about the middle of August. Meanwhile he could take comfort from the brilliant successes of Prince Ferdinand. After expelling the French from Hanover in April the Prince had set up his headquarters at Münster in Westphalia and on 13 June his forward troops crossed the Rhine: '*Quelle humiliation, Monseigneur, laisser débarquer 6,000 hommes et établir un pont sur le Rhin,*' wrote the Pompadour to Clermont.[13] The Prince soon had 55,000 men on the west bank and on 23 June soundly beat Clermont at Crefeld, some fifty miles east of Düsseldorf; 5,200 Frenchmen were killed or wounded and 3,000 taken prisoner, to only 1,800 German casualties. The Austrian Netherlands were threatened with invasion and raiding parties penetrated as far as Charleroi and Louvain.

Prince Ferdinand's campaign was supported by an attack upon St Malo. Thirteen thousand soldiers were conveyed across the Channel in 150 sail, accompanied by twenty-two ships of the line and eight frigates, the naval and military complements totalling 34,000 men. This fleet commanded by Saunders, who had received his training in Anson's circumnavigation, was not intended merely as escort; the purpose was to provoke the French navy into an engagement. The convoy was commanded by Admiral Richard Howe, younger brother to the gallant Lord Howe. The 3rd Duke of Marlborough commanded the troops; his second was Sackville, who this time agreed to serve but was on the worst of terms with the Admiral. The expedition left the Isle of Wight on 1 June and landed on the east coast of north Brittany four days later. Great things were expected; moreover, information had just reached London that the French trading station on the Senegal river had been taken. As Elliot put it to Grenville: 'The landing of troops at Cancale Bay, six miles from St. Maloes, tallies very exactly with Prince Ferdinand's passing of the Rhine; and these two pieces of news are not ill supported by the accounts we have this day from the coast of Africa.'[14]

Pitt could not help writing to Amherst, of whose arrival off Louisbourg he was eagerly awaiting news: 'There is the greatest reason to hope, that this fortunate coincidence of Events will not fail to have the best Effects in Disconcerting the Views of the Enemy, and Distressing the French in such distant Parts.'[15] St Malo however proved a disappointment. Marlborough was a keen enough soldier but without that swift intelligence that can discern the opportunity for seizing a victory. A vast quantity of enemy stores and equipment was destroyed but the establishment of a bridgehead was not attempted. After cruising off the French coast for a month and taking a look into Cherbourg, the expedition returned home on 1 July. There were unpleasant stories about Sackville, who angrily retorted 'he would go buccaneering no more'.[16]

In view of the victories in Germany, Pitt decided on a complete reversal of his veto upon the use of British troops in Europe; Prince Ferdinand must be maintained upon the left bank of the Rhine, a constant menace to France. That Pitt, who had refused Cumberland a single regiment, should allow one British soldier to set foot in Germany has been paraded by his detractors as proof of political dishonesty. His change of front was evidence not of wavering principles but of that strength of mind that can discern and grasp a novel opportunity. Pitt saw that so long as Frederick could keep Austria and Russia at bay, Prince Ferdinand by keeping the enemy busy could leave Britain free to conquer the entire French overseas empire. The young politician who had harried Walpole and Carteret for Hanoverian counsels had become the mature statesman who realised the possibilities presented by a broad canvas. But Pitt was slow to recognise that Leicester House would not like the change. During June he had several preparatory conversations with Bute and on 23 June committed himself to a letter announcing that he had suggested to Newcastle the despatch of some British cavalry to Germany: 'Such a succour I believe will effectually tend to prevent repassing the Rhine, which, *at some moments of low spirits*, I confess I apprehend.' The letter did not mention that Pitt had also won Newcastle's agreement to sending 6,000 infantry. Bute laid down that the cavalry should be the limit, but Pitt went on to persuade the House of Commons to pay for six squadrons of cavalry and six battalions of infantry, 8,000 men in all. On 27 June Pitt wrote triumphantly to Grenville: '. . . I hope to share a sprig of German laurel very soon.'[17]

This new policy, despite the substantial addition to the cost of the war, met the mood of national optimism. Even the cautious Jenkinson noticed how Britain's finances, 'her real intrinsic power', were gaining in buoyancy. Prince Ferdinand and his Hanoverian army had become so popular that people did not mind the cost; as Jemmy Grenville expressed it to his brother George: 'I am told it was said in full circle that there are no better troops in the world than the Hanoverians when they have a good general at their head: that the greatest obligations are due to the King of Prussia for giving Prince Ferdinand to that army: that Prince Ferdinand loves that army, and the troops adore Prince Ferdinand.' Such was not however the mood at Leicester House, where the rage of the Prince of Wales and Bute at what they thought to be Pitt's doubledealing knew no bounds: '. . . when I mount the Th[rone] I shall be able to form a M[inistry] who can have the opinion of the people.'[18] By a simulation of respect Pitt might have toned down the irritation in the mind of the Prince who could not bear to see his 'Dearest Friend' ignored. Pitt's outlook was not however likely to be modest, for that week news came from Halifax that Boscawen had set off for Louisbourg.

The expeditionary force intended for Germany was entrusted to Marlborough and Sackville, with the Marquis of Granby, heir to the 3rd Duke of Rutland and member of Parliament for Cambridgeshire, in charge of the cavalry. Sackville now had a real chance to achieve a martial distinction that would better his political prospects, but he was a nuisance from the start. He departed without taking leave of the King. Then, because as a purely temporary measure the troops had been put under General Edward Bligh's command, he wrote to Pitt asking to resign. Once in Germany he maintained a most indiscreet correspondence with Bute, highly critical of Prince Ferdinand.[19] The French War Minister, Belleisle, stood firm despite the disaster at Crefeld where his son had been killed. He superseded Clermont with Contades, a better general; Broglie was ordered to make a detour through Hesse and invade Hanover, so exposing the Prince's left flank. Soon Prince Ferdinand found himself in a position similar to that of Richelieu at the end of 1757: detachments for garrison and supply had reduced his field army to a mere 20,000 men and the campaign had told heavily upon their clothing and equipment. Contades attempted to catch him in a trap at Roermond by forcing his army to fight against superior numbers with their backs to neutral Holland. Prince Ferdinand was compelled to stage a planned withdrawal northward whilst in a subordinate campaign around Cassel Broglie won a hard-fought and bloody victory at Sandershausen on 29 July. The Prince pressed Pitt to send an expedition to the French coast, even at the cost of some diminution in the size of the British expeditionary force, which was not due to arrive until 15 August.

By the last week in July Pitt had selected Cherbourg as a suitable target and appointed Bligh for the command, supported by Admiral Howe. Owing to a premature rumour that Louisbourg had fallen the national mood was one of extreme optimism.[20] All that Pitt yet knew was of the disembarkation on Cape Breton Island and that from a French source. But he had no doubt of the outcome and on 28 July, the day after Louisbourg had in fact capitulated, he ordered Boscawen to winter ten of the line with proportionate frigates and stores at Halifax.[21] Three days later the Cherbourg expedition set sail and the town surrendered in a week. Pitt in a burst of enthusiasm wanted to hold Cherbourg until the peace; Newcastle was aghast at this idea, which Ligonier quashed by pointing out that the place had no landward defences. The entire harbour and fortifications of Cherbourg were razed and the brass cannon removed for a grand parade from Kensington Palace to the Tower.[22]

On 10 August Captain William Amherst, brother to the General, arrived in London with news of Louisbourg, but a week later Pitt received Abercromby's account of Ticonderoga. He was deeply cut at the loss of Howe: 'He was, by the universal voice of the army and the people, a character of ancient times: a complete model of military virtue in all its branches.' Temple wrote to Pitt full of enthusiasm: 'My dear Louisbourg Pitt, a hundred thousand methods of congratulation to you upon this great and glorious event – the salvation of Europe . . . nothing but congratulations to you, my dear brother Louisbourg – I shall never call you by any other name except by that of Quebec in due time.' The Prince of Wales wrote of his sorrow over Howe to Bute who, in a touching way, polished the note and showed it to Pitt. Pitt in his letter to Grenville of 22 August wrote: 'Amherst will be felt, I trust, wherever he goes, perhaps even to Quebec, though the season is far advanced for such an operation.'[23] On 7 September a procession marched to St Paul's carrying the Louisbourg trophies. News was still awaited of how Forbes was faring in Pennsylvania.

Although full provision would probably have to be made for the conquest of Canada, Pitt decided that next year the British expeditionary force to Germany should be even more powerful, especially when news came that Frederick in Germany had destroyed a Russian army at Cüstrin (Zörndorf) on 25 August. Pitt's confidence would have been even greater had he known that in India Lally's attempt to take Madras had miscarried; d'Aché had attempted to blockade the harbour, but when Pocock appeared on 3 August he declined an action and pusillanimously withdrew to Mauritius for a refit. Pocock took his chance to retire to Bombay for the monsoon season. To the north Clive had sent Colonel Forde into the Northern Circars, where Masulipatam was recovered and the British controlled the entire coastline between Calcutta and Madras. The French never regained the initiative in India and Lally was restricted to maintaining his position at Pondicherry.

Then the year which had gone so gloriously turned awry. At the end of August Bligh and Howe were once more sailing in the Channel and decided to attack St Malo. It was Bute who, because the Prince of Wales's younger brother Edward was with the fleet, prevailed upon Bligh to undertake this venture. Bligh had general instructions to attack the French coast but Pitt, Ligonier and Newcastle were not specifically consulted. No more foolish notion could have been cooked up because, as St Malo had already been attacked that year, the enemy would be ready. Soon after the landing on 3 September the weather turned foul, a re-embarkation was ordered and the British, caught on shore, suffered heavy casualties. When on 28 September Bligh attended Court the King turned away from him. Bute complained angrily and accused Ligonier of wilful persecution. At this Pitt lost patience; as he himself, Ligonier and Newcastle had all been kept in ignorance the blame lay elsewhere.[24]

This silly episode had been all the more needless in that Pitt was coming to the conclusion that coastal raids should be avoided so as to give scope for preparations for an attack upon Martinique, chief of the French Windward Islands. Hitherto the war in the West Indies had been limited to the negative aim of commerce protection: now Pitt proposed passing to territorial aggrandisement. Ligonier worked out that 6,000 men would be required and the 3rd Earl of Albemarle, a great favourite with Cumberland, was chosen for the command with Barrington's younger brother John as his second. On 7 September Ligonier wrote to Pitt from Baldock, where he was inspecting troops for the expedition, that the King had approved these arrangements. Barrington was not particularly happy at his brother being selected, but Pitt and Ligonier refused any alteration. They could not however prevent Albemarle backing out, so Bligh was considered, but St Malo finished him. The next choice was a friend of Bute, General Granville Elliot, who asked for sick leave at Bath. Ligonier had to go to the King with a new list and the story ran that while they, Newcastle and the ministers were debating their choice Pitt stalked in: 'Perhaps', he observed with humorous sarcasm, 'my presence lays you under difficulties but I object to no one. Pray consider who is most proper and I shall be for him.' The King made the most unexciting choice of General Peregrine Hopson, a very senior officer and one-time Governor of Nova Scotia; fortunately Barrington was kept on.[25] On one point there was universal agreement – Abercromby must go. On 18 September Pitt sent a circular to the Governors of North America announcing Abercromby's replacement by Amherst, who received his notification by a despatch of the same date. Abercromby was treated merely to duplicate copies of these and a formal acknowledgement of his despatches of 29 June and 17 July.[26]

The year had been glorious but not quite complete. As in

North America, so too in Germany, a final effort would be demanded for 1759. Frederick, repeating his mistake at Kolin in 1757, over-reached himself and attacked the strong position Daun with his Austrians had taken up at Hochkirch in Saxony. The result was a resounding defeat, though fortunately Daun neglected to press forward. Then on 10 October Broglie won a further success at Lutterberg in Hesse. Belleisle's strategy paid off and in order to avoid being outflanked Prince Ferdinand had to re-cross the Rhine and fall back upon Münster. Contades was not sufficiently strong to invade Westphalia, so that when the Prince settled down to his winter quarters the campaign was ended. The net result had been the expulsion of the French from Hanover and the reconstitution of the Electoral army. George II granted the Prince an income of £2,000 p.a. for life, secured upon the Irish revenues, and Frederick made him a Field Marshal in the Prussian army. Then on 28 October Marlborough died suddenly at Münster. Sackville succeeded to the command but, to his chagrin, his Instructions did not give him the power to issue commissions Marlborough had enjoyed. He wrote to Pitt complaining at this 'personal disapprobation', but Pitt and the King knew how bad were his relations with Prince Ferdinand, loyalty to whom was the first consideration.[27]

On 16 October Pitt drafted Hopson's orders for the attack on Martinique. His departure from Portsmouth was delayed by storm damage to the transports. Pitt decided to give him a reinforcement of seven companies of Highlanders, who once Martinique had been reduced were to join Amherst on the mainland. The expedition of six of the line and 6,000 men left on 12 November. On the last day of the month Pitt sent an express to Hopson that provisions for 7,000 men and the Highland companies were to leave in a month and rendezvous at Barbados.[28] The British Caribbean stations alone would have at their disposal fleets equivalent to Byng's at Minorca in 1756. Also Pitt organised a small squadron to capture Goree and complete the elimination of French slaving stations of the coast of west Africa.

Above all, plans were laid for the capture of Quebec. On 30 October Pitt received news of Bradstreet's success against Niagara. Ticonderoga was outflanked and all was ready for the assault upon Canada from the land and by the St Lawrence. Pitt sent out 2,000 regulars and 1,000 Highlanders to replace casualties. Amherst's responsibility was for the operations from New England and by his Instructions of 29 December Pitt ordered him to proceed along Lake Champlain to Quebec, or from Niagara up the St Lawrence to Montreal; alternatively he was free to attempt a thrust in both directions. The Quebec expedition was entrusted to Wolfe, universally regarded since Howe's death as Britain's finest soldier. On news of Louisbourg Pitt had ordered him to stay put but already Wolfe was on the water, hoping to join the army in Germany. Within a month of his arrival Pitt had given him command of the Quebec expedition. Although only thirty-two, his health was wretched. His temperament was noticeably highly-strung and his outspoken ways made him enemies. When someone remarked that Wolfe was mad, George II commented: 'Then I wish he would bite some of my generals.' On 1 December Wolfe wrote to a friend: 'I have this day signified to Mr. Pitt that he may dispose of my slight carcass as he pleases.' Amherst's Instructions comprised the measures necessary for Wolfe's support. Transports of 20,000 tons were shortly to leave England for New York and in case of delays and deficiencies Amherst was to provide a further 6,000 tons from North America. All the forces for the Quebec expedition were to rendezvous at Louisbourg by the third week of April, so that Wolfe might proceed for the St Lawrence by about 7 May. Durrell, whom Boscawen had left in charge at Halifax, was to set up a blockade of the St Lawrence as soon as the ice lifted, so as to anticipate any attempt to put men or supplies into Quebec.[29]

As his lieutenants Wolfe selected Monckton, the victor of Beauséjour in 1756, James Murray and George Townshend. Since his quarrel with Pitt Townshend had devoted himself to the militia and with his approval had during the spring of this year piloted through the House of Commons a bill to amend and enforce the Act. Then in May he had applied for reinstatement in the army to which Pitt agreed and now he had his chance of glory. Colonel Isaac Barré, an Huguenot professional soldier who had already served with Wolfe at Rochefort and Louisbourg, was Adjutant-General and Guy Carleton the Quarter-

Master. All the general officers were under forty. The King took exception to some of Wolfe's colonels and Pitt retorted: '. . . in order to render any general completely responsible for his conduct he should be made, as far as possible, inexcusable if he should fail; and that consequently whatever an officer entrusted with a service of confidence requests should be complied with.'[30] Boscawen, in view of his service at Louisbourg and because his family was politically influential, could not be refused his request for the Mediterranean station. The command of the Quebec fleet was given to Saunders who had commanded the ships in the raid on St Malo. The Quebec expedition was Pitt's masterpiece and the entire direction and strategy were his.

The Address at the opening of Parliament on 23 November was proposed by Sir Richard Grosvenor, one of Pitt's most stout Tory supporters. He described the Pitt and Newcastle administration as 'the glory of this country' and 'ended with particular compliments to Mr. Pitt, who was the shining light or rather the blazing star of this country'. This was indeed a suitable prologue to Pitt's defence of the presence of British troops in Germany, which he undertook on 23 November. The House of Commons voted supplies totalling £12,705,339 for the coming year against the £10,471,007 voted at the end of 1757. On 18 November Colonel Forbes had taken Fort Duquesne, which he renamed Fort Pitt and subsequently became known as Pittsburg. When on 6 December Pitt moved the Thanks of the House of Commons to Amherst and Boscawen, Sir John Philipps urged that no British government should ever give up these conquests and found a seconder in Beckford. On the following day the subsidy to Frederick the Great was renewed for a further year.[31] The continuation of the Prussian treaty drew the attention of Leicester House. By this time the Prince of Wales was borrowing Pitt's old nickname – 'The Orator': 'Indeed my Dearest Friend he treats both you and me with no more regard than he would do a parcel of children, he seems to forget the day will come, when he must expect to be treated according to his deserts.'[32] For two years the Prince had been resolved on his accession to place Bute at the Treasury instead of Newcastle and by the end of 1758 had decided that this change must involve Pitt's downfall. Pitt's position had originally had three bases:

Newcastle who could never be depended upon; Leicester House whom he had since alienated; and military success. This last factor, and the public esteem that thereby followed, was from now on his sole platform, though as yet this consideration was not apparent to him. Temple was no help when in September he had sprung a demand upon Newcastle to be made a Knight of the Garter. Newcastle, who knew full well how George II hated the man, vaguely promised that the matter would be considered in the next promotion, but this did not satisfy Temple, who talked of absenting himself from Court on the King's birthday. Jemmy Grenville, together with 'a letter from Mr. P.', prevailed upon Temple 'not to put myself wrong in the opinion of my best friends'.[33]

The year had seen the vindication of Pitt's naval strategy in North America, the African coast and India. Abercromby had been a mistaken choice dictated to Pitt by considerations of seniority, but the soldiers of the war for North America, Amherst and Wolfe, were now in command. During the autumn Cardinal de Bernis had made some vague noises about peace. An exchange of Louisbourg for Minorca with a return to the *status quo ante bellum* had some attraction for Newcastle and Leicester House. But at the end of 1758 Pitt had the House of Commons completely behind him, even in respect of his expeditionary force for Germany. The coastal raids had been the only aspect of Pitt's strategy that might be deemed a wasteful misuse of resources: not a French battalion had been taken out of Germany in return for the very substantial concentrations of men and ships required for the expeditions against Rochefort, St Malo and Cherbourg. The French fleet had not been drawn into open combat. But even on the Continent the French strategy had lost its purpose. That December de Bernis was superseded at the Foreign Ministry by the Duke of Choiseul, who on the last day of the year signed a new treaty with Vienna by which France withdrew her subsidy but had to forgo the prospect of annexing West Flanders. Choiseul's one hope was to disentangle his country from the war into which Kaunitz had inveigled Louis XV without the complete loss of his overseas empire.

CHAPTER 9

Pitt's War: Annus Mirabilis and the Death of the King

'Come, cheer up, my lads! 'tis to glory we steer,
To add something more to this wonderful year;
To honour we call you, not press you like slaves,
For who are so free as we sons of the waves.
　　Heart of oak are our ships,
　　Heart of oak are our men,
　　We always are ready,
　　Steady! Boys! Steady!
We'll fight and we'll conquer again and again.'

David Garrick.[1]

From the New Year Pitt continued to organise victory in
North America to the last detail, with his mind fixed upon the
rendezvous at Louisbourg for April. Hardly a day went by
without a directive. His orders to Saunders of 12 January
opened: 'His Majesty having directed the Lords Commissioners
of the Admiralty to take up Twenty Thousand Tons of Transport Vessels, & to cause the same to be victualled with Six
Months provisions for the ten thousand Men, & to be provided

with Bedding and fitted in every way for the Reception of
Troops, at the rate of one Ton and a half a Man; . . .'. Saunders
was to send the transports to New York under an officer of his
own choosing – an unusual concession from Pitt; artillery and
stores on the Thames were to go at once to Spithead. Next day
Pitt forwarded to Amherst Wolfe's suggestion that molasses be
bought for the manufacture of spruce beer, the antidote to
scurvy. At New York Amherst anticipated few obstacles – the
difficulties supposed to attend the navigation of the St Lawrence
were more imaginary than real.

On 19 January Pitt received Forbes's account of the taking of
Fort Duquesne. He at once ordered its restoration and asked the
colonial governments to contribute materials. Pitt pointed out
to Amherst the importance of seizing Presqu'il, so that Canada
would be completely cut off from the Ohio valley. For the
service of the year the assemblies of the northern colonies voted
over 17,000 men and the southern over 4,200.[2]

In the West Indies Hopson and Barrington had arrived off
Barbados on 3 January. In the course of the passage eleven ships
became separated, including 'the Great Hospital Ship' and the
transport carrying the engineers. Notwithstanding, Hopson and
Sir John Moore, who already knew the West Indies and had
taken over the naval command when the expedition arrived,
left for Martinique on 13 January. Two days later every battery
at Port Royal was silenced and the troops put ashore without
opposition. Hopson, finding the terrain far more mountainous
than he had been advised, lost heart and embarked his men.
Moore, sooner than see the expedition wasted, pointed out that
the acquisition of Guadeloupe would be a very adequate
alternative. Hopson therefore made for Basseterre the capital
which during 21 to 23 January was destroyed by naval bombardment. The troops were put ashore but serious sickness
broke out which decimated the Highland battalions. Hopson
could either have withdrawn or attempted to penetrate the
interior but instead stayed put, the worst thing to do. Barrington, though highly critical of such wasteful inactivity, was
powerless until by chance, towards the end of February,
Hopson's death gave him the command. He and Moore decided
to move the troops by sea to the other side of Guadeloupe.[3]

In London Pitt was taken with a sublime mood of confidence. On 10 February he wrote to Amherst pointing out the need to assemble provisions for the men who would winter in Quebec seven months hence. He was back on his hobby horse of an attack upon Mobile and Mississippi: 'whether, towards the end of the year, when operations in the more Northern Parts of America must necessarily cease . . .'. The seventy-four sail of transports left Spithead with an escort of six of the line and nine frigates on 14 February. Midway across the Atlantic they ran into a severe gale and only fifty-three were able to keep together. Wolfe was supremely confident of his ability to win a victory that would prove to be a decisive event in the history of the world. The evening before his departure he had dinner with Pitt and Temple and as usual ate frugally and drank only to support a toast to victory. He then disconcerted his hosts by stalking round the room waving his naked sword in the air and boasting of the wondrous deeds he would perform in Canada. Saunders accompanied Wolfe in his flagship *Neptune*, with ten of the line and some auxiliary vessels.[4] While they were cruising from British waters, Kempenfeldt on 16 February relieved Madras from Lally's siege. The first good news of the year to reach London was of the capture of an island in the Senegal river by Commodore Keppel on 28 December last.

All Pitt knew of happenings in the West Indies was Hopson's account of the destruction of Basseterre. This he acknowledged on 3 March in a despatch practically assuming that Guadeloupe was taken and ordering the seizure of St Lucia as the preliminary to a renewed attempt upon Martinique; the four months supply promised at the end of last year was on its way. Pitt had wind that Chef d'Escadron de Bompart had left Brest on 9 March with seven of the line but had every confidence in Moore's ability to manage, 'wherever its destination may be'. By the time Pitt was giving out these orders for the West Indies Saunders had reached Louisbourg and at once ordered Durrell to the St Lawrence. Forbes had died on 11 March, unfortunately before he could have received Pitt's letter acknowledging the compliment of Pittsburgh: 'I cannot conclude without adding my particular acknowledgements for the very great undeserved Honour, you have done my Name!'[5]

Choiseul knew the chances of saving Canada or the smaller French West Indian possessions to be slender. His sole resort was the daring project of an invasion of England, combined with a successful campaign against Prince Ferdinand. It was the general expectation that Frederick could not survive another year at war. Cüstrin and Hochkirch had ruined his best regiments, which were patched up with mercenaries and prisoners, officered as well as might be. Prince Ferdinand came out of winter quarters early in March and took Cassel. But Broglie beat the forward section of his army at Bergen on 13 April, inflicting heavy loss. He then retook Cassel and pushed forward in company with Contades with the intention of turning Prince Ferdinand's left and preventing Frederick from receiving succour. Faced with a combined French army twice the size of his own, the Prince was forced to retreat. Sackville's contribution lay in hostile and bitter criticisms of Prince Ferdinand in letters to Holderness, and worse still to Bute, who complained to Pitt at his not being given full powers. Holderness, as in duty bound, emphasized the complete confidence of the King in Prince Ferdinand.[6]

Choiseul did not aspire to the capture of London or the occupation of several counties; he placed great faith in the damage to the British system of credit that must follow upon any effective landing. Only partial success was required to ensure the stoppage of men, supplies and subsidies to Prince Ferdinand and Frederick. De Vaudreuil, the Governor of Canada, and Montcalm were instructed to hold Canada for the duration of the war, even if within very constricted limits, 'since the conditions of peace would be very different if the French King's forces were still maintaining themselves in a part of the country, however small'.[7] Pitt refused to be drawn into altering his overall strategy. Hawke, with the home fleet at the mouth of the Channel, guaranteed protection for the Atlantic convoys. The French with only twenty-seven of the line at Brest could not contemplate invasion unless the Toulon fleet got out of the Mediterranean. Boscawen with Thomas Brodrick as his second was therefore sent to Gibraltar. Through a diplomatic leakage from Sweden, the French plans became known in London. There was to be a three-pronged invasion, the main blow coming from Ostend with Malden in Essex as the point of disembarkation, supported by diversionary moves against the Clyde and Northern Ireland. If the British army and militia were compelled to concentrate around London the disembarkation of small French detachments in Scotland and Ireland would cause chaos. But the French plan was founded upon a fallacious appreciation of naval strategy. If they could cover a landing in Essex, so complicated and wasteful a scheme as attack from three directions was pointless; equally, if their navy was unable to keep the British at bay, the project was so grandiose as to invite bloody destruction.

On 1 May Saunders sent word to Pitt that Louisbourg was yet ice-bound; the Quebec campaign must be put off till the second half of the year, with all the anxieties entailed by the approach of winter. Saunders left Halifax on 13 May and his departure from Louisbourg for the St Lawrence took place on 4 June. Of the 119 ships in convoy more than half had been supplied from the merchant marine and ship-yards of North America. On the mainland Amherst had sent expeditions against Oswego and Niagara and was assembling an army at Crown Point for the capture of Ticonderoga. On 5 May Pitt, who was under the happy presumption that the April rendezvous at Louisbourg had been met, received the reports of Barrington and Moore of Hopson's death and the stalemate on Guadeloupe.

But better news was on the way. On the arrival of de Bompart at Martinique early in April, Moore withdrew his ships to Dominica, from where he could at once look after the Leeward Islands sugar convoy and, he supposed, keep an eye on the enemy. The Frenchman gave him the slip and was off Guadeloupe on 2 May, but too late. Barrington had sent his second, John Clavering, into the interior and he, acting with real pluck, had forced the French to capitulate one day before de Bompart got there. Moore was free to withdraw to Antigua and despatch home the grand sugar convoy of 300 sail. Although de Bompart caused terrible havoc to British shipping around Barbados he had to set forth for Brest with nothing strategical achieved. Clavering was deservedly entrusted with the despatches from Barrington and Moore to Pitt announcing their triumph. The

French were assembling their troop flotillas in the Channel and Biscay ports, whilst Pitt urged the Lords Lieutenant to make returns of the militia. The arrival of Clavering, the hero of Guadeloupe, on 14 June turned the mood of apprehension into one of gay rejoicing. The Annus Mirabilis had in truth begun.[8]

Pitt's pride in victory was enhanced by the birth of his second son William at Hayes on 28 May: George Grenville was invited to be a godfather.[9] But soon Pitt suffered a great sorrow in the death of his dear friend Potter on 17 June. A mountebank to the end, Potter had been deep in an electoral intrigue with Bedford. The scheme was that Potter should relinquish his constituency of Okehampton, become member for Bedfordshire, turn that county over to his son at his coming of age and then he himself would return to his one-time seat at Bath! The consideration that Pitt and Ligonier were the sitting members seems not to have come into it and, of course, Bedford with his patronage in Devon and Bedfordshire was a very necessary party.[10] It had indeed been a strange friendship between Pitt the rigorist and Potter the drunkard, the womaniser and the opportunist. Potter was succeeded in the Recordership of Bath by Pratt.

When on 4 July Pitt received word of the departure of Saunders and Wolfe for Quebec, the possibility of invasion was absorbing his hourly attention.[11] Hubert de Brienne Conflans, the French Admiral at Brest, would be superior to Hawke in number, though not in the quality of his ships, provided the Toulon fleet under de la Clue could slip past Boscawen into the Atlantic and de Bompart arrive safely from the West Indies. When in July George Rodney successfully raided the flotilla in Le Havre, the French might have guessed that their entire plan would founder: "Tis hot work at Le Havre, and Quebec too by this time,' wrote Lyttleton's brother Richard to Grenville, 'Good success to Wolfe and Townshend is my toast also.' On 17 July the King reviewed the Norfolk militia in Hyde Park. Rumours of a French landing in Kent proved unfounded, but the news from Germany was disconcerting; Prince Ferdinand had retreated to Osnabrück, it was hoped with the intention of drawing Contades into a trap.[12]

Whilst Pitt was preoccupied with the safety of the country,

Bute thought up a neat tit-for-tat for his neglect of Leicester House. That July the Prince of Wales asked for permission to join the army: the post of Captain-General had been vacant since Klosterseven and the heir to the throne could at twenty-one fairly expect to be offered what his uncle Cumberland had been given at twenty-three. Newcastle was so flustered that he was unable to concoct a suitable rejoinder. Pitt, while he readily admitted that the isolated condition of the Prince's upbringing was unfortunate, had no intention of handing military patronage to Bute; no commission of any kind would be appropriate just now, though an occasional inspection of the Guards in London or the troops at Chatham and Portsmouth in Ligonier's company would be permissible. The Prince was furious at Newcastle delaying a reply: 'The King', he wrote to Bute, 'and those he has consulted have treated me with less consideration than they would have dar'd to have done any Member of Parliament. . . .' Towards the end of the month Bute, possibly not knowing that Pitt had laid down the law, arranged to discuss the matter with him as an introduction to the Prince's audience of the King arranged for 30 July. Pitt fobbed Bute off, which was not difficult, for the objections to the Prince or him interfering in military matters were obvious. Great was the young man's indignation: 'I am not much surpriz'd at this insolence of Pitt's, he has long shown a want of regard both of you my Dearest Friend and consequently of myself.' From his grandfather he gained nothing: according to Newcastle his audience 'lasted some seconds' – in other words the Prince got a flea in the ear.[13]

Prince Ferdinand, forced to abandon Minden and Münster, made up his mind to turn and face the enemy. Contades would rather have waited for reinforcements but was under pressure from Versailles to press forward. The armies engaged in the Battle of Minden on 1 August. Broglie opened with an attack upon the Prince's left but then held back upon orders from Contades, who saw six British and three Hanoverian infantry battalions advancing upon his centre. Possibly this movement originated with a misunderstood signal, but the battle was thereby decided. The British red-coats, despite heavy fire from the enemy artillery, advanced in line unshaken and repulsed attack after attack from the French cavalry, inflicting heavy loss, a singular triumph of bayonet over sabre. Prince Ferdinand, the opportunity for complete victory in his grasp, ordered Sackville with his twenty-four squadrons of cavalry to fall upon the enemy. To his utter astonishment the order was ignored. Granby tried to take matters into his own hands and moved forward but was commanded by Sackville to halt. The French suffered 8,000 to 10,000 casualties against only 3,000 British and German, and lost forty-three guns, but the opportunity to destroy the enemy completely was lost.

Prince Ferdinand's Order of the Day on the morrow of the battle contained no direct reference to Sackville but included these words: 'His Serene Highness further orders it to be declared to General the Marquis of Granby he is persuaded that, if he had had the good fortune to have him at the Head of the Cavalry on the Right Wing, his presence would have greatly contributed to make the day more complete, and more brilliant. . . .' Sackville tried some explanation, but the Prince demanded his immediate recall. He retorted with resignation and the King with his own hand struck Sackville's name from the army list. Granby took command of the British forces in Germany and Sackville was given leave to return home, but was now a civilian.[14] No sufficient explanation of Sackville's conduct will ever be agreed. Accusations have oscillated between mere cowardice and jealousy of Prince Ferdinand, or even a concoction with Bute to disgrace the British army in retaliation for Pitt's not allowing the Prince of Wales to become Captain-General. Considering an opportunity comparable to a Blenheim had been let slip, Sackville could expect little sympathy from Pitt but already the benevolence of Leicester House was enlisted on his side. The day after he resigned Bute wrote to Pitt asking for his friendly intercession, to receive a very guarded reply: 'I shall continue to give him, a most unhappy man, all the *offices of humanity* which, our *first*, *sacred*, object, my dear Lord, the public goodwill allow. . . .'[15]

Minden was rapidly followed by the first great naval victory of the year. Early in July Boscawen had learned that de la Clue at Toulon had ships sufficient to establish an equality. When on 17 August de la Clue with ten of the line slipped through the

Straits of Gibraltar, Boscawen put to sea in three hours and was extraordinarily lucky. Owing to a misunderstood signal the French rear squadron under de Castillon put into Cadiz and de la Clue, unaware of the mistake, sailed northwards, confident that his remaining ships were coming up. Boscawen came upon the Frenchman off Lagos in the Algarve and, undeterred by the consideration that the enemy was in neutral waters, destroyed him. Without reporting home for orders Boscawen hastened to the Channel to join Hawke's blockade of Brest, leaving Brodrick off Cadiz with a force adequate to watch de Castillon.

Prince Ferdinand's victory was a godsend for Frederick, who had suffered a terrible disaster. During the spring of 1759 the Russians had overrun East Prussia and defeated a Prussian army at Poltzig on 23 July; by the end of the month they were only forty miles east of Berlin. In August they were joined by an Austrian army and Frederick's nightmare of a junction between the Russian and Austrian armies within his territory became a reality. Leaving a small force in Silesia and Saxony, which Daun ought to have set upon, Frederick marched to the Oder and with 50,000 men attacked 48,000 Russians and 18,000 Austrians at Künersdorf. He was completely defeated and suffered sleepless nights for months, alternately contemplating suicide or addressing sonnets to his favourite sister Wilhelmina. Yet with his wonderful resilience, within a week he was issuing orders for the formation of another army, though from very poor material. He sent an urgent message to Prince Ferdinand begging for help, but as Münster was still in French hands only a token force was sent; then he met with two further defeats in Saxony.

In the first week of September Sackville arrived in London and wrote to Holderness requesting a court martial and even to Pitt asking for his protection. Pitt returned a bleak answer on the 9th: 'Give me leave, then to say, that I find myself . . . under the painful necessity of declaring my infinite concern at not having been able to find . . . room, as I wished, for me to offer my support, with regard to a conduct which, perhaps my ignorance of military questions, leaves me at a loss to account for.' But the Prince of Wales, more than ready to espouse Sackville's cause, was writing to Bute on the very day of this rebuff:

'I think it is pretty pert for a little German Prince to make publick any fault he finds with the English Commander, without first waiting for instructions from the King in so delicate a matter.'[16] The Prince was forgetting that Sackville's disobedience had been so brazen that only frank confrontation could have sustained the self-respect of Granby and his officers. It was Sackville who had requested a court martial and in his reply of 10 September Holderness pointed out that as he had not demanded a trial while in Germany the matter must stand over until the officers who might act as witnesses were free to come home. Meanwhile the country was calling for Sackville's blood and Pitt condemned even his attendance at the opera. Horace Walpole assessed Sackville to be formidable: 'With his parts and ambitions it cannot end here; he calls himself ruined but when Parliament meets he will probably attempt some sort of revenge.'[17]

Wolfe and Saunders had left Louisbourg on 1 June to find that owing to the negligence of Philip Durell – the local naval commander until Saunders's arrival – a French convoy had already reached Quebec, commanded by Louis Antoine de Bougainville, one day to become one of the greatest explorers. Durell had since tried to make up by sending his ships up the St Lawrence to Coudres, sixty-five miles from Quebec. The French placed their faith in a great natural barrier; forty-five miles down river from Quebec lay the treacherous shoals of The Traverse, believed to be unnavigable except by small ships and then only with the aid of local pilots. Durell managed to take three ships of the line over The Traverse into the Quebec basin and by 26 June the entire British battle-fleet with scores of transports lay opposite Quebec, a very remarkable achievement in navigation. To Montcalm, sure in the belief that an attack by way of the St Lawrence was impossible, this spelt disaster, but de Bougainville had intercepted a despatch of Amherst so that some defences at Quebec were put up which frustrated the possibility of a *coup de main*.

Montcalm had 12,000 men, three-quarters mere colonial militia, to Wolfe's 8,000 regulars. Saunders had every intention that his men and guns should play their part on land. Montcalm adopted a strict defensive; he had only to hold on until the winter freeze. He took up a series of positions along five miles of the Quebec side of the river and in order to take the city Wolfe would have to defeat him in the field. An approach to Quebec direct from the water was forbidden by the Heights of Abraham, which Montcalm considered so inaccessible that only a few sentinel posts were necessary; the batteries of Quebec harbour would prevent the British making any progress up-river and protect his supply lines from Montreal.

Wolfe split up his army so as to face Montcalm's encampments and intended to tempt the enemy into sallying forth to fight. He could then use Saunders's ships to concentrate his men, and the Frenchman would be at his mercy. The campaign was a straight duel of wits, each commander testing the steadfastness of the other to the utmost. Wolfe was perplexed at Montcalm's fortitude and on 23 July held a council of war. No minutes were taken but the attack upon Montmorency, a promontory outflanking the city, which took place on the last day of the month, must have been decided upon. The British were beaten off with a loss of 800 men. Wolfe did not send Pitt an account of his reverse. On 10 August he issued a proclamation declaring his intention to lay waste the country. In New England Amherst had taken Ticonderoga and Crown Point whilst a detachment from his army had captured Niagara; Montreal lay open to approach. In the last week of August reports of these successes reached London.[18]

The season was running out and on 28 August Wolfe summoned a second council of war. He was suffering from a fever and in a moment of despair authorised a movement with which he did not agree, to force the enemy lines one mile above the town. He had completely lost the confidence of George Townshend, who was utterly disgusted at the warfare upon civilians.[19] At this point Wolfe wrote to Pitt for the first time since disembarking below Quebec on 27 June. His despatch of 2 September was a confession of failure and left open little hope that Quebec would be his.[20] Then, as by a miracle, Wolfe regained health and confidence. A reconnoitre on 9 September convinced him that the Heights of Abraham were vulnerable: Montcalm's weakness lay not on his flanks but at the centre. Wolfe made up his mind to scale the Heights and gain access to the plateau above Quebec. His brigadiers were appalled at what they considered an almost insanely dangerous venture; if the French noticed anything before the entire army was drawn up on the plateau, Wolfe's men would be massacred piecemeal as they gained the top of the cliffs. They drew up a formal remonstrance, but Wolfe was undeterred at finding himself in a minority of one: 'I have the honour to inform you today that it is my duty to attack the French army. To the best of my knowledge and abilities, I have fixed upon that spot where we can act with the most force, and are most likely to succeed. If I am mistaken, I am sorry for it, and must be answerable to his Majesty and the public for the consequences.'[21]

On the night of 12 September 4,500 red-coats, in three successive detachments, scaled the Heights of Abraham which were still unprotected apart from routine sentries: a challenge was answered in French, to the effect that commissariat boats were coming down river. Subsequently George Townshend gave Pitt an eyewitness account:

'Just at daybreak another most fortunate circumstance contributed to the success of this critical operation, when the first corps for disembarkation was passing down the N side of the River & the French Centries on the banks challeng'd our boats, Capt. Fraser who had been in the Dutch Service & spoke French, answered – la France & vive le Roy – on which the French centinels ran along the Shore in the dark crying – laisser les passer ils sont nos gens avec les provisions – which they had expected for some time.'

The blue-jackets hauled the guns up the precipice and by dawn the British were drawn up in line upon the plateau overlooking Quebec. Montcalm knew that he had no choice but to fight a pitched battle. He led his men, mostly irregulars, in a charge against Wolfe's grenadiers who waited motionless until the enemy was thirty paces distant – then came three volleys. Montcalm's Canadian militia, broken by the deadly fire, fled to the protection of Quebec. Wolfe led the charge and, although twice wounded, ran on to receive a mortal shot in the breast. At almost the same moment Montcalm received the wound from which he would die the following day. The entire action had taken only fifteen minutes and the British suffered 650 casualties to 1,500 Frenchmen killed. Wolfe's death in the hour of glory was a tragedy unparalleled until the death of Nelson. But Quebec ranks among the decisive battles of the world, a turning point in the history of North America.

On the following day George Townshend, upon whom the command had fallen, had his anxieties which did not altogether spring from his natural turgidity. Monckton, Barré and Carleton had been severely wounded. The citadel of Quebec still held out, whilst at Cape Rouge lay de Bougainville with 2,000 men, and de Lévis might come up from Montreal. Without Montcalm, however, there was no spirit in Quebec, which surrendered on 18 September. Two days later Townshend sent his despatch to Pitt:[22]

'The 17th a flag of truce came out with proposals of capitulation about noon before we had any Battery erected. I sent ye officer who had come out, back to town allowing them four hours to capitulate or no further treaty. He returned with terms of capitulation, which with ye Admiral were considered, agreed to, & signed on both sides by 8 o'clock in ye Morning ye 18th instant.'

Whilst tidings of victory were coming over the Atlantic the ministry was threatened by a crisis over personalities. The occasion was unfortunate, for Newcastle felt a sincere appreciation for Pitt's achievements, recording in his notes on 4 September: 'Mr. Pitt – More popular every day than ever; even in the country and with the Old Whigs.'[23] The upset occurred when Temple renewed his request for the Garter, even though Minden had made certain that Prince Ferdinand must be of the next election. Newcastle in his usual cowardly way asked Devonshire to see what could be done. When on 11 September Devonshire broached the subject the King exclaimed: 'No My L<u>d</u> I will not do it, ye fellow has had too much from me. I will never do anything more for him.' Devonshire gently pointed out that Pitt felt 'obligated' towards Temple and considered that he himself had done more for the King than any other subject: if this sole request was granted he would readily promise never to ask anything more. Devonshire put things more directly than Newcastle would have dared: 'now S.ʳ if Mr. Pitt thinks himself bound by his obligations to follow his Brother-in-Law, & wd. resign, your affairs would fall into ye same confusion they were in three years ago.' Parliament was due to meet in five weeks and, Devonshire pointed out, without Pitt, Newcastle neither could nor would carry on. He then cleverly suggested that the King might honour Temple, yet at the same time make it clear to all that he was prompted solely by the desire to show a public respect to Pitt. Yet the King still refused; he feared that 'ye world would see his situation & yt. he was no King'.[24]

None the less Pitt was able to look after another old friend. On 6 October Ralph Allen drew his attention to the vacancy in the see of Gloucester. 'I have', Pitt was soon able to write to Warburton, 'the particular satisfaction of thinking this residence will not carry you out of reach of Prior Park, and that as a man of Bath I am not a little interested in the vicinity.'[25]

When on 16 October George Townshend's despatch describing the battle for Quebec arrived, Pitt knew the war to be won. Whilst the country went mad with delight, Pitt took his chance to insist upon the Garter for Temple. The King's obstinacy had irritated him beyond all sense of proportion and on the 26th he went prattling to Devonshire about a dramatic resignation to coincide with Temple's receiving his stall at Windsor. Two and a half weeks later Devonshire very nearly surmounted the difficulty through the agency of Lady Yarmouth: 'the D. of Newcastle could not stay without Mr. Pitt & indeed if he was to ask my opinion, I sd. tell him yt. he would endanger his head if he attempted to stay in, for ye success we had had this last year had made Mr. Pitt so popular throughout ye kingdom yt. no Ministry could be form'd without him.' That evening Lady Yarmouth talked to the King and on the day following she reported to Devonshire his readiness to give a promise of the Garter at the end of the parliamentary session. Temple on 13 November sent a very proper letter to Pitt thanking him for his good offices. When next day Devonshire had his audience the King did not mention Temple, but on leaving the Closet there was a rude awakening: 'met Ld. Temple in the outward room who told me he was going to resign'. George II had been thoroughly alarmed when Lady Yarmouth had told him that if Pitt went Newcastle would be out next day, and did his utmost to dissuade Temple without success. He told Devonshire to give Pitt an account of his conversation. Devonshire reached the conclusion that Pitt's resignation would be unlikely. Bute wrote to Temple expressing his pain and shock, whilst at the Levee next day the King went out of his way to be civil. That evening Devonshire saw Temple who agreed to take the Privy Seal back and talked pompously of accepting the Garter as a mark of favour and never upon terms.[26]

Pitt's encomium upon Wolfe in the House of Commons on 20 November was unfortunate. Gray had his censure: '. . . a studied & Puerile declamation on funeral honours (on proposing a Monument to Wolf) in the course of it he wiped his eyes with one handkerchief & Beckford (who seconded him) cried too, & wiped with two handkerchiefs at once, who, was very moving. the third was about Gen. Amherst, & in commendation of the industry and ardour of our American Commanders, very spirited and eloquent. this is a very critical time, an action being hourly expected between the two great fleets, but no news yet.'[27] London was tense with daily fear of invasion. Newcastle was croaking away and expostulated in sarcastic vein to Granby's father Rutland: 'We who are not *bled* with a militia should do something to show our zeal and to serve our country in this time of danger, as effectually and perhaps more so than if we had a militia.'[28] Pitt readily approved Grosvenor's looking after the Cheshire militia instead of attending the parliamentary session: 'as you are manifesting your zeal for his Majesty and for your country in so essential a manner where you are, it would be unpardonable selfishness in me to express the regret which losing the pleasure of seeing you must always occasion.'[29] In fact Newcastle's contempt for Pitt's militia was not all that misplaced. The idea never caught on and despite the invasion scare only half the 32,000 men provided for came forward. The security of Britain lay with Hawke and the fleet.

At Brest Conflans, a humane man, considered the condition of his ships and the rawness of his crews rendered the hazard of putting to sea unjustifiable. Rough weather hardly known in living memory prevented Hawke intercepting de Bompart, who arrived in Brest that November: his effigy was burned by the London mob. But de Bompart's return sealed the fate of the Brest fleet, for though after the double Atlantic voyage his ships might be unseaworthy his sailors, in good training and discipline, could well be pressed into placing their lives in jeopardy for the forlorn prospect of covering the invasion. Conflans, his judgement overruled by orders from Versailles, left port on 14 November with instructions to collect the troop transports along the Morbihan coast and invade Britain. Ligonier had no doubt as to the outcome: 'We expect to hear every moment that Hawke has thoroughly slashed Conflans.' Finding Hawke set upon attack, Conflans took refuge in Quiberon Bay, hoping that the British would never dare to enter those rock-strewn waters amidst the storms sweeping the Brittany coast. Undeterred, Hawke descended upon the enemy and on 22 November six French ships of the line were destroyed, four wrecked on shore and 2,500 sailors killed or drowned, to the loss of only two British heavy warships.

Six days later the guns roared in salvo at Hyde Park and the Tower; two hundred members of Parliament attended St Paul's to be elevated by a sermon to the text of Psalm XCV, verses 1–2: 'O come, let us sing unto the Lord, let us make a joyful noise to the rock of our salvation.' Throughout Brittany, whose boys had provided most of the French complement, there was hardly a village without a sign of mourning. On 16 January Hawke anchored in Plymouth Sound after withstanding thirty-five weeks at sea, a terrible strain on a man of fifty; he received the Thanks of the House of Commons and a pension of £2,000 p.a. but not the peerage surely his due.[30]

Pitt's talk of resignation was comic opera. Indeed he was bent upon leading the country through to a victorious peace, which the fall of Quebec must indicate a matter for common sense with the rivalry in North America decided in favour of Britain. The quarrel between Frederick and Maria Theresa over Silesia could obviously be treated separately. But the possibility of an early peace with France was overshadowed by the change of attitude towards Britain at the Court of Spain. Shortly after Minden Ferdinand VI had died, to be succeeded by his brother

Charles III, King of the Two Sicilies, who had no reason to love the British: in 1742, in his capital of Naples, he had been subjected to an ultimatum demanding his withdrawal from the War of the Austrian Succession. Charles III had seated in his mind a picture of himself as mediator between Britain and France which Pitt indignantly turned down: 'That as to the rest, such had been the Blessing of God upon His Majesty's Arms, that it was more natural for France than for the British King to turn their thoughts towards the Good Offices of Neutral Powers in procuring a Peace.'[31]

Whether or not by coincidence, the approach from Charles III was shortly followed by advice from another quarter. The Princess of Anhalt-Zerbst was, as the mother-in-law to Peter, heir to the Russian throne, a lady of consequence. She wrote to Hardwicke's younger son, Joseph Yorke, Ambassador at The Hague, about a possible overture for peace. Without informing Pitt Newcastle passed this suggestion on to the Prussian Ambassador but Holderness let the cat out of the bag. Pitt at once taxed Newcastle, to meet with the disclaimer that a tiresome female correspondence need cause him no alarm and deception was not intended. Pitt rejoined: 'I believe it, for if you did, you would not be able to walk the streets without a guard.'[32] Over what the details of a peace negotiation might be Pitt at this time was surprisingly moderate. Whilst the squabble over Temple's Garter was raging he chatted to Devonshire who thought him 'really desirous of peace this winter'. Minorca Pitt recognised public opinion would insist on and in Canada certain forward positions must be annexed for the security of New England: 'As to Quebeck, Montreal & Louisbourg, they were points to be treated of & not given up for nothing.'[33]

The attempted intervention of the Princess of Anhalt-Zerbst was shortly matched by an approach from Choiseul. After Minden, with Quebec lost, the West African settlements taken and the prospect of further reverses in the West Indies and in India, Choiseul felt obliged to consider a separate peace. The French treasury was so exhausted that there were weekly difficulties over paying the army in Germany. Choiseul wrote to Kaunitz of his country's desperate condition. It was not a French interest to maintain a large army in Germany to prosecute the dismemberment of Prussia. Choiseul forwarded a series of proposals to Britain through the government of Denmark. At this stage he practically proposed a return to the *status quo ante bellum*, which hardly took account of the fact that Quebec and Guadeloupe were in British hands. Charles III's offer to mediate could not be set aside without a polite appearance of consideration. Pitt took up Frederick's clever suggestion of a European Congress, which was forwarded to Paris on 25 November. At the same time the British Ambassador at The Hague was instructed to inform the French and Austrian ministers that Britain would be prepared to treat for peace in general terms, though only at a heavy cost to France. Pitt had no intention of abandoning Prussia and would certainly have insisted upon a French evacuation of Germany as a condition of peace. Frederick commented: 'I am willing to leave my fate in the hands of England and am rejoiced to see it in the good keeping of Mr. Pitt.'[34]

Pitt's distrust of Newcastle, evinced in the Anhalt-Zerbst episode, was not altogether well-founded. Newcastle, on 27 November, wrote of him to Granby: 'He is a man. A man of great merit, weight and consequence, it is for the service of the publick to be well with him; to aid and assist him.'[35] Newcastle, proud to see himself Prime Minister of a victorious country, was more than ready to forget old scores: that Pitt must always be a power in the Whig party he freely acknowledged. Unfortunately Pitt was blind to Newcastle's admiration and to spurn the hand of friendship was folly in view of the enmity of Leicester House, largely of his own provoking. In the event of the King's death Newcastle and Pitt could not survive long without each other.

On reaching Saragossa en route for Madrid, Charles III despatched a Memorial to the Spanish Ambassador in London, Felix d'Abreu, which was handed to Pitt on 5 December; the British King and nation were congratulated upon their glorious successes, but at the same time it was pointed out that the King of Spain, who had the largest interest in America, could not regard with indifference the threat to the balance of power established by the Treaty of Utrecht. Charles III formally offered his good offices as mediator. Pitt forwarded an urgent despatch to the 2nd Earl of Bristol, British Ambassador at

Madrid: the Spanish King, he pointed out, had acted before a discussion with his government had been possible; Britain could not enter negotiations without consultation with her allies; French aggression had destroyed any respect for a balance of power established by the Utrecht Treaty, 'the fearful infractions of which over a long succession of years, had been the only cause of the present war between the two Crowns'. Britain, it was made clear, would not scruple to use her strong position to dictate such terms as would prevent a recurrence of the present struggle.[36]

At Madrid Wall, the Prime Minister, was most upset at seeing all his endeavours to keep Spain out of the war placed in jeopardy by his new King. Bristol considered the suggestion of a Congress far from welcome to Charles III, who felt his sense of self-importance diminished. Distinct possibilities of friction were indicated when Spain revived points of dispute dormant since the 1751 Treaty with Britain; that the right of British lumber-men to cut logwood along the shores of the Gulf of Honduras, recognised by the Treaty of Utrecht and worth £100,000 p.a., had been carried beyond the agreed limit had some truth; the time-worn arguments about the right of search, let alone a claim to participate in the Newfoundland Fisheries, never before exercised or even seriously asserted, looked ominous.[37] If Charles III carried his resentment to the point of a threat to intervene, the war might prove as lengthy if not as fruitless as the War of the Austrian Succession. Pitt was right to make clear, though with all courtesy, that advice from Spain was not required. On 17 December he assured the House of Commons that Frederick must on no account be left the victim of his enemies as a result of Britain and France making a separate peace.[38] Pitt's ability to fulfil his word must, however, depend upon the life of the King and Newcastle's friendship.

By common consent 1759 stands, with 1588, 1704, 1815 and 1940, as one of the greatest in our modern annals. To Pitt the months had had their disappointments and indeed moments of alarm; the final endeavours had fallen considerably short of his sanguine expectations of the spring season; the French were still in Montreal; in the West Indies Guadeloupe alone had been taken. Pitt had underestimated obstacles capable of baffling even Wolfe's genius. But the overall achievement was none the less most impressive and irresistible to the pride of the nation. The destruction of the French navy at Lagos and Quiberon Bay meant that French Canada could almost certainly never be restored and possession of the Ohio Valley, which had been the *casus belli*, must pass to Britain. The French Windward Islands lay at Pitt's mercy whenever he chose to mount an expedition. In southern India the elimination of French power was merely a matter of time and Clive's agent John Walsh had pointed out to Pitt the possibility of acquiring an empire of fabulous wealth. Minden had been the salvation of Frederick, though Prince Ferdinand warned Pitt that the survival of his army in fighting condition for another year must be in doubt. That William Pitt the Younger should have been born in the year of his father's triumphs is one of the most singular coincidences furnished by history.

When on 7 January 1760 Pitt addressed a circular to the Governors of North America calling for men, money and supplies, he may have reflected that the war for Canada, which he had expected to be a settled thing by the end of the preceding summer, still presented considerable prospect of bloodshed and expense. That day, too, Pitt wrote to Amherst, to whom he left every latitude in choosing measures for the reduction of Montreal. Amherst's plan was that Murray ascend the St Lawrence from Quebec, supported by flanking movements from Lake Champlain commanded by William Haviland and from Niagara directed by himself in person. As always Pitt went into considerable detail about batteaus for Lakes Champlain and Niagara, supplies of fresh meat and pork and the despatch of additional tents from home. Finally, in a charming postscript Pitt passed on a request from the Duchess of Aiguillon that the Hotel Dieu at Quebec be looked after: the nuns had shown tireless solicitude for the wounded after the Battle of Quebec.

In the expectation that the Montreal campaign would be swift and simple, Pitt ordered Amherst to send 8,000 men to Guadeloupe, with the reduction of Martinique, and perhaps of St Lucia and Dominica too in view. Pitt knew Amherst had artillery to spare and convoys would be sent from England to North America to convey the expedition to the Windward Islands. These instructions, duly acknowledged by Amherst on

8 March, were shortly followed by an order for the complete destruction of the fortress of Louisbourg of which the utility was superannuated. Saunders was summoned home to the Mediterranean command and was replaced by the 7th Lord Colville.[39] During the spring Pitt was still engaged in his tiresome negotiations with Charles III of Spain who, concerned to step back a little, recalled d'Abreu and sent Count Fuentes as Ambassador. While at home Pitt organised the *coup de grace* for French Canada, in India Sir Eyre Coote soundly beat the enemy at Wandewash on 21 January, which confined the French within the walls of Pondicherry.

The ministerial bickerings, which had thrown rather a shadow over the glories of 1759, continued; the King hankered after compensation for the ruin of his Electorate; the affair of a certain nobleman's blue ribbon, which should have been laid to rest, still rankled. Newcastle, full of imaginary complaints about ill-treatment from the King and Lady Yarmouth, made matters worse by pressing the King to give Temple the Garter at once instead of waiting until the recess. Temple was furious at Newcastle's interfering and the King disgruntled. At the same time a minor constitutional question arose when Beckford, Sir John Philipps and a group of Tories persuaded Pitt to endorse a Qualification bill which would require members of Parliament to take the oath as to their property on taking their seats as well as before election. Hardwicke and Mansfield were both of the opinion that the request could not reasonably be turned down. On 30 January Devonshire saw the King and tried to smooth matters. His Majesty pooh-poohed Newcastle's grumbling and complained that he was always trying to manoeuvre for position. Devonshire strongly advised him to get the affair of Temple's Garter over with. The King was nettled:

'You know I promised to do it at ye end of the Session. I will keep my word, why am I to be plagu'd? I don't care to do it sooner.'

'Good God S^r,' exclaimed Devonshire, 'what can it signifye to yr. Majesty whether you do it now or three months hence, is it worth while to risque putting yr. affairs into confusion for such a trifle?'

Devonshire went on to point out that the reign owed all its

glory to Pitt, to which the King retorted that it was he who was giving support to popular measures such as the Qualification bill. Devonshire rather cunningly indicated that Pitt, by giving way to the Tories in a matter of no consequence, enabled himself to support further the King's continental affairs: Tory measures were the price for Prince Ferdinand's army and cheap at that. He ended the audience by once more urging that Temple be given the Garter promptly: 'I c'd not get a promise but we parted in very good humour.'

On the following day Devonshire saw Lady Yarmouth, who thought Newcastle's grumbling 'quite childish', and when on the next and last day of the month he again saw her she said the King would give Temple the Garter without delay. Devonshire was with every ground annoyed on receiving that afternoon a letter from Temple declaring that after all that had passed he must decline: 'I put it in my pocket & from Court went to see Mr. Pitt, told him wt was done & complained of Ld. Temple's manner. . . .' But Devonshire and Newcastle decided it were better to overlook Temple's cross-grained impertinence and each wrote him a fulsome letter of congratulation. The 31 January ended with George II giving Newcastle a humorous reprimand: 'The King ask'd D. of Newcastle how he cou'd be such a Fool as to think him chang'd, which satisfy'd his Grace.' Temple was appointed a Knight on 9 February and, to keep matters even, a young and very rich Newcastle Whig, the 2nd Marquis of Rockingham, who had since 1751 been a Lord of the Bedchamber, and Prince Ferdinand were similarly honoured. The Prince of Wales thought Temple 'childishly overjoyed at the thought of what I call his dishonour'; even so Bute sent his felicitations.[40] There was a story that the King, instead of laying the ribbon decorously upon Temple's shoulder, cast it over his back and turned away with mutterings of disgust at his new Companion.

The Temple affair had been private: popular attention was riveted upon Sackville, whom the King had decided should be court martialled. At the end of February he was placed under technical arrest, but now came a difficulty. No formal charges had been prepared, so at the request of Pratt and Yorke Holderness wrote asking him upon what counts he proposed offering a defence. Lord George joined issue with the very proper request that he be prosecuted for any crime of which he might be thought guilty. When on 7 March the trial opened, Sackville was charged with his failure to obey Prince Ferdinand's order and he defended himself with an altogether arrogant self-confidence. The trial ended on 5 April and conviction was a foregone conclusion, but his civilian status, the consequent legal doubts and no doubt the influence of Leicester House, saved him the fate of Byng. He was left unpunished apart from being 'adjudged unfit ever to serve his Majesty in any military capacity whatsoever'. So as to expose Lord George to the gravest possible insult the King ordered that the sentence be read out before every contingent in Europe and in America, 'so that officers may be convinced that neither high birth nor great employments can shelter offences of such a nature'. Sackville, to Newcastle's indignation, appeared at his seat in the House of Commons: 'I did not hear that his Lordship had any acceuil from anybody.' Horace Walpole however shrewdly observed: 'I think this is not the last we shall hear of him.'[41] Although the King had forbidden Sackville the Court, on 18 April Lady Yarmouth warned Newcastle that Leicester House proposed receiving him. The King sent Devonshire with a command that Sackville was not to be countenanced. The Prince kicked out with a petulant letter to Bute, replete with discontent at being told whom to receive in his own house.[42]

Bute chose this inopportune season to come out into the open with Pitt about his taking control as First Lord of the Treasury on the death of George II. When on 30 April Elliot called upon Pitt to prepare the ground, Pitt indicated that it would be in the national interest that Newcastle should continue in power; there was no reason to suppose Bute acceptable to the Whig party. At once the Prince of Wales ardently affirmed his intention to get rid of Pitt: '. . . the late instance in the transaction with Mr. P. is perhaps the strongest that ever happened to a man of your strong sensations; he has shown himself most ungrateful and in my mind the most dishonourable of men, I can never bear to see him in any future Ministry; . . .'.[43] Evidently the Prince and Bute considered that Pitt ought to foster Bute into the highest place in return for their support in the past.

Elliot, who fancied himself as a bit of a king-maker, was distressed at the possibility of a breach between his friends. To him
Pitt gave a lecture on his concept of his ministerial duties and
made clear that he would never find in Bute a workable
colleague.[44]

Pitt knew he had to bring the war to a successful conclusion.
On 3 April Russia and Austria had made clear to Choiseul that
negotiations which included Prussia would be construed as a
breach of the alliance. In the following month the plan for a
Congress was abandoned. Frederick was convinced that
Choiseul did not intend peace and urged Pitt to carry on the
naval war. Pitt was planning an expedition to the East, although
not on the lines Clive had suggested. The plan was to take
Mauritius, the naval base upon which the French position in
India ultimately rested. He envisaged an army of 10,000 men
and a fleet commanded by Keppel, on the model that had
proved so successful in seizing Guadeloupe. The assemblage of
so large a force and its rumoured destination alarmed Versailles
and d'Aché was ordered not to leave Mauritius for the relief of
Pondicherry when the monsoon ended. The doom of Lally and
of French power in India were made certain.

During the spring and summer the great ministry passed
through its Indian summer and such disputes as took place were
more Pitt's fault than Newcastle's. The mood of the nation was
one of united self-confidence; during the year trade to the value
of over £400,000 poured in from Guadeloupe. Quiberon had
freed troops held for home defence and Newcastle was set upon
reinforcements for Granby: 'I am now in hope to send you a
good body of infantry. Three or four good and strong battalions
are certain: but I will not be contented without six, and I hope
to succeed. Mr. Pitt is very reasonable but he has his apprehensions at home.' Granby's army was increased to 22,000, a greater
contingent than had served under Marlborough during the
War of the Spanish Succession. But French troops, too, were
released by the collapse of Choiseul's plan of invasion and they
had 100,000 men to the Prince's 80,000. Broglie was the best
general ever sent against Prince Ferdinand and popular with
his men, though much disliked at Versailles where there were
constant intrigues for his dismissal. Consequently he had always

to consult Belleisle, whilst the Prince had the advantage of operational independence.

Both the Hanoverian and French armies were late in taking the field. The Prince blamed his delays upon the failure of the treasury to refurbish his magazines and complained to Pitt behind Newcastle's back. The inevitable squabble blew up in April with an indignant rebuttal of the Prince's allegations by Newcastle in a letter to Granby: 'I little expected this, and that the charge – heavy as it is should be conveyed to Mr. Pitt, and not one word said of it by his Highness to me, though he had then before him one or two letters from me unanswered.' Newcastle blamed the shortcomings of his department upon his agents in Germany, though he generously decided against any dismissals. He was given no consolation by Pitt: 'Mr. Pitt will not say a word upon it. *It is not in his department.*' Broglie was in no position to take advantage of Prince Ferdinand's difficulties. He could not open his campaign until May because he was hampered by a shortage of money and Hesse was so devastated that he had constant forage problems.

The truth was that a general war-weariness was beginning to affect all the combatants. Newcastle tried to prod Prince Ferdinand into vigorous action: 'If you can, strike a good blow, before they begin with the King of Prussia, I shall have the greatest hopes of the success of the campaign, and of a good peace at the end of it.' Newcastle, genuinely keen on the German war and wishing to convince Prince Ferdinand of his goodwill, wrote triumphantly to Granby in June: 'I hope the Prince sees there is no want of money *at present* – £158,000 l. in cash and £150,000 on the road cannot be called a want of money. Mr. de Broglie would rejoice at half as much.'[45]

Although Amherst had made every preparation for the final blow, things were not destined to move as smoothly as he and Pitt were anticipating. Surprisingly, the weak spot lay at Quebec, where Murray was in command; cold and scurvy had killed 1,000 of his men and put a further 2,000 into hospital. At Halifax Colville had his ships in readiness to put men and provisions into Quebec, but foul weather confined him to port. De Lévis came up from Montreal with 10,000 men with the daring intention of avenging Montcalm's death by recapturing

Quebec. Murray could muster only 4,000 and brave if fool-hardy sallied forth to give battle on the Heights of Abraham on 28 April. The fight was appallingly bloody, Murray having one third of his army killed or wounded and the French suffering 2,500 casualties. Forced to abandon his guns to the enemy, Murray was confined within the walls of Quebec. During the first week in May he managed to send out word of his predicament to Amherst, who forwarded news of the disaster to Pitt in a despatch of the 19th which arrived in London on 17 June.[46]

Pitt was already depressed by the lack of enthusiasm of the North American Assemblies now that 'Notions of Peace' were rumoured. Murray's defeat came as a complete surprise. With his swiftness of tactical vision Pitt saw clearly and with horror the precarious situation of the Quebec garrison. All depended upon Murray's being relieved and that must rest with the hazards of navigation in the north-west Atlantic. There was certainly nothing Amherst, still less Pitt, could do and the further danger was that a French naval squadron might reach Quebec before Colville could come in from Halifax. Full of foreboding that the issue must in any case already have been decided, Pitt in his reply to Amherst of 20 June expressed complete confidence that Colville could stop French help reaching Quebec. If it turned out that Murray had been forced to surrender, the St Lawrence must be blockaded. At Quebec the hopes and fears of Murray and de Lévis were exactly as Pitt had perceived. Each lay in daily expectation of help from the sea and neither was strong enough to force an issue unaided. But the Atlantic storms which had kept Colville idle also held up the flotilla expected by de Lévis. When on 9 May a ship appeared it was HMS *Lowestoft*, which had left England on 3 March. A week later Captain Swanton arrived with several men-of-war, and de Lévis broke up camp and retreated to Montreal with only half the gallant 10,000 who had accompanied him. On the following day Colville, with the main fleet, lay off Quebec.[47]

When on 27 June word arrived in London that Quebec was safe, Pitt exclaimed by letter to Lady Hester: 'Oh! happy day, my joy and excitement are indescribable.' Newcastle entertained Pitt at Claremont and, like the sound patriot he was, wrote to Temple: 'Everything looks well in that part of the world.'[48] Pitt knew that Amherst could carry out his pincer movement against Montreal with complete decision. Whilst Amherst and Haviland closed in from the west and the south, Murray with 2,000 of his garrison, accompanied by the regiments taken from Louisbourg, set out down river. On 8 September de Vaudreuil, the French Governor, surrendered all Canada to the British Crown. Under the Capitulation the free exercise of the rites of the Roman Catholic church was guaranteed. The French army was accorded full honours of war and the undertaking of conveyance home by the British navy subject to parole. That day Amherst sent Pitt the last despatch of the campaign, which he entrusted to Barré, who had been Wolfe's Adjutant-General.[49] At the same time he asked permission to return home.

Decisive victory in Germany was the only way by which the French might win compensation for the loss of Canada. Broglie's lieutenant du Muy was defeated on 31 July at Warburg when Granby led one of the most celebrated cavalry charges in British history, but this reverse was more than counterbalanced by the French capture of Cassel. That autumn Prince Ferdinand attempted without success to take Frederick's fortress of Wesel on the Rhine, which the French had occupied since the beginning of the war. Frederick could not have been expected to do more than hold his own against the Austrians and Russians by whom he was completely outnumbered. He led a life of constant personal danger, nightly changing his quarters for fear of capture by Austrian patrols. On 23 June a Prussian army was beaten at Landshut with the loss of Saxony and most of Silesia. Fortunately for Frederick the Russians did not, as in 1759 at Künersdorf, attempt to move in concert with the Austrians but concentrated on the investment of Colberg on the Pomeranian coast.

Through 1760 the British victories had continued and Pitt was the hero of the nation. Under the provisions of the Septennial Act a new Parliament was due to be elected in the summer of 1761 and Newcastle saw in Pitt's popularity a factor to be reckoned with. To Hardwicke Newcastle poured out his anxieties at great length, his chief worry being that Pitt, from some motive of ill humour, might want to put in a great many

Tories; he quaintly remarked: 'Whereas, if Pitt was really in good humour, I am persuaded he would leave it all to me, and not trouble his head about it, with only perhaps desiring some of his particular friends to be taken care of, which to be sure is reasonable.' Having no serious desire to let Pitt into his confidence over the entire general election, Newcastle ruefully recalled how Fox had buckled under in 1754. Hardwicke sympathised with him about not consulting Pitt but at the same time pointed out: 'Mr. Pitt's situation in the House of Commons and in the Ministry, which is very different to what Mr. Fox's was.'[50]

Towards the end of 1760 there were strong peace parties in Vienna and Paris; Choiseul would have been ready to consider a separate treaty with Britain and there was little doubt that negotiations would be held during 1761. Although Prince Ferdinand had lost momentum, Frederick, as in the great days of Rossbach and Leuthen, saved his kingdom by a brilliant campaign in Saxony. At Leignitz in September he survived the concentric attack of three Austrian armies. Then, ignoring a raid on Berlin, Frederick, with 50,000 men, beat Daun with 63,000 at Torgau on 1 November. Pitt decided that above all Prince Ferdinand must be supported. In a sudden burst of enthusiasm he discarded his plan for an expedition to Mauritius and decided on the capture of Belleisle off the coast of the Morbihan.

Newcastle was full of complaints; a raid upon Boulogne he was prepared to consider, but the huge expense entailed by holding Belleisle, once captured, he would not countenance. Pitt, however, won over the King and accordingly demanded of the Admiralty transport adequate for 10,000 soldiers. Newcastle tried to persuade Anson and Ligonier that it was too late in the year, but Anson thought the good weather might hold till the middle of November and Ligonier suggested putting forward the embarkation date: 'I expected to have been supported by my Admiral and General,' wailed Newcastle, 'but that was not my good fortune.' Keppel gave evidence to the Cabinet that the Belleisle beaches were covered by the guns of the citadel and that shallow water went out too far for men-of-war to offer a supporting bombardment. Newcastle fussed, so Pitt asked Anson to get a report from Hawke.[51] The Belleisle project was turned by the Prince of Wales into further occasion for suspicion of Pitt who he thought, once he had the troops, would divert them to Germany. On 5 October he wrote to Bute: 'I hope this nation will open her eyes and see who are her true friends, and that her popular man is a true snake in the grass.'[52] The controversy received what Pitt must have considered a most welcome interruption by the arrival of Barré on 8 October with Amherst's announcement of the Capitulation of Canada. Nothing could have given Pitt more pleasure than the Address of the City of London: '. . . big with a million in every line', wrote he to Grenville.[53]

Anson went beyond what the Cabinet had authorised. When on 9 October he asked Hawke to report upon the feasibility of the Belleisle enterprise, which was all Pitt wanted, he had Clevland enclose a covering letter which contained this sentence: 'His Lordship depends upon your thoroughly considering what prospect there may be of success, and would be glad to be favoured with your private thoughts in a separate letter on this subject.' From his flagship in the Channel Hawke, with considerable naïveté, answered both Anson and Clevland in one report of 17 October. He thought the whole idea of Belleisle a waste of resources: 'But suppose it be taken, will the possession of a place detached by water from the Continent draw troops from any part of that Continent to retake it, while we are masters of the sea. . . .' Hawke went on to propose a quite different scheme for placing a permanent bridgehead on the Morbihan coast; the French could not treat with indifference an establishment upon their mainland.[54] Characteristically, 24 October found Pitt acknowledging Amherst's despatch of 8 September and pressing him to move against Mobile and Mississippi: that request to return home was not referred to.[55] That day Anson, with Hawke's letter in his pocket, went to see the King. Newcastle, already in the antechamber, was delighted to hear what that document contained. Whilst Anson was in the royal presence by himself, Pitt arrived to be told by a triumphant Newcastle that the Belleisle scheme was scotched. Pitt was indignant at not being shown the letter first and when Anson came out refused to enter without reading it. Newcastle went in next and afterwards Pitt, to be greeted by the King with these words: 'Sir Edward Hawke thinks the scheme is impracticable and I will not send my troops *à la boucherie.*' Pitt joined Anson and Newcastle and ran down Hawke over what he thought a singular piece of impertinence; the Admiral was 'a very good sea officer but no minister' and the letter deserved to be read out in the House of Commons.[56]

That evening Pitt went to see Lady Yarmouth to persuade her. But the commands of George II mattered no longer, for 24 October was the last day of his life. At half past eight next morning he was found dead in the lavatory by his valet de chambre, with whom the Prince of Wales had already arranged a way of proceeding. A royal messenger was sent and he encountered his new Sovereign, who was taking exercise, just before reaching Kew Bridge. He announced that the King had met with an accident, but the true meaning was perfectly taken and the servants were warned on pain of their employments not to gossip of this meeting. Later that morning the Prince received a letter from his aunt, Princess Amelia, giving him an account of the King's death and he at once sent to Bute the following note, his first written communication as Sovereign: 'I am coming the back way to your house. I have receiv'd a letter from my Aunt with an account of the late King my grand-father's death; the coach will soon be ready.'[57]

CHAPTER 10

The New Reign:
Lord Bute the Favourite

'Quoth Newcastle to Pitt, 'tis in vain to dispute;
   If we'd quarrel in private, we must make room for Bute.
Quoth Pitt to his Grace, to bring that about,
   I fear, my dear Lord, you or I must turn out.
Not at all, quoth the Duke, I meant no such thing,
   To make room for us all, we must turn out the King.
If that's all your scheme, quoth the Earl, by my troth,
   I shall stick by my master, and turn ye out Both.'

George Bubb Dodington: lines addressed by him to the
3rd Earl of Bute, 22 December 1760.[1]

It was a Saturday and Pitt's coach was standing to take him
from St James's Square to Hayes when Lady Yarmouth asked
him to Kensington Palace. There he was told of George II's
death by Princess Amelia, the late King's daughter. As Newcastle was at Claremont and Hardwicke at Wimpole, Pitt took
it upon himself to summon all Privy Councillors to town. He
then drove to Kew and was received by Bute before being
admitted to pay his condolences. Newcastle on his arrival
shortly afterwards was also ushered into Bute's presence as the
preliminary to his audience. With all sincerity he assured his
young master of his ardent desire to serve him as loyally as he

had his grandfather, to receive the reply: 'My Lord Bute is your good friend; he will tell you my thoughts at large.' Pitt and Newcastle were put in no doubt that Bute was the man of the occasion.

The Privy Council was held at Carlton House on the north side of the Mall at six o'clock that evening. Although Bute was not a Privy Councillor he was present, an irregularity no one was so indiscreet as to make matter of. George III had his Address ready, composed by Bute but copied out in the King's own hand, which Newcastle was commanded to read out. Pitt stood aghast as he heard the concluding words: '. . . as I mount the throne in the midst of a bloody war, I shall endeavour to prosecute it in the manner most likely to bring an honourable and lasting peace'. Pitt could not allow that phrase 'a bloody war' to pass without protest: to publish the Address as delivered would cause unease at Berlin and satisfaction at Versailles. He asked that 'a bloody war' be amended to 'an expensive but just and necessary war' and the words 'in concert with our allies' be added to 'an honourable and lasting peace'. Bute tried to insist that the public version must follow the spoken but Mansfield ruled that the King might vary his own hand.[2]

By then it was seven o'clock and, according to Elliot's account, 'Lord Bute whisper'd to Mr. Pitt that he wish'd to see him that evening late as it was'. Bute opened the conversation by referring to the occasion six months before when Pitt had firmly rejected any notion of his taking the Treasury. With complete insincerity he told Pitt that he would take matters up 'with the same spirit as if nothing had ever interrupted their friendship' and that, had this meeting taken place last April, 'he would have inform'd him that he had laid aside thoughts of being First Lord of the Treasury, meant to hold the situation of a private man at the side of the King . . .'. Feeling himself challenged, Pitt made clear that meddling in the conduct of the war would not be tolerated: '. . . he too wished to be a private man if he could once see his country out of the present plunge; the only difference between them was that his Lordship would practice his philosophy in a court, and he in a village'.[3]

The death of the old King, together with Bute's intrusion, created a general sense of insecurity. Newcastle had an old crony, Count Viry, the Sardinian Ambassador in London, a keen observer of men, women and things, who welcomed the opportunity to play *éminence grise*. In days a tale got around that Pitt had suggested Bute should take the Treasury with his full co-operation. Probably this story was of Viry's imagination: either the tale of how Pitt 'lowered himself' was utterly false, or the King and Bute judged that the time was not yet ripe and ignored his overtures. Certainly the plan the King had nursed for over four years, to place Bute into the highest office at his accession, was not attempted. But Newcastle, Hardwicke and Devonshire were convinced that Pitt had offered to betray them.[4] Whatever the truth, the King and Bute were merely biding their time: stories true or false that might sow suspicion between Pitt and Newcastle would not find a disclaimer at Court.

The change from the first two Georges, unblushingly lacking affection for the country of their adoption, was generally welcome. The King issued a Proclamation to his peoples containing the satisfactory assurance that he 'gloried in the name of Britain'. The nation was called upon to expect a new era of honesty and virtue, a promise George III was never to break in his personal conduct. It was a time for reconciliation; the King went out of his way to show respect for his uncle Cumberland; the descendants of the old Tories of 1714 were welcome where formerly they had been shunned, a development Newcastle feared would prove advantageous to Pitt. Old stagers too, whose conduct or lack of principle had once incurred censure, turned up; Bath, the traitor to the old Whig opposition, came to Court; Dodington was out for a peerage; Dashwood wanted office; Sackville, too, was standing in the wings.

Pitt, Newcastle and Bute each found his sense of self-interest and concept of honour to some degree at variance. Pitt was the idol of the country, yet here as King was a boy of twenty-two under Bute's thumb. He knew that Newcastle would sacrifice almost anything for his love of power. For his part Newcastle, sixty-seven years of age, pondered whether the time had come to retire gracefully. But his very real patriotism, his affection for the Whig party and his sense of responsibility towards the many for whom he had provided employment, all conspired to

make him decide to carry on. Bute had what Pitt and Newcastle
envied and feared, the ability to manipulate the mind of the
King, but he discerned the jealousies his position must engender.
At the same time Bute was, just as were Pitt and Newcastle, a
man of honour; he sincerely wished his young master to open his
reign well and recognised that the country needed Pitt – at
least until peace was in sight. He knew also that the King, far
from holding Pitt in honour, wanted to be rid of him and to that
end Newcastle could be useful. The King and Bute, however,
had no intention of calling a halt there. To George III Newcastle
was the real enemy and he willed to elevate Bute for the purpose
of decomposing the Duke's tortuous hold, maintained by craft
and cunning ever since the reign of his great-grandfather. Only
the exigencies of the war restrained George III from treating
both Pitt and Newcastle to contemptuous dismissals.

The King's inexperience placed him at a natural disadvantage. Yet he had the telling advantage that although a boy
of his age might fail to outwit the politicians he must be expected
to outlive them. For the present he had but two ambitions,
firstly to marry, and secondly to guide his country firmly along
principles of virtue, for which laudable purpose only one man
from all his subjects was conceivable, Bute. But though Newcastle might be just a corrupt old wire-puller and Pitt an ungrateful hypocrite, the nation felt the victories of the war were
owing to their collaboration. And the young man prided himself somewhat upon taking the character of John Bull – he too
was a patriot.

For the present Bute was appointed a Privy Councillor and
the King ordered his attendance at Cabinet meetings; 'great
court paid to his Lordship', observed Devonshire. Bute repeated
to Temple the assurance he had given Pitt, that he 'wou'd
remain a Private Man'. Then on 27 October Bute conveyed to
Newcastle the King's wish that he should continue at the
Treasury. Newcastle talked to Devonshire of retirement but was
dissuaded: 'I thought he owed it to his friends & ye Whig
party who wou'd be broke to pieces and turn'd adrift.' Devonshire considered that every movement of the Favourite needed
watching and told Newcastle that as Parliament was soon to
meet it would be wiser not to consider resignation until the end

of the session: '. . . by that time likewise he would be able to judge what wou'd become or what was to be done with Ld. Bute who by all yt appears seems not only ignorant of Business but visionary, for it was plain by every step that he meant to be ye Minister over them all & yet had no plan of administration or even thought of ye practicability of effecting it'. Devonshire had summed Bute up precisely. The Favourite was utterly ignorant of the *carte du pays*; he in no way grasped how requisite was Newcastle's influence in the City for raising war loans, let alone such refinements as the Duke's dependence upon Hardwicke.[5] Yet Newcastle, full of forebodings, wrote to Joseph Yorke, Ambassador at The Hague, 'I have lost the best King, the best Master and the best friend that subject ever had. God knows what consequences it may have.'[6] He knew the coming session of Parliament must be followed by the general election, over which he now had the new King and the Favourite to come to terms with, besides the probability that Pitt, the nation's darling, would insist on having a say.

Devonshire cast for himself the role of honest broker. On the second day of the reign he went to Temple and urged upon him that Pitt and Newcastle must work together for the good of the country. He suggested that Pitt might show more regard for the Old Whigs – 'less to his Tories, tho' I did not desire him to quarrel with them'. Furthermore, an accord between Pitt and Newcastle was the one way of checking Bute. Devonshire, however, found Temple's mood distinctly reserved: '. . . convinc'd me that Bute and them were better together and come more to an understanding than he wou'd own to me'. Later that day Pitt, probably at Temple's instigation, came to Devonshire and talked of his willingness to work with Bute provided the German war continued and no countenance was given to Sackville, 'which w^d deservedly give uneasiness to P. Ferdinand'. On the day following his talks with Temple and Pitt, Devonshire saw Viry, who poured out the story of Pitt's self-abasement on the day of the King's accession into ears a little too willing: 'I told him my suspicion that Ld. Bute was agreed with Pitt and Temple, he own'd it was true, yt. immediately on ye death of ye King yt. Pitt humbled himself and was accepted . . .'.

At once Devonshire called on Pitt, who offered counsel so

manifestly in Newcastle's best interests that they should have been reassured. Pitt pointed out that Newcastle must at once close with the King's wish that he continue at the Treasury, for delay would create doubt as to his goodwill. Devonshire pressed the point of view that it was for Pitt and Newcastle to collaborate: 'I found he had some difficulties & at bottom was apprehensive yt. Lord Bute wou'd be jealous if there was too close a union.' Later that day, on meeting Devonshire at Court, Pitt reiterated his advice: 'At Court Mr. Pitt came up to me & said yt. ye D. of Newcastle's indecision wou'd have very bad effects yt. he found Ld. Bute & ye King began to grow uneasy that it had the appearance as if his Grace wanted to fetter them, & that they desired to have his final answer that they might know what they had to depend upon.' There followed a touching scene in which Bute, Pitt and Newcastle came together in a state of mutual accord. Devonshire was witness to the strongest assurances of goodwill between Pitt and Newcastle. Bute promised Newcastle that the choice of the House of Commons at the forthcoming general election would be his. That assurance from Bute was all Newcastle wanted and for the moment quite cured his apprehensions.

The very next day any possibility of a secret understanding between Pitt and Bute was rudely shattered. Sackville turned up at the levee, to be accorded a gracious reception. Pitt told Bute off very roughly and was in no way appeased by the weak excuse that Sackville's appearance had been unexpected.[7] So on 1 November Devonshire called on Pitt with his usual object of soothing ruffled emotions. Bored at Pitt's ranting away about Sackville, Devonshire changed the subject to another *bête noire*, Hawke's letter on Belleisle. Pitt reiterated his condemnation of Hawke and asked Devonshire to speak to Newcastle about a Cabinet meeting; only two questions need be asked, of Anson whether the ships could get near enough to cover a landing, and of Ligonier whether a winter siege was practicable. Pitt was confident of affirmative answers to both and the conversation ended with him in a good way.

Devonshire felt Pitt's indignation over Sackville very understandable. When on the day following he attended Court at St James's Palace, Newcastle at once called over to him about

Pitt's being 'out of humour'. When Devonshire agreed that such was the case, Bute waxed indignant and expressed his complete lack of understanding of Pitt's behaviour. Devonshire decided to put Bute in his place:

'I think it very necessary to have some management for Mr. Pitt, affairs are in such a situation that it is impossible to do without him; you can neither carry on the war nor make peace without his assistance.'

'My Lord,' Bute exclaimed, 'I would not for the world that the King should hear such Language he would not bear it a moment.'

'Not bear it!' retorted Devonshire, 'he must bear it, every King must make use of human means to attain human ends or his affairs will go to ruin.'

Fortunately Bute was at this point summoned to attend the King, who after a while came out of the Closet to return to Carlton House. As the courtiers went down the backstairs to go home Bute turned to Devonshire and said 'I will go this afternoon to Mr. Pitt.' That evening Bute spent one and a half hours with Pitt and Temple and no doubt received a proper dressing down. Temple took the opportunity to remind him that Pitt had been promised a favourable reference to the militia in the King's Speech when Parliament opened. Sackville was soon discreetly told not to attend Court.

Pitt, in a thoroughly unhappy mood, saw Newcastle and Devonshire on 5 November. Devonshire's account ran: 'Pitt said to me My Ld. I can call it nothing but the shell of an administration. I like not the appearance; we can not go on in this manner.' Later that day Devonshire saw Bute and disclaimed the accusation that the Old Whigs wished to dictate to the King. At considerable length he explained why Pitt and Newcastle were indispensable; the triumphs of the war had 'rais'd an infatuation in the minds of ye People' – if Pitt quitted now and the situation in Germany further deteriorated: 'he wou'd have to say that when first I came to be Minister I found this country sunk to nothing & hastening to its ruin, that by proper measures & a proper exertion of its strength ye honour and glory of it is restored: & now other measures are pursued yt. he could not agree to, & in consequence our affairs are going back again; this sort of Language which wou'd undoubtedly be held wou'd raise such a Flame as could not be withstood.' But, continued Devonshire, just as Pitt's popularity had to be taken into account, equally Newcastle commanded circumstances conservative and tangible – 'the Principal Nobility, the Moneyed men and ye Interests which had brought about ye Revolution, and had set this Family on the Throne . . .'.

Meanwhile the ordinary business of government had to carry on. That evening Pitt, Bute, Hardwicke and Newcastle discussed the King's Speech for the opening of Parliament. There was no argument until at the close Pitt asked that some words on the militia be included and Bute, mindful of that evening talk with him and Temple three days previous, came out in support. Newcastle and Hardwicke disagreed and Pitt remained firm yet calm; they parted without a decision. On 7 November Pitt saw Devonshire again and expressed the hope that the bare mention of the militia would not be taken amiss. Five days later Pitt showed the final draft of the Speech to the King who gave voice to some disappointment that the militia was not mentioned more strongly 'but saw the necessity of acquiescing'.

There was a Cabinet meeting on 12 November, at which the decision whether or not to attack Belleisle had to be taken. Although Ligonier and Anson gave their professional opinions against the expedition, they declared themselves unwilling actually to oppose. When Mansfield weakly announced his intention of abiding by them, Newcastle lost his temper. As Legge and everyone else supported Pitt, and Devonshire was absent, Newcastle and Hardwicke found themselves in a minority of two. Evidently, uncertain though Pitt and Bute were with each other, generally they agreed over policy. Bute, a novice in the art of government, knew himself to stand in the shadow of the man who had won the war. As the militia and Belleisle were Tory, 'blue-water' policies, it need not have occasioned surprise that Bute should follow Pitt's lead. When Newcastle and Devonshire saw some dark purpose, they were allowing their fears the upper hand.[8]

It was certainly not Pitt's version that he and Temple had Bute in their grasp. On the contrary, he was complaining that although Leader of the House of Commons he was never con-

sulted, not even over the Civil List for the new reign; there was
to be a batch of peerages to mark the King's accession and Pitt
wanted creations for Grosvenor and Spencer, his one-time
ward, 'but yt. they gave him no opportunity of recommending
them'. Furthermore, Pitt much disliked Bath and Dodington
having audiences. On 17 November Pitt's uneasiness led him
into a public quarrel with Bute: 'Lord Bute and Pitt had warm
words at Court.' Pitt went protesting to the King whilst Bute
ran round to Temple asking him to keep his brother-in-law in
order. The King sent for Bute to sort matters out, but his summons was ignored: 'rather extraordinary behaviour to a King,
particularly one so exact about his being nicely treated', was
Devonshire's comment.[9] Pitt's colleagues were becoming restive
at his displays of temper and his ignorance of what went on
between Bute and the King led him to undervalue the importance of Newcastle's friendship. To Bute the King stressed how
fatigued he was at having to soothe 'every ill humour of a
certain man'. He reiterated his intention to force Pitt from
power and felt certain of popular support: '. . . besides I rely
on the hearts of my subjects, the only true support of the Crown;
they will never join a man who from his own ambition, pride
and impracticability, means to disturb my quiet and (what I
feel much stronger) the repose of my subjects; if they could be
so ungrateful to me who love them beyond anything else in life,
I should then I really believe fall into the deepest melancholy
which would soon deprive me of the vexation of life'.[10]

On 25 November Pitt, Newcastle and Legge met to arrange
the Civil List; their recommendation of £800,000 p.a. as a
reasonable figure was accepted by the King, although his
grandfather had been far better off. There then blew up a real
squabble between Pitt and Newcastle. The members of the
Household of the King had already been selected and their
names published when, a week later, on 4 December, five
additions were announced – all Tories.* Newcastle had not even
been informed and enquired of Devonshire whether it was truth
or rumour, only to be told the whole town knew. Next day
Newcastle remonstrated with Bute, 'and Pitt coming from ye

---

* Lords Bruce and Oxford, George Pitt, Norbonne Berkeley and Northey
became Lords and Grooms of the Bedchamber.

King join'd them & took it up strongly owned himself ye advisor & thus it was the wisest step yt. could be taken to preserve ye unanimity & make ye King's reign quiet'. Then Pitt called on Devonshire and expressed his surprise that Newcastle and the Whigs could possibly take umbrage at a few Tories being taken into the King's service as 'supernumeraries'; no one had been turned out to make way for them and 'when people of such character offer'd their services they ought to be accepted'. Devonshire acidly replied that he had understood the new appointments to have been unsolicited. With some weakness Pitt claimed to have advised only as to the measure and not as to the individuals. The whole thing, Devonshire snapped back, had been badly done; Newcastle had been cruelly treated and to make these additions, a week after matters had been settled, made it look a royal measure undertaken without ministerial advice. Pitt agreed about Newcastle, but 'as to the other it was a refinement'.

Pitt did not come out of this episode with credit. He had lost what little suasion he had with Newcastle and Devonshire, whilst Bute was telling Newcastle how he preferred his methods to Pitt's – 'he could feel what his Grace had endured for two years'. Newcastle plunged straight into the choosing of the new Parliament: 'Ld. Bute reply'd yt. ye King desir'd to see a List of his own Burroughs that the King he suppos'd was to have ye nomination to them, that His Majesty was against spending any Money & so was Mr. Pitt, who said ye King ought to have a Parliament composed of all his People, as they were all unanimous for him.' Newcastle and Devonshire took this to indicate a Tory bias that would let in many of Pitt's supporters. Devonshire therefore advised Newcastle to prepare his own schedule for a Parliament with full explanations for any money required, lay it before the King and, if he met with any substantial objection, resign.[11]

Bedford's arrival in London at this juncture was a further portent of difficulty for Pitt. He was not, as Lord Lieutenant, obliged to stay in Dublin for more than a year consecutively and had no wish to resume residence. In the hope of securing a little independence for the Irish Parliament, the Lords Justices in Dublin sent over two minor pieces of legislation for the royal consent, unaccompanied by the customary money bill. At a Cabinet of 2 December Bedford insisted that the usual principle be observed, despite disagreement from Pitt who, without dividing the meeting, refused to sign the letter of remonstrance approved by the ministers. The Dublin mob burned Bedford's effigy, though the effect upon the Irish parties, always balanced between a search for popularity and a very practical interest in bounties from administration, was short-lived. But Bedford never returned to Dublin, was entitled to attend Cabinet meetings in London and had no cause to thank Pitt for making his path more awkward.[12]

On 6 December Viry, intent on mischief, called on Devonshire to assure him that Pitt and the Court were far from united: 'the temper of Pitt was not to be borne nor submitted to, yt. ye King was quite tir'd of him, but that they must keep him to make the Peace and then they hoped to be in a situation to get rid of him, that therefore in regard to choosing ye Parliament they meant to consult ye D. of Newcastle for that if he did not do it, Mr. Pitt would get greater weight and become more formidable and more troublesome'. Devonshire saw the chance of Newcastle's settling the new Parliament in conjunction with Bute and more or less cutting Pitt out. That evening Newcastle, Devonshire, Hardwicke and their cronies confabulated quite after the manner of old times. Devonshire advised Newcastle to join up with Bute, though 'keeping fair with Mr. Pitt'. Next day, determined to strike while the iron was hot, Devonshire saw Bute at Court and told him that he had advised Newcastle to stay in office provided he could concert measures for a new Parliament. Bute eagerly promised to meet Newcastle's wishes more than half way, at which Devonshire uttered a word of warning: 'I laid great stress on its being done in such a manner as should not give umbrage to Mr. Pitt, who wou'd grow jealous if he saw that they were agreed, & that it would be impossible to go on without him. he assented but shewed great dislike to that set of men.'[13]

Clearly the unity which had marked the great ministry was at an end. Pitt in no way allowed the gyrations of Bute and Newcastle to deter his intention to carry the war either to Mobile and Mississippi or the French West Indies. So that British

regulars stationed in North America might be released for
service elsewhere, Pitt on 17 December addressed the Governors
with the request that they maintain their militias at two-thirds
of the complements of 1759. Amherst was warned to prepare
himself and Pitt sent him detailed orders on 7 January. The
principal aim was to be the capture of Martinique which, however, could not be practicable until the hurricane season ended
at the close of September. The interval might well be filled in
by an attempt against Dominica and possibly St Lucia, too, and
for that purpose Amherst was to draft two thousand men to
Guadeloupe at once. He was given the choice of commander
and already had ample artillery. All, however, must depend
upon the arrival of the expedition at Guadeloupe by early May:
it would be to no purpose for the attack upon Martinique to
miscarry because troops were tied up in a subsidiary endeavour.
For the entire service in the West Indies Amherst need send no
more than 8,000 men from North America and adequate
transports were leaving London for New York.[14]

In Europe, apart from continued support for Prince Ferdin-
and, Pitt had also his expedition for Belleisle well under preparation and that was the deciding factor in the campaign for
Pondicherry. There Lally was on his last legs awaiting the sight
of d'Aché's ships. Then he had word from Mauritius that no
help would be forthcoming, for d'Aché was tied by his orders
from Versailles to prepare against a great expedition from
Britain. So as to bolster morale Lally gave out that a great
reinforcement was on the way but he knew the end had come.
Pondicherry capitulated to Coote on 15 January and the
French no longer held anything in India. There can be no more
striking example of the influence of sea power than the im-
mobility of d'Aché's fleet, waiting in vain for an enemy that in
the event never proceeded further than the Bay of Biscay.

Bute was secretly restless at attending Cabinet meetings
without having the authority of office. Grenville and his friend
Jenkinson had every interest in currying favour and very
probably prompted Bute with the idea to become Secretary of
State and Pitt's equal as colleague. Holderness, despised by
both Newcastle and Pitt, clearly was vulnerable. On 10 January
Viry sounded Devonshire, not ostensibly as an emissary from the

Court but merely throwing out in his gossipy way that the King was displeased with Holderness and would like to see Bute in his place. Devonshire advised Viry to be extremely cautious over what he himself thought a most dangerous undertaking, especially as Pitt's point of view was very material. When five days later Newcastle, Devonshire and Hardwicke met at New-castle House, they were not clear whether Viry was acting off his own bat or at Bute's prompting: 'ye latter opinion prevailed'. After the conference Devonshire saw Viry and played the ball back; Bute had better talk the matter over with Pitt – the last advice the Court wanted. Newcastle agreed to a pourparler with Bute fixed for 20 January, though he was very clear that 'Mr. Pitt must not be displeased, and that nothing must be done in which he does not readily concur'.

When that day came Bute pleaded a cold. At the beginning of the third week in January Newcastle called upon Pitt to find out whether he might actually be at the bottom of Bute's desire for office. Newcastle could see from Pitt's manner that he had some inkling of what was afoot but his fears of some intrigue were utterly dispelled by the ferocity of Pitt's reaction to the idea of Bute as Secretary of State. There had been favourites before in history but the nation would never suffer them to be ministers: *'he for one wou'd never consent or lend a helping hand to make him one'*. When that evening a somewhat bewildered Newcastle reported these words to his friends, Hardwicke acidly pointed out that this declaration was very different from Pitt's conduct at the time of the King's accession. Devonshire mused that it was probably Elliot who had leaked to Pitt what was going on. Newcastle shrewdly discerned that Bute in person would never dare to beard Pitt and he and Devonshire made up their minds to do nothing for the present.

When therefore next day Viry suggested to Devonshire that Newcastle broach the subject with the King, he got the very proper reply that without some knowledge of Bute's wishes and of Pitt's concurrence no such move was possible. Why should not Viry, who appeared to concern himself so much in all this, sound Pitt out himself? Viry was floored: 'as an honest man he cou'd not advise the measure to Mr. Pitt or if he was question'd say that Ld. Bute means Pitt well & to act in confidence with him . . .'. Then out of the blue Devonshire hit on a thought which might please Bute; the man to whom Viry should turn was George Grenville, candidate for the Speakership and completely au fait with the Court, for the King had just agreed to his request to be of the Cabinet also. Devonshire sketched out the lines along which Grenville could be tackled; Bute might stress his reluctance to take office but the King's wishes deserved the first consideration; next Grenville should talk to Pitt in terms of his being the only minister to be consulted, a condescension that must be an earnest of the Favourite's goodwill. At such ingenuity Viry was so entranced that an unwonted mood of candour took hold of him: in reality, he told Devonshire, the aversion of the King towards Pitt, Temple and all the Grenvilles 'grew stronger every day'. This information confirmed Devonshire in his wish to have nothing to do with making and unmaking ministers: if Bute and Pitt were to have a collision let not Newcastle be involved. He was not, however, surprised when on 27 January Viry told him that Bute did not wish to sound Grenville; nor was he in any way deceived into accepting that this hesitancy sprang from diffidence.

Devonshire went straight from Viry to Pitt, whom he found full of original ideas about British relations with Prussia. Although Pitt had no intention of betraying Frederick, he was certain that the Government should move warily before giving him an unconditional renewal of the subsidy treaty; it could never be a British interest that Maria Theresa be overwhelmingly defeated or for that matter a French interest that Prussia be truncated. Pitt was far from ready to provide an open cheque for Frederick, who must be content with Silesia and not expect more acquisitions with Britain footing the bill. Evidently Pitt saw himself firmly at the helm and was not likely to listen to Bute. When therefore, two days later, Viry at last plucked up courage to call upon him with the suggestion of Bute as Secretary of State, Pitt affected surprise, 'grew cool', and pretended to take it as a hint that he should resign: 'for his part he sh'd be glad to retire from Business himself, if the King *wou'd place him in some honourable post in the cabinet he w'd like it if not he cou'd retire & live in ye country*'. But Pitt's bluff was not likely to stem Bute's avidity, which had forced Viry into the open. To Devonshire

Viry confided how very ambitious Bute was and that he had the Secretaryship 'much at heart as the means of making him sole Minister'. Viry had no high opinion of Bute and saw that he lacked courage: 'V—said he was sorry for him that he had a good heart & was a man of honour, but yt. he wanted to govern and had not a head for it & was afraid he wou'd ruine himself. it was G. Greenville that had put him upon being Secretary of State.' This outpour proved decisive, for out of Viry's prattle Devonshire arrived at the firm conclusion that Bute's pretensions were such that no accommodation between him and Pitt was conceivable. Devonshire promptly told Viry that he himself would gladly intervene on Bute's behalf, provided it was clear that the original initiative came from the King and that the Favourite agreed.

When on 4 February Bute saw Newcastle to discuss the new Parliament both were embarrassed: their talk lasted three hours and for a time Bute was unable to look him in the face. They had little real cause for perplexity, for Bute's expectations were very moderate; Legge, who had fallen foul of the Court over an election dispute, must be dismissed from the Exchequer without compensation and Charles Townshend put into the War Office, whilst Newcastle was asked to find seats in the House of Commons for only three new men. Bute also suggested that Elliot be promoted from the Board of Admiralty to that of the Treasury. Devonshire was busy winning Bedford over to the idea of Bute's taking office, which he argued would remove the ambivalent situation of his being Favourite only. Next, on 9 February Newcastle attempted to win over Pitt, who said flatly that he would not continue in office if his right of access to the King was to depend upon Bute. Bute's position was, however, further strengthened when two days later Grenville was admitted to the Cabinet. The situation had changed greatly over the past fortnight; in his opposition to Bute Pitt could depend only upon Temple.

In an attempt to bring about a final settlement Bute offered Temple the Lord Lieutenancy of Ireland with the assurance that he had no thought of using him and Pitt only to make the peace but that 'a permanent system' was his intention. Newcastle grumbled to Devonshire about there being too good an

understanding between Bute and the Grenville clan but
Devonshire had no fear: 'I assur'd him there was no danger of it
& I approv'd much what L⁴ Bute had done.' Temple now
behaved with all the senseless vanity he had displayed at the
time of the crisis over his Garter. To Viry of all men he chose to
confide his megalomania: '. . . if they had had a proper consideration for him, why did they not offer him first Ld. of the
Treasury or Secretary of State, he believed he shou'd not have
accepted either but to make him yt. was Lord Privy Seal, Knight
of ye Garter e.t.c., so Popular in this Country such an offer, it
was an affront'. Puffed up beyond all sense of balance, Temple
went on to declare that Newcastle could be destroyed by the
Court at any time, whilst Bute in his turn depended upon the
Grenvilles: in short his family were 'Masters of the Country. yt.
at a proper time they wou'd show it tho they might perhaps
temporise for the present'. All this Viry reported word for word
to Devonshire who told him to do the same by Bute, so that the
King and the Favourite 'might see how fortunate they had been
in not throwing themselves into the hands of such a set of men'.

In fact, so far from being 'masters of the country', Pitt and
Temple were rapidly losing ground. Everything was turning to
the advantage of Bute, who furthermore, by the death of his
father-in-law, had become one of the richest men in England,
with land and minerals worth £20,000 p.a. and £700,000 in
ready money. On 21 February Newcastle took in Elliot, who
had hoped to keep his old friends together, but 'Mr. Pitt had
held such foul Language in regard to Ld. Bute that he had
given up the Idea & should always think himself under obligations to his Grace'. Then on 23 February news came that Pitt
had been taken seriously ill at Hayes. Yet Bute simply lacked
the stomach to engineer his own appointment. Once more he
sent Viry to Devonshire to urge that Newcastle might be jogged
into proposing the matter to the King. Bute's idea was that he
should appear as taking office at the behest of the great Whig
lords. But under no circumstances would Devonshire allow
Newcastle to fall into this trap.

Bute became indignant at the reluctance of the Whig dukes to
propose him as Secretary of State. But with Pitt out of the way
ill Newcastle, Devonshire and Hardwicke were bound to feel the

position changed and on 3 March they decided to give in. Three days later Newcastle saw the King and proposed that Bute be made a Secretary of State; a united administration, he urged, was essential for the management of Parliament, raising the money to fight the war and for concluding the peace: 'yt. Mr. Pitt's ill-health was such as rendered it impossible to do business with ye King for weeks & months at times'. The King replied that he had thought of Bute as minister since the day of his succession, which was perhaps the one completely honest remark made by anyone during the whole complicated course of this affair. Devonshire was instructed to tell Pitt of the change that had been decided. But still Bute held back, till Newcastle had to tell him that after all the trouble the King's intention must be carried out: '. . . he was only apprehensive of Mr. Pitt's Temper, yt. therefore he must know before he engag'd whether he might in case they differ'd depend upon the support of him and his Friends. His Grace assured him that he might.' Bute took his cue to run down Pitt, whose popularity was sunk and who might be persuaded to stand down with some honourable provision, for gain the King he never could.

At two o'clock on the afternoon of 19 March Pitt received Bute and far from thought of retirement was full of plans for the war; he had changed his mind about sending an expedition so far distant as the East, for if war with Spain broke out 'we would need our great ships here'. He was, however, keen to send an expedition to take the neutral islands in the West Indies, 'for the French talk much of making Peace on the terms of Uti Possidetis, now they are certainly in possession of them'. Bute was thus confronted with Pitt's determination to wage a *guerre à outrance*. That evening Bute reported this conversation to Devonshire; both men must have considered Newcastle's promise of support in the event of disagreements to be of the utmost importance.[15]

On 24 March Pitt sent Amherst his confirmatory orders for the West Indies.[16] Next day Bute's appointment as Secretary of State for the North was made public. Holderness, who had been Secretary of State without interruption since 1751, was paid off with a pension of £4,000 p.a. George Grenville's friend Jenkinson became Bute's under-secretary of state. The other important changes were Bedford's resignation from the Lord Lieutenancy of Ireland and Legge's dismissal from the Chancellorship of the Exchequer. Bedford did not receive any other office but stood high in the favour of the King and as a Privy Councillor was still summoned to Cabinet meetings; the change marked, not his decline, but his continuation at the centre of things. Bute, always a snuffler, pretended to have nothing to do with Legge's undoing. In truth no one was sorry, for as Newcastle remarked to Fox: '. . . you despise him, and there is the Duke of Bedford hates or despises Legge, and Mr. Pitt hates or despises Legge, and I don't care a farthing for Legge (you know I have no reason) . . .'. Thus ended the long career of a politician empty of any claim to statesmanship, with too much ambition and too little fidelity. But Newcastle was not the gainer, for the new man at the Exchequer was Barrington, always the exemplary servant of George II and as devotedly loyal to his grandson. As Bute had suggested, Charles Townshend, no friend to Pitt or Newcastle, succeeded Barrington at the War Office, his first important post. The palace revolution was rounded off when Dashwood for the first time in his life received office as Treasurer of the Household and was sworn of the Privy Council, an earnest of better to come. Old age precluded Dodington from employment, but having placed his borough interest at Bute's disposal he became Lord Melcombe and was hugely pleased.

So far as Pitt was concerned these promotions and honours were in no way outweighed by the peerages given to his recommendations, Spencer as Viscount, in 1765 to become Earl Spencer, and Grosvenor as Baron. Already Grosvenor, once one of Pitt's most staunch supporters, was moving over to Bute, who alone could secure him the Lord Lieutenancy of Cheshire.[17] So long as he left the war to Pitt Bute could do pretty well as he liked and to the average man patronage in the hands of the King's personal adviser was nothing to be frowned upon. Bute's position was bound to be progressively strengthened and he knew full well that almost up to the last neither Newcastle nor Pitt had given the slightest encouragement to his appointment as minister; he might find them necessary for a time but had no occasion for gratitude.

CHAPTER 11

Pitt Resigns Office

'The King has no Subject who rejoices more than I do at the success of His Majesty's arms, of which I most sincerely congratulate you, permit me to add, Sir, no one can be more sensible than I am how much the auspicious openings of the present Reign are owing to the Administration which so gloriously closed the last.'

Major-General Jeffery Amherst to William Pitt, Secretary of State for the Southern Department, addressed from Staton Island, North America, on 25 October 1761, twenty days after Pitt in London had resigned.[1]

Pitt's eclipse, originating from the deaths of the Kings Ferdinand VI and George II, and given illustration in Bute's mighty waxing, received additional momentum when Louis XV's most adroit statesman, Choiseul, attained undivided control following the death of Belleisle. On 31 March Prince Galitzin, Russian Ambassador in London, approached Pitt with the suggestion of a European Congress to include all the powers, together with an independent negotiation between Britain and France over colonial interests. This overture coincided with the setting forth of Pitt's Belleisle expedition; 9,000 infantry under General Studholme Hodgson were conveyed to the Morbihan in one hundred transports, escorted by ten of the line, eight frigates, and numerous auxiliary vessels commanded by Augustus Keppel. They arrived off Belleisle on 6 April: the strength of the defences had been underestimated and a first attack was thrown back into the sea with the loss of 500 men. Pitt sent out reinforcements and a good many of the transports intended for New York to convey an army to the Windward Islands had to be held back.[2] Belleisle was soon completely cut off: surrender was only a matter of time.

When on 9 April Newcastle called upon Pitt they talked round possible peace conditions. Pitt had some set ideas; the Cabinet must be agreed upon terms before plenipotentiaries were appointed; Hanover must be safeguarded but at no sacrifice to British interests and the first of these was 'all North America and the Fishery on the Banks of Newfoundland'. Newcastle at once objected that the Newfoundland Fishery 'wou'd be difficult to be got'; the French would never sacrifice a point so essential to their marine and the powers of Europe might well challenge a British monopoly of 'the Bacaloo trade',* which Spain could take as a *casus belli*: 'Mr. Pitt answer'd he was resolved that he wou'd immediately insist on knowing the sense of the King's servants on this subject &, if he was over-ruled he should desire to retire.' Pitt went on to suggest Temple as the most suitable emissary and delineated his own and his brother-in-law's traits of character in revealing fashion: 'that he was an odd mixture of a Creature the most obstinate on the one hand & the most difficult on the other, that Ld. Temple was a man of the greatest abilities & the most distinguishing head, that except one or two, he was fitter to determine a difficult case in ye Court of Chancery than anybody there barring the knowledge of the terms and forms of law'. As to Bute, Pitt concluded, 'he should have advised him to stay where he was'.[3] Evidently Pitt's intentions on the subject of peace had hardened very considerably since the end of 1759.

In May 1760 Jenkinson had drawn up for Grenville a memorandum on the Newfoundland Fisheries, in which a right to participate had been reserved for France under the Treaty of Utrecht. In time of peace no less than 3,000 of their craft manned by 15,000 seamen found thereby employment yielding a profit of £500,000 a year and furthermore the sailors were kept in training for the next emergency – 'the Bacaloo

* Bacaloo trade: i.e. Cod trade.

trade' of peace provided the naval complements of war. Pitt meant to deprive France of the means of reconstituting a navy: Lagos and Quiberon Bay were to be historically final decisions. If on this point he and Newcastle were disagreed, they were united over the annexation of Canada. A pamphlet controversy was raging over whether Guadeloupe, with its lucrative sugar industry, might be a more fruitful acquisition than Canada, which offered only the fur trade and a small market for British exports. The sugar argument influenced neither Pitt nor Newcastle, whose principal adviser on commercial matters, Sir William Baker, was firmly for holding on to Canada and on 13 April submitted a paper pointing out that here the security of the Thirteen Colonies was involved.[4] With Wolfe enshrined in his country's heroic tradition, there was never a possibility of Canada being sacrificed.

As April went by Pitt's temper became more and more irascible. Prince Ferdinand, though in no serious danger, lost tactical advantages to Broglie for which he blamed the commissariat, 'ye want of care and economy in the Treasury & plainly shew'd an intention of attacking it'. On 19 April Pitt had an audience of the King – his fear that Bute might interject his right of access was unfounded – and he reiterated the peace terms he had outlined to Newcastle: 'all Canada, Cape Breton & Islands & Harbours & Fisheries & particularly ye exclusive fishery of Newfoundland, yt. if he was ever capable of signing a Treaty without it he shou'd be sorry for it yt. he had got the use of his right hand again'. Pitt next railed against the commissariat and demanded an enquiry, to which the King agreed. Returning to the coming negotiations, Pitt accused his fellow ministers of fomenting a stiff-necked obduracy at Versailles by opposing his will in Council. The King calmly replied that his Government ought not to make any firm declaration until it was known what the French had to offer. Devonshire learned what had passed in the course of this unequal conversation when later in the day he was with the King and Pitt, with Bute present. He described Pitt's humour 'as bad as unjust as hostile & as impracticable as possible'.

Three days later Devonshire called upon Pitt and asked him to clarify his policy; was it his idea that the French should be presented with terms already unanimously agreed by the Cabinet, without any introductory talks? To this Pitt assented and Devonshire retorted that in his opinion such an approach would retard peace rather than secure it:

'Mr. Pitt was rather warm. he said he could not allow what I said, that either we were in a situation to receive the Law or to give it, that he thought the latter was our case, that therefore it was our business to propose terms & tell France on what conditions they were to have Peace, that it was so at the Peace of Utrecht & it would be absurd to act otherwise.'

Newcastle, thoroughly put out at the prospect of the Cabinet meeting fixed for the day following, 23 April, sent a message by Rigby to Bedford, who was at Woburn nursing a fit of gout, to come to town and give him support against Pitt. Rigby at once wrote off, ending with the just comment: 'The truth is, that his Grace and the rest of them are afraid of him, and want you to stand the brunt.' Bedford did attend the Cabinet and in the event, as an aide-mémoire from Choiseul was expected, peace was not talked of and the discussion ran upon the defaults of the commissariat. Tempers ran high: Pitt demanded the formal enquiry to which he had secured the King's agreement, but the ministers suspected his real interest lay in holding a sword over the heads of Newcastle's minions at the Treasury Board. Bedford accused Prince Ferdinand of blaming his want of generalship upon the commissariat – not a remark calculated to soothe Pitt. Yet there were moments of humour; Bute suggested dismissing the entire commissariat, whispering to Devonshire that they were all Prince Ferdinand's appointments. 'Ld. Temple made a long speech entering into ye state of ye war from ye beginning of their Ministry, nothing to ye present purpose, but prepared for some other occasion.' Although Hardwicke and Mansfield gave their support for an enquiry, the sense of the meeting went against Pitt and Bute was ordered to find out Prince Ferdinand's requirements. Pitt was very hurt but did not draw the prudent conclusion that by browbeating the ministers over demands of questionable justice he might unite them into obstruction on major issues. Newcastle's gratitude to Bedford was such that next day he embraced Rigby – 'I have heard much of the Duke of Newcastle's kisses, but never had one from him till today . . .'. Confronted by a request for information the Prince disclaimed any wish to overturn the commissariat and asked merely for some alterations.[5]

Choiseul's aide-mémoire met with the King's approval but not with Pitt's and a stormy Cabinet meeting on 27 April resulted. That of 14 May, to consider new instructions to Prince Ferdinand, was the occasion for further dispute. By this time the formal arrangements for peace negotiations were well under way. Temple did not wish to go to Paris and instead prompted Hans Stanley to ask to become British plenipotentiary and to this Pitt agreed. An expert on international law with a first-hand knowledge of the French Court, Stanley was a 'know-all' but made up for his pomposity by a genuine willingness and Pitt formed a very high opinion of him. As special French envoy Choiseul sent François de Bussy, who arrived on 31 May. Nine days later Belleisle surrendered, which Choiseul did not think significant and ordered Bussy to illuminate his residence in London.[6] Pitt wrote in triumph to Amherst and expressed the hope that he would soon be learning of the reduction of Dominica. The transports detained for the Belleisle operation would soon be crossing the Atlantic. At New York Amherst had chosen to command the Dominica expedition the 5th Lord Rollo, a Scots peer of modest estate who had served at Louisbourg and Montreal. For the main thrust against Martinique his selection was Monckton, one of Wolfe's brigadiers, and for the naval responsibility Sir James Douglas was already at Guadeloupe. Amherst assured Pitt of his ability to spare the further 6,000 men required for Martinique and Rollo embarked from New York on 26 April.[7]

Choiseul's suggestion as a basis for negotiation was the mutual retention of conquests to which Pitt's reaction was guarded; British interests would be poorly served if the French held on to Minorca. In a letter to Bute of 13 June Bedford laid down his principles; the French willingness to negotiate a separate peace, from which both Prussia and Austria would be left out, their agreement to the *uti possidetis* and their treating lightly the affair of Belleisle, all this deserved appreciation. Bedford did not

consider that the capture of Belleisle, 'as much part of France as
the Isle of Wight is of England', made a jot of difference: 'I am
aware that it may be observed that it is not meant finally to
retain Belleisle, but that it will be a good thing to carry to
market, to obtain better conditions, than we should otherwise
have; to this I reply, we have too much already – more than we
know what to do with; . . .'.[8] To these views Bedford would over
the next months stick with an utter doggedness, in opposition
to Pitt's notion of 'what we have we hold'.

On 17 June Choiseul made some concrete suggestions:
France would return Minorca in exchange for Guadeloupe and
Goree; Britain would keep all Canada, with the southern
boundary limited by the Great Lakes, but France would keep
Louisiana with the Ohio, and Cape Breton Island would be
handed back as a French *abri* for the use of the Newfoundland
Fisheries; finally, the French army would evacuate Prussian
territory in west Germany. The British reply was drawn up at a
Cabinet meeting of 24 June attended by Pitt, Bute, Newcastle,
Bedford, Hardwicke and Granville. The ministers were
unanimously opposed to any limitation upon the boundary of
Canada, which must include the Ohio: 'all that is not Canada
cannot be Louisiana'. Goree and Senegal must both be held and
Minorca restored. The four islands in the West Indies declared
neutral by the Peace of 1748 should be equally divided. But all
except Temple were opposed to Pitt's dogged policy over the
Fisheries. The ministers readily rejected Choiseul's request for
the return of Cape Breton as being a large island close to the
coast of Canada. But access in some form to the Fisheries must
be conceded. Then Bute suggested that the permanent exclusion
of the French from the Fisheries should be projected but not
made a *sine qua non*. Two days later the King gave his support to
this idea, especially as City opinion would certainly be behind
Pitt.[9] On 26 June Pitt wrote to Stanley but in terms too strong
to please anyone.

Bute's support for Pitt was not destined to hold. At the end of
the month he was complaining of Pitt's insolence to Newcastle,
who at once assured him that he would be only too ready to
'concert previously with his Lordship the measures to be taken;
our point was to do nothing that might prevent or delay the

peace'. At once Newcastle let Bedford know that Bute might be considered an ally. Choiseul's answer to Pitt was in Newcastle's opinion as conciliatory as might be, especially as Stanley thought France would waive Cape Breton provided they were given an abri 'under our influence and command, to dry their fish . . . as is permitted by the treaty of Utrecht'. On 9 July Bedford wrote to Bute insisting that this chance of a peace more advantageous than any since Agincourt must be seized. It was manifestly impossible to deny France with her long coastline the privileges of a great maritime power: '. . . the endeavouring to drive France entirely out of any naval power is fighting against nature, and can tend to no one good in this country; but on the contrary must excite all the naval powers of Europe to enter into a confederacy against us; . . .'.[10]

Newcastle, yet haunted by the spectre of a secret pact between Pitt and the Court, went wailing to Devonshire: 'what would become of him with Mr. Pitt against him & perhaps his Lordship [Bute] & of course the King'. On 11 July therefore Devonshire invited Bute to his house in Piccadilly and asked him to take a stand, either for peace or war. Bute mouthed platitudes 'being all for unanimity & would consent to a moderate peace even if he knew a better peace might have been obtainable'. But then his feelings of ambition got the better of his sense of discretion and 'he confess'd that if ye D. of Newcastle was overruled and war was to continue, *he should not be surprised to see him quit the Treasury*'. Devonshire challenged Bute with his customary directness; a position as Favourite, he observed, could easily take a dangerous turn and if the succession to Newcastle was the object in view, this could be obtained only with the consent of the Whigs which must rest with the friendship of Pitt and Newcastle – 'he could not do without both'. Bute came down to earth and confessed that he thought Pitt had gone wrong over the Fisheries and that the Utrecht precedent should be followed. The day following Bute wrote to Bedford committing himself to the Utrecht basis. He thought that his views and Bedford's coincided nearly enough and believed France so exhausted that a conclusion on these lines ought easily to be obtainable.[11]

Dining at Claremont on 18 July Devonshire found Newcastle

'much out of humour over Bp. of Lincoln not getting London &
the Queen's household'. The King's betrothal to Charlotte of
Mecklenburg-Strelitz had been announced, and to be ignored
over the selection of her ladies and overruled in ecclesiastical
patronage weighed with Newcastle every bit as much as the
Fisheries.[12] He despairingly told Devonshire and Hardwicke
that he saw no alternative to resignation, an idea crushingly
disposed of by Hardwicke in his letter of 8 August:[13]

'If your Grace quits now it must be either upon reasons of
personal usage, or of *public measures*. Forgive me to say that the
promotion of the Bp. of Norwich to the See of London, contrary
to your opinion and advice, will not be thought a sufficient
justification by the public, or by the Whig Party.'

While Newcastle brooded over his grievances great news
reached London. From India came tidings of the surrender of
Pondicherry in January. On 20 July Pitt had before him Rollo's
account of the surrender of Dominica on 8 June after a token
resistance. An attack upon St Lucia, which Pitt had also thought
might be feasible, was considered inadvisable because the
Governor of Martinique had thrown in strong reinforcements.[14]
    Pitt would not choose the path of weakness in negotiations
but in Minorca Choiseul had the bait to induce the Court of
Madrid to undertake a gamble. That January, two months even
before Galitzin had approached Britain, he had proposed a
military alliance and had continued these talks while receiving
Stanley with every mark of condescension. On 20 July Choiseul's
reply to a series of British proposals reached London: even Bute
was shocked that he still insisted upon Cape Breton Island.
When three days later Bussy submitted a statement of footling
Spanish grievances on the lines of what had been indicated
towards the end of 1759, the Cabinet was dumbfounded and
unanimously consented to Pitt's reply of 24 July that Spain
could not be a party to any negotiations between Britain and
France:[15]

'His Majesty will not suffer the disputes with Spain to be blended
in any manner whatever in the negotiation of peace between the

two crowns; . . . that it will be considered an affront to His Majesty's dignity . . . to make further mention of such a circumstance. Moreover it is expected that France *will not* at any time *presume* a right of intermeddling in such disputes between Great Britain and Spain.'

The next day Bute sent Stanley a list of points for Choiseul and a secret and separate letter which contained an ultimatum: Britain would insist upon retaining Canada and Cape Breton; a compromise over the Fisheries would depend upon the reduction of the Dunkirk fortifications to the Utrecht level; Guadeloupe was to go back to France and the neutral islands be divided equally; Senegal and Goree were both to be ceded to Britain; Belleisle and Minorca would each be restored. With regard to India a new arrangement should be the subject of an independent negotiation between the respective East India Companies. France was to evacuate Prussian territories and finally both powers were to abstain from aiding either side in 'the particular quarrel for the recuperation of Silesia'. That offer was as close to meeting Choiseul that Pitt was prepared to contemplate and the French reply of 6 August was not a serious attempt to bridge the gap.[16]

Newcastle was appalled at the possibility of war with Spain. On 7 August he wrote to Hardwicke: 'I know my Lord Bute and Mr. Pitt despise Spain. The latter carries it so far as to fling out that we shall be better able, by our captures, to carry on the war, with Spain against us, than without it.' Two days later Newcastle was again writing to Bedford about the Fisheries, which 'is and has been almost the sole obstacle to peace; . . .'. At the same time Pitt was writing to Temple: 'You will see by the Ultimatum of France that the pleasing prospect of approaching peace is extremely clouded, and I fear at an end.'[17] Newcastle had a considerable flair for judging public opinion. In 1739 he had rightly sensed that the nation wanted war with Spain, and in 1757 he had yielded to the popular demand for Pitt's services. In 1761 he knew peace and reduced taxation to be the desideratum. In four years the navy had expanded from 134 ships to 412, and the complements from 12,000 men to 85,000. The annual supplies increased from £8.5 million in 1757 to

£19.6 million in 1761. The landed gentry, accustomed to a
2s. in the £ land tax in time of peace were discontented at the
4s. rate when the war had evidently been won. By the end of
1761 loan finance had increased the national debt from £72
million in 1755 to nearly £150 million. The general sense of
unease was reflected in a best-seller pamphlet by Israel Mauduit,
Considerations on the Present German War, which appeared with
Hardwicke's approval and made a deep impression upon the
thinking public. Thomas Gray, who always took a lively and
chatty interest in public affairs, described the new temperature
of opinion to his friend Thomas Wharton: 'The Ministry are
much out of joint. Mr. P.: much out of humour, his popularity
tottering, chiefly occasioned by a Pamphlet against the German
War, written by that *squeaking* acquaintance of ours, Mr.
Mauduit: it has had a vast run.'[18]

This war-weariness never turned into any public campaign
against Pitt, who for the remainder of his days would be
worshipped by his countrymen. Amherst was commissioning
some pictures of the Niagara Falls as a gift to Pitt: '. . . three
views of water . . . I think them very pretty, and I shall try to
get some more of the same sort'. Owing to the carelessness of
an ADC this consignment miscarried but in the end views of
Niagara and of the Chohos on the Mowhawk river found their
way to Hayes.[19] This was a mark of esteem from a man who
had been importantly concerned with winning Pitt's war, but
his position was very different with the King and the politicians.
Bute was every day becoming more powerful; his luck during
the late summer of 1761 astonished all. On the death of his
uncle, the 3rd Duke of Argyll, he obtained 'the management' of
Scotland for his brother James Stuart-Mackenzie, whose
popularity was such that the bulk of Scots members returned at
the forthcoming general election looked to Bute as leader. Then
in September Bute's daughter married Sir James Lowther, 5th
Bart, the richest commoner in England and uncrowned king of
Cumberland and Westmorland, who put into Parliament the
ubiquitous Jenkinson.[20]

On 15 August 1761 the French and Spanish governments
signed the second Family Compact of the eighteenth century
between the Bourbon powers. By the terms of the secret Special

Convention, Spain was to enter the war by 2 May 1762 and to garrison Minorca from that date. The long delay between the treaty and the proposed declaration of war was needed to give the Spanish treasure fleet, the Flota, time to enter Cadiz. From Paris Stanley gave warning that war was practically unavoidable. On the day the Family Compact was signed the Cabinet met to consider Pitt's letter on breaking off the negotiations, which Granville sneeringly called 'a fine piece of oratory'. Pitt flew into a rage: 'he would not suffer an *Iota* of it to be altered and would tell the King that he would sign this letter and no other'. He went on: 'yt. he wou'd not bear the treatment he met with he averr'd he had stuck literally to ye sense of the Council on all occasions & he wou'd not bear insinuations to ye contrary, yt. he saw combinations of great lords against him but for his part he w'd go his own way, yt. he was a British subject & he knew he stood upon British ground, yt. he had learnt his Maxims and Principles under ye great Lord Cobham and ye Disciples of the greatest lawyers and generals of K. Williams days, namely Lord Somers and of D. of Marlbro'. At this diatribe Bedford walked out. Bute read an intercepted letter of Choiseul's, offering to prolong negotiations for six weeks, probably so as to wait for the Spanish galleons. When the Cabinet came to vote on Pitt's letter Devonshire abstained; as nobody's opinion had been invited 'it could not be said to come under their deliberations'. Six, including Bute and Temple, voted for the letter; Bedford, Granville, Hardwicke, Newcastle and Mansfield were against. Two days later Bedford announced that he would no longer attend Cabinet meetings except at the King's express desire.

When next morning Devonshire had an audience, the King expressed himself most hurt at Bedford's withdrawal. He insisted that the point of the Fisheries must be further explored and Devonshire suggested that though Cape Breton was too near to Canada for its use as an abri to be compatible with safety, a small island at a greater distance should present no difficulty: to this the King agreed and suggested convening another Council, at which Bedford might be present, to draw up a satisfactory despatch to Stanley. From Court Devonshire went to Granville's where he met Bussy, who told him Pitt's letter was far too high but that he would not forward it at once. On 19 August a meeting to draft new instructions to Stanley was held in the King's presence; Pitt, Bute, Devonshire and, at the King's command, Bedford, were there and Bussy was especially invited. Pitt gave an account of all the negotiations: 'Bussy presented a Paper marking the Bounds of Louisiana which took in the Ohio and a great part wch. they used to call Canada, & yt. France wou'd insist upon it; he said they had a Right immemorial to fish in the Gulph of St. Lawrence.' To this Pitt retorted: 'yt. ye Rivers & Gulphs & Territories gave a Right, therefore they could not have it previous to their Conquest'. Bute, realising that the first turning point in his master's reign had come, announced that for his part he was willing to bow to whatever the majority of the Cabinet decided. There was a further meeting of the Council on 26 August, which Bedford refused to attend and at which Pitt was as obdurate as ever. Further despatches from Stanley were unsatisfactory; he doubted Choiseul's sincerity and though Newcastle thought peace might still be had, the possibility was shrinking.

By the second week of September Pitt was once more threatening to resign and this time was credited. He was in despair at his position in the Cabinet, faced as he was with the obstruction of 'the great lords' who wielded such influence in the House of Commons: 'It was', he told Bute, 'impossible for him to remain that for ye sake of Unanimity he had gone as far as his conscience or even his *Sleep* wou'd permit him, & therefore as he cou'd not execute any orders for making further concessions, he must throw himself on the King's Generosity for the case of himself & his Family'.[21] Though Newcastle pooh-poohed Pitt's talk of resignation as a 'menace', Bute did not take the prospect with equanimity. During the autumn life had once more shone for Newcastle, because Bute had been recommending all his ecclesiastical protégés: 'The King, I should have said *first*, is most gracious to us all.'[22] Intoxicated at Bute's politic flirtatiousness and the King's grace, Newcastle almost believed the days of his old master George II had once more descended; provided he could feel *au fait* with the Court, the prospect of Pitt's resignation was not too alarming.

On 11 September Pitt repeated his threat to Newcastle and

Devonshire, roundly abused Bedford and assured them that on his retirement he would give no opposition and 'not appear in ye H. of Commons the next session unless he was calumniated'. Two days later Newcastle was writing to Bedford: 'Whether there was any reality in it at all, or whether it was meant only in the case of a peace being to be concluded on lower terms than those last offered, or whether it meant to comprehend all events either of peace or war, I will not pretend to determine; but, to be sure, in the present circumstances of the nation, it is an important consideration.'[23] Four days later, on 15 September, the Cabinet decided upon Stanley's recall, when Pitt unexpectedly hesitated: ought not some conditions be laid down which might be the basis for negotiations hereafter? Nevertheless, that evening he wrote to Bussy summarising the causes for the breakdown. Hardwicke considered the dictatorial tone of this final letter went beyond anything the Cabinet had authorised.[24] Had the treaties between France and Spain been known to the public, Pitt's position would have been greatly strengthened; the City of London welcomed the prospect of war with Spain.

The Cabinet of 18 September was decisive; Pitt opened the proceedings with a Spanish aide-mémoire, stating that the Bourbon courts would never renounce the right to uphold one another in their international disputes. This was followed by a Notification, describing the talks between Pitt and Fuentes on the accession of the Spanish King, which had ended in the claim to participate in the Fisheries, which Britain refused. These preliminaries over Pitt began the discussion; the situation was 'dangerous and arduous' and the course to be taken – and that systematically – was the one least attended by risk. Mansfield asked if there was any proof that Spain was engaged with France: 'None', answered Pitt, 'but ye strongest Union express'd & Mr. Stanley's Letter mentioning their undertaking for the defence of Martinico.' Pitt continued that to him there was no doubt 'yt. Spain is France'; there was a union in the House of Bourbon and whatever was dangerous now would become more so six months hence. 'Ye Fact is prov'd ye treatment we have had shews w^t we are to expect.' He ended by asking for the Council to give their opinion before he finally formed his own. Granville took up the point of the great value of British merchant establishments in Spain; if Britain could deliver a mighty blow the risk might be worthwhile, 'but where are we sh'd we fail?' Hardwicke followed: 'I am not for proceedings with too great delay, nor with too much precipitancy'; – a union of the Bourbon House was not ground for attack without proof that Spain was engaged to declare war: 'Mr. Stanley hints at it, I don't know on what authority' – but passages in intercepted letters were not enough. Pitt did not think the argument concerning trade with Spain valid, because no power was more vulnerable to the British navy: 'I am still of opinion yt. an immediate action gives us ye best chance to extricate ourselves.' Every Spanish flag on the high seas ought to be taken – 'If the means to do this are doubtful will it not be more so next Spring. I am for it *now*.' Only Temple spoke in support and when Pitt formally proposed that Bristol ask for his passports he was voted down. He accordingly produced a Paper containing his arguments and declared he would hand it to the King with his signature, to which Temple asked to join his. The Cabinet ended with a decision to increase the Windward Islands squadron to nineteen of the line and to send there 3,000 men released by the taking of Belleisle.[25]

George III refused to consider Pitt's Paper until Stanley had returned from Paris. Had Pitt known of the King's true feelings towards him, his conduct of the crisis might have been very different. On the following day the King wrote to Bute: 'I highly approve the part my Dearest Friend took yesterday, it was the only way of keeping up the honour of the British Crown, of acting with justice, and of overturning Mr. Pitt's black scheme.'[26] At a further Cabinet meeting of 21 September Pitt, in child-like mood, threatened to abandon the business of his department to Bute, yet that day he was writing to Monckton informing him that a strong reinforcement was on the way from England under the command of Rodney.[27] The next day saw the Coronation of the King and his bride of ten days. Soon after eight o'clock in the morning George III was at the House of Lords to prepare and asked Devonshire what Pitt's next move might be; if the war was to be prolonged, his continuance in office would be desirable. Devonshire thought Pitt and Temple would find little support in Parliament. In Paris Stanley, though expecting his recall, was desperately trying to save the peace. In a last effort the King wrote to Choiseul in terms which would allow him to restrain Stanley's departure if he so wished.[28]

It was clear to all that the negotiation with France had fallen down over the Fisheries and that Pitt's intransigence had made the Family Compact certain. Newcastle had been a Cabinet minister under George I; Hardwicke had become Lord Chancellor of England when Pitt had been in Parliament only two years; Granville had been a Cabinet minister long before Walpole had cashiered 'that terrible cornet of horse'; Anson had been circumnavigating the globe while Pitt's fulminations against Walpole were falling upon deaf ears; Bedford was already First Lord of the Admiralty when the King had with reluctance admitted 'the orator and his junto' to minor offices. If the ministers were open to a charge of ingratitude, Pitt was most impolitic to ignore the public expectation, reinforced by the advice of the Cabinet, that the war must be brought to an honourable conclusion. All were ready to provoke Pitt into resignation, and if Temple went out with him so much the better. On 23 September, after attendance at Court, Newcastle, Bute, Devonshire, Anson and Mansfield gathered at Devonshire House 'to consider what was to be done to justifye our dissent from Mr. Pitt'. At first they thought a joint minute to the King would be best but this was decided to be an unfortunate precedent. It was settled that each minister should wait upon the King and deliver his opinion, which on the following day was done. Newcastle observed to Hardwicke: 'The King seems every day more offended with Mr. Pitt and plainly wants to get rid of him at all events.'[29] His sole anxiety was lest the public gain the impression Pitt was being forced out.

Two days later Bute, Newcastle and Devonshire met to thrash out the question of Pitt's successor. For the first time in his life George Grenville was mentioned for Cabinet office. For long his subordinate situation had irked him and Pitt's distress gave him an opening. In his friend Jenkinson he had a foot well placed in the Bute camp. Bedford would have liked to succeed Pitt, or so Devonshire told Bute and hinted to the King. The King at once declared himself ready to accept Grenville if only to keep Bedford out. Bute had every intention that Grenville should be promoted and did not think he should remain in London 'to seem in a state of expectancy'. Grenville therefore departed for Wotton, his Buckinghamshire seat, on 26 September. London bristled with rumours, the Hanoverian Minister Münchausen telling the King that the Prussian Ambassador Frieherr Dodo von Knyphausen had told him Pitt would go; on 29 September Bute said to Jenkinson the resignation was a certainty, information promptly posted on to Grenville.[30] At the end of the month Stanley and Bussy each returned home. On the last day of September Stanley had an audience of the King, in which he expressed his belief that Spain was about to declare war, but he declined to disclose his source of information; that evening George III wrote to Bute: 'Upon the whole I could perceive he had been tutor'd silence by Mr. Pitt or else that awe prevented his speaking out; for he would never name the authors of what he alleg'd indeed I never down right asked him who they were.'[31]

Pitt met the Cabinet for the last time on 2 October; all were conscious of the dignity of the occasion, which they knew was the prologue to the resignation of the greatest Englishman of his day. Pitt stood by his Memorial to the King: 'You are *now* at war with the House of Bourbon, but, for open war with Spain you are prepared and she is not.' Bedford was not present and the other lords, Granville, Devonshire, Hardwicke, Anson, Ligonier, Mansfield, Bute and Newcastle held to their former opinions. Temple left the Council, leaving Pitt to address the ministers in a long speech which ended with these decisive words:

'Without having ever asked any one single employment in my life, I was called by my Sovereign and by the Voice of the People to assist the state when others had abdicated the service of it. That being so no one can be surprised that I will go on no longer since my advice is not taken. Being responsible I *will* direct, and will be responsible for nothing that I do not direct.'

Granville, the senior statesman, alone spoke, firstly to pass an encomium upon Pitt's services but then to reject as utterly unconstitutional his refusal to endorse anything not of his own making: '. . . I find that the gentleman is determined to leave us, nor can I say I am sorry for it, since he would otherwise have certainly compelled us to leave him'. True it was that the King and the Secretary of State might undertake a foreign measure but once an issue had been referred to the Council the majority vote determined the point, each giving his opinion according to his conscience. In the House of Commons, Granville concluded, Pitt might talk of his responsibility to the people but at the Council table his duty lay only to the King.[32]

There was justice in Pitt's claim to owe his position to the Voice of the People: popular demand had forced George II to entrust him with power and the successes of the war had confirmed the verdict. Yet this was an emergency situation not correspondent with ordinary eighteenth-century practice. This famous clash between Pitt the Great Commoner and Granville, who nearly twenty years earlier had lost power owing to an excessive dependence upon the monarch, illustrated an unbridgeable gap in constitutional principle. Granville believed in individual ministerial responsibility. Pitt always had the deepest reverence for the Crown, yet by virtue of his career he stood also for the 'Voice of the People'. To join authority with popular demand might seem to approach the concept of a modern Prime Minister. No such idea occurred to Pitt, but he appeared to his colleagues as thrusting himself into the position of 'sole minister'. Such presumption Granville rebutted as a usurpation of the rights of the Crown and of the Cabinet. At four o'clock that afternoon Newcastle penned his description of the meeting to Bedford: 'Mr. Pitt in a long speech showed the impossibility of his going on in office and *in effect* quitted.'[33]

Pitt went to Hayes for the weekend. That evening Jenkinson was busy writing to Grenville on Bute's behalf, demanding his immediate presence in London. The letter arrived at Wotton at two o'clock in the morning of Saturday 3 October and two hours later Grenville set off. On the road between Amersham and Chalfont he ran into Temple on his way to Stowe. Grenville stopped the chaises, got into Temple's and proceeded to explain in a halting way his situation. Temple tried to set George's mind at rest; he himself had resigned only because he had no desire to continue attendance at Council: 'that he did not see another person in the kingdom who ought to resign from the same cause; that he himself would not have resigned but from the peculiarity of his situation, and that he was going to write to this effect to Mr. James Grenville as soon as he got to Stowe . . .'. Grenville thought he had received his elder brother's permission to do whatever Bute asked. On his arrival in London it cannot have been a surprise when Bute offered him the Secretaryship of State which Pitt was about to leave, but none the less he declined and expressed the hope that his future position as Speaker be confirmed.[34]

On Monday, 5 October, Pitt arrived back in London to hand in his resignation. That day Amherst wrote from Staten Island informing Pitt that Monckton's army was embarking for Martinique.[35] A call from Grenville went off very civilly. Later Pitt saw the King; the occasion was of the utmost dignity and redounded to the credit of both. Never before in English history had a minister resigned when at the height of his powers and on the very crest of his triumphant progress; Wolsey had been disgraced; Burleigh had died in harness; Clarendon had been dismissed; Marlborough had fallen from favour; Walpole had lost his majority in the House of Commons – though not his Sovereign's confidence – and here indeed was a difference. Pitt laid down office whence no one, King or colleague, would have dared order him out because he had the support of Parliament. He explained to the King that he felt bound to follow his own convictions and declared his intention to keep away from the House of Commons, apart from giving his support to the Address and the great measures of supply. Otherwise he would attend only if he found himself calumniated. The King expressed his sorrow at this turn of events, but pointed out that had the Cabinet been behind Pitt he would have found himself in as difficult a position, being dragged into a further war which he felt was unjustified. The King hoped Pitt would accept any honours or emoluments which he could with propriety bestow. Pitt, face to face with his young Sovereign, perceived that his decision to withdraw his services, however clothed in soft words, 'was naturally offensive to majesty. He burst into tears, and could only say he was penetrated to the very soul by such manifestations of bounty and goodness to him, and should only pray that such rewards might be bestowed upon his future, not his past services.' His audience over, Pitt returned Grenville's call of the morning and spoke with 'great decency and gratitude of the King', whilst his brother-in-law assured him how glad he was that there should be the bestowal of a royal mark of favour.[36]

Next morning Bute wrote to Pitt putting forward two suggestions; what the King would like would be to make him Governor of Canada at £5,000 p.a. with special legislation to enable him to continue in the House of Commons; the alternative was the Chancellorship of the Duchy of Lancaster with the salary made up. Then Bute went to see Elliot and as he recounted the parting scene between the King and Pitt, 'the tears stood in his eyes'. Both men realised that this was an heroic tragedy above petty jealousies and personal vendettas: ' – great ambition disappointed, an office of the first consideration and profit resigned, a King offended yet not resentful, Rivals in power doing justice to each other, and even softened to gentleness while acting under passion'.

There were, too, men outside the main scene dumbfounded at Pitt's going and of these was Barrington who called at St James's Square to find Pitt out. His message read: 'I shall take the earliest opportunity of waiting on you again, in the mean time permit me to say, that no man living can esteem, respect & venerate you more than myself, or be more earnestly desirous to shew it.'[37] Elliot, utterly distressed at the turn of events, had asked Pitt for an interview and been told to call at seven that evening. To him Pitt was frank and expressed his bitter awareness of a superiority to the ministers who had deserted him – they were only just starting to think for themselves – 'Show me the man', said he, 'that I ought to follow and I am ready to do it.' Pitt saw a gloomy future for the King and the Favourite: 'The noble Dukes and great lords of the Cabinet he passed slightly over, but insisted their influence and authority were so widely spread and so artificially woven, that they had only to chuse the time to overthrow Lord Bute and fetter their Sovereign.' As to Canada or the Duchy of Lancaster Pitt would take neither but would find very welcome a peerage for his family, together with a suitable endowment: 'He did not wish peerage to himself, saying the simplicity of his character made him satisfied to carry to the grave the name of William Pitt.' He hoped the pension attached to the title would be secured upon the quit-rents of America, which were absolutely in the King's gift and independent of the civil lists of Britain or Ireland.[38]

The 8 October found Bute writing to Pitt, offering the title and a grant of £3,000 p.a. on the plantation duties, payable to Pitt himself and any other two lives he might name. The 9 October saw Temple's resignation – he had probably hoped for a dramatic dismissal – and that evening George Grenville, his conscience still uneasy, went to see his brother. On the next day the *Gazette* announced the resignations and Lady Hester's peerage as Baroness Chatham together with a pension of £3,000 p.a. attached to the lives of Pitt, his wife and their eldest son.[39] George III and Bute were accused of some fell design in the announcement of the resignation, the peerage and the pension on the same day. But these happenings fell naturally together: Pitt had in no uncertain way indicated a necessity of 'throwing himself on the King's generosity, for the case of himself & his Family'.

Pitt, it seemed, felt far from rich and at once set about reducing his establishment; his splendid coach and six were put up for sale and he announced his intention of giving up the lease of No. 10, St James's Square, where on 24 April 1761 his youngest child and third son, James Charles, had been born. These were laughed at by some as the gestures of a perverted sense of pride. The press had some acid comments to make on the pension and the peerage – *Lady Cheat'em* for Lady Chatham – but Pitt showed no false modesty over defending himself: his acceptance of a pension from His Majesty, 'as his thanks to me', was on a level with the City's bestowal of its Freedom, 'an example so extensively followed . . .'. Pitt justified himself further in a public letter to Beckford, which the King thought 'ungrateful'. To Warburton, too, he made the situation clear in a letter of 15 October, asking that his position be explained to Allen and his Bath constituents.[40] On no other occasion since 1688 has the fall of so great a man produced so little consequence. Apart from a few intimates such as Temple and Beckford, no party

formed around Pitt. Jemmy Grenville, Cofferer of the Household, was the only member of Parliament to resign office in
sympathy. At no time under the British parliamentary system
has public opinion carried weight unless reflected in the division
lists of the House of Commons. Only a nervous system strained
almost past endurance can explain Pitt's tragic error of
judgement.

Newcastle and Bute were not agreed over who was to succeed
Pitt. Both knew his resignation might well be vindicated by the
outbreak of war with Spain and then the House of Commons
must be asked to find the money. Although Bute had always
done his best to instil in George III the deepest mistrust for Fox,
he suggested none other than he to be Pitt's successor. Newcastle
questioned whether Fox would be generally acceptable and
returned to the idea of George Grenville. Bute did not see
Grenville standing up to Pitt and proposed him instead as
Chancellor of the Exchequer, but to this Newcastle was utterly
opposed: 'The first thought, I believe,' wrote he to Bedford on
6 October, 'was to persuade me to consent to bring George
Grenville into the Treasury as Chancellor of the Exchequer: I
believe your Grace will not wonder that I could not consent to
that.' Bute next pressed Grenville to accept the seals as Secretary
of State, to meet with another refusal. Instead Grenville
recommended his wife's brother, the 2nd Earl of Egremont, one
of the richest landowners in England but a relative newcomer
to the scene and politically colourless. To this Newcastle agreed
and Egremont became Secretary of State for the Southern
Department. His first task was to carry out the King's order to
instruct Bristol that an explanation of the new Family Compact
must be demanded of Madrid.

But a new Leader of the Commons had still to be found. The
King insisted that Grenville give up all idea of being Speaker
and manage his parliamentary business. Grenville buckled
under and so became Leader of the House while remaining
Treasurer of the Navy, at the same time joining Newcastle, Bute
and Egremont to constitute an inner Cabinet.[41] Thus matters
were settled on 8 October but an arrangement which left Grenville Leader of the House of Commons without effective office,
the situation of Pelham as Paymaster in 1742–3, would not last

long. Grenville was bound either to go forward a long way or fall by the wayside. His days as partner with Pitt and Temple in the Stowe firm were done with and he would have to fend for himself. Hesitant and even timorous though Grenville might appear, he had hidden courage. A devoted student of the procedures of the Commons, his long experience of junior office had given him a most impressive understanding of the national finances.

Although Newcastle welcomed a smaller Cabinet he did not relish his prospects with Bute and his gnomes Egremont and Grenville, though Hardwicke, Granville, Devonshire and Mansfield continued to attend Cabinet meetings. Temple's position as Lord Privy Seal had yet to be filled and on 9 October Newcastle suggested Hardwicke but Bute would not have that. Newcastle expostulated to Devonshire:

'My Lord Bute has got rid of his rival Mr. Pitt; who dared to contradict him; and will make everybody else as insignificant as he can. This is certainly his scheme. My resolution is taken,

Holles-Newcastle.'

'I don't mean to quit immediately.'

Bute's candidate as Lord Privy Seal was Bedford, but for the time being this suggestion was kept private 'as seeming too pacific'. Every day brought a row over some job. On the afternoon of 11 October Pitt was seen at Court seemingly contented with his lot while Temple glowered round the Levee. Two days later Bute and Newcastle had a long argument: 'His Lordship', Newcastle wrote to Devonshire on the 14th, 'is always talking of getting *friends, and preferring his own friends.*' That night Bute sent Elliot to George Grenville with a letter promising the King's support; this he insisted upon having returned forthwith – but it was not sent back before Mrs Grenville had taken down 'the heads of it immediately . . .'. The words were so rude about Newcastle – 'crazy old man' – that it is not surprising Bute wished to keep it.[42] The expectation that Newcastle would resign was not shared by Rigby. He advised Bedford of his certainty that Newcastle would carry on provided he could depend upon him and Devonshire: '. . . he confessed the dread

the whole council used to be in lest Mr. Pitt should frown, and
that you were the single man who dared to deliver an opinion
contrary to his, though agreeable to every other person's
sentiments present . . .'.[43]

Grenville, despite a terrible row with Temple, who forbade
him ever to set foot in Stowe again, did not think Pitt a danger:
'He did not imagine that Mr. Pitt would have any great following of the Tories, that Ald. Beckford and Sir John Phillips
pretended to answer for them but could not; and that Sir
Charles Mordaunt and the soberer part of them were sick of
Mr. P's measures of war, more especially the continental, and of
the immense expense.' Grenville was really afraid of Fox's
jealousy, but Bute was certain of bringing the Paymaster to heel
and told Newcastle: 'He shall comply. I know how to deal with
Mr. Fox. His removal would be as popular, as the removal of
others may have been otherwise.' Fox's price, a peerage for his
wife Lady Caroline, was agreed to the extent of an oral undertaking that she should be included in the next batch of creations.
These wrangles did not imply any sense of regret at Pitt's
resignation. The ministers were somewhat alarmed at the
responsibility thrust upon them but Pitt had made full preparations for hostilities with Spain. All were agreed that to carry out
his plans as vigorously as possible was the right course as the
sure way to an early peace. While Bute was browbeating Fox,
Newcastle summed up the situation in a letter to Devonshire:[44]

'I am sorry to observe that our new Secretary of State talks
war . . . much more than I think . . . he should do. I will repeat
it again. *Out war Mr. Pitt* we cannot. And *we* [*with?*] *the nation*
have no ground to stand upon, but to get a good peace, as soon
as we can; and God grant it may be soon, or we shall all be
undone.'

CHAPTER 12

The Peace of Paris

'*1 Citizen.* Pray now, what do you really think of this Peace?
2 Citizen. That it is a damned bad one to be sure!
Physician. Damned bad one? Pray what would you be at? Have you not had all that you wanted? Did you not begin the war to settle your boundaries in North America? And have you not got that done, as Mr. Pitt the great champion of the opposition acknowledged in the House, better than could have been expected? Have you not got a large tract of territory ceded to you? Is not the line of division plain and straight?
Boswell. Suppose, Sir, I went out a-hunting with intention to bring home a hare to dinner, and catch three hares. Don't you think that I may also bring home the other two? Now, Sir, I grant you that we began the war with intention only to settle our boundaries in America and would have been satisfied with that and nothing more. But, Sir, we have had uncommon success. We have not only got what we intended, but we have also picked up some other little things, such as the Havana, Guadeloupe, &. I should be glad to know why we are to part with them?'

James Boswell: 'A Dialogue at Child's';
11 December 1762.[1]

Pitt's resignation carried the prevailing consequence that Bute assumed the management of foreign affairs. On 17 October, only twelve days after Pitt went out, Viry with Bute's authorisation wrote to the Bailli de Solar, Sardinian minister at Versailles, requesting an approach to Choiseul with a view to the resumption of the negotiations Pitt had broken off. Here indeed was the seventh heaven of Viry's celestial career at the Court of St James's. In Bute's judgement the differences between Britain and France would admit an easy reconciliation once the matter of the Fisheries was adjusted. This move was apprised by the King alone and Newcastle was not even informed. Jealousy, without doubt, was in part the cause of his being kept in ignorance or, as he would have put it, deceived. But a truer reason lay in the wide disagreement between him and Bute, not over the desirability of peace but as to the means of attainment. Bute and the King were all for a high tone towards Spain, short of declaring war, and a speedy end to the costly and sterile war in Germany. In his zeal for the Continent Newcastle appeared almost more German than British. That school derived from the days of William III and Marlborough when Britain had been fighting an efficient French monarchy in defence of her proper independence. Pitt by the employment of naval power had revealed the decay of the Bourbons. Newcastle, though conscious that his ideas were out of date with the younger generation, sensed that without Pitt global war was impracticable: 'With all his faults, we shall want Mr. Pitt, if such a complicated, such an extensive war is to be carried on; I know nobody who can plan, or push the execution of any plan agreed upon, in the manner Mr. Pitt did. . . .'[2]

Bute felt himself and his young master to be in an alarming circumstance of isolation. Whereas until recently his importance had been known to few, Pitt's resignation unveiled him; a Scots birth was no recommendation, let alone the family name Stuart of accursed memory. Bute was painfully apprehensive that the national adoration for Pitt, a paramountcy that must always stay with him, was distinct from that respect proper to the throne. Whereas Elizabeth I had revelled in the glories of her reign and Queen Anne participated fully in Marlborough's triumphs, nobody associated Pitt's war with the young King and the Favourite. Bute discerned that safety lay in Pitt's 'blue-water' war; as Devonshire observed: 'his L^dsp wants to have ye Popularity of carrying on ye war in Popular Places'.[3]

Pitt's talk of keeping away from Parliament was not credited. Fox mused that the ministry might founder and Pitt return 'sole minister', except that after what had passed in Council nobody would sit with him: that claim to *'direct'* was far from forgotten. But the people were incensed at the downfall of their hero. Parliament was due to meet on 3 November and Pitt had regained his popularity in the City. When the Common Council voted him an address of thanks, Newcastle commented to Bedford: 'Mr. Pitt's most extraordinary and unwarrantable letter has had a most extraordinary and unanswerable effect, and has brought to him his mad noisy city friends, who were for a time displeased with him.' The members of Parliament for the City were instructed to promote an enquiry into war expenditure and to consent to no peace without the retention of conquests. 'I never doubted', wrote Newcastle to Bedford on 22 October, 'Mr. Pitt's resentment would be turned upon me in the manner it now appears to be.'[4] Yet Newcastle and Bute could not bury their mutual suspicions which George Grenville described in racy style: 'they had got into a sort of Piqueering the one saying you are Minister for you have got both Houses of Parliament, the other you have the King'. When on 9 November the King drove to the Lord Mayor's banquet at Guildhall the mob shouted for Pitt. Addresses to Parliament from Exeter, Chester, York, Norwich, Stirling and Dublin paid tribute to his greatness. The City of Cork commissioned a statue, the work of Joseph Wilton, which Pitt prized above all other likenesses of himself in stone or on canvas.

To enable George Grenville, newly Leader of the House of Commons, to collect himself the meeting of Parliament was put off a week. Over the following months Newcastle and Bute would each measure his standing with Pitt as yardstick. At the Cabinet of 10 November Grenville made a bad start by suggesting that papers relating to Spain be laid before Parliament. Finding himself unanimously overruled he suggested giving extracts only and was put in his place by Newcastle: 'yt. Mr. Pitt w'd say they were unfair extracts & w'd take upon himself to prove it that he wou'd then be forced to give them all in his justification. it ended in their being refused.'[5] Parliament met on 13 November with many new members returned at the general election, though the political character of the new House of Commons was little different to that of 1754. Grenville was so nervous that Newcastle had great difficulty in coaxing him into taking the lead at the eve of session Cockpit meeting.[6] Charles Townshend, jealous of Grenville, criticised the King's Speech for omitting a reference to the Militia Act, due for renewal. The King ordered Bute to bring Townshend to heel or Grenville could not be expected to carry on.[7] In the debate on the Address Pitt made no attempt to criticise administration; he defended his resignation in the very terms he had used to the Cabinet and the King and urged the virtues of the Prussian alliance:[8]

'America has been conquered in Germany, where Prince Ferdinand's victories have shattered the whole military power of that great military monarchy, France. Recall the troops from Germany and I should be robbed of my honour, while England by deserting her allies, would be deserted by God and man.'

Temple despised Pitt's reticence and aroused the King's wrath by a bitter attack on Bute in the Lords. With that habitual lack of judgement, he spent nearly an hour of the evening of 15 November lecturing Hardwicke upon how happy he and Pitt would be to coalesce with Newcastle. Next day Bute showed Devonshire 'a very extraordinary despatch' from Bristol: on being asked to explain the French treaty, Wall had gone into such a rage that war might come at any time: 'Ld. Bute was very desirous that we should instantly return a strong & spirited answer, or else Mr. Pitt wou'd justly charge us with giving up the honour of the Nation.' Devonshire had no doubt that Newcastle must stand firm and ignore the popular clamour for Pitt. He took it upon himself to explain to Grenville how Newcastle might be kept in tow: 'Ld. Bute might very easily manage him by a little attention & confidence & early communication of w^t was doing & a Smile from H.M. wou'd do more than all . . .'.[9]

On 25 November Bedford's appointment as Lord Privy Seal
was completed. In the House of Commons all was at sixes and
sevens. On 9 December Pitt attended to see Charles Townshend
introduce the vote of £1 million for Prussia. Townshend defended the German war in terms far too buoyant for the Court,
ending with an enconium upon '*Mr. Pitt's divine plan*' – 'such a
divine spirit has been infused into our councils, that the French
were lost in America and hopeless in Europe'. When Pitt got up
he had already been met more than half-way from the Government side and Grenville went complaining to the King. But
Townshend was not seriously contemplating a leading part and
got down to War Office detail.[10]

Pitt was not present when next day the discussion of the
Prussian subsidy produced something of a sensation. Sackville
took the opportunity to make his first speech since his disgrace,
but surprisingly attracted little notice: 'He was heard as quietly
and replied to as civilly . . . as if nothing had happened.'[11] Then
thunder such as the House of Commons but rarely had to suffer
descended in an Irish brogue from the lips of Barré, who two
years ago had delivered to Pitt Amherst's despatch on the
Capitulation of Canada. To his indignation his application for
promotion was turned down by Pitt on grounds of seniority. He
was taken up by the 2nd Earl of Shelburne, a most brilliant and
wealthy young man who, having made his mark with Prince
Ferdinand's army, had become aide-de-camp to the King.
Intent upon cutting a figure in politics, Shelburne was of the
Court and the friend of Bute, whilst his professed contempt for
the German war could not be attributed to lack of bravery or
resentment at want of notice. But he could never be of the
House of Commons, for which his only remedy was to use his
borough interest to put in Barré as mouthpiece.

After Sackville had sat down without raising more than a
whisper, Barré essayed his maiden speech with a gusto conceivable only in a man without experience. He denounced the
German war as costly pandering to German interests, and Pitt,
the prime object of his venom, he depicted as 'a dangerous,
profligate and abandoned minister, who had thrust himself into
the closet upon the shoulders of a deluded people; who, like a
chameleon, had turned himself into the colour of the ground on

which he stood'. But as Pitt was not present, Barré was rudely called to order. Next day Pitt in his seat had to endure the repeat performance but certainly did not care about this impudent gas-bag. The adventurer Barré's unorthodox rhetoric did not go down with the House but he was favourably received at Court, made Colonel of a Regiment, Adjutant-General to the British army and Governor of Stirling Castle.[12]

No matter what Pitt's popularity 'out-doors', he was out of fashion not only at Court but with the 'Old Whigs' too. Hardwicke had never liked seeing his son Charles Yorke Solicitor-General in second place to Pitt's favourite, Pratt the Attorney. At first Bute, such was his anxiety not to displease Pitt, appeared to favour Pratt, upon whom a knighthood had been conferred on 22 November. But the death of Sir John Willes, Lord Chief Justice of the Common Pleas, gave Hardwicke his opportunity to change the picture. He proposed that Pratt succeed Willes and the next Attorney-General would obviously be his son. At first Pratt consented, but reflection led him to see that he was being got out of the way. He affirmed an unswerving loyalty to Pitt that must compel him to stay in the House of Commons, then muttered protests that opposition he would never contemplate, which drew from Hardwicke the sardonic comment: 'I remember a certain lady once writ me she could not answer my letter, *till her nerves were unfermented.*' Bute told Pratt that his choice lay between acceptance or no office at all. On 22 December Pratt became a Lord Chief Justice and had to leave the House of Commons. Next month Yorke was promoted Attorney-General.[13]

That Pitt by resigning had ill-served his country was proved conclusively when on 19 December Spain declared war. Charles III, in making the mistake of his reign, let himself be carried away by wild dreams of annexing Portugal and Brazil and so recreating the grand Iberian Empire of Philip II. His fleet comprised many superbly built and very heavily gunned men of the line, but the quality of command was extremely poor and the French navy in no condition to give support. To speculate whether Charles III would by Pitt's remaining in power have been deflected would be pointless. Certain it is that Pitt, had he bided his time six weeks, would have been standing

before Parliament and the nation with the unassailable authority
of a man proved right, ready to fight Spain to her knees. As it
was Bute's negotiations would continue in deep secrecy but not
of the stuff that Pitt would have purposed. In the House of
Commons Pitt abstained from the temptation to have his tit-for-
tat and called for a united effort regardless of cost. Choiseul was
not venturing beyond hope of compromise peace and to that end
Pitt's downfall was his surest gain: a war-weary people was
presided over by a young King and a weak-willed Favourite.
But to safeguard the House of Bourbon from utter humiliation
some great success such as might shake those pliable men Bute
and Newcastle was imperative. France and Spain had in the
West Indies some thirty men of the line and either Jamaica
might be captured or the British sugar convoy destroyed.
Gibraltar was open to attack and finally Choiseul was still
banking upon that hoary ace of trumps, some sort of glorified
raid upon the south coast of England, resulting in the collapse
of British credit. But his mood was far from optimistic: 'Well do
we know that, in spite of the wide distribution of their fleet
which they have always maintained throughout the war, they
have always shown themselves in a position to face every danger
with which France threatened them.'[14]

When on 6 January Bute held a Cabinet meeting at his house,
he was confronted with news of the fall of Colberg, the important Prussian port on the Baltic. He was appalled at the seemingly endless prospect of paying for Prince Ferdinand with
Frederick a liability, but was all for vigorous war against Spain.
None could deny that honour required the despatch of an army
to defend Portugal. Bute also carried agreement that a project
to take Havana, which originated with Pitt and Anson had
planned in detail, should be put in motion, much though
Newcastle quavered at the expense. Bute did not raise the
question of Frederick's subsidy, but he did suggest the withdrawal of British troops from Germany. Newcastle and Devonshire pointed out that Britain would thereby for ever forfeit her
reputation and if the French army were not tied down in
Germany an attempt to invade Britain might follow. When two
days later Devonshire saw Bute, he was smilingly confronted
with the revelation of the peace feelers put out through Viry

and the Bailli de Solar.[15] And that very day Bute penned a despatch to Mitchell instructing him that Frederick must seek his own salvation.[16] But on 30 January a despatch from Mitchell revealed that the international situation had been completely transformed by the death of the Czarina Elizabeth on the last day of 1761. Her successor, Peter III, a fervent admirer of Frederick, not only ordered his army out of Prussia but even prepared to turn it against Austria. Bute saw his chance; Frederick might be asked to accept an end to British assistance without loss of honour, Newcastle would be nicely out-manoeuvred and Pitt find difficulty in winning an audience favourable to Prussia.

Frederick was badly informed of the state of parties in London. Asked by Bute to lay before the British Government his future plans, he replied with a brief letter 'breathing war more than ever'. To Frederick the revolution in Russia was the blessing from heaven that would win him not only Silesia but even Bohemia and he expected Bute and Newcastle to find in the Spanish intervention a parallel suited to Britain. Bute's mood darkened when in an intercepted and deciphered despatch from Frederick to Knyphausen, the British ministry were recommended for Bedlam. The Prussian minister blandly requested that Frederick's subsidy of £670,000 be renewed in unamended form. Matters were made worse when Knyphausen, with an extraordinary lack of discretion, approached Pitt for advice upon how to procure a change of government and then blabbered to Bute:

'Kniphausen told Ld Bute yt. he had talked with Mr. Pitt & ye heads of all ye factions in this Country & they were all for his Master, Ld Bute replied that he w^d do better to talk to ye King's Ministers & not cabal with Factions. they quite quarrell'd.'

Even Newcastle was taken aback at such temerity and told the Prussian minister that to use happenings at St Petersburg as a means to further war was a grave mistake: 'yt. ye subsidy did not press and must be delay'd till we had answers from Mr. Keith and Mr. Mitchell with an account w^t use ye King of Prussia meant to make of this Event in Russia.'[17]

Bute was veering round to the sensible standpoint that the withdrawal of British troops from Germany might be treated separately. At a Cabinet of 22 February he asked Newcastle whether money could be found to maintain an army of 70,000 men in Germany: 'he replied if the Expence of Portugal does not go beyond w^t appears at present & there are no other expences I am of opinion I can support them for this present year, but cou'd he for another year, he c'd not tell he c'd only answer for this year'. At this Bute was 'well pleased'.[18] On 6 March 1762 Pocock, d'Aché's gallant opponent in the Indian Ocean, sailed from Britain bound for Havana, having first taken his leave of Pitt.[19] His fleet conveyed 4,000 soldiers commanded by Cumberland's favourite, the 3rd Earl of Albemarle, and a reinforcement from North America was planned too. Pocock was to rendezvous at Barbados with Rodney, who might perhaps by this time have taken Martinique.

As the Havana expedition went its way Bute sent his terms to Paris and their generosity aroused Newcastle's warm approval. That Canada and the Ohio should be British and only Louisiana proper French was not open to question. But France would be allowed access to the Newfoundland Fisheries outside territorial waters, with St Pierre and Miquelon as abris, subject to a non-fortification clause. In the West Indies Guadeloupe would be handed back and the four smaller Windward Islands be divided equally in full sovereignty between the two powers, and here Bute knew full well that the situation might change altogether if Martinique or Havana fell. In West Africa either Senegal or Goree would be retroceded. So far as concerned India, the renewal of the leases of the French factories, principally Pondicherry, Karikal and Chandernagore, was freely granted. The points of difference between Britain and Spain were academic and should present no obstacle. It followed logically that in Europe there should be a return to the *status quo ante bellum*, with Minorca returned to Britain. The future of Silesia did not fall within the compass of the negotiations. But Choiseul was not in a moderate frame of mind and when in April he offered his terms even Bute had to describe them as insolent. Choiseul naturally recognised that in respect of Canada the fact of conquest must be accepted and welcomed the concession of the

Newfoundland Fisheries. With regard to the French East India
Company Choiseul knew himself fortunate to find terms. It
therefore came as an unpalatable surprise to Bute that Choiseul
should in respect of the West Indies ask for conditions in no way
warranted by the outcome of the fighting. Choiseul belonged to
the school of rigid mercantilism and, the Newfoundland
Fisheries apart, the Caribbean sugar plantations were the only
colonial interests he considered useful. In respect of the division
of the neutral islands he made the significant variation that the
most important, St Lucia, and one other pass to France.
St Lucia was essential for the protection of Martinique, which
then, in the event of future war, would still constitute a valuable
base. All Britain stood to gain from her costly West Indian
campaigns would be the choice of two of the three least fertile of
the Windward Islands. Bute and Egremont prepared an answer
leaving Choiseul an opening to write further, but that letter was
not sent.[20]

A fortnight later came glorious news from the West Indies.
Rodney, with his expedition against Martinique, had arrived
off Barbados on 22 November and was met by eighteen ships
of the line, a score of cruisers and transports carrying 13,000
men commanded by Douglas and Rollo. Martinique surrendered on 15 February and Grenada and St Lucia soon
followed; a French reinforcement under Chef d'Escadron
Blénac had come too late. France had lost her entire West
Indian empire except Haiti and Britain held to ransom a great
trade in sugar and Negro slaves. Pitt welcomed news of
Martinique as further evidence of God's design for the British
nation and wrote to Warburton: 'May our Country stand in the
smile of Heaven, and may shortsighted silly man, if it does not
know how to improve at least not be able totally to reject the
proferr'd blessing.'[21] Though such complacent certitude may
have a maleficent ring to the modern ear, Pitt's age believed
prosperity to be the divine reward for virtue. After Martinique
Bute could hardly confront Parliament and the nation with
terms substantially less than what Pitt had been ready to consider the year before. When on 26 March the Cabinet met at his
office, he was relieved that Egremont's reply to Choiseul had
not gone off, 'for w^t wou'd People say if we had made such an

offer after ye success of Martinico & therefore he imagined the negotiation of Count Viry shou'd be dropp'd'. Newcastle, Hardwicke and Devonshire wanted a letter sent to Solar and Bute complied with a meaningless draft which left open further communication.[22]

Though the negotiations with France were shelved, the votes for foreign subsidies and the war in Germany had to be decided upon before Parliament was prorogued for the summer recess. Here Bute saw that a resounding defeat for Newcastle would force his resignation. For some time Samuel Martin, Secretary to the Treasury and originally a Pitt appointment, had been covertly supplying Bute with details of the Treasury accounts. Since about the middle of March Newcastle had had his suspicions and at his request a Cabinet was held at Egremont's office on 10 April. Newcastle insisted that a vote of two millions for foreign subsidies and the army in Germany was the least he could ask for. Grenville, who had Martin's figures, held that with the savings from the capture of Belleisle and the reductions to be anticipated in America, one million was sufficient. The atmosphere was unpleasant and bitter, with Grenville hinting at 'such immense frauds' in the Treasury accounts. The Council broke up without a decision.

That evening Newcastle wrote to Hardwicke of his belief that Grenville was planning to supplant him at the Treasury: 'Let Mr. Grenville carry on his Maritime War, as he pleases; and much good may it do him!' It was no surprise to Newcastle when on 12 April Bute revealed Martin's treachery. Their inevitable altercation was couched in terms of the public attitude to Pitt's resignation. Bute pointed out that opinion would accuse them of levering Pitt out and then carrying on with his 'Continental War'. To this Newcastle had an easy rejoinder: 'I will tell your Lordship what *they say*, that Mr. Pitt went out, because we would not declare war against Spain; and as soon as he was out, we did the same thing; and that being the case, Mr. Pitt would carry on his own measures better than anybody.' The King, underneath his hero-worship for Bute, did not lack pluck and on 15 April wrote to him of his indifference to Newcastle: '. . . in my conscience I don't believe he would have ten followers if out of place'. He also suspected that Grenville had an eye on the

Treasury, which he found quite laughable. On the evening of 25 April Martin presented Newcastle with a paper proving that Prince Ferdinand's army and the war in Portugal could in fact be met with only one million. Grenville's case was proved and the ground cut from under Newcastle's feet.

Newcastle told Bute on 7 May that recent events made his resignation imperative. He promised not to oppose the vote for one million only but to instruct Barrington, the Chancellor of the Exchequer, to put it to the House of Commons. When Bute expressed anxiety that his departure might weaken the possibility of peace, Newcastle promised not to oppose that either: 'I also said smiling I extremely approve *your peace*; I wish I could approve as much *your war*; meaning his ridiculous maritime war.' Next day Newcastle saw the King and announced his intention of laying down office. Newcastle fondly believed his resignation need not affect his 'friends'; he asked them not to quit their employments but 'continue to act with me, in the same conduct, as when I was in business . . .'. Things, however, were not what they had been during the Pitt and Devonshire administration when George II had hated his ministers and wanted Newcastle back. For six years George III had wanted Newcastle out and Bute in as soon as might be after his accession. Hardwicke saw his old friend's mistake and told him frankly that he must either withdraw from public life or wholeheartedly oppose.[23]

Newcastle had kept Pitt at arm's length for as long as he dared. Then such had been his power that Pitt, against his real feelings, had been forced to join with him in order to win the war. To Newcastle Pitt had been the intruder to whom he had been compelled to grant almost an equality but without ever understanding him. Newcastle never really comprehended Pitt's 'blue-water' war. Pitt on his side had come to accept that the German front could serve as a diversion and Newcastle had with magnanimity acknowledged that his efficient ability to organise the army and navy had secured success. But Newcastle, motivated by greed for power, had by acquiescing in Pitt's resignation sealed his own downfall.

Bute was Prime Minister at last and George Grenville naturally succeeded him as Secretary of State for the North. As his Chancellor of the Exchequer Bute appointed Dashwood in place of Barrington, who made no complaint at being shifted to the Treasurership of the Navy. Dashwood's appointment was welcomed by Grenville: 'I rejoice extremely as I am convinced that his behaviour will be full of honour and spirit towards the publick.'[24] The palace revolution set in motion on the death of George II had achieved finality. Parliament was prorogued for the summer holiday without the subsidy for Frederick being renewed. Czar Peter III's reign shortly ended when he was deposed and murdered with the connivance of his wife and successor, Catherine II the Great, who withdrew from the war altogether. Sweden, unable to shoulder the burden of the northern front alone, rapidly made peace. Frederick had nothing to fear from fighting Austria alone.

Bute had somehow to make a peace the House of Commons would accept in the face of Pitt's certain disapproval and possibly, too, with Newcastle turned enemy. He knew that his administration could never win the popularity that by right appertained to Pitt *solus*. The loss of Martinique did not influence Choiseul into budging in respect of St Lucia. He knew Bute would yield much rather than the negotiations break down and pointed out the advantages of moderation; no victor looking for a stable peace could hope to retain all the spoils; that Britain, with a population of six millions, should press her advantage fully over a nation with twenty-five million peoples must excite the apprehension of Europe and invite a war of retribution. Bedford especially appreciated the logic of Choiseul's common sense, but he could afford to despise public opinion where Bute was susceptible. With unusual acumen Bute hit upon a brain-wave which brought agreement nearer: the Mississippi as dividing line between Britain and France in North America would allow the restoration of Guadeloupe and Martinique. At heart he would have liked to reserve all four neutral islands for Britain but was not ready to fight over St Lucia.

At a Cabinet of 21 July Grenville, newly appointed Secretary of State, showed himself a stumbling-block over an easy peace. Therefore, with the connivance of the King, Bute and Egremont, without letting Grenville know anything, intimated to Choiseul that Britain would not allow St Lucia to be an obstacle. At this deception Bute felt uneasy and set that old fox Viry into hinting to Newcastle he would be welcomed into the Cabinet. Newcastle weakly professed himself content with the thought of being Lord Privy Seal but with 'a Treasury of friends'. Hardwicke would not allow Newcastle to be fooled and on 28 July told Bute that he could not come in unless measures were regulated his way. By that time the King and Bute had decided that before long Grenville had better be pushed downstairs.[25]

Outside the haven of power he had so long enjoyed, Newcastle felt completely lost. Since that fatal day of Klosterseven Cumberland had had nothing to do but breed Arab racehorses and stand idle whilst others gathered the laurels; that in Fox he had backed the wrong man and found more than his match in Pitt could not be gainsaid. But in the situation arising from Newcastle's downfall he saw a chance of recovering some semblance of his old prestige and no doubt entertained a hearty contempt for the daffodil Favourite his nephew had foisted upon the country. Windsor Lodge was only a few miles from Newcastle's suburban palace Claremont and a royal invitation had shortly followed the change of ministry. There could be little doubt that the Duke advised Newcastle to seek an understanding with Pitt.

Towards the end of July, Pitt and Granville had a political discussion at Bath and from Viry and Mansfield Newcastle got wind that Pitt was not prepared to contemplate an alliance with the Old Whigs. He was correct, and the grape-vine reached Bute's ear that Pitt 'would support his measures in Parliament as a friend to his country tho' an enemy to himself'. Of Pitt's real motives the King was highly sceptical: '. . . Mr. Pitt's placidity is certainly occasion'd by his looking on the next session as not a time for disturbance, for his goodwill if that were possible is not what can be rely'd on.' During August and September Bute again tried to win Newcastle over and sent Lyttleton with offers which included the Great Seal for Charles Yorke. There were occasions of comedy. All his life the King in conversation was apt to switch subjects and chop sentences in disconcerting array and of his interview on 3 September Newcastle could not help commenting upon the regal confusion between the Mississippi and the Ganges: 'As I am far from knowing exactly the state and limits of those countries I said nothing farther upon that head.'

The appointment of Bedford as special ambassador to France was a sure indication of the British desire for peace. He was worrying lest good news from Havana upset matters, and on 23 August Bute told him that Egremont and Grenville were most insistent that if Havana was taken there must be compensation and mentioned Florida or Porto Rico. When on 3 September Bute sounded Cumberland, he received the very honest advice that though the return of St Lucia to France would be criticised by the parliamentary opposition, the country wanted peace. By this time the popular rage against Bute occasioned at the time of Pitt's resignation had revived in full: Martinique, and the dismal failure of the Spanish invasion of Portugal, were not likely to be attributed to this ministry. In a couple of months Bute would have Parliament to deal with and, as Grenville certainly could not be relied upon, Fox's support was enlisted. Soon Fox, only too eager to indulge his envy of Pitt, was busy writing to Cumberland pointing out that his own interests would best be served as mediator between the King and the politicians rather than as head of an opposition; otherwise Bute might make a pact with Pitt, 'who would bring such popularity with him to the King as has never yet been seen'. Pitt, 'sole minister', would be no service to the royal family.[26]

On 29 September news reached London that Havana had surrendered to Pocock and Albemarle on 14 August. The British flag flew over the Queen City of the Indies after an uninterrupted Spanish occupation of more than two centuries. Fourteen Spanish ships of the line, one-fifth of the entire Spanish navy, were destroyed and one hundred merchantmen were taken together with a booty of £750,000. The Spanish empire was paralysed; with Havana lost and Cadiz blockaded it would be impossible to bring home the annual treasure fleet upon which the entire machinery of government depended. The conquest of Havana deserves to rank with Anson's circumnavigation of the globe twenty years earlier as an epic achievement in the annals of the British navy. The greatest First Lord of the Admiralty of all time, Anson was on the verge of ending a life which had shed such glory upon the reign of George II and Pitt's name.

Havana brought more unpopularity to the ministry and in the Cabinet gave determination to Grenville. When next day Cumberland called to congratulate his nephew, the King was exceedingly gracious, but the Duke had no intention of being a buttress for Bute; on the contrary he was 'much soften'd towards Mr. Pitt'. Bute was so alarmed at the popular clamour that on 22 September Bedford was ordered to demand Porto Rico or Florida.[27] Newcastle was toying with a formal alliance with Pitt for the purpose of ousting Bute with a vague scheme of himself, Hardwicke and Devonshire directing affairs, but without taking office; 'but, in this, both Mr. Pitt and Mr. Legge must be principal parts'. Hardwicke drummed in the emptiness of this; ministers would not accept direction from men outside the Cabinet: 'And how does your Grace think Mr. Pitt would quadrate with it, if he were to be one of the Ministers?' In his lust for the trimmings of power Newcastle was deceiving himself: originally it had been he, Hardwicke and Devonshire on the pacifist wing and Bute acting John Bull to Pitt's lead. As Devonshire pointed out, Bute's peace was so near to what they themselves had been ready to agree as made no difference. Newcastle was hazarding his character as the oldest friend of the House of Hanover.[28]

When Grenville suggested that the preliminaries should not be signed until after Parliament had approved them, Bute's patience gave out. Fox was asked to take Grenville's place as Secretary of State and Leader of the Commons but lacked the stomach for a situation so prominent: 'It would be adding unpopularity to unpopularity, of which there was enough; . . .'. It was made clear to Fox, however, that if he wished to remain Paymaster he must undertake to see the peace through as Leader of the Commons and to that he capitulated. Lord Halifax therefore became Secretary of State for the Northern Department instead of Grenville who was pushed into the subordinate post of First Lord of the Admiralty, though remaining of the Cabinet. Fox, in his tough way, knew exactly what had to be done to see the peace through and gloated over the prospect of turning out any friends of Pitt and Newcastle not disposed to trim their sails.[29]

Already the King's rage had become incensed when Devonshire ignored a summons to attend a Council on the peace terms. 'These proud dukes', as he termed them, were out to exploit divisions within his government. On the evening of 28 October Devonshire called at Kew to hand in his resignation and, having been refused an audience, left his wand. Two days later Rockingham, one of the greatest Whig magnificos, resigned his place in the Household. On 3 November the King struck Devonshire's name off the Privy Council roll with his own hand. That December Devonshire, Rockingham and Newcastle were dismissed from the Lord Lieutenancies of their respective counties, which had for so long been their family preserves. The King was in no difficulty, for there were other noblemen. The 3rd Duke of Portland succeeded Rockingham at the Bedchamber and the King happily pointed out that Granby's father Rutland could well take on the Lord Lieutenancy of Derbyshire.[30] That a Newcastle or a Devonshire should no longer find favour at Court was without precedent since the Glorious Revolution. To them an interpretation founded upon the King's being inculcated with Tory principles by Bute and the Princess Dowager was very understandable if misconceived. Newcastle, seeing his friends discomfited, began urging his supporters to resign.

The preliminaries of the Peace of Paris were signed at Fontainebleau on 3 November 1762. French Canada was recognised as British. That great colony, founded when Cardinal Richelieu was Prime Minister, nurtured during the reigns of Louis XIV and Louis XV, and for which great men, Duquesne and de la Galissonière, had devoted their energies and Montcalm had given his life, passed into oblivion; the seigneurs, peasants and priesthood, sixty thousand in number, born Catholic subjects of His Most Christian Majesty, became British nationals, with the free exercise of the Roman Catholic religion the sole reservation. The Mississippi became the permanent frontier between British and French territory, with a divergence at the mouth to allow the inclusion of New Orleans in Louisiana. The French were conceded participation in the Newfoundland

Fisheries outside territorial waters, with St Pierre and Miquelon as abris. On Choiseul's insistence Spain agreed to give up Florida in return for Havana. Britain was mistress of almost the entire western sea-board of North America from the St Lawrence to the cays of the Bahamas, with access to the Gulf of Mexico at Mobile. The capture of Manila was not yet known in Europe, otherwise the terms offered Spain would have had to be more severe. But in the West Indies Choiseul won hands down. Guadeloupe and Martinique were handed back to France, Britain receiving only Grenada in return. The neutral Windward Islands were divided in full sovereignty, St Vincent, Dominica and Tobago to Britain and St Lucia to France. With regard to the less important points of negotiation, the French retained Goree while Senegal became British territory. Those factories in India recognised as French on 1 January 1749 were restored, but the fortification of Chandernagore was forbidden. In Europe the *status quo ante bellum* was adhered to. Choiseul had won terms far better than anyone could have expected at the outset. He had taken over Louis XV's affairs when the war was already lost to France. Without the opportunity to prove himself war minister, in foreign affairs he had no peer but Kaunitz.

The summoning of Parliament had been put off from 11 till 25 November. Newcastle, unable to credit that his sway was completely ended, approached Pitt, using as intermediary Thomas Walpole, member of Parliament for Ashburton and a banker with a government contract for remitting money to the army in Germany. Pitt took the opportunity to discount the old tales of how he had 'lowered himself' to Bute and the King at the opening of the reign. He also made clear that he was not prepared to concert an opposition to the treaties with Newcastle. Pitt was still smarting at the memory of that combination of 'noble Dukes and great lords of the Cabinet' which had forced his resignation. On 13 November, and again four days later, Cumberland saw Pitt who disclaimed any intention of speaking on the occasion of the Loyal Address. Very shortly Pitt was seized with a terrible attack of gout.[31] The King, however, was in for a shock which for a very young man must have been far greater than any Newcastle had suffered in recent months. Bute, with a cowardice almost unbelievable, was proposing to resign and may not have perceived the deep hurt he was inflicting. George III, obsessed at his own sense of inadequacy, had not yet realised that Bute was not only mortal man but also something of a funk. What would become of those youthful dreams of he and Bute hand in hand purging the country's politics of vice? So blind was the King's faith that when the mob pelted Bute's coach with mud on his way to Parliament, he even pondered a coalition with Pitt.[32] It seems George III did not recognise that to 'gain Mr. Pitt' was completely incompatible with passing the treaties.

Fox did his work well. After the Cockpit meeting of 24 November he told Bute: 'The Torys see the situation of the King in its true light . . . we shall not only have numbers, but, which I more doubted of, and value more; a most eager co-operation of those we have.'[33] Next day, the Address, very tactfully worded, passed both Houses without an adverse vote. Beckford compared the preliminaries to Utrecht and dwelt especially upon the inutility of Florida. He was smartly answered by Charles Townshend, who in private had condemned the acceptance of Florida but now maintained that these treaties bore no resemblance to the treacheries of 1713.[34] Temple was writing to Wilkes: 'Mr. Pitt lies now in bed, tortured with a most violent fit of gout; God knows when it will end; when it begins so early in the winter, it generally lasts very long.'

At this time Wilkes's journal *The North Briton*, which Temple was paying for, was winning great publicity; No. 25 contained an attack upon the peace preliminaries expressly intended to annoy Bute and Newcastle as much as possible. Wilkes described his mood as 'Pitt-bitter', whilst Temple got down to constructing division lists and calculated that some fifty peers and one hundred and fifty commoners might be expected to divide against the Government. Pitt had however declared himself 'a single man', and was in no state of health to play politician.[35] When on 29 November the peace preliminaries were laid before the House of Commons, Bamber Gascoyne, listed by Fox as 'Tory' and 'Pitt', moved that they be read. Next day Dashwood carried 9 December as the day for the debate by 213–74 and Fox in a letter to Bute suggested Townshend as a possible mover or seconder. But on the day before the great occasion Townshend resigned from the War Office and many expected him to vote with Pitt against the administration.[36]

After Fox introduced the Peace, Pitt delivered his speech of condemnation: 'He began by lamenting his ill state of health, which had confined him to his chamber; but although he was at this instant suffering from the most excruciating torture, yet he was determined, at the hazard of his life, to attend this day, to raise up his voice, his hand, and his arm against the preliminary articles of a treaty, that obscured all the glories of the war, surrendered all the interests of the nation, and sacrificed the public faith by an abandonment of our allies.' His illness seemed to overcome him to such a degree that at the unanimous desire of the House he continued his speech sitting – a concession without precedent. To Pitt the fundamental principle of British foreign policy was 'that France is chiefly, if not solely, to be dreaded by us in the light of a maritime and commercial power. And therefore, by restoring to her all the valuable West-India islands, and by our concessions in the Newfoundland fishery, we had given to her the means of recovering her prodigious losses, and of becoming once more formidable to us at sea. That the fishery trained up an innumerable multitude of young seamen; and that the West-India trade employed them when they were trained.' Between the wars France had excelled Britain in the volume of her sugar trade, a commerce which afforded the home governments a constantly expanding revenue. By retaining Martinique or Guadeloupe Britain could have strengthened her marine and her national finances to a degree that the trade with North America could not possibly offer. The West African interest was inextricably bound up with the West Indian, yet Goree, essential for the safety of Senegal and which de Bussy had agreed should remain British, was to be abandoned. A great Atlantic trade, which ought to have been centred wholly upon Britain, was to be handed back to her inveterate rival. In India, where the French had nothing to offer, their old trading factories were returned them. Florida was no equivalent to Havana, by the capture of which 'all the Spanish treasures and riches in America, lay at our mercy'. For Minorca, the only conquest France had achieved, we 'had given the East Indies, the West Indies, and Africa'.

The oft-derided German war, Pitt continued, had kept the French army in Europe. It had been infinitely more economical for Britain to subsidise Prussia and maintain her own force on the Rhine than to despatch and supply even more men to North America. France had been drained of cash in subsidies to her allies, who had given her nothing in return – 'if we except the honour of burying above 150,000 of their best troops in Germany'. Pitt then went on to denounce the base desertion of the King of Prussia, who had been trifled with over his subsidy and then left wanting.[37] Here was no dwelling for compromise: Pitt wanted a peace founded upon the retention of conquests, to debar France for ever from the oceanic trades. Allowance must be made for the natural exaggerations of a statesman out of office: Pitt in power might have made greater concessions than his speech indicated. Even so, he would have been ready to continue fighting, no matter what the expense, because he was confident that only at this point in history could the Bourbon powers be brought to their knees.

His speech ended, Pitt left the House immediately. Fox replied and was followed by Charles Townshend who, to the surprise of many, 'spoke strongly and handsomely for the Peace, and was deservedly applauded'. As Rigby told Bedford: 'I never heard Pitt so dull in my life . . . Charles Townshend replied to him *after he was gone*, and made the finest speech I ever heard in my life.'[38] Barrington, too, commented of Pitt that he 'never made so long or so bad a speech'.[39] Pitt's open disclaimer of the least pretension to opposition restrained many who might have joined Newcastle's following in voting against the treaties. That evening the House divided 319–65 in favour of the peace. Great was Bute's relief and he wrote to Grenville: 'Millions of congratulations upon your very great, very able and manly performance: this will do, my dear friend, and shows you to the world in the light I want, and as you deserve.' On the following day there was a further vote of the Committee of the whole House, attended by less than 300 members, with Pitt absent. Opposition was led by Legge and the Commons divided 227–63 in support of the administration. In all only ninety-seven members voted against the terms – of the minority of sixty-

three on 10 December, thirty-one had been away the day
before.[40]

Only a handful of those who voted with the opposition could
be termed followers of Pitt and they included Beckford, Jemmy
Grenville and Wilkes, who acted as teller. The vote was made
up overwhelmingly of 'Old Whigs'. Newcastle, Devonshire and
Rockingham, although the peace really followed the lines they
had freely agreed to until Bute had become Prime Minister, did
their utmost to marshal their forces against administration and
with a marked lack of success. Although the general election of
1761 had returned a House of Commons at the time satisfactory
to Newcastle, only relations, very close friends and borough
clients remained loyal. Of the independent gentlemen of
England only fifteen county members voted against the peace.
There had indeed been a revolution in politics since the King's
accession. Countess Temple commented to her husband: 'I find
there are people that think if Mr. Pitt had not said he was a
single man, Charles Townshend, *cum multii aliis*, would never
have voted for the Peace, and that it was impolitic to make that
declaration when there was no occasion for it.'[41]

Fox had pushed the peace through, but too much should not
be made of personal pressures on members of Parliament. The
country wanted the end of war. Whereas the settlement of 1748
lasted only until 1754, that of 1763 lasted until 1778, fifteen
years compared with six. There is no reason to believe that war
would even then have broken out between Britain and France
but for the revolt of the Thirteen Colonies. Had the British
nation not become divided against itself, the Bourbon monarchies would never have had the spirit to embark on a war of
revenge. The long peace after 1763 and the unique circumstances which led to another French war in 1778 are decisive
evidence of the wisdom of the terms of the Peace of Paris. To a
by no means inconsiderable extent the Bute administration can
be regarded as credit-worthy.

After speaking against the peace Pitt went to Hayes and
rested his gout, downcast over Bute's triumph. He found a
welcome diversion in a correspondence with Thomas Hollis, a
rich eccentric of versatile interests. Hollis was reputed a 'repub-
lican' in that he refused to use his fortune to enter Parliament

and too an 'atheist' because he attended no church. Hollis was in fact a stout Englishman: he had approved Pitt's conduct of the 1761 peace negotiations and deplored his resignation. On 21 December 1762 Hollis informed Pitt by letter that Count Algarotti, the Italian dilettante, had left him a collection of drawings. In his customary artificial style Pitt replied in the third person: 'Little did he dream that his name was to live to Posterity, before Count Algarotti, by joining it with his own, forbid it to dye, till Litterature shall be no more; Thus giving him to be indeed. Immortal.' The drawings were a long time in coming and at one point Pitt sarcastically questioned the existence of such a clause in Algarotti's will. But after two years, to Pitt's great delight, the drawings appeared. The friendship with Hollis proved one of a lifetime.[42]

Despite the unswerving loyalty of the King and commanding majorities in both Houses of Parliament, Bute was still bent upon abandoning his post. While he dithered over how to contrive his exit with dignity, Fox set about the 'Massacre of the Pelhamite Innocents'. Obviously any of Newcastle's parliamentary following who had voted against the peace lost their places. But Fox extended his attack to Newcastle's many protégés among government employees throughout the country and instances of genuine hardship did occur.[43] Newcastle and Hardwicke were looking for a respected House of Commons man to keep together the remnants. Legge, his concern as always being for his own skin, was ready to hazard opposition provided he had the support of Charles Townshend and Attorney-General Yorke. Townshend, by reason of his chucking up the War Office, seemed an obvious recruit and in Parliament shone brilliantly, quite captivating Rigby: '. . . I could not help making comparisons in the House between him and Pitt, rather injurious to the latter'.[44] Yorke was in a dilemma, for his father wanted him Lord Chancellor. Plainly the only course for Newcastle and Hardwicke was to seek a reconciliation with Pitt.

Near Hayes, at Frognal, lived Thomas Townshend, a man of about thirty and member of Parliament for Whitchurch, Salop. 'Young Tommy Townshend', as he was known with a quite universal affection, was a cousin to George and Charles and, being Newcastle's great-nephew, was of the Whig hierarchy.

His vote against the peace had cost him his place in the royal household. But being a private man of fortune Tommy Townshend was not subservient to Newcastle and always considered his loyalties to lie with Pitt. Obviously he was the man to try and bring the two together. On 24 December 1762 Pitt and Townshend had a conference at Hayes. Townshend found Pitt still hurt by the desertion of so many Tories and deeply averse to the Bute and Fox regimen but not, however, ready to join Newcastle in the sense of making a party, though on 'all great occasions' he was ready to act with him. Newcastle and Rockingham, too, were pleased with what Pitt had to say but Hardwicke thought it all pointless: 'I cannot say I am much edified with Mr. Pitt's discourse with Tommy Townshend jun^r.'

Pitt stayed put at Hayes and Hardwicke, when he ran into Temple at Cumberland's on 1 February 1763, got no hint as to his intentions. As Pitt's absence was not at this time due to ill-health Hardwicke concluded that there must be a '*motive*': 'Whether that motive be an aversion to join with us, a desire to keep his connection with the Tories or some management for the Court, I am not wise enough to determine. But I am sure his conduct will not serve to carry on an opposition . . .'.[45] Shortly the Court received what appeared to be an accession of strength when Charles Townshend accepted the Presidency of the Board of Trade. With peace made the Cabinet was considering the rationalisation of the American establishment in respect of finance as the primary call of business. Townshend, a one-time member of the Board of Trade, might have some useful suggestions, though from the start the King had his doubts, writing to Bute on 10 February 1763: 'He will ever be so fickle that no man can depend on him.'[46]

Hardwicke and Newcastle were of the out-going generation and at the New Year Granville had died at Bath in his seventy-fifth year. He whom Pitt had denounced as 'the Hanover troop-minister' had lived to pass the epigram upon his resignation. Chesterfield's judgement upon 'The King's minister' who watched the withdrawal of 'The Great Commoner' deserves to be recalled: 'He would have been a great first minister of France – little inferior, perhaps, to Richelieu; . . .'. But Pitt at the end in no way belittled Granville's gifts: 'in the upper departments of government he had not his equal, and I feel a pride in declaring that to his patronage, to his friendship, and instruction, I owe whatever I am'.

On 10 February the Peace was signed in Paris by Bedford, Choiseul and Grimaldi. Meanwhile, Frederick and Maria Theresa had come to an agreement which was signed at Hubertusberg, a hunting lodge in Saxony, on 15 February. Frederick retained all Silesia and his territories on the Rhine were restored to him. The third world war of the eighteenth century had ended. In his attempt to recover Silesia Kaunitz had to face failure. Yet the course of events was not without logic; the fighting opened in North America and the primary outcome was the transfer of Canada from France to Great Britain. No matter what Pitt's views, Bute could congratulate himself on peace with honour.

With the spring Pitt recovered his spirits and came to realise that his authority could be rebuilt only by a reconciliation with 'the great lords' who had forced him into resignation. Pitt opined that the surest way to Newcastle's friendship would be by the employment of his most telling invective against the ministry in the House of Commons. The debate on the army estimates of 4 March gave him a pretext to attend and his appearance after an absence of almost four months was eagerly awaited. His speech, urging moderation in the reduction of the military establishment, passed by without event. Three days later he again appeared when the Chancellor of the Exchequer Dashwood introduced his budget, which included an additional tax on cider. Sensing danger Grenville, although First Lord of the Admiralty and so not directly concerned, rose to point out that any who criticised must suggest some equally remunerative alternative. This brought Pitt to his feet and though what he said had little to do with cider or taxation many thought 'that he *had* answered, and knew more of the matter than his antagonist'. Grenville, in an attempt to wind up the debate, plaintively asked the House where else a tax could be laid: 'I say, Sir, let them tell me *where*! I repeat it, Sir, I am entitled to say to them, tell me where!' Pitt looked at Grenville and hummed a popular ditty: 'Gentle shepherd, tell me where,' whereon the House collapsed with laughter and Pitt walked out.[47] Next evening Pitt attended a great Whig banquet at Devonshire House.

Two days later Newcastle wrote joyously to Hardwicke: 'What he [Temple] had been about, unsuccessfully, for Six months, viz. The bringing Mr. Pitt and us together, is now come about as It were of itself; That nothing could be better.'[48] The Government, alarmed at the prospect of Pitt in active opposition, decided to reduce the cider tax and place it on the retailer, but this gave opposition the opening to raise the dread word excise. The City of London aroused an agitation, and as might be expected the south-western counties followed. On the main debate of 13 March Pitt again dilated upon cider and found himself joined by William Dowdeswell, the Tory member for Worcestershire, but the division produced a Government majority of 138–81. Although for over seventy years the established convention had been that the peers should not tamper with a money bill, Pitt asked Newcastle to refrain from letting the cider tax through without a division. This extraordinary tangent Cumberland considered the height of folly but Newcastle, anxious to keep his new-found friendship with Pitt, gave in. Hardwicke spoke and voted against the cider tax, his last speech in Parliament. On the division the opposition fared even worse than in the Commons and the budget was passed.[49]

To the world Bute's administration appeared solid, but he was on the verge of collapse: 'If I had but £50 per annum I would retire on bread and water, and think it luxury compared with what I suffer.' Plainly he was under an obligation to find his own successor and had nothing better to suggest than Fox. Rather than that the King was ready to make 'Mr. Greenville' a peer and place him at the Treasury. Fox, only too eager to ditch Grenville, started his political map-making and on 14 March the King reluctantly consented that Bute might commission Fox to form a government: 'I know the soundness of my D. Friend's judgement . . .' was George III's truly astounding comment. But Fox showed himself reluctant to transcend his Pay Office riches and seize power as First Lord of the Treasury and Leader of the House of Commons, proof sufficient that he could never have been Pitt's equal. The door was ajar for Grenville, especially as the King had a fixed notion against Pitt's ever coming back: 'As to Mr. Pitt and Mr. Legge,' he wrote to Bute, 'they are more obnoxious to me than any men, no misfortune could drive me to act with them; their conduct is not to be parallel'd.' Elliot, not for the first time in his life, acted as Bute's go-between. To Grenville was put an arrangement originally of Fox's baking, that he take the Treasury but, so as to prevent too great a concentration of power in one family, his brother-in-law Egremont be replaced as Secretary of State by Shelburne. At this condition Grenville demurred so in desperation Bute replied on 23 March with a strong hint at Fox: 'I must in a few hours put other things in agitation.' Grenville, however, had his justification: Egremont could certainly be dropped, provided he freely consented, but that Shelburne, bright though he was, should enter the Cabinet at twenty-five must excite an insufferable jealousy. To this reasoning Bute yielded, so Egremont stayed on. Shelburne's promise was given recognition with Charles Townshend's Presidency of the Board of Trade. Townshend had made himself a thorough nuisance by trying in the House of Commons to stampede the Cabinet into rearranging American taxation before the facts relevant to legislation had been compiled. Notwithstanding, he was offered the Admiralty and on his refusal went away empty. On 2 April Bute attempted to round off the new Cabinet by writing to Bedford, who was still in Paris, offering him the Lord Presidency of the Council.[50]

The new arrangements were finalised at an audience accorded Grenville on 4 April. To the world in general it was put out that Bute had never wanted the Treasury and had served only in order to secure a satisfactory peace. To Grenville the King gave Bute's health as the pretext and promised his new minister every support. Bute's last ministerial act was to appoint his brother Stuart-Mackenzie Lord Privy Seal for Scotland, whose recommendations for the Northern Kingdom, Grenville was told by the King, must be accepted.

On 8 April Bute completed his resignation and on the following day Pitt penned to Newcastle his acid but just comment: 'As to the event of the day, I think it rather sudden than surprizing; Lord Bute's Undertaking seemed to me the Matter of Astonishment, not his Lordship's Departing from it.' However, Bute received a letter from the King couched in the most glowing terms: 'As I now write I can't help expressing how I feel his conduct yesterday, his openness on that most unhappy occasion (for I shall ever think it so) has more endear'd me to him than any one action of his life; I don't use plainer words because I am sure he understands my meaning...'. The position of Bute was indeed dangerously ambiguous, for on the very day that the King was writing his praises he informed Charles Yorke of his intention to be a private man, an undertaking completely inconsistent with the King's attitude and the favour shown Stuart-Mackenzie.[51] For the present he departed for Harrogate but might expect a summons if the King found himself in a quandary. This was the first danger in Grenville's mind as he surveyed the scene from the top of the tree.

CHAPTER 13

Pitt and the
Grenville Administration

'He took public business not as a duty which he was to fulfil, but as a pleasure he was to enjoy; and he seemed to have no delight out of this house, except in such things as some way related to the business that was to be done within it. If he was ambitious, I will say this for him, his ambition was of a noble and generous strain. It was to raise himself, not by the low pimiping politics of a court, but to win his way to power, through the laborious gradations of public service; and to secure himself a well-earned rank in parliament, by a thorough knowledge of its constitution, and a perfect practice in all its business.'

Edmund Burke's Tribute to George Grenville
in his Speech on American Taxation, April 1774.[1]

George Grenville followed the examples of Walpole and Pelham by annexing the Exchequer to the Treasury. Dashwood was happy to take household office and go to the Lords by the termination of the abeyance of the ancient le Despencer barony. Fox remained Paymaster but was forced by the King in a personal interview to accept a peerage as Lord Holland. The first disappointment for Grenville came with Bedford's reply to Bute of 7 April refusing to remain in the ministry: 'For God's sake persuade his Majesty to widen the bottom of administration, and if he has a mind to keep those out of his cabinet who have behaved to him with the least respect, [i.e. Pitt and Temple] let the Dukes of Newcastle, Devonshire, and Grafton, Earl Hardwicke, &c., be called again into his Majesty's service.' Pitt, too, had no confidence in the administration and on 9 April wrote to Newcastle suggesting a meeting. On 22 April Bedford formally resigned from his post as Lord Privy Seal and Granby's refusal to succeed him was a further blow, though he was pleased to become Lieutenant-General of the Ordnance.[2]

Temple, only three weeks after Grenville had taken office, set off a firework that would foul political life for the ensuing ten years. He was still subsidising the *North Briton*, with Wilkes editor, and No. 45 contained an attack upon the King's public veracity together with the usual silly and untrue innuendoes against his mother and Bute. The King, instead of leaving Wilkes to stew in his own juice, personally ordered Grenville to prosecute for seditious libel.[3] The Secretary of State Halifax issued what was known as a 'general warrant', which was a blank cover for the arrest of anyone suspected of printing, publishing or distributing No. 45, without any names being specifically inserted. This sweeping and savage procedure, used in seditious libel cases only, had arisen since the Glorious Revolution, but with the peace and prosperity of the eighteenth century prosecutions had become a very rare exercise in a reserve power and plenty of offences were passed by. But there was enough libel in No. 45 to satisfy any lawyer of Wilkes's guilt; he was a specially impudent fellow, and from the King's point of view had the added undesirability of a connection with Stowe. Wilkes and over forty journalists and book-sellers were hauled in, he being taken to the Tower – there was no question of a great nobleman such as Temple being brought to book. Undesirable publicity was bound to follow from Wilkes being the only member of Parliament ever prosecuted for seditious libel. Grenville, a man of the world, should never have allowed his young Sovereign to fall for such bait.

The first act in the drama opened when Charles Yorke, Attorney-General, prosecuted Wilkes before Pratt in the Court of Common Pleas. As parliamentary privilege carried immunity for a misdemeanour, Wilkes was discharged three days later. Although Pratt had merely executed the law, the circumstances of his career, having been promoted by Pitt and his long rivalry with Yorke, aroused much comment. Wilkes used the occasion to pose as the persecuted protector of 'the middling and lesser sort' and made himself the focus for the endemic unpopularity of the powers that be. The King dismissed Temple from the Lord Lieutenancy of Buckinghamshire. The new Lord Lieutenant le Despencer persuaded Quarter Sessions to vote their congratulations to the King upon the Peace, a courtesy Temple had studiously omitted and to which Wilkes and a few others refused to put their names.[4]

Grenville's worst fault was a lack of imagination with people. He made no attempt to flatter the good intentions of a young King, to whom he talked down in pompous manner: 'When he has wearied me for two hours he looks at his watch to see if he may not tire me for one hour more.' Grenville had been in office only a month when, instead of allowing him a decent chance, George III embarked upon a course of intrigue excusable only by his youth. Bute came back to London, found his feet, and was soon a frequent caller at the house of Hardwicke's son Lord Royston. On 13 May and again in June, at the King's command, Egremont engaged in long conversations with Hardwicke, who made clear that he was not going to desert his friends.

It next occurred to the King that, if Pitt could be persuaded to join his brother-in-law's ministry, the protection he looked to from the Old Whigs would be unnecessary. Towards the end of June Bute went to see him, but beyond the formal courtesies Pitt would not budge. So as to make sure that the right impression was landed with Newcastle, Pitt gave Charles Yorke every assurance of his favour, provided 'everything might be done with civility to my Lord Ch. J. Pratt'. The 30 June found Newcastle writing to Hardwicke of his complete confidence in Pitt. But the King and Bute did not grasp the situation. Granville's death had left vacant the Lord Presidency of the Council, which on 1 August Egremont offered to Hardwicke, with a hint at a court place for Newcastle. To Egremont Hardwicke made the position clear: 'Lord Hardwicke at once rejected the offer and said they would never come into office, but as a party and upon a plan connected with Mr. Pitt and the great Whig Lords, as had been practised in the late King's time.'[5]

The King had to recognise that Pitt and the Old Whigs would neither parley without the other. Although he and Bute had in 1761 and 1762 employed every device to undermine Pitt and Newcastle in turn, George III now resolved to push Grenville out and restore the great ministry of the Seven Years War. On 2 August he gave Grenville a very cold hearing and asked for ten days in which to consider his position. Grenville, Egremont and Halifax were mystified; some machination of Bute was discerned, and rightly.[6] Bute wanted to help the King get rid of odious Grenville but was not in a position to approach Pitt or Newcastle in person. But over the Peace he had worked cordially with Bedford, who had only four months before refused to join Grenville on the ground that his ministry had not comprised the Old Whigs. Bedford was the man to get hold of and as his emissary Bute selected John Calcraft, who had had a most successful and remunerative career in the Pay Office where many years ago he had been Pitt's junior. Calcraft went on a secret mission to see Bedford, who was at Blenheim Palace, the seat of his son-in-law the Duke of Marlborough. Bedford's advice was that Pitt be sent for. That day Calcraft wrote to Temple asking how he could get in touch with Pitt and enjoining secrecy. Temple was journeying to the west country and Calcraft's letter caught up with him at Hackwood Park, the Duke of Bolton's seat in Hampshire. Temple advised a direct approach to Pitt, who would soon be returning to Hayes for the rest of the summer.

On the morning of 14 August Calcraft repaired to Hayes and engaged in a conversation with Pitt lasting three hours which both undertook should remain private. Pitt emphasised that he was completely committed to Newcastle and did not stop there. He utterly rejected Bedford's intervention and vetoed the participation in either active or household office of any man who had been associated with the Peace of Paris. Considering that it was at Bedford's instance that Calcraft was at Hayes, Pitt could not have been more insulting. When Calcraft, on his return to London, saw Bedford's intimate Rigby he confined himself to the observation that Pitt could not move without the Newcastle

Whigs.[7] But he did not maintain the same reserve with Bute, so that the King heard of what had passed. Then on 21 August Egremont died of an apoplexy at his London house; a new Secretary of State had to be found.

Bute, finding his plan to use Bedford a cul-de-sac, steeled himself to an interview with Pitt. Beckford arranged the meeting which took place in Jermyn Street on Thursday, 25 August. Where Pitt had no intention of breaking with Newcastle so as to bolster up Grenville, a total change of ministry was another matter. Bute came away well pleased and Pitt was commanded to attend the King early in the afternoon of Saturday the 27th at the Queen's House, which did not become known as Buckingham Palace till George IV's day. Pitt's audience lasted nearly two hours; the authors of the Peace of Paris were to be dismissed and their places taken by the Newcastle Whigs; a new alliance with Prussia was to be negotiated. He was commanded to call back on the Monday. On this second occasion Pitt's expectations with regard to places were very stringent and he even rejected the King's suggestion of Granby as Commander-in-Chief in favour of Albemarle.

Grenville arrived whilst Pitt was still with the King and gloomily wrote to Halifax of their expected dismissals: 'I do not know the particulars, but by what I collected, the measure is fully taken.' On Pitt's leaving Grenville went in and got no change; the interview was very brief and that evening gossip told him 'that carte blanche is given, which account tallies with such observations as I could make'. Next morning Pitt saw Newcastle at Claremont and summoned Devonshire from Chatsworth: 'Whatever issue it may lead to I beg you will be assured that I shall, finally, take a share in nothing which does not carry with it the Duke of Devonshire's approbation, countenance and co-operation, and unless the system be so form'd that the great Revolution-Principle Families of the Kingdom shall return to be, where they ought to be; about the Throne and in the Councils of His Majesty.'[8]

But Pitt was counting his chickens too hastily. Elliot and Jenkinson, feeling great apprehension at the employments of Bute's friends being placed in question by Pitt's dogmatism over the Peace, went to Kew and put the wind up him so thoroughly that he yielded to their entreaties to keep Grenville on. At eight o'clock that Sunday evening Grenville was once more at the Queen's House, stayed half an hour, and that night wrote to Halifax: 'A new scene has been opened in consequence of the extraordinary terms demanded yesterday.' On Monday, 29 August, the King, instead of dismissing his old ministers and appointing the new, put everything back. The first thought of the ministers whose necks had been spared was retaliation; supposing Newcastle had not at heart endorsed Pitt's demand for wholesale dismissals, it might be possible to detach him 'and leave those worthy gentlemen, Lord Temple, Mr. Pitt, and their attached friends, in the lurch'. Elliot saw clearly that Bute as instigator of the attempted upheaval was in a most invidious situation and the last day of the month found him giving Grenville the following assurance: 'He seems extremely desirous that you may be armed with every degree of power so necessary at this juncture.' Grenville made clear that Bute must leave the royal counsels for ever, by which a withdrawal to Scotland was indicated. Bute left Court but shortly purchased the estate of Luton Hoo in Bedfordshire. A successor to Egremont was found in an old friend of Bedford's, the 4th Earl of Sandwich.[9] Pitt had let slip his chance. That he should lay down an international treaty, which could never be reversed, as a schismatic principle was as impracticable as impolitic. George III, by the rash promotion of Bute into the highest office, followed by his shabby treatment of Grenville, took first responsibility for the choppings and changings of this decade. But Pitt too, sullen and vindictive, from this point shares much of the blame.

On the day after the negotiations broke down Pitt and Temple flattered Calcraft with a visit. Calcraft acknowledged the compliment in a letter to Pitt: 'I never can forget the confidence you have placed in me, or be insensible to your approbation of my conduct.'[10] Calcraft the Pay Office tycoon and Pitt may appear incongruous companions. Yet Calcraft, like Potter and Beckford, became an intimate of the Pitt household. Very shortly Shelburne, the most promising young man in politics, convinced that Pitt's presence was necessary for any stable ministry, resigned the Presidency of the Board of Trade. His allegiance to Pitt was the decision of his life. A great landed proprietor in England and

Ireland with the right to sit in both Houses of Parliament, he was possessed of a lively and original intelligence and a consistent ambition together with a capacity for hard work. Shelburne brought with him his protégé Barré, one of the most noisy and pugnacious members of the House of Commons.[11] Pitt found another disciple in the young 3rd Duke of Grafton, who frequently called round for a chat about men and affairs.[12] Memory of the debacle of Pitt's resignation was fast fading and he found himself in fashion with the coming generation.

Pitt's obduracy towards all connected with the Peace of Paris cost him his friendship with Warburton. Already their relations had become strained when Warburton had published a most pompous pamphlet, for which he sought extra publicity in the form of an 'Advertisement' in praise of Pitt. Though the laudation was not rejected, Pitt took exception to two points in the text; firstly the placing of Puritanism upon a level of objection parallel to Popery; secondly the advocacy of a general law for the regulation of the press, as dangerous to liberty as irrelevant to the Bishop's subject. The episode was of some interest as indicating Pitt's attitude to religious and civil liberty. Warburton accepted the rebuke and amended the second edition. But when that September the clergy of his diocese passed a vote of congratulation to the King on the Peace Pitt never forgave him.[13]

Grenville knew that when in a couple of months time Parliament met he would be faced with the concerted opposition of Pitt and Newcastle. The case of Wilkes, so much in the public eye, would afford ample ground for contention. A ruling from the House of Commons upon parliamentary privilege in cases of seditious libel was clearly demanded. Grenville was blind to the consideration that to tamper with privilege merely to hound Wilkes wore an appearance of dishonesty and would merely keep him in the news. He could be confident of the support of Bute's following, bound to uphold a respect for the royal family. Grenville looked around for further support and saw Bedford easily open to recruitment. The King was irritated at Pitt's obduracy, which had brought the negotiations to nothing and saddled him with Grenville without respite. He therefore, through the agency of Sandwich, made certain that Bedford found out about Pitt's intransigent attitude towards him with Calcraft. Bedford, deeply incensed, accepted the Lord Presidency of the Council on 12 September. So as to make one more enemy for Pitt the King told Granby how during the August negotiations Albemarle had been preferred as Commander-in-Chief.[14]

The Wilkes furore could have been embarrassing to Pitt, because of Temple's involvement. Pitt had no intention of being dragged down into a personal defence of Wilkes, but was wholeheartedly opposed to any limitation of the privileges attached to membership of the House of Commons. During September he kept in touch with Newcastle and on 14 October wrote to him expressing the hope that Charles Yorke, still Attorney-General, might be influenced into upholding parliamentary privilege. Pitt felt Mansfield to be behind the prosecution: 'All I will say, is, that My Resistance of Lord Mansfield's Influence is not made in Animosity to the Man, but in Opposition to his Principles . . .'. Yorke was not sympathetic to Pitt's views on the law, but nor did he wish to face him in debate. After consulting with Newcastle, Devonshire and Rockingham, he resigned on 3 November.[15]

When Parliament assembled on 15 November, Wilkes was the first call of business in both Houses. The Secretary of State Sandwich produced before the House of Lords a versification printed on Wilkes's press entitled 'Essay on Woman'. This piece was an indecent parody of Pope's 'Essay on Man', with scurrilous notes impudently attributed to Warburton, and the author had probably been Potter. Although the exposure was probably the result of theft by government agents, the House of Lords voted 'Essay on Woman' a blasphemy and a libel against the Bishop of Gloucester. In a division lobby of the House of Commons Horace Walpole ran into Pitt, who indignantly exclaimed: 'Why do they not search the Bishop of Gloucester's study for heresy?' That day the House of Commons, immediately following the Speech, considered a message from the King delivered by Grenville that one of their number was the author of 'a most dangerous and seditious libel'. The *North Briton* was unanimously voted 'a false, scandalous and seditious libel' and burning by the common hangman was ordered. Samuel Martin, Secretary to the Treasury, used language so insulting that next day he met

Wilkes's challenge to a duel. Wilkes was wounded and found a withdrawal to Paris on the plea of ill-health convenient.

A government motion of 23 November, that parliamentary privilege did not cover seditious libel, brought Pitt to his feet. He carefully dissociated himself from any sympathy with Wilkes and condemned the whole series of *North Britons*: 'The author did not deserve to be ranked among the human species – he was the blasphemer of his God and the libeller of his King.' But the abandonment of privilege Pitt denounced as subversive of the popular liberties the House was pledged to uphold. When a complaint was made against a member the House could always give him up: 'This privilege having never been abused, why then is it to be voted away? Parliament has no right to vote away its privileges.'[16] Wilkes never forgave Pitt, the quondam companion who had used to smile at his witticisms, the strictures he employed that day. In his autobiography Shelburne was to accuse Pitt of hypocrisy: 'He depended upon taking quick turns, which was his forte: example Wilkes.'[17] Yet as a patriotic statesman Pitt was right to drop so dangerous a man and by leaving him to his fate was free to put his views without embarrassment. The House of Commons relinquished privilege in the instance of seditious libel by 243–166: the minority included almost every member who had voted against the Peace. Shelburne and Barré, and General Henry Seymour Conway too, were deprived of their army commissions for voting against the ministry. Particular resentment was aroused in the instance of Conway, younger brother to the 1st Earl of Hertford, one of the most opulent landowners in England and Ireland and a great man at Court. Despite an indifferent career in the Seven Years War, including participation in the Rochefort fiasco, Conway was a favourite with Cumberland and very close to Rockingham and Grafton.

After the debate of 12 November Pitt was seized with the worst fit of gout ever and withdrew to Hayes. During the Christmas recess he wrote to Newcastle: 'I will say but little upon Evils – beyond all Remedy; let those of happier Complexions hope; I confess, I despair; – Having seen the Greatness of England, by a strange Fatality, thrown away; & seeing now the Constitution expounded into whatever the purpose of the

Day may render Expedient.'[18] Pitt was not in London to witness the final act in the amazing drama of the *North Briton*. The mob intercepted the common hangman in his incendiary duty: 'The cry was "Wilkes and Liberty!" A jackboot and a petticoat – the mob's hieroglyphics for Lord Bute and the Princess, were burned with great triumph and acclamations.' Wilkes, who remained in Paris, was held to be in contempt by the House of Commons, expelled and outlawed. But in truth the round went to him because Pratt's decision in *Leach v. Money*, where an innocent man had been apprehended, made the further use of a general warrant impracticable, if not illegal. Pitt was able to attend the debate in the House of Commons of 13 February to speak in favour of a motion declaring general warrants against the law, but the ministry carried the day 232–218. This substantial majority included not only all the friends of Pitt and Newcastle but too Sackville, the Townshend brothers and many back-woodsmen who contributed to make one of the fullest houses of the period.

Pitt's attack of gout would preclude further activity for many months. The pitch was left to Grenville for the Old Whigs had never shown the least ability to concoct an opposition without Pitt. On 6 March 1764 the death of Hardwicke deprived New-castle of his oldest friend and best adviser. Though for many years Hardwicke had distrusted Pitt's ambition, he had come to respect him as an honest man above petty interests. Above all, the greatest Lord Chancellor of the century had added states-manship to legal eminence as the architect of the great Pitt and Newcastle ministry. Newcastle felt even more desolate when the following November Devonshire died at the early age of forty-six; he had never been strong. A life-long friend of Fox he had been reluctant to serve with Pitt in 1756 but did his duty. He had come out at his best when after George III succeeded and Bute came to the fore he tried to keep Pitt and Newcastle in harmony. The losses of Hardwicke and Devonshire made certain that in any further negotiation aimed at unseating Grenville the King would turn to Cumberland.

To Grenville 'Wilkes and Liberty' had been merely a tiresome interruption to what he considered the main business of his Government, the reconstruction of taxation. From April he had in Thomas Whateley, an expert on Shakespeare and gardening, a Secretary to the Treasury of his own choosing. Grenville realised that after the trouble over the cider tax serious financial innovations were not practicable and therefore set about improving the existing system by economies and efficient administration. Though he could not reduce the land tax to 3s he had by the end of 1764 rendered additional loan finance unnecessary. The King, set against anything Grenville did, made the acid and rather snobbish comment: 'That gentleman's opinions are seldom formed upon any other notions than such as may be expected to originate in the mind of a clerk in a counting house.' Grenville next turned to the question of the American revenues. In justice to the British tax-payer he was resolved that the Thirteen Colonies and the West Indies should contribute towards the cost of the military establishment overseas. Britain had shouldered the burden of the war which had given the colonies their security and furthermore, by a special Act of Parliament, their governments had been repaid their expenses. Grenville first proposed a skilful reorganisation of the American customs. As Walpole's molasses duty of 6d on foreign sugar had always been systematically evaded, Grenville reduced it to 3d and employed the navy as collector. His 'Sugar Act' was the preliminary to the Stamp Act of 1765.

Grenville had no intention of imposing an onerous, still less an unjust or unconstitutional burden upon the American colonies. He planned only a marginal shift of taxation and would have preferred the colonies to offer a voluntary and self-imposed contribution. As no local Assembly offered to tax its electors, Grenville on 6 February put before the House of Commons a bill to tax the colonies directly by imposing a stamp duty upon newspapers and documents similar to that in Britain. Shelburne's follower Barré was one of the few to oppose the Act in a celebrated and oft-quoted peroration. Despite protests from four out of the Thirteen Colonies and from Jamaica, the Stamp Act passed through the Commons by 245–49 and through the Lords without even a debate. Benjamin Franklin, who had just arrived in England, proceeded to recommend a few of his friends as stamp collectors.

Amidst his gouty sufferings Pitt had encountered a piece of

fairy-tale luck. There was in Somerset an octogenarian baronet of irate spleen, Sir William Pynsent of Burton Pynsent. In Queen Anne's last Parliament he had voted against the Treaty of Utrecht. His natural heir was a distant relative, Frederick Lord North, who with his large family could have used the money, but on hearing that his kinsman had voted for the Peace of Paris – another Utrecht! – Pynsent cut him out and left all to Pitt. After a protracted lawsuit Pitt's title to the entire property, worth £3,000 p.a., was upheld. Together with the £3,000 pension already entailed upon his wife's peerage, Pitt had become a rich man. Amherst addressed to him a charming letter of congratulation upon his good fortune.[19] Pitt set about the 'improvement' of his estate with enthusiasm; as might be expected the changes he wrought were picturesque and completely uneconomic – a substantial annuity would have been a far better inheritance than this costly toy. But the joys of landscape gardening and pretending to farm helped to lift his mind out of the depression which had engulfed him for the last eighteen months. In the early spring Pitt came up to Hayes.

In Pitt's recovery Newcastle saw hope of resurrecting an opposition and towards the end of March prevailed upon Rockingham to undertake the arduous task of visiting him. Rockingham's obvious starting point was the dismissals of Conway, Shelburne and Barré for their votes over Wilkes. Pitt, while sympathising with the injustice, doubted whether a question so close to the royal prerogative was suitable parliamentary material: 'He had never urged the subject being mooted at all.' Pitt then dug up all his old bitterness over Newcastle's abandoning 'his war'. Rockingham went away feeling Pitt's return to parliamentary activity might be injurious rather than of advantage. Newcastle, though very hurt at these old scores being re-engaged, none the less prudently pointed out that without Pitt no opposition would come about: 'Let them say what they will, Grenville will have *champ libre*, and nobody to oppose him.'[20]

Time had not improved the King's feelings for Grenville, who had shown an extraordinary lack of sympathy when early in the year he had been smitten with a series of feverish colds. On one occasion Mansfield had been sent to give the young man a

general ticking off: this, as it ruined the King's Sunday afternoon, was impolitic as well as impolite. But then Grenville did
not accept that he was below par: 'The King's confinement
makes a great deal of talk, as few people believe him to be as ill
as is given out by Lord Bute's friends.'[21] But George III was
never a malingerer and prudently requested Grenville to prepare
a scheme of Regency in the event of his infant son succeeding as
a minor. To the King as much as to Newcastle Pitt's return to
the scene was a welcome portent that Grenville might be got rid
of. The suggestion he hit upon as leader of a new ministry, the
2nd Earl of Northumberland, may have been a little surprising.
Inheritor by marriage of the Percy title and half their estates,
Northumberland was intelligent, respected and endowed with
a discriminating if sumptuous taste in the visual arts. Pitt was
too infirm and Newcastle too old to undertake the Treasury:
Northumberland as figure-head would be eminently respectable, though a disadvantage was that his eldest son had recently
married one of Bute's daughters. Cumberland's guiding hand
was brought in.

On Easter Day, 7 April, the Duke, about to set off for his
Newmarket stud, received an unexpected summons to the
Queen's House. Since the Peace George III and his uncle had
not met in private and the Duke's health and appearance had
sadly deteriorated. Gluttony had settled his weight at twenty
stone, his sight was poor and the leg wound incurred at Dettingen made movement painful. On this occasion the King limited
his observations to the coming Regency bill, without entering
upon what the arrangements might be. Cumberland suspected
his nephew had more on his mind.[22]

With regard to the proposed Regency Grenville and the King
were soon at loggerheads. The King wished to reserve the right
to nominate the Regent himself, which Grenville suspected to be
a plot by Bute to nominate the Princess Dowager. Grenville
made what appeared to be the simple suggestion that the Queen
be Regent, but this annoyed Cumberland, who had been
included in the Act of 1751. While the bill was before the House
of Lords an amendment was carried to include all the male
descendants of George II, being British subjects, in the Regency
Council, which would include Cumberland and the King's

younger brothers. But the King's mother was therefore left out, a stupid affront which aroused general indignation. In the House of Commons her name was inserted and the King was naturally enraged at finding himself associated with so maladroit an episode.

At Newmarket the Duke was busy with his horses when he received an unexpected caller in Northumberland. The talk soon moved from racing: both agreed that the state of business was lamentable and the Duke showed anger at the indignities which 'the gentlemen in power' heaped upon his nephew. Through April they kept in touch until on 6 May Northumberland committed himself with the King's spoken order that the Duke should open a negotiation with Pitt, Temple and the great Whig families. Next day Cumberland spoke to Newcastle and Rockingham of the outlines of the proposed ministry, Northumberland at the head with Pitt and Charles Townshend Secretaries of State. Newcastle and Rockingham were enthusiastic to see this plan come to light. It was agreed that Pitt be tackled by Albemarle, the victor of Havana, to whom Cumberland gave this message: 'the eyes of the whole nation are now all looking up towards him, and that should he not come to the relief of his King and country, at this time both in danger, I greatly feared that he would no longer preserve that weight in this country which he so justly bore'.

At Hayes on 7 May Albemarle, the plain soldier, had to endure four hours of Pitt at his most difficult. Pitt set about making demands of the utmost stringency; the restoration of Conway and displaced officers 'as well as many others who had been displaced for their opposition'; ample justice and favour for Lord Chief Justice Pratt; a disclaimer of the use of general warrants and amendments to the cider tax; the regulation of military and naval promotions by merit and 'not for dancing attendance'. Finally, and in his eyes most important, Pitt asked for a 'foreign system of affairs', meaning the end of British isolation by means of a Prussian alliance and this, he expected, 'would not render the closet more favourable towards him'. That evening Cumberland summoned Temple and Grafton to town.

Grafton refused all thought of office with the specious excuse that as the plan must succeed his engagement in business was unnecessary. On the evening of 10 May Cumberland received Temple and was not pleased at what he found: 'At six we accordingly met, and I cannot help saying that I think he was more verbose and pompous than Mr. Pitt; nor do I think so near concluding.' Temple more or less reiterated what Pitt had said, with the rider that meeting their demands would constitute no guarantee of their taking office. At this impudence Cumberland came near to losing his temper. Temple went to Hayes and on his return saw Cumberland once more, merely to repeat his previous bombast. Cumberland reasonably assumed him to be speaking for Pitt too, and met with the demand that 'Lord Albemarle would make one more jaunt to Hayes, to know whether Mr. Pitt's answer would be of the same nature . . .'. Pitt told Albemarle that neither he nor Temple would consider office unless their points were met. Cumberland could see the unfortunate King in thrall to Grenville and Bedford for ever. But at this point Rockingham screwed up his courage, dropped all reserve and offered to serve the King in any capacity asked for. This open declaration of a sense of duty proved the turning point in his career, for Cumberland could perceive that here was a man who might head a ministry. The King was impatient to hear what decisions had been arrived at, but when at eight o'clock on the Saturday Northumberland called on the Duke he was confronted with nothing better than Pitt's compliments and doubts: of him and Temple Cumberland spoke with extreme indignation. As there was no hope of the Old Whigs serving without Pitt, the Duke could only lament his inability to be of service.

At five o'clock in the afternoon of Saturday, 11 May, Cumberland sat down to dine at the house of his sister Princess Amelia. The proceedings were interrupted by Rockingham and Albemarle, who had a message from Northumberland, conveying the King's wish that the Duke go to Hayes in person; he might take a military escort to lend publicity to the visit. For a royal duke to honour the house of a subject was fairly unusual and, after Pitt's coldness and Temple's insolence, it was not surprising that Cumberland decided firstly to see his nephew. A little after six he arrived at Richmond Lodge and stayed till ten.

The King, in a most agitated condition, recounted every happening since Bute's resignation, a habit of self-justification in time of crisis that would remain with him through life. He pressed his uncle to see Pitt and next day, the Sunday, between nine and ten o'clock in the morning, Cumberland set out for Hayes with Albemarle in attendance. He left a message with Temple to be at Hayes by eleven.

Cumberland spent one and a half hours in *tête-à-tête* with Pitt: 'I repeated to Mr. Pitt the King's most sincere desire of seeing affairs at home and abroad carried on with more spirit and activity than he was able to do with this present Administration.' Pitt admitted that, though practically an invalid with gout, 'he had still vigour and strength of mind to undertake business, if he saw a probability of success; . . . '. But then he was certain that his policy of a system of alliance against the Bourbon House was disliked at Court and probably suspect to the public at large. And there were the further points of the officers dismissed 'for their *opinions in Parliament*' and 'something must be gone into to put people's minds at ease with regard to the *illegality* of the warrants'. Cumberland went away believing that Temple was aiming at a ministry of the Stowe fraternity, which with Grenville's parliamentary following together with Pitt's prestige was no impossible ambition.[23]

If Grenville thought he might draw comfort from Pitt's obduracy he was mistaken. When on Sunday, 19 May, the minister waited on the King the following colloquium ensued:[24]

'There is no hurry,' said the King; 'I will have the Parliament adjourned, not prorogued.'

'Has your Majesty any thought of making a change in your Administration?' enquired Grenville.

'Certainly,' was the reply, 'I cannot bear it as it is.'

'I hope your Majesty will not order me to cut my own throat?'

'Then', said the King, 'who must adjourn the Parliament?'

'Whoever', the minister retorted, 'your Majesty shall appoint my successor.'

When that day the King went to the House of Lords to give his assent to the Regency bill, he was confronted by the Spital-fields weavers. The largest industrial section in London, they were out in protest against Bedford's securing the rejection of a bill prohibiting the import of French silks. When the mob laid siege to Bedford House, the ministers saw a chance to cause a breach between the King and Cumberland. On 20 May Halifax wrote to the King suggesting that Granby take command of the troops. The King ordered Halifax to summon a regiment from Chatham and forwarded his note to his uncle, together with the request that he should take command as Captain-General. This Cumberland, of course, was very ready to do and made sure Pitt and Rockingham got to know of Halifax's impertinence. Pitt thought the King perfectly right to turn to his uncle but did not consider there was reason sufficient to turn out the ministers who had merely advised in the light of their judgement. Nor did Pitt think there was any possibility of his serving: 'On the contrary, my Lord Bute, whose influence was as strong as ever, and whose notions of government were widely different from his, would disincline the King to his system; . . .' Pitt expressed the wish that Cumberland might persuade Newcastle and his friends to undertake a ministry, though he offered no guarantee of his imprimatur.

Grenville and the ministers thought they might checkmate the King by a concerted resignation on the Tuesday following. The King again summoned Cumberland and hit on the truly mad expedient of asking Lyttleton to form a ministry. As might be expected Lyttleton got flustered and, quite unable to take command of himself, begged to consult Pitt and Temple. The King refused to accept defeat. Such was his fear of Grenville that he again sent Cumberland to Newcastle and his friends. During the whole of 21 May and again on 23rd they were in consultation, but the Old Whigs in no way felt strong enough to accept office by themselves. Cumberland saw that for the present the King had no alternative but to recall his ministers.[25] Grenville and Bedford took their revenge by removing from office Bute's brother Stuart-Mackenzie, the most popular man ever to 'manage' Scotland, an injustice which caused a resentment second only to the instance of Conway. Holland came to the end of his active career when his Paymastership was given to Charles Townshend. The ministers plainly intended to force the King into an intolerable dependence. Towards the end of May the

King wrote to Bute complaining of his feverish lack of sleep, occasioned by having to deal with 'the men I daily see; . . . excuse the incoherency of my letter; but a mind ulcer'd by the treatment it meets with from all round is the true cause of it'.[26] On 30 May Pitt entertained to dinner at Hayes George Grenville and his wife, Temple and Jemmy Grenville. It was an occasion of reconciliation, a covenant of forgiveness to bury the memories of Pitt's resignation. When he made clear that politics had nothing to do with it, Grenville readily concurred.[27] Towards the other side of the map, Pitt was gaining much ground among Newcastle's young followers. As Richmond observed to Holland on 8 June: 'Many of the party are now quite Pitt's men.'[28] And here was every presage of practical opportunity for Pitt before so very long.

On 12 June Bedford reprimanded the King over his lack of confidence in his ministers. Although the story current that he read out a set piece was almost certainly an exaggeration, the King was so incensed that he decided to treat him and Grenville as a caretaker administration. That evening, seething with indignation, he wrote to Cumberland: 'the world will see that this Country is not at that low Ebb that no Administration can be form'd without the Grenville family'. He assured Cumberland of his deep respect for 'those worthy men, Ld Rockingham, the Dukes of Grafton, Newcastle and others; for they are men who have principles and therefore cannot approve of seeing the Crown dictated to by low men'.[29] The ministers knew the end to be near and over dinner at Grenville's, Bedford, Halifax and Sandwich offered to place their seals at his disposal. Elliot, who had witnessed the making and unmaking of every ministry since ten years back he had introduced Pitt to Bute, turned upon Grenville full of complaints at Cumberland the bully and Bute the teeterer. On Sunday, 16 June, Grenville repaired to Wotton and next day was cordially received at Stowe. From town Sandwich sent word that the ministry had but a few days to live: Grafton was expected to see Pitt and declare his unreserved loyalty to him and Temple. At Stowe Lyttleton called round to assure Grenville in his usual ineffective way that, whatever Pitt might think, he personally approved Stuart-Mackenzie's dismissal.[30]

Cumberland strongly advised his nephew to ask Pitt to form a ministry. On the evening of Tuesday, 18 June, the Duke went to Hayes and was with Pitt until four o'clock next morning. Later on the Wednesday Pitt went to the King and over a conversation lasting two hours they reached agreement about 'Measures' or policy: 'The first were principally a treaty with Prussia, the repeal of the Cyder Tax, and the question about General Warrants.' Pitt was strongly critical of the taxation of the colonies, the unfunded debt, measures taken against smuggling in America, and Stuart-Mackenzie's being turned out. Afterwards the King saw Lord Chancellor Northington, who advised him to leave his ministry as it was, counsel which it was made clear would not be taken. Newcastle considered the position of himself and his followers to depend entirely upon 'Mr. Pitt; and the Great and Little Whigs; I mean the Whole Whig party, There is my heart; and There shall be my wish. The Duke of Cumberland is, and ought to be at our Head.'[31] While Pitt was settling 'Measures' with the King, Jemmy Grenville sent word to his eldest brother to hold himself ready to travel to London at any moment: 'Lord Temple determined not to go upon this notice.' That evening Grafton, who had left London before Pitt saw the King, had dinner at Stowe and confabulated with Temple. Next Friday, 21 June, Grenville returned home to Wotton and late that night received a letter from Temple, quoting Jemmy as bringing word 'that all Mr. Pitt had said to the King was *ad referendum*, and that he was to see His Majesty again on Saturday'.

Pitt did attend the King on Saturday, 22 June, and they came to an agreement over 'Men'. It was to be a composite ministry, with Pitt at the centre and the trimmings made as agreeable as might be to Newcastle's Old Whigs and Bute; parliamentary backing and the royal countenance might therefore be guaranteed. Pitt together with Grafton were to be Secretaries of State, with Temple at the Treasury; the backbone of the ministry secured, Newcastle was to be Lord President of the Council and Sir George Savile, member of Parliament for Yorkshire and a stalwart friend of Rockingham, Secretary at War: 'Mr. Mackenzie some office equivalent in value to that he had quitted, but without power, in Scotland; and all Lord Bute's friends to keep their offices.' Pratt was to be made a peer, a hitherto unknown distinction for a Lord Chief Justice of the Common Pleas. Finally Bristol, sometime Ambassador at Madrid, was to be Lord Lieutenant of Ireland. In the light of these arrangements the King ordered Pitt to summon Temple to appear at the Queen's House on Tuesday, 25 June, at ten o'clock and then His Majesty went out of town for the weekend. Pitt sent an express letter to Stowe: '. . . things have advanced considerably. . . . Upon the whole I augur much good, as far as intentions go . . . '. Temple at once set out for Hayes but at the same time sent his wife to Wotton with a note asking Grenville to see him before his audience of the King.

Temple arrived at Hayes early on Monday, 24 June, and what passed between him and Pitt at that fateful meeting is speculation. At the same time Grenville made the short journey to Woburn, where he found Bedford 'in the most friendly dispositions imaginable towards him . . . '. Next day Temple, before his appointment with the King, entertained his brother George to breakfast in Pall Mall: 'His conversation was of the most cordial and affectionate kind to Mr. Grenville, but he appeared under great agitation.' On going to the King, Temple declined absolutely to enter his service: 'The reasons he . . . assigned for not accepting the offer the King made him were two, the first of which was the difficulty of forming a proper plan with regard to the House of Commons; the second was of a tender and delicate nature, and which he therefore desired not to explain. The King pressed him to come into his service, and wished him to consider upon it.' An hour later Temple sent a note to Grenville telling him what had happened. Next Pitt saw the King and conveyed his own refusal to form a ministry. Temple spent the evening with Grenville in London and 'then related more at large what had passed. . . '. The day was not yet over, for Cumberland was with the King and late that night Grenville was sent word by Temple 'that one of the King's grooms had just called at his house with a letter from the King to Mr. Pitt, and was gone with it to Hayes'. Pitt, as the letter demanded, saw the King next morning, Wednesday, 26 June, and reiterated his refusal to accept office. The King's next caller was Lord Chancellor Northington, who passed straight on to the Levee and 'told everybody that the negotiation with Mr. Pitt was broke off'.[32]

Cumberland and Pitt were thoroughly out of humour one with the other. The Duke wrote to Albemarle with some irritation: 'I fear by what I understood last night from His Majesty, that we are all afloat again, Lord Temple having most peremptorily and determinately refused bearing a part in any shape, great or small, in the Administration to be formed. This declaration of Lord Temple's prevents Pitt taking a share, which indeed most thoroughly and heartily he had done . . . '.[33] A misunderstanding there had certainly been, and the King made to look a fool. Temple has been blamed for indulging a jealousy for Pitt. Unlike Newcastle and Rockingham, Pitt could never be head of his family connection and he was always far more loyal to Temple than Temple to him. But the important preliminary of consulting Temple before nominating him for the Treasury seems not to have been carried out by Pitt with the necessary exactitude. The reason 'of a tender and delicate nature' which inhibited Temple's acceptance was simply loyalty to his brother. As Burke commented in a letter to a friend: 'You know, that by the defection of Lord Temple to his Brother George, the minority is divided; Pitt will not part from his family; but declares much obligation and gratitude to the King; and a resolution in consequence not to oppose.'[34]

If Grenville judged the King to be in a quandary he was mistaken. Following the Levee of Wednesday, 26 June, the King saw his ministers on usual business. Next day Temple went to Hayes in the morning and came back to London on the Friday, having dined with his brother: 'Mr. Grenville received fresh assurances every day from a great variety of people of their indignation at the ill-treatment he has received, and of their determination to follow him through all situations.' Grenville would not have been so self-righteous had he known of Cumberland's assurance to the King on the last day of the month: 'I am engaged from dutty and inclination, and as long as the rope will hold I'll draw.'[35]

CHAPTER 14

Pitt and the Rockingham Administration

'A man worthy to be held in remembrance because he did not live for himself. . . . He far exceeded all other statesmen in the art of drawing together, without the seduction of self-interest, the concurrence and cooperation of various dispositions and abilities of men, whom he assimilated to his character and associated in his labours.'

Edmund Burke's Memorial Inscription to
Rockingham at Wentworth Woodhouse.

'More childish in his deportment than in his age, he was totally void of all information. Ambitious, with excessive indolence; fond of talking business, but dilatory in the execution, his single talent lay in attracting dependants: yet, though proud and self-sufficient, he had almost as many governors as dependants. To this unpromising disposition, he had so weak a frame of person and nerves, that no exigence could surmount his timidity of speaking in public; and having been only known to that public by his passion for horse-races, men could not be cured of their surprise at seeing him First Minister. . . .'

Horace Walpole.[1]

Cumberland, set upon forming a ministry from the 'Old Whigs' without Pitt, commanded Newcastle and Conway to attend at Windsor Lodge on Saturday, 29 June. Following his audience of the Duke, Newcastle convened a conciliabulum of seventeen of his friends at Claremont. The 'Old Whigs' were not one bit enthusiastic and the demand that Bute's influence be eradicated so clamorous that Cumberland was inclined to give up. But Newcastle, pained at seeing the juicy prospect of power once more eluding him, thought again. Reassured by Rockingham and Conway, he saw Cumberland and urged him to persevere. The scheme to save the King, which Cumberland and Newcastle were undertaking, would have to include men such as Grafton, whose loyalty lay to Pitt but were disconcerted at his tergiversations. To follow the words of Newcastle's Memorandum on 'Measures': 'The Plan of Administration should, in General, be made as palatable to Mr. Pitt; and as agreeable, as possible, to his Notions, and Ideas.'

By Tuesday, 2 July, Cumberland had decided that the new First Lord of the Treasury was to be Rockingham. Though the new Premier was only thirty-six he had matured early; a wealthy sportsman with few intellectual tastes, he compensated for a certain dullness and a decided laziness by plain honesty and goodness of intention. The most admirable aspect of his life was his friendship with Edmund Burke, who had entered Parliament in 1765 and soon became his private secretary and mentor. Though Rockingham's popularity in his own county of Yorkshire was immense and he was widely respected, he in fact exercised a loose leadership only over those Whigs who had been ousted with Newcastle. He was Prime Minister by default, because Pitt had refused to serve without Temple. From the outset the 'Old Whigs' were governed by fear of Pitt's possible displeasure. As yet these were early days and when Keppel and Saunders visited Pitt at Hayes on 4 July he gave his opinion that Rockingham ought to undertake administration – 'and that he would show his approbation'. As Rockingham was a peer the choice of Chancellor of the Exchequer was most important. After Charles Townshend, Conway and Newcastle's City friend Baker all declined, Cumberland fell back upon Dowdeswell, who despite his Tory antecedents had many friends among the

'Old Whigs' and moreover had won Pitt's approval for his opposition to the cider tax. The Secretaries of State were to be Grafton for the Northern Department and Conway for the South, who both expected a junction with Pitt to be a matter of time. Newcastle became Lord Privy Seal with ecclesiastical patronage attached and Pratt was given a peerage as Lord Camden.[2]

By Monday, 8 July, Cumberland and Rockingham had completed their arrangements. Grenville was summoned to the King at half-past ten on the morning of 10 July to deliver up the seals. His handling of the occasion was unhappy. He chose to go over in detail the events of the past two months, was so indiscreet as to refer to Stuart-Mackenzie and expressed his lack of understanding of why he had lost the King's confidence: 'The King said in general that he had found himself too much constrained, and that when he had anything proposed to him, it was no longer as counsel, but what he was to *obey*.' Grenville 'started at that word' and went on to make matters worse by entering into the situation of Bute, but the King retorted that he had no hand in the present changes. Grenville concluded with the most solemn advice that the King should on no account yield over the taxation of the colonies.[3] Here he showed prescience, for the Stamp Act was not to come into force until 1 November and no more than a mutter of discontent was anticipated.

When that afternoon the new ministers kissed hands and the major appointments became public, the general reaction was one of derision. Charles Townshend, still Paymaster, had his witticism upon a 'Lutestring administration', matched by Lord Chancellor Northington's jibe at 'a damn'd silly system'. Rockingham and Grafton were better known at Newmarket and Ascot than at Westminster and their administrative innocence was quite laughable: 'Persons called from the *Stud* to the *State*, and transformed miraculously out of Jockies into Ministers.' A devotion to the Turf might appear harmless enough in gentlemen of fashion but ill befitting the gravity of aspiring statesmen. But the Rockingham ministry found some praise the other side of the Atlantic. Conway had opposed the Stamp Act and the new men were fully expected to do anything in their power to discredit Grenville. As Franklin put it: 'Some we had reason to doubt of are removed, and some particular Friends are put in place.'

From the start Cumberland was head. Obviously he could take no civil employment and was not even Captain-General; he had acted as such during the Spitalsfield riots but no formal appointment was made. He presided over Cabinet meetings either at his house or Grafton's and in his absence a minute was promptly supplied. Subject to Cumberland's scrutiny things were run by Rockingham, Grafton and Conway, who consulted their colleagues only departmentally. For Cumberland to govern military patronage was natural enough but he chose the new Ambassador to France, the 3rd Duke of Richmond, and over bishoprics invaded even Newcastle's domain. That a member of the royal family should act as though he were Prime Minister has been unknown before or since but Cumberland had no alternative. Newcastle was hurt at being left out of things and harked back to what had been the good old days: 'as Mr. Pitt told me when we were Ministers, and Something like it together – My Lord I must be in the the first *Concoction* of Things.'4

Cumberland had the summer to consolidate Rockingham's position in Parliament, where Grenville's financial astuteness was respected. Though many of Bute's followers were in minor office, he was plainly set for retirement and, after all, he had manifestestly deserted the ship in the first place. Rockingham might therefore have set himself to bury the bitter memories of the massacre of the Pelhamite innocents and conciliate the Tories, especially Bute's party. Burke had no doubt as to the prudent course: 'I call, taking in Lord Bute, or at least not quarrelling with him, and enlarging their Bottom by taking in the Tories, and all the men of Business of the house of commons not listed against them, acting wisely.'5 But Rockingham and Newcastle, no less than Grenville, were convinced of the hold Bute had over the King and every whit as jealous: their vociferous hatred was noted by the press. Cumberland, who had other views, could not even obtain Stuart-Mackenzie's reinstatement. Blind to the consideration, recently exemplified in Grenville's downfall, that the power of the Court had to be taken into account, Rockingham and Newcastle thought of 'out-doors' popularity, especially in the City, where Grenville was well-liked. Newcastle was bent upon putting things back where they had been before 1762. It was natural enough that the Lord Lieutenancies be restored and those who had lost their places at the Boards of Treasury, Admiralty and Trade be reinstated. But the broom applied to many obscure posts in government and on 27 July Newcastle wrote: 'The Restitution of all our Sussex Friends is near over; and I own, It will give me the greatest pleasure, To see Them Reinstated, Gay and Happy, after all their Sufferings *on my Account*.'[6] But the parliamentary future of the new administration depended not upon marshalling the 'Old Whigs', which was easy enough, but upon securing the allegiance of Bute's following and to that end the countenance of the Court was very relevant. Only his hatred for Grenville had induced the King to take back the 'Old Whigs' and time would tell whether tolerance might ripen into affection.

Although Pitt's value in terms of court favour was very questionable, his blessing was made the main desideratum. That Shelburne should refuse the Presidency of the Board of Trade and therefore Barré a minor post might have been taken as a danger signal.[7] Instead Newcastle remarked to Grafton on 11 July: 'If Mr. Pitt is not kept in good humour, nothing will go on well.' The measures Pitt had made *sine qua non*, a Prussian alliance, the repeal of the cider excise, the reinstatement of the dismissed officers and a parliamentary declaration against the use of general warrants, were all to be slavishly adopted. Of a Cabinet decision of 22 July to make an approach to Prussia Newcastle's comment was: 'The Minute of The Other Night, If carried into Execution, as I hope, It will be, will give Him full Satisfaction upon That Point.' Cumberland approved and the first preliminary had to be an exchange of ambassadors; the British chargé in Berlin was given instructions and the co-operation of Prince Ferdinand of Brunswick requested.

The ministry had entered upon merely the preliminaries of an existence when at the end of July news came from America of resistance to the Stamp Act. At the end of May the Virginia House of Burgesses had 'rung the alarm bell for the entire continent' and declared that the people of the colony possessed an ancient right to be governed by their own laws with regard to internal taxation and policy – a right hitherto always recognised by the King and mother country. The spirit of protest took hold of the Thirteen Colonies. But the initial reaction of the Cabinet was leisurely, for the pillage of the property of royal officials at Boston and the general wave of protest and disorder were not yet known. Not till 30 August did the Cabinet discuss the Virginia resolves and Conway's despatch of 14 September to the Governor was drafted in the belief that the squall would blow over.

That autumn Rockingham was far more concerned about the coming session of Parliament. His expectation was that opposition in the House of Commons would not number more than one hundred but Newcastle pointed out to Albemarle: 'I admit, That the Administration *may* have a Considerable Majority in Both Houses: but that Majority must be made up of their Enemies, Creatures of the Two last Administrations, and such as are influenced only by their Employments, and Their Interest.' One reverse and clearly the ministry would be in trouble. During September a general election was seriously considered, with the avowed object of using Crown influence to the maximum, but Cumberland made clear that there was to be no dissolution of a Parliament that still had three years to run. Then, during the first week of October, tidings came of the Boston riots and the plans for the systematic boycott not only of British goods but also of government authority. 'All America is in confusion', wrote Conway to Rockingham on 10 October.

Cumberland was not a man to tolerate the flouting of authority. Conway was soldier enough to insist upon respect for the powers that be. Following a Cabinet meeting of 13 October in Cumberland's house he wrote to the Governor of Massachusetts ordering him to 'inforce a due Obedience to the Laws, and to take care that His Majesty's Revenue suffers no Detriment, or Diminution'. The Commander-in-Chief in North America, General Thomas Gage, was ordered to support the Governors. But by law the employment of the military required the request not only of the Governor but also of his Legislative Council. American Councillors were not ready to bring down force upon their own countrymen with whom many agreed. Gage had to report home that, to his regret, he had received no requisition for soldiers. It was plain that government in America had broken down and that the Stamp Act would be impossible to impose.

The intention was to hold a Cabinet on the last day of October. Cumberland attended the Drawing Room looking remarkably well, but at about eight o'clock in the evening had a seizure and was dead in five minutes. Next day the King met the situation with calm magnaminity and gave Rockingham every assurance of his fullest support. As Newcastle remarked: 'The King behaves like an Angel, upon This Occasion.' Even so, the ministers were stunned. Grafton's suggestion that Pitt be approached was adopted at a Cabinet meeting of 7 November and strongly endorsed by Newcastle. But George III had not forgotten Temple's insolence only five months previously and forbade a negotiation with Pitt. The King's veto was bad luck for Rockingham, for here was the meeting of Parliament round the corner and no politician of mettle willing to parley; Halifax preferred to await Grenville's return to power; Stanley refused reinstatement at the Board of Admiralty; Lord North, who had done well as a junior minister under Bute and Grenville, would not serve. Rockingham felt so anxious that he offered Charles Townshend Leadership of the House of Commons with a seat in the Cabinet but had to inform Newcastle: 'Charles Townshend continues professing the most Favourable Intentions – but does not seem to chuse to be now called to the Cabinet.' When that December Pitt went to Bath all Rockingham could do was to tell his wife to establish social relations: 'If a *Real Great Man* comes there, I would have you consider him as such and am not afraid of your Conversation with him as I don't believe it will be *Criminal.*' By chance the Duchess of Newcastle, too, was at Bath and had similar instructions from her husband.[8] The one effectual move Rockingham accomplished was the most injudicious conceivable. Sackville, desperate for rehabilitation, would accept office from any ministry. Accordingly, on 20 December, he was restored to the Privy Council and made joint Vice-treasurer of Ireland, which Shelburne believed was solely to meet considerations of parliamentary convenience. Pitt was so disgusted that all possibility of his lending Rockingham a supporting hand was obliterated.[9]

Cumberland's death also had drastic consequences for American policy. Even in October Rockingham had been lukewarm about repression, preferring simply to blame Grenville for the troubles. During the week following the Duke's death Savile and Barlow Trecothick, a merchant very prominent in the North American trade, advised him that persistence in enforcing the Stamp Act would be utterly destructive of commerce. Rockingham, great magnifico though he was, thoroughly appreciated the significance of business and mercantile opinion, because his most remunerative interests lay midway between the fast-developing West Yorkshire and Humber areas. Unfortunately Grenville's tightening of the Navigation Acts had coincided with a recession and he was blamed for blizzard conditions which were only slightly, if at all, the results of his legislation. Rockingham was easily convinced that a reversal of policy was imperative, provided a formula could be found dealing with the right of Parliament to tax America.

By the middle of November rumour was rife that moderation was to be the rule and on 28th Grenville wrote to Bedford of his expectation that the Stamp Act would be repealed.[10] The non-importation agreements passed in New York, Philadelphia and Boston to take effect at the New Year goaded the mercantile community into action. On 4 December a new London North America Merchants Committee came into being, which circulated the leading commercial and industrial centres. Rockingham could draw encouragement from the consideration that rumours of his liberal intentions were welcomed in the industrial north. On 11 December Sir William Meredith, member of Parliament for Liverpool and a most enlightened man, wrote to Burke: 'I am just come from Manchester, and am happy to tell you, that Mr. Pitt was never more popular, than L Rockingham and the present administration.' By the end of January some twenty-five cities and boroughs, comprising every centre of importance with the exception of Norwich, had petitioned the House of Commons in these words: 'We mean to take for our sole Object, the Interest of these Kingdoms it being our Opinion, that conclusive Arguments for granting every Ease or Advantage the North Americans can with propriety desire, may be fairly deduced from that Principle only.' In the face of economic self-interest the constitutional questions raised by the resistance to imperial authority were happily brushed aside.[11]

Though Rockingham had much popular backing for repeal he lacked the unanimous support of the Cabinet. Conway had in any case opposed the Stamp Act and he was followed by Grafton and, a little reluctantly, by Newcastle. But Northington, Charles Yorke and Charles Townshend had been in office when the Stamp Act was passed and were more than ready to defend not merely the principle of Grenville's policy. For an eighteenth-century Cabinet to propose the repeal of legislation so recent was constitutionally a very serious matter. The condonation of flat disobedience to the authority of the Crown, which repeal would clearly imply, was distasteful: 'America would boast she had conquered Britain.' As was inevitable under a weak ministry, Lord Chancellor Northington had immense influence and after a Cabinet meeting of 11 December had no hesitation about writing to the King declaring in the strongest terms his dissent from yielding 'to the Insurrections and Clamours . . . '. Although the King was not happy at Rockingham's proposal to back down altogether, he agreed that enforcement was undesirable and was certainly not ready to obstruct his efforts to secure parliamentary consent for repeal. That Grenville and Bedford were going to oppose the ministry in any event was certain and the divisions within the Cabinet were something of a boon. If to the Thirteen Colonies the stamp duty appeared the precursor to some truly burdensome imposition, from Grenville's point of view theirs was an illegal resistance to a just and moderate enactment approved by both Houses of Parliament and the King. Grenville had select though not very able advisers in the young 12th Earl of Suffolk, Whateley and Charles Lloyd, as well as intelligent henchmen in Hans Stanley and Bamber Gascoyne. He could depend upon sixty regular supporters in the House of Commons. Bedford's 'Bloomsbury Gang' comprised some twenty to thirty members of Parliament and a dozen peers, well marshalled by his ambitious Duchess and Rigby. If reinforced by Bute's following and a substantial defection from the government benches, the Grenville and Bedford parties would become dangerous to Rockingham.

Parliament was to meet on 17 December and Rockingham's

ability to overcome dissidents within the Cabinet must depend upon Pitt, who took care to make known his support for repeal. As Beckford declared: 'In the American matter he does *not* doubt indeed.' George Cooke, member of Parliament for Middlesex, had had conversations with Pitt at Burton Pynsent. Newcastle, sensing the way of the wind, plumped for repeal. So as to placate Pitt, Cooke was asked to second the Address. As might be expected, Grenville attempted a preliminary skirmish with an amendment to the Address bitterly reproachful of the ministry for vacillation towards America. But he found so little support that he withdrew and in the Lords Suffolk was defeated 80–24. Men like Jenkinson, Elliot, and Charles Townshend were not proposing to endanger their standing with the King by siding with Grenville so soon. But that was no guarantee of their violating their consciences over the Stamp Act if they genuinely believed that the legislative authority of Britain must be asserted at all costs.

Rockingham formed what was for practical purposes a secret committee. He held dinners at his house with Conway and Dowdeswell to thrash out American policy. Charles Yorke at an important conclave of 27 December suggested that an Act asserting by declaration the legislative supremacy of the Imperial Parliament was the solution. He was the author of the plan eventually adopted to repeal the Stamp Act but, at the same time, in his own language, 'to Assert the Authority of Parlt in general words'.[12]

Rockingham was so unsure of himself that he resolved to waive the leadership of the ministry in Pitt's favour. At the New Year Tommy Townshend was sent to Bath with authority to say 'not only that we requested to be favoured with Mr. Pitt's opinion on the measure then under consideration, but that we desired much to receive him at our head, now, or at any time he should find it suitable with his views for the public'. Pitt gave 'young Tommy' more than a flea in the ear; indeed his attitude was quite monstrous. Newcastle must be dismissed and Temple placed at the Treasury. Newcastle, though stupefied at such churlishness, with true patriotism offered the King his resignation. But Rockingham was beginning to enjoy being at the head of affairs and the King would not truckle to this type of nonsense:

'so loose a conversation as that of Mr. Pitt and Mr. Townshend is not sufficient to risk either my dignity or the continuance of any administration, by a fresh treaty with that gentleman; for if it should miscarry all public opinion of this ministry would be destroyed by such an attempt'. The King, brushing aside prattle about resignation from Grafton, told him not to write to Pitt until 'the Person comes to Town'. On 10 January he made clear to Bute that he expected his followers inside the Government to support Rockingham's American measures so far as their honour or conscience would allow.[13]

Parliament was to reassemble on 14 January and Pitt wrote to his friend Thomas Nuthall, Solicitor to the Treasury, of his intention to 'deliver my mind and heart upon the State of America'.[14] But after his surly rejection of Rockingham's offer to place him at the head, Pitt could not be expected to oppose the Stamp Act with a view to propping up the present administration. To the contrary, he had plainly decided to let them topple over of their own accord. The ministry decided to hold their hand with regard to the Stamp Act and hear what Pitt had to say. The King's Speech, drafted by Charles Yorke, was so moderate that men as different as Elliot and Sandwich anticipated that the plan for repeal had been shelved.[15] Conway presented to the Commons papers on the American disturbances. Pitt then rose in his place, his first appearance in the House of Commons since the debate on general warrants of 14 February 1764. Burke had his epigram: 'Last Tuesday we drew up the Curtain and discovered the Great Commoner, attended by his Train, *solus.*'[16]

The occasion was solemn and historic. The spell of Pitt's oratory gave vision to the revolutionary constitutional doctrines he put forward. Where a plea for the repeal of the Stamp Act had been generally anticipated, the eighteenth-century House of Commons had never before heard their electoral foundations called in question or the regulation of their legislative powers proposed:

'It is my opinion that this kingdom has no right to lay a tax upon the colonies. At the same time, I assert the authority of this kingdom over the colonies to be sovereign and supreme, in every circumstance of government and legislation whatsoever. They are the subjects of this kingdom, equally entitled with yourselves to all the natural rights of mankind, and the peculiar privileges of Englishmen: equally bound by its laws and equally participating of the constitution of this free country. . . .

'Taxation is no part of the governing power. The taxes are a voluntary gift and grant of the Commons alone . . . when therefore in this House we give and grant, we give what is our own. But in an American tax what do we do? We your Majesty's Commons of Great Britain give and grant to your Majesty – what? Our own property? No. We give and grant to your Majesty the property of your Majesty's Commons in America. It is an absurdity in terms. . . .

These words might be taken as battering down Yorke's clever device to quiet the conscience of the House of Commons with an Act declaring the legislative authority of Parliament. Pitt passed on to the subject of representation in general:

'Would to God that respectable representation was augmented to a greater number! Or will you tell him [an American] that he is represented by any representative of a borough – a borough which perhaps its own representatives never saw? This is what is called "the rotten part of the constitution". It cannot endure the century. If it does not drop it must be amputated. The idea of a virtual representation of America in this House is the most contemptible idea that ever entered the head of man: it does not deserve a serious refutation.'

'It cannot endure the century.' With these words Pitt recognised the changes of his own time. A whole new middle class, what Wilkes had aptly dubbed 'the middling and the lesser sort', had come into being. The industrial sights of the Midlands were among the wonders of the time and at Birmingham for example there had come into being a new urban centre, which, however, could exert political influence only through the medium of elections for Warwick county. Pitt warned the House of Commons that the old franchise could not continue without criticism. He thus adumbrated the principle of parliamentary reform and also indicated how such could best be achieved, by weakening or even abolishing the representation of private boroughs. He was the first major statesman since Cromwell to advocate the rationalization of the franchise.

Conway indicated that the ministry would adopt Pitt's opinion that American taxation must be discontinued. Grenville then rose to defend the Stamp Act and to denounce as breeders of sedition those who sympathised with resistance. Pitt was provoked into rising from his seat for the second time that evening and after rebutting the accusation of sedition as an infringement of the right of free speech, he reiterated his principle that internal taxation without representation was unconstitutional, as distinct from external taxation for the regulation of trade:

'If the gentleman cannot understand the difference between internal and external taxes, I cannot help it. But there is a plain distinction between taxes levied for the purpose of raising revenue and duties imposed for the regulation of trade for the accommodation of the subject, although in consequence some revenue may accidentally arise from the latter.'

Pitt pointed out that Britain, by virtue of her profit from the colonial trade of two millions a year, received ample return for the protection of the colonies in time of war:

'Upon the whole I beg leave to tell the House what is really my opinion. It is that the Stamp Act be repealed absolutely, totally and immediately; that the reason for the repeal should be assigned, because it was founded on an erroneous principle. At the same time let the sovereign authority of this country over the colonies be asserted in as strong terms as can be devised, and be made to extend to every point of legislation whatsoever: that we may bind their trade, confine their manufacturers and exercise every power whatsoever — except that of taking their money out of their pockets without their consent.'

Pitt insisted that a complete distinction existed in principle and in law between taxation for the regulation of trade and taxation for revenue. The Navigation System fell within the imperial responsibilities of Parliament but by a prescriptive right under English constitutional law, taxation for revenue or the power of the purse lay with the representative legislatures in the colonies. Conway and Dowdeswell hardly intervened in the debate, though the former bent over in his compliments to Pitt and his willingness to change places with him. The Address was carried *nem. con.*[17]

The following day Rockingham reported to the King: 'That the events of yesterday in the House of Commons have shown the amazing powers and influence which Mr. Pitt has, whenever he takes part in debate, and That your Majesty's present administration will be shook to the greatest degree, if no further attempt is made to get Mr. Pitt to take a candid part, is much too apparent to be disguised.' But the King had no intention of calling on Pitt and considered asking Northington to take the Treasury. This was not merely a manoeuvre, for had Northington accepted then a shift of policy in favour of modification rather than repeal must follow. Northington, however, had no wish to abandon the security of the Woolsack for the hazards of Premier and even Charles Townshend advised that Pitt be summoned.[18] On the evening of 17 January Pitt had the pleasure of hearing Burke's maiden speech upon the Manchester petition complaining of the decay in the North American trade. Dr Johnson remarked that Burke had 'gained more reputation than perhaps any man at his first appearance ever gained before. He made two speeches in the House for repealing the Stamp-act, which were publickly commended by Mr. Pitt and have filled the town with wonder.'[19]

A couple of days' reflection made the King realise that he had to allow a further negotiation with Pitt. Rockingham and Grafton visited Pitt on 18 January to find out his conditions and above all whether, as last summer, a refusal by Temple would bind him also. An accommodation with Pitt would shelve Yorke's plan to sugar repeal with an Act declaring the legislative authority of Parliament; moreover the Stamp Act would be withdrawn in terms considerably more apologetic than any the Rockingham administration had been prepared to consider. Pitt expressed himself ready to co-operate with Rockingham, Grafton and Conway, provided Newcastle resigned: 'that Duke was of so irksome and meddling a nature that He would marr and cramp all Councils'.

Temple had been keeping George Grenville's company, where no correspondence was to be found with Pitt's policy towards America. There Pitt had to restrict himself to Delphic utterances at his most maddeningly obscure: if Temple wanted to bring in 'some of his new *Associates*' Pitt would decline: 'he must be excus'd declaring any thing of his own conduct if Ld Temple would not accept'. It was hardly surprising that Rockingham decided to go ahead and risk Pitt's displeasure. Following a Cabinet meeting at his house next day, he wrote to Charles Yorke: 'The Ideas we join in are nearly what I talked of to you this morning. That is – a *Declaratory Act* – in General Terms afterwards to proceed to *Considerations of Trade* e.t.c. – and finally *Determination* on the Stamp Act – ie *a Repeal* and which its own Demerits and Inconveniences as *felt here* will justify.' During the third week of January a further Cabinet meeting and an assemblage of Whig peers confirmed Rockingham's resolve. Despite the expected opposition of Bute's friends he expected the House of Commons to produce a great majority: '*If it does* – we shall then show *how* we stand *as Administration*. – If it does not – I wish no Man so great a Curse – as to desire him to be the Person to take Administration and be obliged to Enforce the Act.'

At this point Pitt made a mistake which destroyed the small possibility of the House of Commons leaving the right of Parliament to tax America to go by default. On 27 January George Cooke produced the petitions of the Congress colonial committees at New York praying for repeal, which directly denied the right of the British Parliament to tax. As Conway saw clearly that petitions in these terms would weaken the case of administration, he and Dowdeswell advised their rejection outright. Pitt then spoke strongly in favour of the petitions and declared that '*the Original Compact with the Americans was Broke, by the Stamp Act*'. Then, conscious of having upset the feelings of the House, he said no more. The petitions were quietly ignored. The first ministerial resolution later to be embodied in the Declaratory Act, presented on the last day of the month, read: 'The King in Parliament had, hath and of a right ought to have, full power and authority to make laws and statutes of sufficient force and validity to bind the colonies and people of America *in all cases whatsoever.*' These last four words Pitt, supported by Barré, attempted to have cut and so by implication make an exemption of taxation. He could not even persuade the House to divide. When in the Lords Grafton proposed the declaratory resolution Camden's objections were soundly routed by Mansfield. No justification in law has ever been considered to lie at the basis of Pitt's distinction between taxation for revenue and taxation for the regulation of trade.

At the beginning of February Bute's friends came out in opposition to repeal. On the 4th of the month they combined with the followers of Grenville and Bedford to secure a minor Government defeat in the Lords and, ominously for Rockingham, Northington voted with them. The King was unjustly suspected of plotting Rockingham's downfall but next day told Newcastle: 'I am; I was always against enforcing it. I have thought some middle way might be taken, but I am now convinced that nothing but the repeal will do.'[20] Although Grafton wanted the ministry to resign, Rockingham decided to stand his ground and back their reputation on securing repeal.

The 7 February yielded Rockingham a singular triumph, when Charles Yorke's motion for the Chairman to leave the chair in the committee on the American papers was carried 274–134. Pitt left the House before the division but that evening, at Rockingham's instance, Burke wrote informing him of the result: 'I take the Liberty of congratulating you on this Event; Nothing could add so much to the satisfaction, I dare say, of all who divided in that Majority, as to find that their Conduct had your approbation, and that their Success gave you pleasure.'[21] It was only to be expected that Rockingham should take the opportunity of an encounter with Nuthall in Palace Yard to reopen the prospect of Pitt's heading a ministry. As Nuthall reported to Pitt: 'He wished to God, Mr. Pitt would fix upon some plan for carrying on an administration putting himself at the head of it; and that such a plan might be laid before the King . . . '. At this stage Rockingham had no intention of confiding in even Grafton and Conway. Therefore he made clear that the King must be presented with a united plan on which he and Pitt were agreed, or the ministry would fall to pieces. Up till now Pitt had always been ready to hear what Rockingham or his emissaries had to say, and his brusque reply, delivered through Nuthall, must have come as a shock: 'I am under an impossibility of conferring upon the matter of *administration* without *his Majesty's commands*. . . '. Pitt was not willing to undertake any negotiation without the King's commission to form a ministry; under that interdict Rockingham could not long remain minister.[22]

At this time Burke still enjoyed the favour of Pitt's praises: 'Mr. Pitt has been very kind and generous in protecting me by very strong expressions, twice or thrice in publick, and often in private conversations.'[23] But these tributes from an established great man to one just entered Parliament were no olive leaf for Rockingham. To the contrary, when on 4 March the third reading of the bill to repeal the Stamp Act passed 250–122, Pitt marked the occasion with an undisguised bid for support from the King's Friends: though he declared he had no wish to see Bute minister, he thought the proscription of his followers a disgrace and the dismissal of Stuart-Mackenzie an insult to the King. Soon all the world was talking and the King, too, noted these words.[24]

Although the repeal of the Stamp Act allowed the restoration of normal trade, the tolerant harmony of the past relations had been gravely damaged. That pressure of British commercial interests had forced repeal was not evident across the Atlantic, where the institution of a Congress had presented an altogether unprecedented appearance of unanimity. There new theories were current, to allow each colony an autonomous standing; the position of the King in North America should be parallel to his constitutional position at home. The King as convenor of the colonial legislatures, not the King at Westminster, was to be Sovereign. The possibility of an eventual rupture was not contemplated, for self-interest demanded the peaceable flow of trade and there was yet a profound heritage of loyalist sentiment. Pitt appeared to many to be the only statesman who might forge an understanding. Burke was working hard upon a design for the complete revision of 'all the Commercial Laws, which regard our own or the foreign Plantations, from the Act of Navigation downwards; It is an extensive plan'.

The co-operation of the North American and West Indian colonies was enlisted and agreement with their Agents was reached on 10 March. The sun of the Rockingham ministry reached its apogee when on the day following the repeal of the Stamp Act passed the House of Lords by 73–61. Grafton and Richmond spoke with distinction and, Burke thought, Mansfield's opinion contra was more than matched by a long and spirited address from Camden. Burke wrote: 'I do not now look for much opposition; The Spirit of the adverse faction begins to evaporate; Even Mr. Grenville begins to slacken in his attendance; His Language is, I am told, that of despair of the Commonwealth, Prophecies, Omens, ruin &c. &c.'[25]

Burke was completely mistaken in his optimism. The passage of the Stamp Act through the Lords by a small majority had reflected not Rockingham's strength but the influence Pitt was bound to command over any point of imperial significance. Pitt had decided to bring down the ministry and on 14 April, when Conway and Dowdeswell were away ill, he denounced the militia regulations: 'He went to the House, and made a vociferous declamation against the Ministry, who, he said, aimed at destroying the militia; he would go to the farthest corner of the island to overturn any Ministers that were enemies to the militia.'

Four days later Dowdeswell opened his budget. His main innovation, a window tax to replace the cider tax, though strongly opposed by the Grenvilles and Bedfords, went through comfortably. But on any issue Pitt chose to fight, the ministry had no hope in Parliament. In the Lords Rockingham had spoken only twice throughout his ministry and Grafton was mediocre. Conway, apart from his recent and severe illness, was not happy in the Commons and Dowdeswell, though a far stronger character than had been expected, no match for Pitt or Grenville. Pitt had rejected all Rockingham's overtures with scorn, and in consequence that constant deference towards him proved debilitating. Though Burke always overestimated the talents of his leaders, he summed up their weaknesses so far as Pitt was concerned: '. . . by looking to a force exterior to themselves, and leaning on it, they have weakened themselves, rendered themselves trifling, and at length have drawn away from them the prop upon which they leaned.'

Grafton on 21 April asked Rockingham to clarify his attitude to Pitt's joining the ministry, to be told that no such advice would ever be given to the King. The next day Grafton told Conway that he intended to resign. Then on 24 April Pitt humiliated the ministry by persuading the House of Commons unanimously to ignore Dowdeswell's advice that a petition against the high duties on imported foreign sugar be set aside. Four days later Grafton declared to the King his inability to continue. When asked to be more explicit he explained that Rockingham had recently refused to go to the Closet and advise a further approach to Pitt. The King was rather taken aback when Grafton went on to point out that when the previous July the ministry was informed the understanding was that they were to be mere caretakers.[26] Above all George III feared the spectre of Grenville and to his relief Rockingham, Newcastle and Conway were ready to carry on, though Northington considered a coalition with Bute and his friends essential. At this the King wrote to Bute on 3 May expressing his readiness to take in anyone but Grenville, though, other than to quote Grafton, he did not mention the possibility of a Pitt ministry. He was sleeping badly and longed for some definite and long-standing arrangement.[27]

Although Rockingham and Newcastle were absolutely against negotiating with Bute, the King felt little patience with ministers manifestly almost incapable of conducting daily business yet unwilling to put themselves into a position to manage. He just managed to swallow Richmond, whom personally he disliked, as Grafton's successor. As he later explained to Bute, he wanted time 'that I might with some degree of certainty discover whether Mr. Pitt really was desirous of coming into office'.[28] It is very possible that Pitt did not anticipate that he might shortly be called upon to form a ministry, for it was during May, while Grafton was busy resigning, that he sold Hayes to Thomas Walpole. In view of the alterations to Burton Pynsent the decision was financially judicious but left him without a residence in or near London.

Northington, never a friend to Rockingham, initiated the change in the course of a meeting with Camden. He asked whether Pitt would serve, to receive this assurance: 'he was ready to come in if called upon, that he meant to try and form an Administration of the best of all party's and an exclusion to no descriptions; . . . '. A few days later Northington retailed this conversation to the King, who was greatly encouraged. Next Northington announced to the Cabinet his inability to attend further meetings consistent with his sense of honour. At first Rockingham took no notice, so on Sunday, 6 July, the King summoned his Cabinet and announced his intention of seeking other servants. That evening George III drafted his letter to Pitt with the commission to form an administration, which Northington at once forwarded to Burton Pynsent.[29]

CHAPTER 15

The Chatham Administration

'What shall I say to you about the Ministry? I am as angry as a Common Council Man of London about my Ld. Chatham but a little more patient and will hold my tongue till the end of the year. In the mean time I do mutter in secret & to you, that to quit the House of Commons, where lay his natural strength; to sap his own popularity & grandeur (which no one but himself could have done) by assuming a foolish title; & to hope that he could win by it & attach to him a Court, that hate him, & will dismiss him, as soon as ever they dare, was the weakest thing, that ever was done by so great a Man. Had it not been for this I should have rejoiced at the breach between him and Lord Temple, & at the union between him & the Duke of Grafton & Mr. Conway: but patience! we shall see.'

Thomas Gray to Thomas Wharton, 26 August 1766.[1]

Pitt replied promptly to the royal summons, undertaking to get to London as soon as possible. When the King informed his ministers, 'Lord Rockingham and the Duke of Newcastle seem'd thunderstruck, Conway on the contrary said he had ever wished to see him head Administration. . . '.[2] Pitt reached London on 11 July – under three days and quicker than the *Taunton Flying Machine*.[3] Though badly shaken, he had his first audience that day at Richmond Lodge. Before Pitt arrived the King wrote to Bute explaining the course of events, promising Stuart-Mackenzie's reinstatement and to let him know how matters turned out.[4] Here was Pitt's great opportunity. A series of weak administrations had followed one after the other and a chief cause of this long uncertainty had been his reluctance to take office. In truth Pitt was too great a man to share power: now he had the ball at his feet. George III, twenty-seven and no longer the immature boy who had succeeded to the throne, buried all resentments of the past. He generously welcomed the Great Commoner as minister and wished to give him every mark of support. The King looked upon Pitt as the greatest living Englishman, who alone could guide his country to triumph in the arts of peace.

As in July the previous year, Pitt's choice as First Lord of the Treasury was Temple. The King asked for Stuart-Mackenzie's reinstatement as Lord Privy Seal for Scotland, to which Pitt could easily agree. Getting down to business, Pitt chalked out to the King the outline of a ministry to be balanced between that of Rockingham and his own friends, a blending of Grafton and Conway with Shelburne and Camden. Pitt proposed giving a general direction without the daily toil of departmental responsibility and decided to become Lord Privy Seal, an office usually held by a peer and therefore an indication that he intended to go to the House of Lords. He hoped that thereby he might protect his health and be free to concentrate upon great issues of state, 'measures not men', to use his own expression. Admittedly the precedents of almost a century indicated that the Treasury carried with it the government of the country. But Pitt's charisma was unique and there was no doubt that he was to appoint and head the ministry. That night Pitt repaired to the Harley Street home of his kinsman Captain Hood. After taking a complete rest, on the following day he wrote to Shelburne asking him to come to town.[5]

At four o'clock on the afternoon of 13 July Northington summoned Temple by letter. Temple replied that he was coming to London 'with all the dispatch in my power at so short a warning'. He continued: 'No man in the kingdom can wish more ardently than I do to see force and effect given to the King's government, having long lamented for my country, as your Lordship knows, the want of it.' Temple reached London that evening and at once notified the Lord Chancellor, who gave him the royal command to attend at Richmond between five and six o'clock on the evening of 15 July. Early that day Temple went round to Jemmy's. At that moment Pitt, finding the dog-days of midsummer London too much, was on his way to North End, the home by Hampstead Heath of a friend, Charles Dingley. By coincidence, therefore, Temple went to the King without first seeing Pitt, to whom he sent word through Jemmy of his cordial affection with the suggestion of a conference the following day.[6]

Temple saw the King and had his own idea of Gower as a Secretary of State and a Cabinet place for Lyttleton. Although Temple was far too circumspect to mention his brother George, his proposals meant the exclusion of the Rockingham Whigs and possibly a return to Grenville's policies in respect of America. Temple asked the King if the day following, 16 July, might be reserved for a conference between himself and Pitt. To this the King readily agreed, but as soon as Temple was gone he sent a line to Pitt warning him not to expect the slightest accommodation. The King asked Pitt to be at the Queen's House on Thursday, 17 July, at eleven, giving a day or two for him and Temple to attempt common ground.[7]

Pitt saw Temple on the Wednesday and discovered that the King was right. He vetoed Gower and Lyttleton but promised Temple that if he accepted the Treasury on terms agreed with the King, the selection of a Chancellor of the Exchequer and of the Treasury Board would be his.[8] Pitt was disappointed and upset; next day he wrote to his wife: 'The state of my health is not quite what it should be; some fever hanging upon me, and the conversation, from its length and *issue* yesterday, with Lord Temple, having been rather too much for my situation, which was greatly mended, though not quite in a natural state.'[9] On receiving this unhappy letter Lady Chatham packed the children off to Weymouth and hastened to London. The young party, which included William aged seven, had no cause to miss their parents, for at every stage they were reminded of the great man their father. The church bells of Yeovil rang out; at

Weymouth a deputation of Mohican chiefs on their way to present a petition to the King waited on them to pay homage.[10]

Temple had his concluding audience of the King on Thursday, 17 July, at three o'clock in the Queen's House, after the Drawing-room. He explained his motives for declining the Treasury and, as was his wont, his manner bordered on pertness: 'though I was willing to sacrifice my brother George Grenville's pretensions, as he was himself, to Mr. Pitt's indisposition towards him, for the sake of public and general union, yet as that in my opinion was not the plan, I would not *go in like a child, to come out like a fool*'. Temple thought the King lukewarm: 'I stayed with him an hour: very gracious, and I believe not a little delighted with my declining.' The next day Temple went back to Stowe, to find that his cook had taken a nasty fall from his horse through getting drunk at the Assizes, a serious mishap in view of an imminent house party to include the King's aunt Princess Amelia, Bedford and Marlborough with their Duchesses, Gower and Waldegrave.[11]

At Hampstead Pitt had to reconstruct his ideas and this time resolved to carry on without Temple. He decided that the First Lord of the Treasury must be Grafton. As Pitt intended that Conway, Grafton's closest friend, should continue as Leader of the House of Commons, the ministry would have a core of solid loyalty. The new Premier was only thirty-one and the character which emerges in the sometimes unconscious self-portraiture of his autobiography is manly, candid and attractive. Possibly Pitt thought responsibility would cure his notable idleness and at least he could be trusted to obey. When on Saturday, 19 July, Grafton saw Pitt at North End, conscious of his inexperience, he was utterly astonished at being asked to take the Treasury and was even more disturbed when Pitt told him of his intention to take a peerage.[12] That evening Grafton went to his house in Grosvenor Square and saw Charles Townshend who, too, kept a residence in that distinguished venue. Grafton threw out to Townshend the possibility of his succeeding Dowdeswell as Chancellor of the Exchequer, to meet with an eager response.

Next day Grafton drove out to North End and got down to particulars. Pitt decided that the Secretaryship of State for the South should go to Shelburne, with Conway remaining at the

North. Camden was to be Lord Chancellor in place of Northington who, however, was to remain in the Cabinet as Lord President of the Council. Pitt's withdrawal to the House of Lords, together with Grafton's ignorance of Treasury business, was bound to give the Chancellor of the Exchequer a special importance. When, however, Grafton pressed for Townshend's appointment, Pitt was most reluctant and as Grafton later related: 'Mr. Pitt . . . said everything to dissuade me from taking as a second one from whom I should possibly meet with many unexpected disappointments.' Over the years Pitt had observed Townshend's wayward and fickle nature, which was further bedevilled by his too grand marriage to the Countess of Dalkeith, the widowed mother of the young 3rd Duke of Buccleuch. Greatly against his inclination, Pitt yielded, provided Townshend was not given a seat in the Cabinet, which in any event no Chancellor of the Exchequer had ever been allowed since 1710. That evening Grafton sent word to Townshend and set out for Wakefield Lodge, his Northamptonshire seat, thinking the matter fixed.

When on 21 July Townshend saw Pitt at North End, he asked for time to make up his mind. Early next morning Pitt, anxious to settle matters, sent Dingley with a message asking for a decision. At this Townshend sent Pitt an absurdly long-winded letter, throwing himself upon His Majesty's commands, but at the same time asking that he might await the arrival of his brother George, who in 1764 had succeeded their father as the 4th Viscount Townshend. When on Thursday, 24 July, Pitt saw Townshend for the second time, he was left with the strong impression that the Exchequer was settled. At six o'clock that evening, therefore, he wrote to the King, requesting an audience next day. But late that night Townshend went chattering to Grafton, who had returned to Grosvenor Square, asking if he might not after all remain Paymaster. Whilst at eleven o'clock on 25 July Pitt, in complete ignorance of Townshend's tergiversations, was presenting his list of ministers to the King, Townshend sent two highly ambivalent notes to Grafton, who felt he had no alternative but to write to Pitt setting forth all these doubts and hesitations. Furthermore, Grafton had learned that the favour shown Townshend was causing great annoyance in Rockingham's circle because Dowdeswell had not been put right as to his situation. The letter ended with an interesting postscript: Bedford had sent word that he would, without taking any post himself, gladly give Pitt support 'by placing properly a few of his friends'.

That afternoon at four o'clock Pitt wrote to Townshend the most cordial letter. But meanwhile Townshend had been received by the King who, to his astonishment, was faced with a request from Townshend to stay Paymaster. As the King explained to Pitt, Townshend appeared reluctant to accept the loss of salary the change of office would entail and was moreover of the opinion that there was far more chance of Rockingham's 'being quiet' if Dowdeswell remained Chancellor of the Exchequer. At this Pitt's old fire blazed forth; he was not going to have his ministry manipulated by Rockingham: 'Mr. C. Townshend is engaged to serve in that office and I am persuaded will not retract his declarations.' As to Rockingham's 'being quiet', Dowdeswell had better be informed at once that he was not to continue. Late that night Townshend replied to Pitt agreeing at an intolerable length to take office. At nine o'clock on the evening of 26 July Pitt was at last, after six days, in a position to inform the King of Townshend's acceptance. But Townshend was deeply mortified at not receiving the right to sit in the Cabinet whilst Grafton had an uneasy feeling that Pitt would have done better to keep Dowdeswell on.[13]

Lady Hester had arrived in London on 22 July and with some naiveté sent Temple a letter: 'I cannot express to my dear Brother the sensible joy it is to me to understand from Mr. Pitt, that, though you upon the whole did not agree in sentiments upon things in question, yet your differing was with the greatest kindness and friendship imaginable towards him, and which I assure you is felt by no less pleasing satisfaction by him than by me.' On Sunday, 27 July, Temple, who had just returned home from a visit to Blenheim Palace with its new lake, sent his sister a counterblast, making absolutely clear his indignation, which concluded: 'Our reciprocal visits, cannot, therefore, take place as we intended.' To this Lady Chatham sent a most sweet and unaffected reply: 'You know my faith, and I hold it fast, that the blessing of Heaven will still be given to upright and virtuous intentions.' On the day that Temple administered this snub Pitt called on Rockingham, some said to offer him the Lord Lieutenancy of Ireland: 'Lord Rockingham came home while Mr. Pitt's chair was at the door, upon which it was carried into the hall, but his Lordship went upstairs and sent word by his servant to Mr. Pitt, that he was extremely busy, and could not possibly see him.'[14]

Pitt embarked upon his administration with the highest ideals of the quality of statesmanship the times demanded. He was ready to give office to any politician of character, assuring the King of his intention 'to dissolve all factions and to see the best of all parties in employment'. King and country expected Pitt to resolve almost as by magic any difficulty that might arise at home or overseas. Victory in war had been succeeded by a sense of disillusion, with no prospect of land tax falling below 4s and the trade recession causing serious unemployment. Although the Thirteen Colonies had been superficially pacified by the repeal of the Stamp Act, the elusive problem remained of finding the wherewithal for the American establishment in ways acceptable to the House of Commons and the Assemblies.

The influence of the East India Company in Parliament and the City was novel and disturbing. The revenue the Company expected to receive from the *diwani* of Bengal was estimated at £2 million p.a. The statutory renewal of the East India Company's Charter was shortly due and the terms were bound to give rise to dissension. But with Pitt at the helm the mood of hope was general: Barrington wrote to him on 26 July: 'When you resign'd the office of Secretary of State, I troubled you with a Letter expressing the real concern which that Event gave me; and my very sincere wishes that you might soon be restored to the Service of the Crown; allow me at present to express to you with equal truth, the satisfaction I feel from the happy prospect now opening, of returning Stability, Union, Dignity and consistence; the Effects of which will I trust equal the warmest wishes of those, who best love their King and Country.'[15]

His Cabinet-making complete, Pitt set in motion his pet project for an alliance with Frederick the Great, which was to be extended to an understanding with Catherine II of Russia. Whilst British relations with Frederick and Catherine were distant, they had in 1764 reached an accord on finding that their mutual designs against Poland could be satisfactorily matched. Frederick saw no objection to Russian ambitions on the Black Sea as counterweight to Austrian influence in south-east Europe. Although Mitchell was still at Berlin, relations had not recovered since Bute had negotiated the Peace and, according to Frederick, left him in the lurch. The opening attempted by Conway as Secretary of State under Rockingham had made little progress. Every effort was being made to restrain Maria Theresa from maintaining a close connection with France. Sir George Macartney, envoy at St Petersburg, had after much patient effort only just managed to secure a trade agreement. That Britain emerge from her isolation appeared more imperative from the consideration that the possibility of a clash with the Bourbon powers was on the horizon. In his report after his circumnavigation of the globe Anson had recommended the colonisation of the Falkland Islands as a convenient port of call on the Cape Horn and Pacific route to the Far East. Shortly after the Peace the Admiralty resolved actively to enforce this strategy and a British post, Port Egmont, was set up on West Falkland. The French had a similar interest and de Bougainville had planted the French flag on East Falkland. But Spain had always regarded the Pacific as her monopoly and the Falkland Islands, although unoccupied, as her territory. When Pitt came on the scene he decided after some hesitation that Britain should stand her ground.[16]

In his arrangements for his diplomatic offensive in Berlin and St Petersburg Pitt disregarded completely the efforts of the Rockingham ministry. He consulted only the King in his selection as special envoy to both Courts of Hans Stanley, who had acted for him in the 1761 negotiations with Choiseul. Once Conway had been let into the picture, he could see all sorts of difficulties and on 29 July wrote to Pitt pointing out that to accredit Stanley publicly to Berlin would stand in contradiction to an assurance he had just given Vienna that no treaty with Prussia was under consideration; further there were the positions of Mitchell and Macartney to be considered. A talk with Conway put the wind up Stanley, who had not been told by Pitt how poor were relations with Prussia. He therefore suggested

that it might be wiser to proceed to St Petersburg direct. Pitt
decided on a compromise: Stanley should certainly visit Berlin
on his way to St Petersburg, so as to allay any suspicion Frederick
might have at a *démarche* with Russia. But he would not be given
full ambassadorial status and Mitchell must first be asked to
ascertain Frederick's views.[17]

On 29 July, at twenty-five minutes past five, the King wrote to
Pitt from Richmond Lodge: 'I have signed this day the warrant
for creating you an Earl, and shall with pleasure receive you in
that capacity tomorrow, as well as entrust you with my privy
seal; as I know the Earl of Chatham will zealously give his aid
towards destroying all party distinctions, and restoring that
subordination to Government, which can alone preserve that
inestimable blessing, Liberty, from degenerating into Licentious-
ness.'[18] Pitt, in his full titles, became Earl of Chatham and
Viscount Pitt of Burton Pynsent. Among high circles his intention to take a peerage was not by this time unexpected but the
public was dumbfounded, the reaction immediate and vehement. Caricature after caricature depicted the new Earl in
sinister alliance with Bute. Whereas the Thirteen Colonies
usually had the popular press on their side, even Chatham's
American policy for a time shared his unpopularity. Horace
Walpole summed up the phenomenon: 'The people thought he
had sold them for a title.'[19]

'Charles Townshend has a fine game to play,' wrote Albemarle to Rockingham on 1 August, 'if I am not mistaken he will
soon take the lead in the House of Commons.'[20] Albemarle
knew that Conway was really interested in a military career and
unhappy struggling with the tides and uncertainties of parliamentary life. That prophecy must, however, appear to depend
upon Townshend's willingness to submit to Chatham, who
intended to rule with an iron rod. Conway had been treated
with scant consideration and Shelburne's request for an earldom
of Great Britain was ignored.[21] Life with Chatham was no fun
and some forty years later Shelburne would remark in his autobiography: 'I was in the most intimate political habits with him
for ten years, the time I was Secretary of State, included, he
Minister, and necessarily was with him at all hours in town
and country, without drinking a glass of water in his house or

company or five minutes of conversation out of the way of business.'[22]

Even the King got a gentle brushing from the autocrat. His request for places for Northumberland, le Despencer, Sir Fletcher Norton and Welbore Ellis, respectively Attorney-General and Secretary at War in Grenville's government, met with a rebuff: 'they were very fit persons . . . but as they brought no share of abilities with them, they must wait a little'. Chatham's objection to the promotion of men who had been prominent members of the Grenville ministry and owed their start to Bute was very understandable. He was apprehensive lest the King's Friends looked to the King's Friend rather than to the King's Minister. Le Despencer received minor office but Norton and Ellis got no dinner.[23]

Norton complained to Bute, who took it upon himself to expostulate to the King. He received a stiff rejoinder containing accusations of gross inconsistency, at the least, in seeking the employment of his following as the condition of supporting the King's administration. Deeply stung, Bute replied in a long letter of exculpation which contained an attack upon Chatham and his ideas of party, ending with the heart-rending plea: 'I say, Sir, suffer me in this most humiliated situation to possess your friendship independent of your power; . . .'. An immature friendship such as theirs was almost bound to end in bitterness. Bute had not seen the King in private for a year and never more would.[24]

That August Chatham got down to broadening his ministry; his promise to give employment to any man of character irrespective of party must be honoured. The hope that faction might be eliminated was by no means visionary for, despite Dowdeswell's very understandable refusal of minor office, with Grafton and Conway in administration Rockingham could hardly canvass resignations among his friends. A politically sound Commander-in-Chief was found in Granby. Ligonier, despite his eighty-seven years, protested that he was still fit to carry out his duties and certainly was yet well capable in the arts of seduction. He received an earldom of Great Britain as Earl Ligonier and after three years ended his gallant career in this world.[25] Bedford had shown an interest in places for his connection. But when

Gower was offered the Admiralty Bedford made clear that to allow his family and friends to take office a sufficient number must be included to give colouring to the ministry. The King was not surprised and wrote to Chatham: 'I am sorry I have proved so true a prophet, in the course of the various arrangements that have been proposed; but am clear the sounding Lord Gower was right, and must convince the deluded people that the declaration, that no exceptions were made to men, except so far as their own characters pointed it out, was the real truth.'[26] Evidently the King took seriously Chatham's professions, so close to the ideals he himself had cherished at the outset of the reign.

To the Admiralty Chatham appointed Saunders, a Rockingham Whig, but despite his deserved reputation after Quebec his abilities as administrator were not thought on highly.[27] Pocock, of Havana fame, resigned as Admiral of the Red in protest and found his application for a peerage ignored.[28] Conway's brother Hertford, Rockingham's Lord Lieutenant of Ireland, was induced to become Master of the Horse. Bristol, Ambassador to Spain during the negotiations of 1761, was Chatham's choice for Ireland and to him was made clear that a more assiduous residence than customary would be expected.[29] Where Rockingham's neglect to cultivate the Court had been a reason for his failure, with Bute out of the way Chatham got down to including King's Friends in his Government. The choice of Stanley for Berlin and St Petersburg was of a King's Friend and Stuart-Mackenzie was reinstated Lord Keeper of the Signet but, as the King made very clear, without the 'management' of Scotland. Hillsborough and young Lord North, whom Rockingham had turned out, got places.[30] As Shelburne would in his old age record of Chatham: 'He told me himself . . . that the world was much mistaken in thinking that he did not like patronage, for he was but a little man in 1755 and obliged to act the part he did, and he proved very sufficiently that he did, by catching at almost everything that dropped in every department.'[31]

The aggrandisement of the King's Friends perturbed Newcastle but Rockingham was happy for the present, basking in a wave of popularity by way of contrast to the execration which had greeted Chatham's peerage. Congratulatory Addresses on the repeal of the Stamp Act rolled in from the City, Bristol, Lancaster, Leicester, Liverpool and Manchester, apart from his loyal city of York. As the 2nd Earl of Hardwicke put it: 'You are really beating the Great Commoner at his own Weopons and receiving those Eulogiums wch his *Puffs* have hitherto supposed, that No-body was *entitled* to but himself.'[32]

Chatham and Grafton embarked upon the preparatory negotiations for the renewal of the Charter of the East India Company, which had always been the occasion for a capital gift to the Crown. Chatham had every intention that, in view of the acquisition of Bengal, the contribution should be more substantial but wanted, too, a formal parliamentary enquiry into the affairs of the Company. When on 28 August Grafton entertained the Chairman and his deputy to dinner at his house in Grosvenor Square, he had with him Conway and Shelburne. As a special condescension he invited Townshend, who had the churlish impertinence to refuse on the ground that he would not take responsibility for affairs outside his department. The Chairman was given a written paper which stated the intention of administration to promote a parliamentary enquiry.[33] During the first week of September Chatham looked around with every feeling of satisfaction, his government formed, the affairs of a great northern alliance and of India under way, and on 7 September he declared: 'That He was very sensible of The Run There was against Him; But, That It did not affect Him, nor should alter His Conduct; That if his Majesty was pleased, (which He did not seem in The least to doubt,) To continue His Confidence to Him, He would never desert The King; But support Him in all Events, broke, and Old as He was; – That he has not the least Doubt of Success; And That His Administration would be a permanent One.'[34]

One of the disappointments of Chatham's life was not long in coming. Mitchell saw Frederick at Potsdam on 14 September and outlined Chatham's scheme for an alliance between Britain, Prussia and Russia to counterbalance the Family Compact. Frederick could see no reason for such a project; France and Spain were not at the moment in a position to make war; a northern alliance would simply create needless apprehension; treaties concluded with a view to distant events became merely a matter of ostentation. Mitchell countered that the weakness of France and Spain made the immediate present the proper time to provide for the future. He explained how Chatham intended sending Stanley, his envoy to St Petersburg, by way of Berlin in order to secure first the blessing of the Prussian Court.

Frederick had two serious objections to any negotiations; firstly he thought that eventually Britain and France would go to war, in which the interests of Prussia might not conduce him to join; secondly, the instability of British politics made the secure transaction of business impossible. When Mitchell pointed out that the formation of Chatham's government promised a long period of order, Frederick commented: 'I fear my friend has hurt himself by accepting of a peerage at this time.'[35] Stanley was never in a position to embark upon his mission, whilst at St Petersburg Macartney was so bridled at Chatham's interference that he resigned. Frederick had been correct in supposing that France and Spain were not yet ready for war. Choiseul restrained the Spanish Government from interfering with the British settlement in the Falklands, and a crisis was averted.

That summer an uninterrupted succession of rain had destroyed the corn harvest. The price of bread rocketed and in several counties food riots were so serious that the Lords Lieutenant had to call out the army. Shelburne hurried to Bowood, his Wiltshire seat, so alarmed were his servants for the safety of his house. Although the price of corn had not advanced to the level required by statute for an embargo on exportation, Chatham decided on an Order in Council to stop corn ships leaving port. In view of the disturbances he could confidently expect Parliament to consent to an Act of Indemnity. Gout which deprived him of the use of his right hand precluded his attendance at the Council of 24 September, where, however, Newcastle was present as an indication of support from Rockingham.[36]

Grafton was so wearied of Charles Townshend's girlish pertness that he secured Chatham's consent to his admission to the Cabinet. The meeting of 1 October, with foreign affairs the subject, could not fail to interest and Chatham's masterly exposition was of his best. Going home in Grafton's carriage,

Townshend owned: 'Lord Chatham had just shown to us what inferior animals we were, and that, as much as he had seen of him before, he did not conceive till that night his superiority to be so very transcendent.'[37] Townshend's mood of humility did not last long, for within days he was pestering Grafton for a peerage for Lady Dalkeith. The next day Chatham left for Bath where he joined Camden and Northington and composed the King's Speech for the opening of Parliament. The day after Chatham's departure a dukedom was announced for Northumberland, a move likely to dissipate any lingering objections among Bute's following at supporting the Government. Two further dukedoms were conferred upon heads of ancient Houses, Montagu and Leinster, the only ducal creations of George III outside the royal family. Administration would be able to face Parliament in another five weeks secure in the national esteem.[38]

With the Charter of the East India Company coming up for review, Clive's agent Walsh was much concerned at what line administration might take. He therefore called upon Chatham at The Circus in Bath on 11 October and found him more than affable, his admiration for Clive unabated. Over general issues Chatham was deeply angered at the Court of Proprietors who, against the advice of the directors, had raised the dividend from 6 per cent to 10 per cent. The increase had no justification from the balance sheets and irrespective of economic considerations was grossly impertinent when a renewal of the Charter was shortly to come before Parliament. Though Chatham reposed a certain faith in the good sense of the directors he hated the greedy passions of the Court to whom they were responsible. In respect of the parliamentary enquiry, Chatham in no way envisaged even a leadership from administration over so difficult and extensive an affair as the Company, which 'in all cases, must subsist'. Chatham's idea was that the consensus of Parliament be freely taken: 'that by the means of so many gentlemen coming from so many different parts of the kingdom, and turning the subject different ways in their minds, many new lights might be gathered; . . . '. Chatham got a shock when Walsh told him the state of the Company revenues, generally supposed much larger. Walsh reported to Clive: 'This is the substance of my conversation with this great man, who is certainly not only the most vigorous, but the most comprehensive and judicious minister this country ever had.'[39]

By 19 October Chatham could just hold his pen, and at the cost of considerable pain sent Shelburne a reprimand for suggesting that Hillsborough might become Ambassador to Spain; the draft of the King's Speech would be off to Grafton in a couple of days and he expected to be in London by the first week of November. Grafton was fussed about opposition in the coming session of Parliament and wished most to secure the services of Burke. In fact Grafton had little to fear because Chatham had had quite a useful though inconclusive conversation with Bedford at Bath and difficulty need be anticipated only from Grenville.[40]

When Parliament opened on 11 November Chatham was introduced to the House of Lords by Northington and Bristol. His maiden speech was unfortunate; an affected apology for being of the peerage was succeeded by a defence of the illegal embargo so spirited as to imply that Parliament was not concerned; even the name of John Locke was called to witness. A casual explanation in down to earth language would have done far better.[41] Within days Chatham committed an error which could have brought down the ministry. The 3rd Lord Mount Edgecumbe was a man without ambition who had represented the family borough of Fowey for fifteen years without oral record before succeeding his brother. He was, however, proud of his office as Treasurer of the Household and took exception to Chatham's peremptory demand that he become a Lord of the Bedchamber in lieu. Common sense demanded that one of the greatest borough proprietors in Cornwall be treated with consideration, especially as he had just undertaken to introduce Conway's nephew Viscount Beauchamp to the House of Commons. Edgecumbe would take no job to compensate for his dismissal, so that Saunders and a number of minor office holders friendly to Rockingham resigned. Conway, who had never made any bones about his distaste for an active life in the House of Commons, addressed to Chatham a powerful remonstrance at the unhappy situation in which he was.[42] Conway's friendship for Grafton restrained him from the resignation Rockingham would have liked to see.

Conway and Townshend were both put out when Chatham entrusted Beckford with moving the resolution for a parliamentary enquiry into the affairs of the East India Company. Although Beckford's authority in the City might be considered a recommendation, his renowned hatred of monopolies made his leadership far from reassuring.[43] And Chatham might not have taken the prospect of the Rockingham party in opposition so lightly had he known of Townshend's treachery, for under the cover of nominees the Chancellor of the Exchequer was speculating in East India stock to the tune of thousands. He had over the years accumulated a camarilla of unspeakably corrupt protégés. Whilst Treasurer of the Chamber in the Pitt and Devonshire administration, he had appointed as his deputy John Huske, by birth a North American and member of Parliament for Malden. Huske quietly embezzled £30,000 and kept the secret well. Yet more sinister was Samuel Touchet, member of Parliament for Shaftesbury, a big business man with debts in excess of £300,000, though parliamentary privilege protected him from bankruptcy proceedings. Townshend appointed none other than Huske the thief and Touchet the rogue to be his unofficial advisers on the national finances. The Chancellor of the Exchequer, who had a secret pecuniary interest in the East India Company and was in daily correspondence with evil men, took the edge off Beckford's introduction: 'Charles Townshend stated the matter quite new, disclaimed all the offensive parts, and made a very artful, conciliating, able and eloquent speech.' That evening the followers of Rockingham and Bedford joined Grenville in voting in the minority of 76 against 129.[44]

As the support of the Rockinghams could no longer be depended upon, Chatham turned to Bedford, much against the wishes of the King who could not forget or forgive that nobleman's conduct when partner with Grenville. The Admiralty was offered to Gower, who on 28 November travelled to Woburn for Bedford's counsel. The King had no great expectations, for Chatham's talk with Bedford at Bath had yielded nothing positive; before Gower could return to London several vacancies were filled up, including a place for Bute's old protégé Jenkinson. When on 1 December Bedford saw Chatham at rooms he had taken in Bond Street, the places he meant to ask for had substantially been taken and he returned to Woburn with a deep sense of insult. Chatham, very apt to fall back upon airy phrases about the King's freedom to choose his own servants, would have been wiser to attempt nothing.[45] He gave the Admiralty to Hawke, an appointment professionally irreproachable though no buttress to the ministry.

The 6 December was the day appointed for a Cabinet meeting to discuss the next stage of the East India business. Although the King wrote to Conway insisting that the enquiry be set under way, Townshend openly opposed the whole idea. Next day Chatham wrote to Grafton:

'I grieve most heartily at the report of the meeting last night. If the inquiry is to be contracted within the ideas of Mr. Chancellor of the Exchequer . . . the whole becomes a *farce*, and the *Ministry a ridiculous phantom*. . . . Mr. C. Townshend's fluctuations and incurable weaknesses cannot comport with him remaining in that critical office.'

Townshend cringed before Chatham's fury and on 8 December meekly supported Beckford's motion for papers, whilst next day Laurence Sulivan prudently agreed to the enquiry being opened. Evidently Chatham could, by a sharp exertion of his authority, keep his Cabinet in order and, subject to that condition, have his way with the House of Commons.[46]

When the embargo upon the export of corn was again debated in the House of Lords on 10 December, Chatham launched into a heated altercation with Richmond, who had merely pointed out the irregularity of the situation. The embargo was legalised by an Act of Indemnity passed unanimously, but Chatham had bungled a mere technicality. His irritability at any disagreement was acute and, ominous sign, he was spending ridiculous sums upon magnificent equipages and required fifteen servants to wait upon his children at Weymouth. Parliament rose for the Christmas recess and Chatham went to Bath.

On the second day of the New Year, 1767, Chatham received Henry Flood at his house at Bath. Since 1759 Flood had been a member of the Irish House of Commons and had become leader of a movement for reform among Protestant landowners. None of the restrictions, political and economic, upon the Ireland of Walpole's day had been relaxed; the Irish House of Commons elected in 1761 was not due to be renewed by a general election until the death of the King, who was only twenty-seven. Flood laid down to Chatham four essentials, a Septennial Act, a Habeas Corpus Act on the British model, the grant of an appellate jurisdiction to the Irish House of Lords and the reform of the pensions list. Chatham showed deep sympathy with Flood's proposals, though that valiant patriot Lord Charlemont was sceptical: 'Your interview with the Patagonian has turned out pretty much as I expected. It is easier for a camel to go through the eye of a needle, or for a rich man to enter the kingdom of heaven, than for a politician to lay aside disguise, or for a minister *here* to think as we would wish, with regard to our affairs.'[47]

Charles Townshend had remained in town with authority to open negotiations with the East India Company. On New Year's Day he addressed to Chatham a letter informing him that the Court of Proprietors had empowered the directors to treat: 'It must be some time before the directors can, in their committee, either name the persons out of their own body who are to act for them, or prepare for the opening of the business; but if it were not so, I should certainly decline all intercourse, separate from your Lordship, and wait the return of his Majesty's servants.' Chatham was not at all pleased with the wording of the Proprietors' resolution, devoid of reference to the rights of Parliament but concerned with 'extending their commerce, securing their possessions, and perpetuating the prosperity of the Company . . . '. But he had no wish to act from a distance and his reply by return of post was cautious; the resolution was only 'the dawn' though the apparently reasonable wording might conceal 'certain narrow notions'. But Chatham gave Townshend every encouragement to go forward: 'I will, however, hope for the best side of the alternative, and am fully persuaded, my dear Sir, that you and I shall equally share the honest joy, if the desired success crowns the work; and, indeed, by one and the same act, to do the nation justice, and to fix the case and pre-eminence of England for ages, are plentiful sources of many and noble joy.'

Townshend saw the directors and considered their attitude eminently co-operative. He was far from happy about what Chatham's idea of a parliamentary enquiry might lead to: 'the endless difficulties accompanying every idea of substituting the public in the place of the Company, in the collecting, investing, and remitting the revenue . . . '. Faced with such a demand the Proprietors might well 'stand the issue . . . rather than submit to what they might deem severity in the manner, or in the plan'. To this Chatham sent a non-committal answer on 6 January, more or less telling Townshend not to anticipate his fences. While he accepted that 'right' lay with the Company, Parliament had the discretion to decide what proportion of the revenues they might retain. Chatham emphasised that his fears lay with the 'vices and passions' of the Proprietors and when Grafton forwarded to him their resolutions he had no hesitation in dubbing them 'preposterous'.

The date for the opening of the parliamentary enquiry was fixed for 22 January. In a letter to Chatham, Grafton stressed the importance of his attendance: 'I have every reason to desire, whenever the negotiation is to be opened, that it may be in your Lordship's presence: it is of the utmost consequence it should; I mean even in the first overture.'[48] Chatham set out for London on 11 January, but gout in the hand forced him back to Bath. The King at once grasped that Chatham's absence at this juncture must jeopardise the whole East India business.

When on 20 January Beckford proposed to the Commons that the East India papers be printed for the perusal of members, Townshend asked that the motion be deferred 'as he hoped to settle all matters with the East India Company to the satisfaction of the public'. Townshend, all set to cut a figure as author of a treaty between Government and Company, was hinting that the directors make offers so favourable that no administration could reject them, and in consequence forestall the enquiry. Beckford agreed to withdraw his motion for a few days. Two days later Grenville put before the Commons the very eighteenth-century idea that the territorial rights of the Company should be decided, not by Parliament but by the Court of King's Bench. Townshend retorted that the right lay with the Company and the only question was what contribution the Crown should receive in

return for the confirmation of their Charter. On this declaration
East India stock rose six points. Beckford was seriously disturbed
and on 27 January wrote a strong letter to Chatham: 'Your
presence and advice was never more wanting than at this critical
juncture. Possibly you have not heard with precision what has
passed in the House, relative to East India affairs.' Beckford
stressed that Townshend in no way seemed to grasp the principle
that the rights of the Company must stem from parliamentary
recognition and Conway too 'was not so decisive as I could have
wished; although he has a good head, and honest heart'.[49]

The insubordination of the American legislatures was bound
to bring trouble for the ministry from Grenville. The precedent
of the successful combination of the merchant interest in defiance
of the Crown was unforgettable. The Assemblies were not prepared to pass legislation which branded the Stamp Act disturbances as criminal. The Assembly of New York refused to
comply with the Mutiny Act of the Grenville ministry which had
imposed mandatory billeting of British soldiers, at the expense of
the colonial governments. In the course of his long service on the
Board of Trade, Charles Townshend had developed views on
America very similar to those of Grenville, who never wavered
from the principle that the American colonies must be subject to
imperial taxation, a policy clearly understandable and with
appeal to members. Dull Conway, who had opposed the Stamp
Act, was no match for Grenville across the floor. On 26 January
1767, in the course of the debate on the vote for the army
estimates, Grenville demanded that the £400,000 required for
the overseas establishment be defrayed from colonial taxation.
The motion was negatived by 106 to 35, but Townshend
promptly offered to find the money from the indirect, as distinct
from the direct taxation of the colonies. This undertaking was
equivalent to a promise to tax the colonies for purposes of
revenue, albeit in disguised form, yet only Shelburne saw the
necessity to inform Chatham.[50]

By the end of January, Chatham, though still unable to leave
Bath, could take to his coach 'for a little motion and air'. He
fully realised that important opportunities were being wasted
and on the last day of the month wrote to Shelburne: 'My
absence from London, in the present crisis, is afflicting to me

beyond expression; but lamentations are vain, and it is best to look forward.' But he recognised that action had to be conditioned in the light of the commitments Townshend had publicly entered. As Townshend had declared in the House of Commons that the East India Company was about to make an offer, the constitutional question would have to wait. But Chatham did not think himself beaten: 'If the proposals shall be, as I expect, very inadequate, strength will be gained thereby for bringing on the question of right.' Therefore by the same post Chatham asked Beckford to move for a postponement of the debate on the East India papers until he might get to London.[51]

On 6 February Grafton forwarded to Chatham further proposals from the Company which he himself thought inadequate, but was ignored. Shelburne wrote in desperation to Chatham that although the Company had been told by the Cabinet that their terms were inadmissible, Sulivan was proposing to have them confirmed by the Court of Proprietors: 'The situation of the House of Commons,' he added, 'too bad to be described, appears to make what passed in the City very material.' George III was most anxious that the East India business be brought to a decisive conclusion but still looked to Chatham for decisions. Even wry Grenville saw the humour of the situation when he wrote: 'The Earl of Chatham is still at Bath, and consequently the King's administration has got gout and hobbles terribly. Mr. C. Townshend indeed seems to wish to move a little more nimbly and to try to walk a little without crutches.'[52]

On 27 February Charles Townshend asked the committee of ways and means for the renewal of the land tax at 4s., but for one year only, 'to give room for the most brilliant operation for finance this country ever saw . . . '. Dowdeswell moved for 3s. only from an interest substantially factious, for the lower rate could not be afforded unless either through the medium of colonial taxation or some deal with the East India Company alternative funds arose. North the Paymaster-General distinguished himself on the Government side but with the support of Grenville and the Bedford party Dowdeswell carried the day 206–188. Next day Grafton warned Chatham that the treasury operations for that year were crippled.[53] Chatham summoned up strength to travel and after several days' delay at the Castle

Inn at Marlborough arrived in London on 2 March. The King
at once sent him an assurance of support, and Chatham
attempted to assert his authority by asking North to replace
Townshend as Chancellor of the Exchequer, to meet with a
refusal. Instead of seeking an alternative, Chatham remained in
his Bond Street lodgings incapable of exertion, which left the
field to Townshend.[54]

When on 6 March Beckford moved that the East India papers
be printed and the Company's proposals produced, Townshend
and Conway both objected on the ground that the proposals
were incomplete. But Granby and Hawke, unaccustomed to
parliamentary management, indiscreetly let slip that the Cabinet
was hopelessly divided. Townshend rose a second time to
declare himself strongly in favour of agreement by treaty. When
on 9 March the opposition moved against printing the papers,
Townshend absented himself and the Government motion to
adjourn was carried 180–147, a majority of only 33. A few days
later Townshend's speculations in East India stock leaked out.
As Horace Walpole wrote to his friend Sir Horace Mann, the
British consul in Florence: 'What! and can a Chancellor of the
Exchequer stand such an aspersion Oh! my dear sir, his character cannot be lowered.' Townshend's profits were in the
region of £7,000.[55] Quite unabashed he got down to map out an
agreement between the Company and the Government.

At last, on the morning of 12 March Chatham saw the King,
though no business was transacted. When that evening America
came before the Cabinet, Townshend persuaded his colleagues
that there must be an Act of Parliament to deal with the
Assembly of New York and meanwhile the Governor forbid his
consent to any legislation. The next item was the vote of supply
for the American extraordinaries and Townshend declared that
he would not remain Chancellor of the Exchequer unless American expenditure was reduced and a tax levied on some American
imports. Grafton was utterly flabbergasted and next day wrote
to Chatham: 'His behaviour on the whole was such as no
Cabinet will I am confident ever submit to.' Shelburne was
equally disgusted and his letter to Chatham, also of 13 March,
ended: 'It appears to be quite impossible that Mr. Townshend
can mean to go in the King's service.'[56]

Over the next few weeks Townshend went into some pretty tricky political manoeuvring, hinting to Rockingham that he would like to see him at the Treasury. But at the same time he courted Grenville, seeking his company at the House of Commons to abuse Chatham, ridicule the ministry and even discuss American measures.[57] By 26 April Shelburne was losing patience and his letter to Chatham opened abrasively: 'In order to break in as little as possible upon Doct[r] Addington's Injunctions, I beg to say, that the Purpose of this Letter is to *inform* your Lordship of what pass'd on Fryday relative to America.' Various courses to deal with the New York Assembly had come up for discussion, but what stood out in Shelburne's long letter was his insistence that come what may the right of the British Parliament to bind the colonies must be laid down. So as to wipe the slate clean, an indemnity for past disturbances might be combined with an addition to the Declaratory Act making conspiracy to disobey statute or to question the right of the King in Parliament to legislate treasonable offences: 'This to be supported by a Military Power to be occasionally called to aid, as would be done to support any Act of Parliament here.' Shelburne thought the Americans thoroughly unreasonable even on their own principles, 'since the repeal of the Stamp Act was enough to shew them, it was the decided Opinion of Parliament not to make an Internal Tax in point of policy'. Shelburne was however entirely ready to place himself under Chatham's orders: 'I am persuaded your Experience will enable you to fix on that, which has the least evil in it.'[58]

Since his fruitless audience of 12 March Chatham had remained in seclusion at his lodgings in Bond Street. Grafton, Shelburne and Bristol received no reply to letters. Chatham took a daily airing in his coach but was unable to see anyone. The King was so concerned that he sent his surgeon-general to take a look at him and with every kindness suggested a retirement to North End, where would be the facility for equestrian exercise.[59] Charles Townshend took advantage of the hiatus to get down to facts and figures about America with Touchet, for whom he requested of Grafton a sinecure: 'He and he alone has the merit of whatever has been honourably done in this winter for the public and the Treasury in the choice of taxes.' The scheme for indirect American taxation that emerged by the end of April was subtle. Tea and several other articles liable to heavy duties on entry into Britain would be subject to lower duties on re-export to America. But British custom house officers would be sent out to collect and the moneys, though used for the purposes of civil government in America, would not be subject to appropriation by the Assemblies. The proceeds were estimated at £35,000 p.a.[60] As Conway refused to present these proposals to the House of Commons, Townshend decided to take the business in hand and hustled Grafton into compliance by threats to resign.

So elated was Townshend at his handiwork that on the evening of 6 May he became seized with the desire to advertise his pretensions to become Prime Minister. For a full hour he drivelled away before the House of Commons in what was dubbed his 'champagne speech', though the evidence for his being intoxicated is flimsy. Much was to the point; above all Townshend called for 'the restitution in the first point in Administration to the House of Commons' and an end to 'weathercock' government; a new order of things based upon the Rockingham connection with himself at the head was demanded but without the slur of a priority of property over talents: 'The House was in a roar of rapture, and some clapped their hands with ecstasy, like audience in a theatre.' The trouble was that in an age when ministers were still made and unmade by Kings, Townshend was the last person to be putting himself forward. At one and the same time Townshend showed himself fit for Prime Minister, yet in tact and temperament supremely unfit. Only ten months had passed since Chatham had questioned his suitability for Chancellor of the Exchequer.[61]

When on 13 May Townshend moved his American resolutions in the House of Commons he delivered a most business-like exposé of his imperial principles; though he had supported the repeal of the Stamp Act to prevent mischief, the right to tax the colonies was indubitable: 'Should their disobedience return, the authority of Parliament had been weakend; and unless supported with spirit and dignity, must be destroyed.' The New York resolutions were carried 180–98 and the duties passed without a division and almost without discussion. The purpose of the Act, to make provision for the civil government of America, was clearly stated. (7 George III c. 46.) Townshend estimated that the American mercantile interest would never countenance civil commotion and boycott with the consequent loss to trade.[62]

All the ministers, even Townshend, were staggered at the decision of the General Court of the East India Company to raise the dividend from 10 per cent to 12 per cent, against the advice of the directors. Had Chatham been actively concerned this unutterable impertinence, following so soon on the increase from 6 per cent, would have guaranteed that Parliament undertake an enquiry. Indeed, the conduct of the Company was becoming manifestly so prodigal that some Government intervention in the interests of the Proprietors themselves was imperative. A dividend restraining bill was put down as a Government measure. Only Sulivan commanded that confidence with the Company, in Parliament and with administration necessary for any negotiation. He made a shrewd deal with Townshend that the Company should make very handsome proposals and in return the dividend bill would be buried. Sulivan kept his word and the Company's proposals were accepted by both Houses of Parliament without demur. In return for an annual contribution of £400,000 to the Crown, the East India Company was confirmed in the full and autonomous possession of its territories.

The provisions of the East India Company Charter Act of May 1767 were purely financial. The question of sovereignty, which must have been raised as a result of Chatham's proposed enquiry, was never discussed in Parliament. The £400,000 the country expected was exactly the amount required to meet the cost of the military establishment in America. But the viability of that arrangement must depend upon the estimate of the *diwani* truly working out at £2 million p.a. Townshend let Sulivan down because he had not the authority to deter the House of Commons from passing the dividend restraining bill, which imposed a limit of twelve per cent for one year only, though the restriction was expected to be renewed regularly. Subsequent legislation exempted the Company from any contribution to the Crown if the dividend were cut back to six per cent.[63]

During May Rockingham, Bedford and Grenville combined

to attack the ministry in respect of American policy, and Towns-hend's predilections offered easy game. On 26 May the Government majority in the House of Lords fell to only three upon the vote for a committee to consider the papers relating to the disturbances. Grafton in his distress confided his conscience to Camden and Northington, who were convinced that the administration could not and ought not to be carried on. The King was advised accordingly and he directed Grafton to represent this deplorable state of affairs to Chatham. To his request of 27 May for a visit to North End Grafton received a reply in Lady Chatham's hand: 'If I could be allowed but a few minutes to lament that the continuation of his illness reduces him to the painful necessity of most earnestly entreating his Grace to pardon him, if he begs to be allowed to decline the honour of the visit the Duke of Grafton has so kindly proposed.' To a further letter from Grafton of 29 May Chatham replied by letter in his wife's hand that for him business was impossible but begged the ministers to stay at their posts. Grafton and Northington decided a recourse to the King was the sole rejoinder. The King backed them with a personal letter to Chatham setting out in great detail the parliamentary difficulties of the ministry and indicating that Grafton might resign any day. This entreaty Chatham had to meet by inviting Grafton to pay a call. The King was overjoyed and returned to the mood of optimism he had felt when Chatham had first formed his government:

'Your letter has given me the greatest pleasure: though I was certain no indisposition could abate your dutiful attachment to my person, or your natural intrepidity to withstand the greatest enemy of this poor country – faction, I already look on all difficulties as overcome; for the Duke of Grafton, who came to me just after I had received it, on my acquainting him you would see him tomorrow, required no other encouragement to continue in his present situation.'[64]

When, however, Grafton saw Chatham on the last day of the month he was horrified at his condition, worse than his most painful anticipations: 'The confidence he reposed in me demanded every return on my part: and it appeared like cruelty in me to put a man I valued, to so great suffering as it was evident my commission excited.' Grafton ran over the perilous situation of the ministry and alluded in particularly bitter terms to Townshend. He urged the necessity of a union with either the Bedfords or the Rockinghams, to which Chatham assented though expressing a preference for the former. After an interview lasting some two hours Grafton took his phaeton back to town.[65]

Grafton's expedition opened his eyes to the plain fact that Chatham was likely to remain in mothballs indefinitely and might never emerge. The King authorised Grafton to negotiate with either Rockingham or Bedford, though with Grenville he was not prepared to treat. In fact he had no faith in any negotiation and neither did he believe in the irreversible nature of Chatham's gout. On 2 June he wrote to Chatham again, indicating that Conway and Townshend were each on the verge of resignation: 'Upon the whole, I earnestly call upon you to lay before me a plan, and also to speak to those you shall propose for responsible offices. You owe this to me, to the country, and also to those who have embarked in administration with you.'

Grafton approached Gower on 3 June to discover the intentions of the Bedford Party, while on the same day Conway sounded Rockingham. George III did not mean to commission Rockingham to form a new administration and indeed had no faith in his ability to do so, but to graft the 'pure Whigs' on to the existing Government. Although he stated his willingness that Rockingham become First Lord of the Treasury, the King did not vouchsafe an audience. Rockingham correctly surmised that the King was proposing to use him as a figurehead, without amending the administration in any particular. As Rockingham would not enter such an arrangement and Bedford would not act on his own, Grafton's attempt to reconstruct his ministry soon petered out. But not the King's faith in Chatham, to whom on 13 June he addressed a short note pointing out that the fine weather must have amended his ill-health: 'I therefore wish to learn how you now find yourself, and whether you do not flatter yourself soon to be in a situation to see me; . . . '. Chatham replied trying to make clear that there was no hope of his sustaining an audience: 'He is overwhelmed with affliction still to find that the continuance in extreme weakness of nerves renders it impossible for him to flatter himself with being able soon to present himself before his Majesty.' Two days later the King wrote again, suggesting that his court physician might go to the assistance of Dr Addington, who was looking after Chatham, to receive back something of a telling off in Lady Chatham's hand.

On 20 June the King was once more writing, commenting hopefully on a rumour that Chatham's condition was beginning to improve, to be informed by return of post that such was not the case. Five days later the King again urged Chatham to return to duty, for the parliamentary situation was so improved that the ministry might yet be saved. All Chatham could suggest was that Grafton remain at his post, and perhaps find a Chancellor of the Exchequer to replace Townshend. In the event the only minister to resign was Bristol, who had never relished the prospect of a personal attendance upon his duties at Dublin. Once Conway resolved to soldier on, Grafton accepted the obligation to remain Prime Minister.[66]

Chatham spent days in isolation without seeing a soul, not even his wife. His meals were served through a hatch. He developed a mania for building and persuaded his unfortunate host Dingley to consent to the addition of thirty-four bedrooms to North End and to buy up any neighbouring building that affected the amenities of the house. Then he felt a longing for Hayes and convinced himself that only there would he recover his health and spirits. After considerable hesitation Thomas Walpole agreed to sell Hayes back, but only on exorbitant terms. In August Chatham gave a power of attorney to his wife. The King's distrust for Addington,* in whom Chatham and more surprisingly Lady Chatham placed every faith, was well placed. Where Chatham was naturally abstemious and loved riding and fresh air, Addington prescribed a regimen of heavy quantities of beef and mutton with liberal potations of hock, port and madeira, and forbade out-door activities. That August, on Addington's advice, Chatham left London for Somerset. Lady Chatham showed herself the perfect wife; her forbearance at his alarming disregard for money heightened the admirable quality of her constant devotion.[67]

---

* Addington's son, the 1st Viscount Sidmouth, was to succeed the younger Pitt as Prime Minister of Britain in 1801.

Meanwhile the triumph of the opposition on 26 May was proved only a temporary phenomenon. The administration carried the dividend restraining bill through the House of Lords on 11 July by a majority of twenty-one. Charles Townshend, on top of form, appeared about to take the lead from Conway. His wife at last obtained that coveted peerage as Baroness Greenwich and his brother George was that August appointed Lord Lieutenant of Ireland in succession to Bristol.

The choice of Lord Townshend had an indirect connection with his brother's American policy. As the duties could never supply funds sufficient to police a frontier stretching from Canada to the Gulf of Mexico, the Irish army was to be increased from 12,000 to 15,200 men, the extra complement to be used for the American service. So as to win the compliance of the Dublin House of Commons, a programme of reform on the lines Chatham and Flood had agreed was to go forward. Townshend was ordered to reside in Dublin with the title of Viceroy. The Irish Octennial Act, providing for general elections every eight years, was greeted with wild enthusiasm, but then the programme ran into heavy weather. Whereas the Irish expected judicial independence, Shelburne had to make clear that Grafton and the Cabinet would insist upon the appellate jurisdiction of the British Privy Council remaining, even if the Irish judges were given a life tenure. The climate of opinion at Westminster hardened against constitutional change in Ireland while disturbances in America were gathering force; whatever happened there, Ireland must remain a dependency. The Octennial Act alone did not satisfy the patriotic movement and added force to its pretensions.[68] Then the political situation at Westminster was transformed by the unexpected death of Charles Townshend from a putrid fever. His shady political connections tumbled to the ground. Huske, knowing that his peculations must come to light, fled to Paris, though he was declared a bankrupt. Touchet was able to remain in England but his career and prosperity were ended and one day he would die by his own hand.[69] Townshend's death forced Grafton to undertake a new system in the House of Commons and the first step was the appointment of North as Chancellor of the Exchequer.[70]

CHAPTER 16

Chatham and the Whig Opposition

'I never pretended to guess at Ld Chatham's intentions. I never comprehended him. But I did not expect that I should be at the same loss about his words. Yet I am assur'd (by several ear-witnesses of veracity) that in one speech in the House of Lords, he said, "That the Livery of London was a most respectable part of the Constitution: older than the King, Lords and Commons. And that Androgeous was Lord Mayor of London when Julius Caesar came here." Where did he find this? And what could he mean by a Lord Mayor and Livery, when every body went stark naked?[1]'

Henry Fox Lord Holland to John Campbell of Cawdor,
21 June 1770.

When Parliament met on 24 November Grenville plunged into a pointed attack upon the American policy of the Rockingham party. The ensuing quarrel between Rockingham and Grenville convinced Bedford that, as a united opposition could never come into being, his following might as well take office. He approached the Court on 29 November, expressing his willingness to support the ministry provided Gower and the 3rd Viscount Weymouth were of the Cabinet and Rigby provided for. Conway readily entered on a retirement by resigning as Secretary of State for the North in favour of Weymouth. North, Chancellor of the Exchequer, became Leader of the House of Commons. Bedford's union of his party with Grafton was his last political decision before his death three years later. Blind and saddened by the loss of his eldest son as the result of a riding accident, he had reached the end. Though none too industrious and a little too conscious of his position, Bedford was one of the few to feel no fear in Pitt's presence. He, more than any other, had forced Pitt into resignation in October 1761 and his firmness helped Bute complete the Peace.[2]

The King considered that Grafton as Premier still secured for the ministry the magic protection of Chatham's name. But both disliked and distrusted Chatham's most loyal adherent Shelburne, whom they would gladly get rid of. That December Grafton revived an idea current for years that a third Secretaryship of State be set up with special responsibility for America. The consideration that America was part of Shelburne's cure at the Southern Department was an added attraction. But Shelburne did not allow any impulse of mortification trick his conscience into resignation and readily agreed to the division of responsibility. Grafton next pressed him to accept the new Secretaryship for which his principles with regard to America were suited but Shelburne insisted upon remaining where he was. The appointment of Hillsborough tilted the balance of opinion in the Cabinet in favour of men who had originally supported the Stamp Act.[3]

Parliament, having run the seven years prescribed by law, was dissolved on 14 March. The poll that summer was as little controversial as that of 1761, the issues local rather than national and the taxation of the Thirteen Colonies of little interest. As Grafton neglected electoral business, the Rockingham Whigs enjoyed a few successes. Holland had the pleasure of seeing his brilliant younger son Charles James Fox enter the House of Commons. The one exception to the quiescent norm was the election of Wilkes for Middlesex. Over the years he had remained in France but the diversions of Parisian society were no compensation for the stark fact that exile meant penury: 'What the Devil have I to do with prudence? I owe money in France, am an outlaw in England, hated by the King, the Parliament, and the bench of bishops. . . . I must raise a dust or starve in a gaol.' Although still an outlaw he returned to England and Grafton sensibly decided to ignore his presence. But Wilkes could not afford obscurity, so he contested one of the four seats of the City of London and was soundly beaten. Temple, always happy to cause trouble, bought him a freehold in Middlesex to qualify him to stand for the county. To represent the three thousand electors of Middlesex, which then included much of modern London including St Marylebone, was an honour jealously regarded. That Wilkes was returned head of the poll was due partly to the recession, which had worsened after the Rockingham administration and in 1768 struck bottom. Memories of No. 45 served Wilkes well with 'the middling and lesser sort'. He found useful auxiliaries in the thousands of workless artisans in the streets and byways: even by eighteenth-century standards his election was remarkable for physical intimidation. Burke acutely summed up the reasons for his triumph: a weak and disunited Government taken by surprise; the hatred for Bute as strong as ever; and above all Chatham's occultation had left the mob no hero.

George III despised Wilkes with the distaste for a debauchee natural to a man of regular life with a marked streak of priggishness. His determination to prevent the demagogue taking his seat was prompted by personal hatred, but the circumstances of Wilkes's election were open to objective criticism. The Cabinet agreed on 20 April to have Wilkes expelled, but decided first to allow the law to take its course against the outlaw. To ask the House of Commons to throw out a convicted criminal would be more regular than to propose his expulsion before he had stood trial. To Wilkes prison was a splendid opportunity to win a martyr's halo. He surrendered to Mansfield's jurisdiction in the Court of King's Bench on 27 April and in June was sentenced to twenty-two months in gaol for his libel in *The North Briton*. Meanwhile Parliament had met on 10 May amidst riots which, though primarily motivated by economic distress, clearly demonstrated his popularity.[4]

Grafton, not satisfied with cutting down Shelburne's importance, wanted to oust him altogether. That June the treaty with Bedford was completed with the appointment of Rigby to the office he coveted, the Paymastership. Camden was won over from Shelburne to Grafton's side. News from America was very bad, of riots in Boston and Virginia against the Townshend duties. The world was abuzz with talk of Grafton having to come to terms with Grenville, or of a union between Bedford and Rockingham with a nominal Prime Minister, for instance Northumberland. All added up to nothing and that September Grafton sought Chatham's approval of Shelburne's dismissal. Chatham retorted by himself resigning at the same time as Shelburne, and the administration, so long defunct in practice, thus formally came to an end. This event was regretted by many and not least by Barrington, still at the War Office, who on 23 October wrote to Lady Chatham: 'Last post brought me . . . a confirmation of Lord Chatham's resignation of the privy seal; very unpleasing news to me, who have most ardently & without intermission, wish'd his return to health and to business.'[5] His resignation was Chatham's first lucid action for the past eighteen months. Weymouth succeeded to Shelburne's office and the Secretaryship for the South was given to the 4th Earl of Rochford. Grafton felt an obligation towards the King to remain at his post, particularly as the question of Wilkes's future had yet to be settled. He and Camden would have served their own interests better had they resigned together with Chatham and Shelburne, but loyalty to the King deflected their judgement.

Two months after Chatham's resignation Newcastle died. He and the Great Commoner could never have been friends: the one represented the conservative forces of the Whig party founded upon great property and the Revolution settlement, the other embodied the spirit of national adventure and as a patriot rose above party. Newcastle had closed the door upon the progress of the man he made a natural enemy as long as he dared and showed all the self-preserving pettiness most irritating to a genius consumed by the desire to prove his greatness before the world. Yet Newcastle, though ridiculed by Granville, Chesterfield and Chatham too, was a deal more formidable than some allowed. The words of Horace Walpole do him justice:[6]

'His life had been a proof that even in a free country great abilities are not necessary to govern it. Industry, perseverance, and intrigue, gave him that duration of power which shining talents and the favour of the Crown could not secure to Lord Granville, nor the first rank in eloquence and the most brilliant services to Lord Chatham. Adventitious cunning repaired Newcastle's folly, rashness overset Lord Granville's parts, and presumptuous impracticability Lord Chatham.'

Wilkes served his sentence in Newgate prison after the manner of an imprisoned nobleman; each day he received his distinguished callers – peers, members of Parliament and literary celebrities. At a fixed hour he would bow from his prison window to a throng of admirers. Grafton would have preferred to handle Wilkes with caution. Camden pointed out the tangle that would result were Wilkes expelled from the House of Commons and then re-elected for the same constituency. But he lacked the character to persuade his colleagues to let the dog alone. Thereafter, if ever Wilkes was mentioned, Camden feigned sleep or shuffled out of the room. When in January 1769 Wilkes presented an impertinent petition to the House of Commons, complaining of Mansfield's conduct of his trial, the ministry obtained his expulsion by a large majority. His re-election by an overwhelming number of the Middlesex electors was characterised by the usual mob brawling and he was once more expelled. Wilkes was elected and expelled three times in all. Finally, in May the House of Commons deemed his defeated opponent, Colonel Henry Luttrell, to have been returned member for Middlesex; no writ for a further election could be issued. The expulsion of a member of Parliament by a vote of the House had ample precedents; to declare his defeated opponent to have been returned instead was of dubious validity. The balance of votes in favour of Luttrell's co-optation was small and made up of placemen. Grenville, always a legalist, considered the rights of the Middlesex freeholders to have been illegally set aside and Rockingham too was critical of the proceedings. Their motives were honourable and to use Wilkes as a peg for a factious opposition was the last consideration.

Wilkes, set upon establishing a popular party to champion his cause 'out-doors', discovered an enthusiastic votary in the

Rev. John Horne, the unconventional Rector of Brentford, Middlesex. They founded the Society for the Bill of Rights and Wilkes chose London for his platform. He became an Alderman of the City and found wealthy supporters ready to subscribe large sums for a popular agitation. Beckford, though he disliked Wilkes and refused to join the Bill of Rights Society, readily persuaded the livery to vote a petition to the Crown on the Middlesex election. That October Beckford was elected Lord Mayor.[7]

Towards the middle of 1769 Chatham's mind began to heal and he returned to an awareness of his surroundings. Having been closeted in Somerset for one year and nine months he came to London and on 6 July saw the King. Their conversation lasted about twenty minutes and Chatham came out in great good humour.[8] Burke had no great expectations and commented to Rockingham:[9]

'If he was sent for, the shortness of the conference seems to indicate that nothing at all has been settled. If he was not sent for, it was, only, humbly to Lay a reprimand at the feet of his most gracious Master, and to talk some significant, pompous, creeping, explanatory, ambiguous matter, in the true Chathamic style; and thats all.'

Burke thought possibly Chatham would be used to reconstruct the ministry but did not expect a competent administration to emerge or think Rockingham should join: 'The Court alone can profit from any movements of Lord Chatham: he is always their rescourse when they run hard.'

Yet Chatham's return could not fail to be the event of the day. Camden called it his 'wonderful resurrection' and on 14 July Barrington called on Temple to present his congratulations.[10] Chatham was indeed presented with a scene of turmoil, with the news from America and the outburst of indignation over the Middlesex election. The completion by the French of the conquest of Corsica showed that now was no time for Britain to be divided. The petition of protest by the City to the King, followed shortly by Surrey, started a snowball. On 28 July Chatham proceeded from London to Stowe. In fine form, he held the reins of a Jimwhiskee, drawn by two horses, one before the other, followed by two coaches and six containing Lady Chatham, the children, and some twenty servants. Soon Chatham, Temple and George Grenville announced to the world their political accord and were dubbed 'The Triumvirate'.[11] By the end of August Temple had drafted a petition to be adopted by Buckinghamshire Quarter Sessions: Whateley, invariably cordial towards Burke, let him have a copy. The implication that 'The Triumvirate' would welcome alliance with the Rockingham Whigs was manifest.[12] A petition endorsed by the twenty thousand enfranchised freeholders of Yorkshire would resound nationally. Rockingham was no democrat but Burke and Dowdeswell, aiming to put the wind up Grafton, persuaded him to take the lead.

On 9 January 1770 Chatham addressed the House of Lords, his third appearance as a peer. His old self-confidence thundered forth and in one of his greatest speeches he denounced the conduct of the ministry over the Middlesex election:

'My lords, I acknowledge the just power, and reverence the constitution of the House of Commons. It is for their sake that I would prevent their assuming a power which the constitution has denied them, lest . . . they should forfeit that which they legally possess. My lords, I affirm that they have betrayed their constituents, and violated the constitution. Under pretence of declaring the law, they have *made* a law, and united in the same persons the office of legislator and of judge. . . .'

Chatham returned to the fray on 22 January with a further peroration; while the attention of the ministry and the House of Commons had been whittled away over constitutional issues which should never have been brought up, the Bourbon monarchies were gaining ground.

Chatham was transforming the House of Lords into a platform of debate concerning the principles of the Constitution, a happening unprecedented in the history of England. Grafton shoved the blame for the Middlesex election on to Camden, who had to admit his neglect to impress upon the ministry the impropriety of declaring Luttrell returned, and his resignation followed. Grafton replaced him with Charles Yorke, who after only two days as Lord Chancellor died – it was rumoured by his own hand, though more probably as the result of a brain haemorrhage. Within days Grafton resigned and Calcraft was assiduous in obtaining the resignations of placemen in the name of mighty Chatham.[13] Grafton's three and a half years at the Treasury, where he had cut a sorry figure of indecision and incompetence, were ended. He would live well into the following century and on and off hold Cabinet office, but that he should return to lead the country was never to be suggested by anyone.

If Chatham expected Grafton's resignation to result in his receiving the royal commission to act phoenix by bringing forth a new ministry from the old he was deceiving himself. He had already in 1766 been entrusted with that alchemy with consequences which the King was not minded to forget. George III was in no difficulty, for he could see the natural successor to Grafton in Frederick Lord North, Chancellor of the Exchequer and Leader of the Commons. Although Calcraft's efforts secured the resignations of Dunning, the Solicitor-General, and Granby, there was no question of the new Premier being embarrassed for want of colleagues. The old Cabinet as a whole stayed firm and North effectively took over the administration Grafton had abandoned.

North's accession to power proved a turning point. A very young King is under the disadvantage of having to suffer greybeards as his advisers and such to him had been Grenville, Bedford and Chatham – the last a broken reed; Bute had been a failure and Rockingham far too rich and splendiferous to be liked by Kings. Despite his early lack of assurance George III had an underlying taste for governing men and in his choice of North was shrewd. The new First Lord of the Treasury was only thirty-seven, six years older than the King. The two had always known each other, for North's father the 1st Earl of Guilford had been a courtier to Prince Frederick who had stood godfather to his eldest son. As a child North had joined in those private theatricals which had been a leading pastime at Leicester House. Certainly, there was no pretence of his ancestors having placed 'the present family' on the throne. But North was no Bute, no newcomer to affairs. Member of Parliament for the family borough of Banbury since 1754 he was now in his third Parliament. Yet as George III had been King ten years and North of the Cabinet little more than two, the King need not suffer from the inferiority of inexperience. A devoted son of Eton and Trinity College, Oxford, North had quiet, scholarly tastes, resembling his master's and a friendship came naturally. North, with the seven children of his happy marriage to bring up, could not throw up the job without a thought for the morrow, a situation fully appreciated by the King. He did not to any marked extent exceed his master in agility of mind, and the King certainly had the stronger character. Altogether North suited George III's book as a man who could safely be relied upon to do his duty and follow the royal inclination.

At the outset a coalition between Chatham and Rockingham in opposition to the new administration appeared likely. Shortly after North's appointment, Chatham delivered one of his most important speeches on the Constitution. To him the disfranchisement of the Middlesex electors called for the reaffirmation of parliamentary reform which he had put forward during the debates on the Declaratory Act. He now proposed positively that the knights of the shire be doubled in number, so as to reduce proportionately the influence of the borough members.[14] Chatham approached Rockingham with suggestions of an understanding but met with a lukewarm reception. Greatly though Rockingham disliked any suggestion of parliamentary reform, a coolness was at this stage more the result of personal than political differences. Burke disliked and mistrusted Chatham and doubted whether after the fiasco of his administration his support could be an asset. He also suspected that 'The Triumvirate' would like to use the Rockingham following to make up for their own lack of parliamentary support, an impression confirmed when in the course of a lengthy dialogue with Richmond Chatham suggested Temple as First Lord of the Treasury.[15]

Beckford attempted to use his position as Lord Mayor to form an opposition party. He carried through the Livery a remonstrance to the King for the neglect of their petition of the preceding October, which when presented drew forth a royal rebuke. Hoping to place Chatham and Rockingham in touch

with Parson Horne, he proposed for 22 March a splendid enter-
tainment. Rockingham's distaste for anything of a popular bias
almost prevented his attendance. Chatham warned Beckford:
'He, Lord Temple, and I, are equally of opinion that no new
matters should be opened or agitated at or after the convivium.'
Chatham did not feel up to a feast but Rockingham was present
and not displeased: 'Nothing could be more magnificent or
better conducted than every thing was there; and indeed the
meeting was a very respectable one.' Beckford organised a
further remonstrance and took the occasion of 23 May to
harangue the King on the mistakes of his ministers. Less than a
month later Beckford died of a neglected cold.[16]

George Grenville's Elections Act was a solid reforming
achievement and a fitting close to the career of a great House of
Commons man. Hitherto petitions arising from disputed
parliamentary elections had been tried by the House of Commons and determined according to the interests of the government majority. The Elections Act relegated trials to a committee
of members of Parliament elected by the House and serving
under oath. Abuses were not wholly eliminated and members of
Parliament not altogether suited to the determination of a
judicial process but considerable improvement was everywhere
acknowledged. George Grenville died in his fifty-ninth year on
11 November 1770. Since his entry into Parliament he had been
associated with Chatham, and the nine years of their political
separation, though marked by bitterness, could never erase their
intimate understanding. Grenville had been no leader until the
advent of Bute gave him the opening which led him to become
Prime Minister. He was not a great man and his lack of judgement in his relations with the King produced his dismissal in
little more than two years. His ministry was marred singularly
by two measures which had to be retroceded; the resolution of
the House of Commons that general warrants were legal and
the Stamp Act. But Grenville was universally respected for his
devotion to duty and honesty of mind, qualities to be repeated
in the career of his third son William Wyndham, a future Prime
Minister.

Wilkes found a violent champion in the brilliant and literate
publicist who wrote under the pseudonym of 'Junius'. Also a

notable advocate of the popular cause was John Almon, historian and publisher, an erstwhile client of Temple and also an admirer of Chatham. Controversy concerning the law of seditious libel was reawakened when the Government decided to prosecute the publishers of the *Letters of Junius*, with their bitter invective against the King and the ministry. As the law of seditious libel stood, the province of the jury was to determine only the fact of publication; the decision as to whether or not the document was libellous was left to the discretion of the Court. The separate trials of the three publishers, Almon, Miller and Woodfall, for printing and selling the *Letters* were held before Mansfield. The London jurors showed their sympathies by returning verdicts tantamount to 'not guilty', in flat contradiction to Mansfield's directions upon points of law.

Camden had always believed that the juries had the right to a wider discretion but when it came to practical action he was hesitant and confused. But Chatham, acting on the advice of Dunning, whose abilities he found truly impressive, came to the conclusion that Mansfield's directions in seditious libel cases were erroneous. He therefore urged his friends in the House of Commons to prepare legislation in declaratory form to the effect that the libellous character of a publication should be the province of the jury, not of the Court. The Rockingham Whigs wished for legislation altering the power of juries in a form that would enact a change in the law; no criticism of the judiciary would then arise. Dowdeswell introduced an enacting Libel bill in the House of Commons but was opposed by Barré and Dunning. North easily had the measure thrown out and rejoiced with the King over the squabbles amongst his opponents. When Chatham invited Rockingham to call for the dissolution of Parliament and a general election he was rebuffed and the possibility of joint action was ended.[17]

Wilkes by clever tactics secured an unexpected coup in securing the free publication of parliamentary debates, a practice which though illegal was growing apace. The Mansion House Court, composed of Beckford's successor Brass Crosby, the aldermen Richard Oliver and Wilkes, committed for assault a messenger of the House of Commons engaged in arresting a printer. Crosby and Oliver were sent to the Tower for contempt.

Barré played a leading part in opposing the proceedings and Chatham condemned the ministry as wanton, though he forbade Shelburne to visit Crosby and Oliver in their confinement. The publication of parliamentary debates was never interfered with again.[18] Wilkes, although a brilliant tactician, was too idle to devise a serious policy. His supporters soon found themselves paying for his taste in fine clothes, sumptuous feasts and elegant ladies. His public breach with Horne split the Society for the Bill of Rights and damaged the cause of popular politics. Wilkes's natural selfishness blinded him to the magnificent opportunity of founding a genuine reforming party composed of the unenfranchised sector of the middle class, the better-paid artisans and above all the nonconformist communions. The English nonconformists and the Scots Presbyterians included some of the most acute minds of the age and they maintained constant and warm contacts with their brethren in the Thirteen Colonies. A strong party for parliamentary reform in Britain might have united with American liberalism.

A contributory reason for the failure of Chatham to influence the House of Commons over the Middlesex election was that the Government and nation were mainly preoccupied with the possibility of war with Spain. When minister, Chatham had been assured that Choiseul would never allow his ally to proceed by force in the Falkland Islands. The subsequent weakness of the British Government emboldened Madrid and in the summer of 1770 the Spaniards had descended in overwhelming force on Port Egmont and carried off the garrison in a warship. The honour of both nations was deeply compromised, and had matters been left to public opinion war must have followed. North mobilised the fleet and armed forces and the land tax, reduced to 3s. in February 1767 on Dowdeswell's motion, had to be raised to 4s. He was anxious to pedal softly; war might bankrupt France but would wreck his hopes of placing Britain on an even financial keel.

George III feared a popular demand for Chatham's recall, with all the implications regarding Wilkes and the Middlesex electors he found most repellent. Although the inflamed state of public opinion made secret negotiations essential, Chatham sought to embarrass the ministry as much as possible. On eight occasions he went to the House of Lords to press for information. He chose the occasion of Richmond's motion of 22 November 1770, calling for papers on the negotiations, to make a major pronouncement on the state of the nation: divisions at home must enfeeble foreign policy. Reverting to the shrill note of patriotism of his young days, Chatham passed on to the events leading up to his resignation in October 1761. On this occasion the first preliminary must be confession of guilt from Madrid by the return of Port Egmont: 'But will you descend so low? will you so shamefully betray the King's honour, as to make it a matter of negotiation whether his Majesty's possession shall be restored to him or not?'[19]

Choiseul had in his hands a report from his Ambassador that Britain had only twelve ships in combat condition, which was accurate. He was ready to back Spain to the limit but not so Louis XV, seventy years old and anxious not to end his reign with his people involved in war. In December he wrote in person to his second cousin Charles III of Spain, urging him to consent to 'some sacrifice to preserve peace without injury to your honour'. A month later Louis XV dismissed Choiseul, who retired to exile at his chateau at Chanteloupe, where he was greeted by the carriages of his many admirers come to pay their respects to the great minister who had for nine years conducted his master's affairs with such distinction.

That January a compromise was arrived at. A declaration from the Spanish Embassy in London disavowed the action of the Governor of Buenos Aires and announced that the restoration of Port Egmont to Britain had been ordered, though without prejudice to the prior right of Spanish sovereignty. By a secret agreement a token British garrison, once established, would be quietly withdrawn after a suitable lapse of time. Although Britain reserved her right to re-occupy, the situation really reverted to what it had been before Port Egmont was established. North had come out of the affair with much judgement, for the Atlantic route to the Pacific was not a justifiable cause of war.[20]

Chatham, undaunted at the loss of Rockingham's friendship, in March 1771 once more raised the banner of parliamentary reform. Despite the protests of Richmond, he suggested the repeal of the Septennial Act of 1716, thus limiting the life of a Parliament to three years. He found little support in Parliament, where he and Rockingham, even had they acted in unison, could have little influence, owing to North's personal ascendancy. Though lacking Walpole's tough fibre or Newcastle's greed for power, North handled men with the humour and tact born of a boundless good nature; he could silence a critic with a kindly witticism or gently chide his opponents if their arguments grew too one-sided. North took every opportunity to broaden the basis of his ministry. Grenville's old followers, including Suffolk, sensibly accepted posts. Grafton decided that opposition was useless and became Lord Privy Seal. Above all, North proved himself a skilful finance minister. The Falkland Islands affair over, he cut back land tax to 3s. and even began to reduce the rates of interest on the national debt, achievements made practicable only by economies of questionable wisdom, including naval reductions. North was dexterous rather than profound, but his policies gave him a great hold over the House of Commons, particularly the county members. On 18 June 1772 North was installed a Knight of the Garter, the first Commoner since Walpole. In the following year he was elected Chancellor of his University, which marked the return of Oxford to the establishment. Step by step North consolidated his position and appeared the natural successor to Walpole and Pelham, an insurmountable barrier to Chatham's recovery of power in sickness or in health. George III could for the first time look forward to an era of stability.

Chatham despaired of politics and devoted his time to his family and friends. On 18 December he was writing to Calcraft about commissioning a portrait of Granby from Sir Joshua Reynolds and the purchase of some mares, 'about $15\frac{1}{2}$ hands at three years old . . .':[21] 'I do not wonder you have not frequented the Metropolis, considering how much comfort and pleasure you have at home, and how little satisfaction the Political world affords. The state of things is indeed most pitiable, strange, and contradictory is our situation. Government had lost its *essential Powers*, and the Country has lost its Liberty.'

That the spirit of political dissent kept alive was to a great extent due to the nonconformists, especially the rational dissenters, who also represented freedom of religious thought within a Christian context. Famous for their efficient academies for further education, the rational dissenters included men of great learning in Richard Price and Joseph Priestley, the friends of Shelburne and Benjamin Franklin. Under the Toleration Act of 1689 licences enabling dissenting ministers to preach depended on their subscribing to the Anglican Articles, except those relating to episcopal government. To orthodox Calvinists this requirement presented no difficulty, but it was an obstruction to divines of unitarian persuasion. In fact the law in this respect was not enforced but Price and Priestley felt the presence of repressive legislation on the statute book an affront to their character as good citizens.

Within the Anglican Church the compulsory subscription by the clergy to the Thirty-nine Articles aroused a resentment in the minds of the unorthodox but a petition to the House of Commons for an exemption failed, which was only to be expected. The rational dissenters were, however, emboldened to present a similar petition which easily passed the Commons in April 1772 and success in the Lords was not anticipated. Through Shelburne Chatham conveyed his sympathy to the rational dissenters whom he regarded as worthy members of the community, their petition justified in the light of changed conditions. Price wrote asking him to attend the second reading: '. . . a toleration limited by law to those who believe in the doctrinal articles of the Church of England deserves not the name!' Chatham received Price and though far from well addressed the House of Lords: 'Toleration', he declared, 'is that Sacred right of nature and hall-mark of truth and most interesting of all objects to fallible man.' As everyone expected, the petition was thrown out and the only Bishop to give his support, Jonathan Shipley, Bishop of St Asaph, forfeited for ever his hopes of translation to an English see. In March 1773 a further petition met a similar fate, but Price believed progress had been made; Richmond, Shelburne, Lyttleton, Camden and even Mansfield had all spoken in support.[22]

North faced his real test with the near bankruptcy of the East India Company in 1772. The original causes were a protracted war with that chivalrous warrior Hyder Ali, Maharajah of

Mysore, and a famine that more than decimated the population of Bengal. The hectic jobbing in shares by London investors to the tune of many millions and the vulgar opulence of the British nabobs presented an unpleasant contrast. The false assumptions underlying the grossly misleading accounts were either not recognised or else concealed by the Board. When the Company passed the dividend without notice, the public realised that an institutional investment supposedly second only to treasury stock was wiped out. The directors applied to the Government for assistance and North would have preferred to negotiate privately and enforce an agreement by statute after the example of Townshend in 1767 but public alarm was too strong. Led on by General John Burgoyne, MP, a versatile and headstrong personality, the House of Commons insisted upon an open parliamentary enquiry into the affairs of the Company of a kind that Chatham had wanted but failed to impose. Burgoyne was elected chairman of a committee of which Barré became a leading spirit, and it was he who mounted a personal attack upon Clive's riches and alleged misdeeds. The committee produced three resolutions which the House adopted: that territory could be legally acquired by British subjects only in the name of the Crown; that illegal acquisitions had of late been made in India; and that Company servants should be forbidden to indulge in private trade. Clive defended his conduct with dignity and Chatham expressed his strong disapproval that legislation should apply retrospectively to a great public servant. The House acknowledged Clive's services and exonerated his career.

The King insisted that the opportunity missed in 1767 to set the affairs of the East India Company on a firm foundation must be taken. North knew that in both Houses there was a powerful East Indian interest and used his majority to have elected a committee of members of Parliament drawn entirely from Government supporters with powers to prepare legislation. Their proceedings would be secret, free from hubbub or interested solicitations. Once Parliament had agreed to lend the Company £1.3 million, the old days were numbered. While therefore the politicians continued talking, North's secret committee prepared the necessary legislation during the winter of

1772–3. Obstruction from the Company could be met with the threat to hand matters over to the tender mercies of the Burgoyne committee.

The East India Regulating Act of 1773 vested the territories of the Company in the Crown. All British India was placed under a Governor-General with a Council at Calcutta. The protection of the Bengalese from unjust exploitation was to be secured by the establishment of a Supreme Court. All ordinary patronage remained with the Company and day-to-day administration, subject to the enactments of the Governor-in-Council, was to be carried out as before by Company servants. The Company would continue to function as a trading concern with, it was hoped, profitable results. The directorate remained extremely powerful and the East India lobby in Parliament very influential for many years. Chatham and his friends, in view of his failure to push things through six years before, could say little by way of addition or criticism.

In that Chatham had in 1767 missed the opportunity to establish a precedent for parliamentary intervention, North's task had been made more difficult. To suggest, however, that Chatham's nonfeasance was indirectly responsible for the disasters of 1772–3 would be an exaggeration. A regulating statute under the conditions prevailing in 1767 would not have gone beyond first principles; war, famine and insolvency had been necessary lessons for the public and Parliament to be persuaded of the fitness of more searching requirements. The completion of the 1773 Act, a novel and highly complicated chapter of legislation, deservedly gave North the character of statesman.

An ancillary provision of the East India Act freed the Company's tea bound for America from the British duty of 1s a pound. The Company was allowed to ship tea direct to America, where the 3d duty would be imposed, the net result being to halve the retail price from 2s to 1s a pound. At the same time North announced the abolition of all the other Townshend duties. America would still be subject to a tax as a symbol of British sovereignty, but in a form which, North hoped, would be made palatable by the cheapness of tea; the duty, yielding a mere £16,000 p.a., could hardly be set up as an offence by even the most hardy political free-thinkers. The radical American leaders feared the dilution of the pure fire of American patriotism. When 298 chests of East India Company tea, worth nearly £11,000, reached Boston a gang dressed up as Indian braves threw the entire consignment into Boston harbour.

CHAPTER 17

Chatham and America

'I am not going to make an idle panegyric on Burke (he has no need of it); but I cannot help looking upon him as the chief boast and ornament of the English House of Commons. What has been said of him is, I think, strictly true: that he was the most eloquent man of his time: his wisdom was greater than his eloquence. The only public man that in my opinion can be put in any competition with him, is Lord Chatham: and he moved in a sphere so very remote, that it is almost impossible to compare them. . . . Chatham's eloquence was popular: his wisdom was altogether plain and practical. Burke's eloquence was that of the poet; of the man of high and unbounded fancy: his wisdom was profound and contemplative. Chatham's eloquence was calculated to make them *think*. Chatham could have roused the fury of a multitude, and wielded their physical energy as he pleased: Burke's eloquence carried conviction into the mind of the retired and lonely student, opened the recess of the human breast, and lighted up the face of nature around him. Chatham supplied his readers with motives to immediate action: Burke furnished them *reasons* for action which might have little effect upon them at the time, but for which they would be the wiser and the better all their lives after. In research, in originality, in variety of knowledge, in richness of invention, in depth and comprehension of mind, Burke had as much the advantage of Lord Chatham as he was excelled by him in plain common sense, in strong feeling, in steadiness of purpose, in vehemence, in warmth, in enthusiasm and energy of mind. Burke was the man of genius, of fine sense and subtle reasoning; Chatham was a man of clear understanding, of strong sense, and violent passions. Burke's mind was satisfied with speculation: Chatham's was essentially *active*:

it could not rest without an object. The power which governed Burke's mind was his Imagination; that which gave its *impetus* to Chatham's will. The one was almost the creature of pure intellect, the other of physical temperament.'[1]

William Hazlitt: The Eloquence of the British Senate.

During the autumn and winter of 1773 Chatham had been leading a happy and relaxed life at Burton Pynsent. The death of his brother-in-law Lyttleton on 22 August must have revived fond memories of visits to Hagley in company with Pope and Murray. Lyttleton had in those distant days been the man of promise, and though his political career had shown a complete lack of judgement his domestic qualities had always been admirable and in 1767 he had at long last brought out his *Life of Henry II.*

The true delight of Chatham's life as his late sixties approached lay in his children, now grown up and a source of endless pleasure. The younger William, hope of the family, was sixteen and went up to Pembroke Hall, Cambridge. There he was struck down by a severe illness resembling his father's gout, and confined for two months, looked after by Addington. Chatham's relief when the crisis passed and his son's health began to mend was beyond expression. Chatham, who never knew the support of an affectionate father, understood how the talents of his children could be given confidence by an unfailing attention.

The Boston Tea Party stunned Westminster and Chatham was no exception. Whilst North was preparing legislation to deal with the seditious people of Massachusetts, Chatham held his peace and remained in Somerset. Shelburne sent him regular reports on affairs and during January 1774 their main interest was the proposal of the Irish House of Commons to tax the near £1 million p.a. taken out of their country by landowners normally resident in England. An Absentee Landowners Taxation bill stood a considerable chance. The Earl Harcourt, who had in 1772 succeeded Townshend as Viceroy, gave his approval whilst North was sympathetic. Rockingham, a large landowner in Ireland, used all his influence to secure a veto by the Privy Council at Westminster and was supported by Shelburne, whose Irish estates were even more extensive. Chatham wrote to Shelburne giving his frank opinion that he would apply to Ireland the principle he had laid down for America, that taxation and representation must be indissolubly connected; the intervention of either the British Parliament or Privy Council was contrary to the principles of a free Constitution, to which the Protestant Irish were as much entitled as Englishmen. Shelburne very creditably allowed himself to be converted. But to offend the many peers and members of Parliament with substantial Irish interests was more than North dared. Harcourt was instructed to employ the venal methods customary to persuade the Dublin House of Commons to bury the suggestion.[2]

Chatham began to perceive the dangerous tendency of the crisis between Britain and America when Benjamin Franklin appeared before the Privy Council in the case of the Hutchinson letters. Franklin, acting by casuistry in the cause of patriotism, had purloined and published letters from Thomas Hutchinson, Governor of Massachusetts, advising North to adopt stringent measures. The coarse insults hurled by the jesting Privy Councillors at Franklin for the tricky but condonable befoolment of the Governor alarmed Shelburne as to what North might intend in Parliament: 'Various measures are talked of, for altering the constitution of the government of New England, and prosecuting individuals; all tending to more or less enforcement. The opinion here is very general, that America will submit, that government was taken by surprise when they repealed the stamp-act, and that all may be recovered.' North's first proposal, which came up in March, was the Boston Port Act which closed the port and removed the customs house to Salem. To this proposal, which passed both Houses without dissent, Chatham offered no criticism and Barré voiced his approval. Chatham considered Britain should stop short at exacting reparation from Boston; the Tea Party should not be made an excuse 'to crush the spirit of liberty among the Americans in general, . . . Laws of navigation and trade, for regulation, not for revenue, I should hope and believe, America once at ease about internal taxation, would also acquiesce under, and friendly intercourse be again opened; without which we, not they, shall be undone.'

North's more exacting proposals disturbed Chatham deeply. The Massachusetts Charter Act suspended the Constitution. The Massachusetts Judicature Act gave the Governor a discretion to direct any criminal proceedings away from the courts of Massachusetts to the courts of another colony or even England. Finally, the Boston Quartering Act provided for the billeting of the King's troops upon the householders of Boston without recompense. North considered the situation to entail no more difficulty than quelling a riot in Edinburgh or Dublin and with an airy confidence assured the House of Commons that only a marginal increase in the armed forces already in America would be required. Throughout these proceedings he was warmly supported by Lord George Germain, formerly Sackville of Minden fame, who had changed his name as a condition of acquiring beautiful Drayton Manor in Northamptonshire, under a legacy every bit as fortuitous as Chatham's possession of Burton Pynsent. The House of Commons was deeply impressed by the logical comprehension of Germain's speeches on America. Chatham, urged by Shelburne to come to London, replied that he saw no point in travelling merely to have his words ignored: 'I have too long seen my no-weight to dream any longer on that subject.'

In May, however, the 2nd Lord Lyttleton, son of Chatham's late brother-in-law, pressed him to come to town, adding that the ministers would delay obtaining the royal assent to the Boston Quartering bill in case he wished to address the House of Lords. An invitation couched in these terms Chatham could not refuse and on 27 May he delivered an oration. He pointed out that if it be remembered that the colonies had originally been peopled by men seeking refuge from the tyranny of the Stuarts 'our astonishment at the present conduct of their descendants will naturally subside'. The riots at Boston had been an outrage, but the innocent should not be punished with the guilty and the original fault lay at home: '. . . the moment they perceived your intention was renewed to tax them, under a pretence of serving the East India Company, their resentment got the ascendant of their moderation, and hurried them into actions

contrary to the law. . . .' Chatham declared that he would carry
to his grave the principle *'that this country had no right under
Heaven to tax America'*. He urged the administration not to
provoke armed rebellion, which must play into the hands of
France.[3] North had no difficulty in obtaining majorities of three
to one for his programme.

A new Governor of Massachusetts, General Thomas Gage,
accompanied by four regiments, arrived at Boston on 14 May
and that day Louis XV died. His twenty-year-old grandson,
Louis XVI, appointed as his Foreign Minister the Count of
Vergennes, the last great statesman of the *ancien régime*. Gage
took over authority without incident but soon recognised that
he must avoid provocation: Massachusetts was plainly united in
offering at least a passive resistance. The people of Salem, who
could have benefited from the closure of Boston harbour,
refused to touch British goods and the colonial militia were
quietly storing away arms at Concord. Over the next ten
months Gage's caution was the subject of growing criticism at
home, but he warned North that in the event of bloodshed the
degree of force required had been seriously underestimated.

North, while making arrangements to bring Massachusetts to
heel, had been preparing legislation to provide a permanent
Constitution for Canada. Here the principles could not be set
apart from the polity of North America considered as one. Since
1760 Canada had been under military government; French law
in respect of land tenure had been upheld and the free practice
of the Roman Catholic religion respected. North was confronted
by a problem hitherto unknown in the history of Britain, rule
over Europeans in another continent of a different nationality
and faith who had long been owners of the soil. To the French
Canadians an authoritarian form of government was in tradition, but the hope was to promote British immigration. The
delimitation of the southern boundary was a dangerous stumbling block. If the frontier was to stop short at the Great Lakes the
New England colonies would be guaranteed unlimited freedom
of expansion and their tiresome tendency to asymmetry of
deportment encouraged. On the other hand, the inclusion of
the Ohio valley in Canada would place the future of the central
plains at the direction of Whitehall. Since the Capitulation

some two thousand British settlers had percolated in and were
bound to remain a distinct minority for a considerable time.
The important point was whether these immigrants should be
granted the protection of representative government to which
they would be entitled in any other American possession. But to
include the French Canadians in a grant of representative institutions would give Roman Catholic subjects overseas a privilege
denied them in Britain and Ireland. On the other hand, to
subject the entire country to an Assembly elected by British
settlers only might be denounced by the French as irresponsible
heretic tyranny. The Thirteen Colonies might construe the
establishment of an official and nominated legislature as a
despotic intention towards the entire continent.

North weighed up that the paramount consideration was to
secure the loyalty of the French by an acceptable form of
government, and that opinion in New England might be set at
nought. The whole of the Great Lakes and the Ohio was assigned
to Canada. The Governor was to rule with the assistance of a
nominated Legislative Council which would include French as
well as British Canadians. The administration of French law,
which lacked a jury system, was to continue. So as to enable the
French to serve on the Council or take office under the Crown
with a clear conscience, the Elizabethan Act of Supremacy was
amended, the explicit renunciation of Papal supremacy being
replaced by a simple oath recognising the secular authority of
the British Sovereign. The obstinate vigour of national feeling
was not at that time generally comprehended and the expectation was that one day the French would forget their descent and
become indistinguishable from Englishmen.

Chatham denounced the provisions for the government of
Canada in the House of Lords on 16 June: 'The merely supposing that the Canadians will not be able to feel the good effects
of law and freedom, because they have been used to arbitrary
power, is an idea as ridiculous as false.' The English jury system
he considered an essential guarantee of freedom and the
establishment, as distinct from the toleration, of the Roman
Catholic religion an abomination. Chatham wound up by
referring to the anxiety uppermost in his mind: 'He pathetically
expressed his fears that it might . . . finally lose the hearts of all

his Majesty's American subjects.' Only six peers went into the lobby with Chatham. Although the Quebec Act contributed to embitter relations between Britain and the Thirteen Colonies, the provisions for the government of Canada proved salutary and eminently workable. The model for Crown Colony government later adopted throughout the British Empire together with the East India Regulating Act were North's most constructive achievements.[4]

On 1 July Henry Fox, Lord Holland, died and twenty-three days later his beloved wife followed. He had been of no weight since funking the Treasury in 1763. Holland made the mistake of drawing his chariot too near the sun; his character, though fortified by the greatest abilities, was not worthy of his ambition. He took the gold instead of the glory and even allowed himself a perverse pride in his choice. Ironically, the need to clear the gambling debts of his sons Stephen and Charles and preserve the family honour had eaten into a bit of the Pay Office fortune. Charles's brilliance in the House of Commons was no equivalent for the disclosures inevitable in such emergencies and Holland died a broken-hearted man.

The session ended with the dissolution of Parliament, one year before the Septennial Act required. The arguments for an appeal to the polls were powerful. Chatham, Rockingham and their supporters had made a showing so poor that North had little to fear. The slump and unemployment which had overshadowed the 1768 general election had been replaced by a great expansion of exports which too diminished the fear of American reprisals. As Burke remarked to Rockingham: '. . . in the present Temper of the Nation, and with the character of the present administration, the disorder and discontent of all America and the more remote future mischiefs, which may arise from those Causes, operate as little as the division of Poland.' Burke understood completely that the temper of the country and North's ministry coincided exactly, whilst Chatham he considered even an asset to administration: 'In the mean time they have three great securities. The actual possession of power: The Chapter of accidents; and the Earl of Chatham. This last is the *sacra anchora*.' In Burke's opinion Chatham, instead of presenting himself as a viable alternative, was letting himself be put in a dignified reserve by King, Government and nation as a *deus ex machina* in case of need.[5] Overall the elections of 1774 were as calm and parochial as those of 1761 and 1768. It was only to be expected that the popular party should hold firm in London, Middlesex and Surrey and at Bristol Burke's views on American taxation secured his return. Wilkes, Lord Mayor of London for the year, was again returned for Middlesex. North took the wind out of his sails by his decision to allow him to take his seat. Agitator rather than statesman, he never cut a figure in the House of Commons and his popular days were over. North, unlike Grafton, gave every attention to the hustings and administration gained a few seats.

While the election was in progress Chatham stayed on at Hayes, too troubled at the prospect in America to indulge a retirement to Burton Pynsent. He frequently corresponded with Stephen Sayre, Sheriff of the City of London and a leading America merchant. That August a Congress representative of the Thirteen Colonies assembled at Philadelphia. North was disappointed of his hope that America as a whole, rather than face the inconvenience of a boycott, would leave Massachusetts to her fate. The Congress decided on the suspension of all trading relations with Britain, apart from allowing the southern colonies to dispose of their tobacco crop; the repeal of all parliamentary legislation applicable to America since 1763 was requested. The threat of Gage and his regiments at Boston was bound to play into the hands of the extreme elements, but when Chatham saw Benjamin Franklin during the summer he received an assurance that freedom under the Crown, not independence, was the hope of the Congress.

With the new Parliament assembled Chatham invited Franklin to talk over the proceedings of the Congress, of which he commented to Sayre in his letter of 24 December: 'Upon the whole I think it must be evident to every unprejudiced man in England who feels for the rights of mankind, that America, under all her oppressions and provocations holds forth to us the most fair and just opening, for restoring harmony and affectionate intercourse as heretofore.'[6] Chatham resolved to speak to the House of Lords in the hope of obtaining a reversal of policy. Burke was pressing Rockingham to bring his party out of the cave of secession and give the country a lead after the Christmas recess: 'If it be not thought proper at this time, I confess I cannot foresee a time that will be proper for it.' As Dowdeswell was on the point of death the only possible leader for the Rockingham connection in the House of Commons was Lord John Cavendish, younger brother to that Devonshire who had with Pitt headed the ministry of 1756–7. He, Burke suggested, had better forget fox-hunting and come to town. Despite his deep mistrust for Chatham, Burke felt an understanding in that quarter pertinent, provided Rockingham did not let himself be exploited. In his letter to Rockingham of 5 January 1775 Burke delivered that immortal epigram: 'The least peep into that Closet intoxicates him, and will to the End of his Life.'[7]

Not altogether by coincidence Sayre had for some time been urging on Chatham the advisability of a talk with Rockingham. At the end of the first week of January, whilst Rockingham was staying at his villa at Wimbledon, Chatham had himself announced without notice. Rockingham was at that moment in the drawing room with Lord Verney and Sayre and had Chatham sent up to his dressing room whilst his guests took their leave, 'not doubting but that the affairs of Great Britain and America were in a fair way of being put into a course of healing and salutary measures'. The interview achieved nothing. Instead of exploring the possibilities of concurrence, Chatham read Rockingham a lecture on the iniquities of the Declaratory Act and the rightness of the distinction between '*no* right to tax and *the right* to restrain their trade'. He went on to announce his intention of raising the matter in the Lords, to which Rockingham retorted that the Americans had not themselves asked for that peculiar distinction to be embodied in legislation. Rockingham found neither the man nor his discourse palatable: 'Lord Chatham,' he wrote to Burke, 'in point of looks is very well, and in the outset of our conversation, I thought his *countenance* denoted more than a transient appearance of a tendency to something like cordiality, *but* our interview lasted near a *full hour*, and I confess, that I was neither much edified and perhaps had as little reason to be satisfied, with some of the ideas and some of the expressions which he dropped.' Rockingham urged Burke to repair at once to Wimbledon to discuss what ought to be done lest by way of Sayre some inaccurate account of the conversation become broadcast in America.[8]

Lady Chatham was anxious about rumours of her husband 'that you are *determined* to give yourself no trouble upon American affairs . . .', but he assured her of his fixed intention to go forward 'if gout does not put in a veto . . . '. Chatham kept his plans within his own small circle, while he prepared his speech in the company of his son William. On 19 January Franklin received a card inviting him to attend the Lords debate on the following day as Chatham's guest. At two o'clock on the 20th Chatham introduced him at the Bar of the House with these words: 'This is Dr. Franklin, whom I would have admitted into the House.' That Franklin, reproached by many as a traitor, was countenanced by Chatham caused raised eyebrows among the peers assembled. Chatham proposed an Address to the King praying for the withdrawal of British troops from Boston. He declared the connection between Britain and America to be 'an union, solid permanent and effectual', and assured the Lords that separation was not the object of the American Whigs: 'I contend not for indulgence, but justice to America: and I shall ever contend, that the Americans justly owe obedience to us in a limited degree – they owe obedience to our ordinance of trade and navigation; . . .'.

When Chatham affirmed that the Americans did not seek independence he was still on sure ground, but he was mistaken in his belief that the ancient restrictions of the Navigation System could survive with the authority of the Congress established. Yet he understood the Americans, no longer colonists, to be a nation inspired with the spirit of ordered liberty inherited from their English forebears:[9]

'When your Lordships look at the papers transmitted us from America; when you consider their decency, firmness, and wisdom, you cannot but respect their cause, and wish to make it your own. . . . We shall be *forced ultimately to retract*; let us retract while we can, not when we must.'

Shelburne seconded and, after Suffolk had replied, Chatham spoke once more. Defeat by 68 to 18 reflected the disdain of the

Rockingham party. Burke was critical of the method and the
matter. In a closed letter to the citizens of Bristol he pointed out
that Chatham's move had been unconcerted, which was a
contributory reason for the small minority in which he had
ended up; moreover, the resurrection of the issues of sovereignty
and taxation was a needless reawakening.[10]

Chatham was convinced that a scheme for American conciliation must be drawn up and speedily, writing to Shelburne: 'Not
a moment can be lost, for whoever has anything to offer to the
public, for preventing a civil war . . .'. He drafted his Plan
which was to present a bill to reconstruct the Imperial Constitution. He took only the advice of Camden and discussed the
completed document with Franklin at Hayes on 27 January.
Two days later he called upon Franklin at his lodgings in
Craven Street. Franklin described the scene: 'He staid with me
near two hours, his equipage waiting at the door; and being
there while people were coming from church, it was much taken
notice of, and talked of as at that time was every little circumstance that man thought might possibly any way affect
American affairs.'

On the morning of the following Tuesday Franklin left early
for Hayes, taking with him his prepared memoranda upon the
Plan: '. . . but though I stayed near four hours, his Lordship, in
the manner of, I think, all eloquent persons, was so full and
diffuse in supporting every particular I questioned, that there
was not time to go through half my memorandums. He is not
easily interrupted, and I had such pleasure in hearing him, . . .'.
Chatham had fixed Wednesday, 1 February, for the presentation of the Plan to the House of Lords but he and Franklin
realised that alterations would be required and intended to
invite amendments from America. In an attempt to enlist the
sympathy of the Rockingham Whigs Chatham notified
Richmond of his intentions.

By way of introduction Chatham declared that he would be
the first to resist the Americans in 'the most distant intentions of
throwing off the legislative supremacy and great constitutional
superintending power and control of the British legislature, . . .'.
He recurred to his former arguments on taxation and representation; insisted they were inseparable, and planted so deeply in

the vital principles of the constitution as never to be torn up without destroying and pulling asunder every bond of legal government and good faith. The actual bill was largely a declaratory statement of constitutional principles; the right of Parliament to regulate trade was recognised, 'the deep policy of such prudent acts upholding the guardian navy of the whole British people'. The power of the Crown to order the armed forces to any part of the Empire, in peace or in war, was asserted. The peculiar privilege of the colonies was stated: 'No tallage, tax or other charge for his Majesty's revenue, shall be commanded or levied from British freemen in America without common consent, by act of provincial assembly there, duly convened for that purpose.' Trial by jury must be restored and in future judges in the colonies were to hold office not at pleasure but *Quamdiu se bene gesserint.*

The great innovation was that Congress be recognised as the repository of legislative power, subject to the supremacy of Parliament. Congress was to consider granting the Crown a permanent revenue to be appropriated to the reduction of the national debt, and to settle the quota of each colony. Chatham's bill ended with these brave words:

'So shall true reconcilement avert impending calamities, and this most solemn national accord between Great Britain and her colonies stand an everlasting monument of clemency and magnanimity in the benignant father of his people; of wisdom and moderation in this great nation, famed for humanity as for valour; and of fidelity and grateful affection from brave and loyal colonies to their parent kingdom, which will ever protect and cherish them.'

Grafton's complaint at Chatham's attempt to shove through great constitutional legislation with undignified haste voiced the feelings of the House and indeed the sense of the period. Sandwich saw in Franklin's presence at the Bar of the House an easy rebuttal of the Plan: 'That it appeared to be the work of some American . . . he fancied he had in his eye the person who drew it up, one of the bitterest and most mischievous enemies this country had known.' Chatham hotly disputed Sandwich's

insinuation that the proposals were not entirely of his own
making and went on to denounce the ministry:

'On one reconsideration, I must allow you one merit, a strict
attention to your own interests: in that view you appear sound
statesmen and able politicians. You well know, if the present
measure should prevail, that you must instantly relinquish your
places. I doubt much whether you will be able to keep them on
any terms; but sure I am, such are your well-known characters
and abilities, that any plan of reconciliation, however moderate,
wise and feasible, must fail in your hands.'

The Plan stood no hope of acceptance and was not altogether
adjusted to realities in America. The withdrawal of troops from
Boston would by no means necessarily have been succeeded by
the acknowledgement of the legislative supremacy of the mother
of Parliaments, matters of trade included.[11]
    Within days of his failure to persuade an alteration to the
direction of British policy Chatham was struck powerless by
gout. North could not, however, allow so dignified a plea for a
scheme of salvation to pass without being complemented by
some intelligible advice to Parliament from administration.
Towards the end of the month he proposed in the House of
Commons that imperial taxation be remitted in the case of any
colony offering a contribution approved by Parliament. By this
time opinion at Westminster had hardened to such a degree
that he found difficulty in persuading even members of the
ministry to follow him into the lobby. With more troops on the
way to Massachusetts there was no hope of any American
Assembly deserting the common cause by offering a contribution. In March Burke put forward his plan of conciliation,
based upon the distinction between the legal sovereignty of
Parliament as stated in the Declaratory Act and the exercise of
power, which must be subject to the limitations of natural right.
Burke had never held office and was at this time remarkable
only for his interesting ideas clothed in memorable oratory.
Chatham was the one man with the standing to effect a compromise: certainly he would never have countenanced action by
the British army. But parliamentary opinion in Britain de-

manded in no uncertain terms the visible exercise of sovereignty.

North fondly clung to the hope that any fighting would be confined to some skirmish in which the colonials would stand no chance against British regulars. If a few rabble were killed, those styling themselves rebels would be cowed. Gage had been Governor of Massachusetts almost a year before he tried anything which might bear consequence. In April 1775 he decided upon a test of power and ordered the seizure of the arms stored at Concord by the Massachusetts militia. At Lexington on 19 April the British were repulsed with heavy casualties, followed by the Pyrrhic victory of Bunker Hill on 17 June. Washington was appointed Commander-in-Chief and from New England the colonists invaded Canada. There Chatham's son Lord Pitt was with his regiment and his mother felt the utmost anxiety. General Guy Carleton, the Governor of Canada, tactfully sent him to England with despatches, whereon Chatham at once ordered his resignation from the service.[12]

North set about reconstructing his ministry: Grafton, always a wobbler, resigned in protest against the war. By far the most important accession to the administration was Lord George Germain, who in the debates on the American Coercion Acts had emerged a heavy-weight. Although that October he refused to cross the Atlantic as envoy with full powers, he was a month later given the key post of Secretary of State for America. For the other two Secretaryships North retained Suffolk and put Weymouth into Rochford's place but they were of no calibre.

Germain reiterated the policy originally laid down by Grenville, declaring to the House of Commons on 26 November: 'If the Americans . . . willing to share their common burthen with us, can propose any mode which will make them easy, which will remove their fears and jealousies, I shall be ready to adopt it.' But his deeds belied his professions and he was driven by an overriding ambition to live down Minden, and, as Horace Walpole put it, 'conquer Germany in America'. Barrington, the Secretary at War, warned North that Britain must limit hostilities to a blockade of the American coast. But Germain was confident that in America there existed a loyalist element which might even number half the population.[13] The American invaders of Canada found no friends among the French whose taciturn loyalty had been secured by the Quebec Act, and they were beaten off with heavy loss.

The gout which had crushed Chatham within days of presenting the Plan kept him debilitated for sixteen months. In July 1776 he made his first political pronouncement for well over a year, a brief memorandum in Lady Chatham's hand, addressed to Dr Addington, recapitulating his views on America with a warning against France:

'In a very few years, France will set her foot on English ground. That, in the present moment, her policy may probably be to wait some time, in order to see England more deeply engaged in this ruinous war, *against herself*, in America; as well as to prove how far the Americans, abetted by France *indirectly* only, may be able to make a stand, before she takes an *open* part, by declaring war upon England.'

This admonition was next to prophetic, for on 4 July Congress had declared America independent and Franklin was despatched to Paris to negotiate an alliance.[14] British opinion, taken aback at such temerity, hardened. That November Chatham, not troubled to attend Parliament, retired to Bath. The complete failure of Lord John Cavendish's motion in the House of Commons for the repeal of the Acts of coercion decided the Rockingham Whigs to secede from parliamentary activity. This inactivity was not altogether the fruit of that genial idleness which characterised Rockingham and his friends. Criticism of the war could be construed as unpatriotic and if by chance British arms were successful, a studied opposition might well carry the retribution of keeping the Rockingham Whigs out of office for ever. Out in the wilderness the party was guided by Burke to the view that on grounds of equity as well as convenience American independence ought to be recognised. A systematic opposition was maintained only by Shelburne and his following and the Wilkite radicals. But for a handful of dissidents both Houses of Parliament overwhelmingly supported the American war and North could shelve any inner doubts about the wisdom of his policy.

Germain devoted his undoubted talent for organisation to the despatch and maintenance of a British army on the other side of the Atlantic. By the end of 1776 there were in North America more than double the number Wolfe had commanded at Quebec. But the blunders of employing German mercenaries and the Indian tribes cost a good deal of loyalist sentiment. At the New Year news of Washington's victory at Trenton brought home that America would not be easily subdued. Whilst France and Spain were allowing American privateers to use their ports, North had been forced to put up the land tax to 4s and to raise loans bearing a crippling rate of interest. To end the war quickly was imperative and Germain planned a master stroke. A British army was to march south from Canada and join up with the regiments in New York, thus cutting in two the rebel country. For this grandiose design Germain chose as general that Burgoyne who had figured so prominently in the East India debates of 1772. By May Burgoyne was already on his way southwards towards Lake Champlain, when Chatham returned to London.

Chatham speedily notified Camden of his intention to address the Lords on 30 May: 'Lord Chatham desires to present his affectionate and respectful compliments to Lord Camden. His hand is too weak to write; but as he is enough recovered to hope to be able to crawl to the House of Lords, he means to be there, on Thursday next, in order to move the consideration of the American war.' Chatham also informed Rockingham, and as Burke commented: 'Lord Chathams coming out is always a critical thing to your Lordship.' Burke was not certain what form the intended peroration in the Lords might take but did not wish Rockingham to leave Chatham the field. Provided Chatham showed Rockingham public consideration, his reappearance must be welcomed: 'If he is tender of you, you will naturally be tender of him.'[15] When Chatham went to the House he was accompanied by his son William:

'My Lords, this is a flying moment; perhaps but six weeks left to arrest the dangers that surround us. The gathering storm may break; it has already opened, and in part burst. It is difficult for government, after all that has passed, to shake hands with defiers of the King, defiers of the parliament, defiers of the people. I am a defier of nobody; but if an end is not put to this war, there is an end to this country.'

Chatham hammered home his points with invincible logic: 'What you have sent there, are too many to make peace – too few to make war.' He asked for an Address to the King, praying for a speedy end to a ruinous struggle; so long as no treaty existed between the rebels and France there was yet time for Britain to extricate herself with honour. The essential preliminary was that Britain should unilaterally abandon the right to tax America: 'We have tried for unconditional submission: try what can be gained by unconditional redress.' Answered by the ministers, Chatham replied by explicitly demanding the repeal of all legislation applicable to America passed since 1763 and compensation for the burning of towns and devastation of the countryside:

'Let, then, reparation come from the hands that inflicted the injuries; let conciliation succeed chastisement; and I do maintain, that parliament will again recover its authority; that his Majesty will be once more enthroned in the hearts of his American subjects; and that your Lordships, as contributing to so great, glorious, salutary, and benignant a work, will receive the prayers and benedictions of every part of the British empire.'

Chatham's motion was rejected by 99–28: the decision of the peers reflected what was still the wish of the country, to fight on.[16]

During the autumn Chatham's health mended and when Parliament assembled in November he was strong enough to embark upon a strenuous period. On 20 November in one of the greatest speeches of his career, he warned the peers that France was reaping every benefit while Britain was wasting her energies upon the impossible; where Amherst and Wolfe had fought long and laborious campaigns to defeat a few thousand Frenchmen, the idea that America's millions could be subjugated was preposterous: 'If I were an American, as I am an Englishman, while a foreign troop was landed in my country, I never would lay down my arms – never – never – never.' Although the use of Red Indians had by this time been abandoned, Chatham could not help but condemn such immorality: 'But, my Lords, who is the man that, in addition to these disgraces and mischiefs of our army, has dared to authorise and associate to our arms the tomahawk and scalping-knife of the savage?' Chatham hoped that the central and southern colonies were 'yet sound'; provided the fighting was terminated, the Americans would see through the basic opportunism of the French, bent merely upon securing the greatest possible gain: 'America and France cannot be congenial; there is something decisive and confirmed in the honest American, that will not assimilate to the futility and levity of Frenchmen.' Suffolk rose to defend the indefensible, to receive the rebuke: 'I am astonished! shocked! to hear such principles confessed – to hear them avowed in this House, or in this country: principles equally unconstitutional, inhuman and unchristian!' Chatham's motion was defeated by 93–28.[17]

Late in November Rockingham convened a meeting of his party at his house in Grosvenor Square. Richmond, Grafton and the younger Fox were solicitous that a motion for a committee on the state of the nation be laid in both Houses before news arrived of Burgoyne. To seek a parliamentary advantage from defeat would arouse public resentment. Camden and Shelburne were reluctant to join forces. But Chatham saw no difficulty in combining over national defence and on 2 December seconded Richmond's motion for papers relating to the number of troops and sailors in Ireland and America. Chatham gave warning that the number of men available for the defence of Britain was insufficient and there was no necessary obstacle to the Americans retaliating: 'It is no farther from America to England than from England to America. If conquest of it be the issue, we must trust to that issue, and fairly abide by it.' Chatham then turned upon Sandwich, the First Lord of the Admiralty, and contradicted his statement that between thirty-five and forty-two ships of the line were ready for service: no more than twenty were seaworthy. The night after this debate a man-of-war, *Warwick*, reached London bringing news of Burgoyne's surrender at Saratoga on 17 October. On the following afternoon Barré in the House of Commons wrung from Barrington and Germain a reluctant admission of disaster. Rockingham sensibly expressed to Chatham the hope that Burgoyne's army, which as a condition of the surrender was to be returned home, might be used to garrison Gibraltar.[18]

On 30 January a commercial treaty negotiated by Franklin between America and France was signed at Versailles, followed on 6 February by a defensive alliance. Faced with an imminent French declaration of war, in which Spain might be expected to join, North despaired. He longed to resign and have done with politics, but the King would not have him back out. George III was no coward and believed himself the virtuous defender of Constitution and Empire which at his Coronation he had sworn to maintain. The King reproached himself with having agreed to the repeal of the Stamp Act, which he believed had put backbone into America. He expected, and rightly, that French intervention would revive the warlike spirit of the country; the southern colonies might hold and compensation for the loss of New England be taken by conquests in the French West Indies. But North in his heart knew the cause hopeless. The eminently presentable minister of peace, whose financial policies and legislation for India and Canada had been charted with such wisdom, was squeezed like a concertina between his forceful Sovereign and the expectant loyalty of his majorities in Parliament.

Saratoga recharged the political atmosphere. The Rockingham Whigs returned to activity, set upon overturning the ministry and forcing the recognition of American independence. Chatham, whilst every whit as zealous for a withdrawal from American soil, was not prepared to envisage the rending apart of the mighty empire he had protected against France and Spain. Rockingham and Chatham, though utterly sincere, were each building on foundations erroneously premised. Rockingham expected a United States acknowledged by Britain to abandon the war and leave her to deal with the Bourbon menace. But as Franklin for one recognised, that course must discredit the new American nation from the beginning. Chatham, in his passionate concern for the unity of the English nation, did not visualise that distance together with three and four generations of settlement must breed an instinct for something more than autonomy. The blood of Lexington and Bunker Hill had quickened the seed of independence and Saratoga made the flowering inevitable.

Under the stress of national disaster constitutional reform inevitably became the watchword of the opposition. Rockingham and his party wished to strengthen the aristocratic element in government at the expense of the Crown. The legend was coaxed up that the Parliament which had voted four to one in favour of the coercion of America was dominated by the corrupt influence of pensions and places, charges reminiscent of the ancient Tory opposition to Walpole but not much heard of for thirty years. The Rockingham Whigs demanded that the placemen be pruned down so that the King and his ministers could, as they put it, never again flout the wishes of the House of Commons and the electorate. Barré, and more especially Dunning, joined in the programme espoused by Burke to diminish the 'influence' of the Crown. Chatham had in 1771 indicated his support for triennial Parliaments and a measure of parliamentary reform but societies for reform came into being which went much further. The more extreme advocated universal male suffrage, annual Parliaments and the binding of members of Parliament to written instructions drafted by their constituents. Chatham was described as giving his blessing to the principles of Major John Cartwright, one of the most prominent of the extremists, but never in public went further than his original proposals. For a statesman of his standing to have attempted to head a movement outside Parliament would have been contrary to the political conventions of the time and gravely damaging to his efforts in respect of America.

Although the King was completely unmoved by allegations of unconstitutional deviations, he and North came to a decision that an attempt at peace must be undertaken. On 17 February North announced in the House of Commons that he was ready to repeal all legislation applicable to America passed since 1763, including the Declaratory Act. For this pronouncement the House was in no way prepared. There was no applause, for all recognised the collapse of the policy most members had had at heart for so long, and had endorsed by their speeches and in the lobbies. 'Astonishment, dejection, and fear, overclouded the whole Assembly.' Peace commissioners headed by the 5th Earl of Carlisle, a loose-living young nobleman of extravagant habits, were appointed with secret instructions that independence should be allowed if no other way out proved possible. Even with this final concession the peace offer had no chance of success. For America no parley with any ministry headed by North was conceivable and to accept a recognition of independence through the discreditable byway of a separate peace would be a blunder no European power would ever forgive.[19]

Thinking to render his situation more respectable, North set about an attempt at broadening his ministry. As the Rockingham Whigs were publicly committed to independence for America, he first turned to Chatham. Early in March William Eden, Secretary to the Treasury and one of the peace commissioners appointed to America, was deputed to exchange views with Shelburne. Of Chatham the King wrote to North: 'I cannot consent to have any conversation with him till the ministry is formed . . . should Lord Chatham wish to see me before he gives an answer I shall most certainly refuse it.' Eden proposed that Shelburne should become a Secretary of State and Chatham receive a seat in the Cabinet with some great mark of honour such as the Garter; the basic character of the ministry under North's leadership was not to be altered. There was no possibility of Chatham and Shelburne forfeiting all reputation by even a semblance of consideration. On 15 March Shelburne replied that Chatham must be 'dictator', with freedom to form a coalition including Rockingham and Grafton. The King reacted violently to Shelburne's terms. Referring to Chatham as 'that perfidious man', he commented to North: 'I shall never address myself to him but through you, and on the clear understanding that he is to step forth to support any administration where you are First Lord of the Treasury.'[20]

Already the Rockingham Whigs had privately decided that their differences with Chatham were past resolution and that parliamentary action independent of his imprimatur was imperative. But none the less Shelburne's proposal of Chatham as 'dictator' was not impracticable, granted the King's commission. North had no desire to soldier on and his parliamentary majorities, largely dependent upon the King's blessing, would soon have transferred themselves to Chatham. The Rockingham Whigs, rather than be left out, might well have taken a closer look. Chatham was certainly the only statesman with whom the

Americans would have negotiated and in that sense the King's obstinate contempt for his greatest subject was deepening the divisions in the nation. But whether even Chatham could have saved of the old Empire some relationship analogous to the connection between England and Scotland in the seventeenth century was a more than doubtful proposition. Once the alliance between France and America had come about, no solution which preserved one semblance of unity between the English-speaking peoples was attainable by mortal man.

Shelburne, one week after he had snubbed Eden's proposals, wrote to Chatham of his concern at the parliamentary tactics about to be adopted by the Rockingham Whigs. Richmond's intention was to move in the House of Lords for the withdrawal of British troops from America, and on the following Monday to call for the removal of ministers. Shelburne's letter continued: 'The Duke of Richmond is so convinced of the possibility of detaching America from France, and avoiding both wars, by acknowledging the independence, that he seems determined to take both these occasions of renewing and inculcating this favourite measure, and goes so far, as in case of war being declared, and a change of men taking place, to insist on this preliminary.' Camden and Shelburne believed a recognition of American independence under a threat from France must bring nothing but discredit upon Britain without dissolving their alliance. Shelburne was convinced that to link American independence with forcing a change of ministers upon the King would work endless evil in the politics of the future.

Richmond's proposal of 23 March to withdraw all troops from America was negatived by the Lords by 56–28. Perhaps this reverse decided him to reconsider his decision to press on with or without Chatham. On the Monday Richmond did not proceed to call for the removal of ministers. Instead he waited until 5 April, when he wrote to Chatham enclosing the draft of an Address which he proposed moving in the House of Lords in two days' time, 'entreating his Majesty to dismiss his Ministers, and withdraw his forces, by sea and land, from the revolted provinces'. Richmond hoped sincerely to bridge his disagreement with Chatham: 'I am willing to hope that differences of opinion were more apparent than real, and arose only from want of opportunities to communicate and to explain; . . .'. To this Chatham sent a frigid reply in the third person: 'It is an unspeakable concern to him, to find himself under so wide a difference with the Duke of Richmond, as between the *sovereignty* and *allegiance* of America, that he despairs of bringing about successfully any honourable issue.'[21]

Resolved to make a public answer to Richmond's motion Chatham, accompanied by his three sons, came to London from Hayes on 7 April. After the journey he was helpless with fatigue and Camden described to Grafton how, finding Chatham resting in the Prince's Chamber, he had attempted to dissuade him from attending the debate: 'Your Grace knows how obstinate he is, when he is resolved.' Chatham entered the House swathed in flannels, supported by crutches and leaning on the arm of William; he was 'pale and emaciated. Within his large wig little more was to be seen than his aquiline nose, and his penetrating eye. He looked like a dying man; yet never was seen a figure of more dignity; he appeared like a being of a superior species. Sensing the historic nature of the occasion, all the peers rose in their places.'

Richmond spoke first; as the Americans could evidently not be defeated they were already independent and a recognition was dictated by common sense. After Weymouth had followed for the ministers Chatham rose in his place: 'He took one hand from his crutch and raised it, casting his eyes towards heaven.' His words were faltering and sometimes inaudible: 'He appeared to be extremely feeble and spoke with that difficulty of utterance which is the characteristic of severe indisposition.' Chatham made no attempt to follow the line of Richmond's arguments and spoke only in protest against the proposed disruption of the British Empire: 'My Lords, I rejoice that the grave has not yet closed upon me; that I am still alive to lift up my voice against the dismemberment of this ancient and most noble monarchy!' Chatham collapsed in his seat. Temple turned to him and said: 'You forgot to mention what we talked of; shall I get up?' and Chatham replied: 'No, no; I will do it by-and-by.'

Richmond spoke in answer to Chatham who tried to stand up but 'after repeated attempts he suddenly pressed his hand to his heart and fell back in a swoon'. The Duke of Cumberland, a younger brother of the King, Temple and other peers, together with young James Pitt, hastened to his assistance. 'His Lordship was removed into the Prince's Chamber, and the medical assistance of Dr. Brocklesby, who happened to be in the House, was instantly procured.'[22] Throughout these melancholy proceedings Mansfield, it was said, sat with callous indifference. Burke had his final fling: 'Lord Chatham fell upon the bosom of the Duke of Portland, in an apoplectick fit, after he had spit his last venom.'[23]

Chatham was carried to a house in Downing Street and later that day was conveyed to Hayes. A week or so later he appeared to make a recovery and even wrote a letter to the Prussian ambassador. Chatham lingered on, to die at Hayes on 11 May, almost five months before his seventieth birthday. That evening Barré moved an Address to the King praying for a state funeral. The Paymaster-General Rigby suggested that a public monument would be a more suitable and permanent way of keeping alive the memory of this great man. Dunning met this by proposing that an addition be tacked on to Barré's motion: 'And that a monument be erected, in the collegiate Church of St. Peter's, Westminster, to the memory of that excellent statesman, with an inscription expressive of the public sense of so great a loss; and to assure his Majesty that this House will make good the expenses attending the same.' Burke in a practical way suggested that, as Westminster Abbey was already cluttered with monuments to the noble and famous dead, the empty spaces of St Paul's might provide a more suitable site for a great memorial in marble. At this moment North, who had gone home earlier, returned in haste and expressed his happiness at arriving in time to give his vote for the joint motion of Barré and Dunning, which passed without dissent.

Two days later Lord John Cavendish proposed that the House of Commons should discharge Chatham's debts and handsomely endow his peerage and North joined in the general feeling that no gesture could be too generous. After tributes to his memory from Burke and the younger Fox, Tommy Townshend proposed an Address to the King asking for the settlement of an annuity upon the Chatham earldom and that a fund be provided to meet his outstanding debts. The House of Lords rejected by one vote Shelburne's proposal that the peers should attend Chatham's funeral in a body – a mean decision inspired by the influence of the King.

For two days, 7 and 8 June, Chatham's embalmed body lay in state in the Painted Chamber of the Palace of Whitehall. The coffin rested upon a catafalque, which was draped with a baldachino bearing his coat of arms. The walls of the Chamber were covered with black hangings, relieved by the gleam of innumerable lustres and there was a day and night watch of eight halberdiers and ten torch-bearers. On 9 June the body was borne through Westminster Hall to the Abbey, preceded by a life-size effigy in wax dressed in his robes, with his coronet in the right hand. Chatham was interred by the north door of Westminster Abbey and over his resting place was erected a magnificent memorial to his example and achievements.

CHAPTER 18

Pitt in Retrospect

'Among all these stately figures and famous slaughters we see the central fact of the period, the shameless and naked cynicism of the eighteenth century, which, turning its back for ever on wars of faith and conviction, looked only to contests of prey. And so it continued till the great Revolution cleared the air, and, followed up by the poignant discipline of Napoleon, made way for the wars of nationality.'

Lord Rosebery: *Chatham, His Early Life and Connections.*

William Pitt was bred to an age commonly regarded as a mandarin society little accessible to criticism. After a traditional education at Eton and Oxford and a Continental tour, member-ship of the House of Commons, if not from a motive of ambition at least as a family duty, was the foregone conclusion. Because of his brother's marriage, Pitt was from the outset associated with the Grenville family. Over the century between Pitt's entry into Parliament and the Great Reform Act the house of Grenville enjoyed a most penetrating consequence in public affairs, surpassing even the Cavendishes and Russells in the quantum and eminence of their statesmen. But the illustrious light of the Grenvilles was substantially a reflection of the correspondent greatness of William Pitt, father and son. Bereft of the meteors, the exact, almost pedestrian qualities of a Grenville could never have maintained so durable an ascendancy. In the career of each Pitt lay ample complexity, unique abilities set in a frame of convention, frailties mortal to the average against a map of far-flung achievement, that no Grenville would ever conjure.

After the fashion of successful politicians down the ages, Pitt was typical of his day in his religious beliefs: a conformity to the norm need not denote insincerity. He was a forthright Church of England man, bred to the fear of God, austere, and in his dealings the honour of his word. In every department of conduct Pitt was a model of virtue, impervious to contamination, but no prude and to his friends no prig, as Potter and Beckford well knew. Apart from politics and the art of war, Pitt's love was landscape design, in keeping with the sense of the age; his eye and counsel were, as Thomas Gray observed, highly prized. That impulse to out-beautify nature, the manifestation of an Englishman's love for his soil, moreover gave the opportunity for the great landowners to exemplify their wealth and power. The palladian method and pastoral 'simplicities' of Stowe boasted the primacy of the Grenvilles and not only in their own county, for an easy proximity to London enhanced their import in matters of state. Temple survived Chatham little more than a year, his titles and estates passing to his brother George Grenville's eldest son, another George as 3rd Earl. Temple's churlish arrogance and love of subterranean intrigue gave him an unpleasing reputation, whilst he never scrupled to use Chatham for his personal and dynastic ends – witness the occasion when he informed Viry that his family were 'Masters of the kingdom'. Yet Chatham without a doubt nursed for him and his family the deepest respect and affection.

A lack of movement, even turgidity, may superficially apply to the first half of the eighteenth century. But the Augustan era was remarkable for Anson's circumnavigation of the globe. The Britain of George II was bustling with energy, expansive, and looking to the future with confident anticipation. The startling career of John Wesley evidenced the freedom and intellectual abundance of the time. The final decades encountered the great upheavals, the American War of Independence and the French Revolution, events definitive of the world of the nineteenth century and still more of the twentieth, which no inhabitant of this planet can look back upon with indifference.

Pitt was born in the reign of Queen Anne, when men yet

believed in the divine right of Kings. Bolingbroke and Oxford did not sincerely profess that faith, and the paradox of their leading the party of the High Church was one reason for the destruction of the old Tory party. Walpole was well aware that he ruled a country in which a large minority, if not more, subscribed to Tory principles but for religious reasons were unable to do more than drink the health of a Catholic King over the water. But the peers, gentry and merchants on whose sanction the polity must depend would never after 1688 have countenanced the least emendation to parliamentary rule. Walpole's greatness lay in his perception of this central fact of political life: government by consent must prove superior to Tory sentimentality, so that in time all men of sense became Whig. Walpole established the precedent that the Hanoverian Kings should rule in partnership with the House of Commons, in whose hands lay financial control. To that end a minister firm in the confidence of the monarch and of the great body of members of Parliament was the cornerstone.

From the example of his grandfather the Governor, Pitt learned to despise Tory principles and entered Parliament a Whig. But here from the start was an element of contradiction, for recently his family had entered into opposition to Walpole. The boy politician moved in the circles of Wyndham, Pope and Bolingbroke, with whom Walpole's Whig enemies Chesterfield, Carteret, Pulteney and later Cobham had uneasily coalesced. These initial loyalties were the fruit of accident and connection, not of mature conviction. Pitt's first taste of responsibility was in the service of Prince Frederick's household. Walpole had himself first set the example of using the heir to the throne to bestow respectability upon a formed opposition. Pitt, buoyed along by the ambition to make his mark, took up the opposition cry against corruption and the evil domination of a 'sole' minister. The cleansing of public life by Place Acts and the limitation on the life of a Parliament to three years was to be accompanied by a return to the Elizabethan tradition of maritime glory.

Walpole's policy of peace at almost any price had originated in the need to safeguard the Hanoverian dynasty. Peace led to the blessing of prosperity. But Pitt was of the generation to whom the cut-throat contentions of Queen Anne's day were of distant memory. He embraced the cause of the 'blue-water' school, the Tory antidote to the top-heavy Whig preoccupation with the Continent. The internationally acknowledged but over vast areas undeveloped monopoly of the greater part of America by Bourbon Spain appeared an unjust obstacle to the expansion of British trade. Pitt, from first to last a fiery patriot, nursed the utmost contempt for the foreigner, especially the Catholic monarchies of Versailles and Madrid, whose subjects could not read the Bible and knew nothing of Protestant liberty. He never considered the pagan motive of greed underlying the rivalries between Britain and her Atlantic neighbours a reproach; Protestant Britain was entitled to God's blessing and the rewards of wealth and empire no detriment. Rarely has any nation embarked upon a hazardous enterprise with the enthusiasm of the English for the War of Jenkins's Ear. El Dorado had to be put to one side when Frederick II plunged Europe into chaos, involving Britain in the maintenance of cumbersome armies with subsidies to Maria Theresa and a string of foreign princes, but without a Marlborough to fight the battles. The failure to wage successful war proved Walpole's undoing. Of the Minister's enemies Pitt alone would become a great man, though one day he would acknowledge his debt to Carteret as exemplar.

Pitt and his associates had to swallow a bitter lesson in the true workings of the political system Walpole had consolidated, for changes were limited to men and talk of reform was soon hushed, to lie buried for almost thirty years. Prince Frederick abandoned the cause and after some hesitation the mantle of Walpole fell upon Pelham, his pupil. Pitt and his friends continued their opposition tactics and among them he gradually established an ascendancy. By stages he came to perceive the futility of attempting to change men, let alone conduce policies, across the floor of the House of Commons and that the only road to power and greatness lay through coming to terms with the Whig oligarchs. But Pitt almost wrecked his prospects of office by his personal attacks upon George II and the Hanoverian connection. His parliamentary tactics were so quick, indeed over-subtle, that but for the King's pig-headed indulgence in a ministerial crisis at the height of the Jacobite rebellion, even the phlegmatic Pelham could hardly have stomached him as colleague. The King's power was sufficient to keep Pitt out of the War Office, but soon fate produced a vacancy in the Paymaster-ship, the most politically distinguished office outside the Cabinet.

Pitt had given earnest that no administration could maintain an ignorance of the just pretensions of a true and sustained ambition. He had outstripped his friends and contemporaries in the race of life and Henry Fox, who had climbed the ladder within the establishment, was his only compeer. Pitt's acceptance by the hierarchy had come about as part of a deal between Pelham and the King. Though Pelham always glossed over the events of those months, the plain fact was that George II had been taught his own business; he could wield his authority only through the medium of a minister capable of managing the House of Commons. Pitt, too, had learned his lesson in the makings of power. To Hardwicke and to many the reform of the renegade indicated a man of cool ambition rather than of scruple. But Pitt redeemed himself by refusing the Paymaster's perquisites, the foundation of his reputation for an incorruptible patriotism.

Pitt was now embarked upon the one season of his career which can be called ordinary. His Augustan repose found illustration in the lines of Sanderson Miller of Radway:

> 'A Laurel walk and Strawberry Bank,
> For which the Paymaster I thank,
> The Paymaster well-skilled in planting,
> Pleased to assist when cash was wanting.
> He bid my Laurels grow, they grew,
> Fast as his Laurels always do.'

At Miller's Gothic Tower on Edgehill, overlooking the fields where the armies of Charles I and the Parliament had met their first great engagement, Henry Fielding read out to Pitt and Lyttleton his manuscript of *Tom Jones*.

Pelham built a hold over the Whig party more comprehensive than even Walpole had achieved and Prince Frederick's demise finally dissolved an opposition become desultory. Pitt, provided he stuck to his last, might expect the highest promotion in the event of a vacancy in the ordinary course of resignation or death.

The Austrian war was brought to a grinding conclusion, with Frederick's acquisition of Silesia the important consequence. After the peace Pitt tried loyally to smooth the differences between Pelham and Newcastle over foreign policy. He recanted his opposition principles in respect of relations with Spain and welcomed the treaty of friendship of 1751. His dislike for Newcastle's German subsidies and resistance to Pelham's most extreme naval reductions were the only indications of the Pitt of the future. Here indeed was no suitable season for deviation. So durably integrated was the Whig ascendancy that men had become set in the belief that change was beyond the order of political nature. The perfect Constitution was supposed as immutable as the constellation and a disturbance to the established balance of King, Lords and Commons an affront to all concept of the possible.

On Pelham's death the absence of a comparable successor created a hiatus where George II thought to see his advantage. To Newcastle he made clear there was to be no First Minister and His Majesty's servants were to keep to their departments. He who supposed himself Premier after his brother was cajoled into the delusion that the House of Commons could be managed by a carpet politician such as Robinson, with true responsibility to the Crown and a Cabinet of peers, after the fashion of George I's early years before Walpole's governance. Pitt and Fox were each disappointed of their reasonable expectations. But Pitt had grasped firmly the lesson Walpole and Pelham had abided by, that the finality of decision must lie with the House of Commons. He found initial support from Fox in exposing Robinson a fool in parliamentary procedures, whilst Murray was made to blanche with fear. That Pitt and Fox should harass the ministry whilst remaining in office opened them to much criticism. So accustomed had the Whigs become to a somnolent inertia, that the left-hand regulation of Parliament contemplated by Newcastle aroused barely a ruffle of resentment. At this most trying point of his career Pitt fell upon the happy chance of an eminently satisfactory marriage. Moreover, the match had a most intimate political relevance in that his ties with the Grenville family were strengthened.

When Fox deferred to the King and Newcastle and undertook

their jobs, he had the approval of Cumberland and the Whig dukes; little damage to his reputation was evident. Pitt justly felt himself betrayed but knew that without some twist of fate he had come to a full stop. At this juncture the anxieties of the Princess Dowager for the interests of her son, should Cumberland become Regent, once more bent the Court of the Prince of Wales towards a course of opposition. Pitt, finding to hand the traditional resource of a disgruntled politician, formed an understanding with the Princess and Bute the esteemed courtier. At the prospect of war with France over control of the Ohio, Newcastle fell back upon the time-honoured policy of alliances with the Continental powers cemented by British cash. Here Pitt found intelligent ground for opposition on the ancient 'blue-water' principles; the Austrian war had produced nothing but a stalemate; to fight on the Continent was merely meeting the enemy on his strongest ground. Pitt's advocacy of a colonial war struck home at the real issue, the future of North America.

On the day of his dismissal as Paymaster, Pitt's position was bleak. Newcastle commanded the big divisions, whilst Pitt could rely only upon his Stowe connection, the friendship of Leicester House and the long discredited rump of the Tories. A victory at sea, such as the destruction of the French convoy at the mouth of the St Lawrence, and Pitt would be forgotten for ever. But everything went wrong for Newcastle, and our weakness lay in the areas where Pitt had indicated. Montcalm took the offensive on the Great Lakes with success. There was no more sure indication of Pitt's latent genius in war than his prediction before the House of Commons that Minorca must fall. Finally, Newcastle's Continental system toppled when Kaunitz secured an alliance with Louis XV and George II was confronted with the unexpected and unpalatable prospect of Frederick as ally. Fox, who realised as clearly as Pitt that power could not be exercised without the respect of the House of Commons, resigned in a panic. By his double betrayal first of Pitt and then of Newcastle he forfeited the esteem of contemporaries and posterity.

'Public opinion' in eighteenth-century Britain, a country substantially provincial, rustic and for the most part illiterate, cannot be gauged in terms of a majority of the whole, head by head.

But that Britain should be losing a war at sea, where lay her pride and claim to paramountcy, must incite the conceit of every man capable of vision beyond the furrow and the loom. No country gentleman could express an indifference to the violation of His Majesty's dominions by the hereditary enemy. The mood of anger following Minorca and Oswego echoed loud through London and the large urban centres. The Whigs, too long accustomed to the security bred by the absence of criticism, had been overtaken by disaster in war. But equally there was no lack of confidence in the institutions of government. Pitt's refusal to parley with Newcastle compelled the King to accept him as minister, a situation not endorsed by the House of Commons where was the feeling that His Majesty's hand had been forced. Devonshire undertook the Treasury as caretaker for one session before a Parliament where caution alone restrained Newcastle from using his majority. To the surprise of many the squalid intrigue promoted by Cumberland to turn Pitt out did not work in Fox's favour. The rain of gold boxes evoked by Pitt's dismissal settled that Fox could not form a government.

Hardwicke saved the day by negotiating the great ministry, representative of all sections, his true achievement as statesman. The coalition with Newcastle which Pitt had to accept was the unavoidable compromise with a system of government no one disapproved. Even so, Pitt had been called to power by the suffrages of the 'people', the first minister in British history chosen by acclaim. Pitt's integrity and force of character convinced men that he alone could save the country, a capacity he himself never doubted. The call for the services of Churchill in 1940, and the co-operation he too had to welcome from old enemies of bitter blood on both sides of the House, is the irresistible parallel. During the second half of 1757 the war continued to go so badly that any administration save this must have foundered. Parliament rallied unanimously behind the Government and opposition seemed beyond relevance. Pitt stood master of the House of Commons, just two years after the King and Newcastle had thought themselves to be rid of him for ever. Cumberland's disgrace, though not altogether deserved, strengthened Pitt because the control of the army was divorced from political considerations.

Where the command of Louis XV's army and navy was suffering a barren period, Pitt had Frederick as ally and in Prince Ferdinand one of the greatest generals of second rank. As Secretary of State he encountered good fortune in finding tried and experienced leadership at the top. Ligonier proved himself a great staff officer and at the Admiralty Anson was one of the greatest naval directors of all time. For command of the fleet Pitt was fortunate to inherit Hawke, much though he underestimated him. Though Mordaunt and Abercromby were failures and Sackville a disaster, overall the quality of senior British officers was superb. That Wolfe should be so established in the loyalty of the army as to constitute the only choice for Quebec was a godsend, and in Amherst lay the ideal coordinator. Pitt's errors can indeed be recounted; the amphibious operations on the French coast were for the most part costly failures; his darling militia was never popular and contributed nothing to the outcome. Against the miscarriages must be set the galaxy of admirals and generals of the second rank, Clavering at Guadeloupe, Boscawen at Lagos, Saunders at Quebec, Rodney and Rollo at Martinique, Pocock at Pondicherry. Only Pitt could have gathered such an assortment of talent to yield so glorious a harvest.

The testimony of Newcastle, Amherst and Barrington attributed to Pitt the credit for Annus Mirabilis and victory, which established him in the heart of the nation for all time. Undeterred by the threat of invasion, Pitt pressed forward with his plans for North America and even the West Indies as well, where lesser men would have been mesmerised by fear of the savage penalties of failure. The country was consumed by a flame of glorious anticipation. Each day was expected to bring forth some further token of national achievement. James Brindley cut the first sod of his great canal and aqueduct, one of the wonders of the age. Laurence Sterne could choose no object for his homage other than Pitt when he dedicated the best-selling edition of *Tristram Shandy*. Henceforth Pitt and his immediate family would be treated with a deference almost attaching to royalty, a situation calling for tact on his part of the most keen delicacy.

Even in time of war Pitt as colleague was ticklish. There was

his absurdly irrelevant squabble with Hardwicke over Habeas
Corpus in impressment cases. Legge he could not abide and in
March 1759 even attacked his budgetary proposal to increase
the tax on sugar. When some fledgling humorously deprecated
the use of parliamentary time on so mundane a subject, Pitt
thundered forth: 'Sugar Mr Speaker, Sugar Mr Speaker, Sugar
Mr Speaker!' Then to a hushed assembly he put the rhetorical
question in his most dulcet tone: 'Who dares to laugh at sugar
now?' Pitt's pugnacious espousal of Temple's demand for the
Garter was placing family loyalties before Government soli-
darity. Pitt showed little appreciation of Newcastle's grudging
yet honest admiration and, still more dangerous, forfeited by
lack of tact the goodwill of the Prince of Wales and Bute.

The year 1760 saw the completion of the conquest of Canada:
the future of North America would lie with the English-speaking
peoples. But that October George III succeeded to the throne.
Although Pitt's dominance of the House of Commons was at
first unshaken, Bute's entry into the Cabinet made men take
stock of the position that might follow on a peace. Newcastle's
enthusiasm for the war steadily diminished, because he genuinely
feared the cost of Pitt's limitless plans. Pitt cared nought for
expense and reckoned the continued expansion of trade provided an adequate return. But Newcastle's intuition that the
nation was tired of war had justice. Yet more compelling was his
desire to cling to power. Newcastle saw clearly that, the objects
of the war achieved, the customary factors in the political scene
must become reasserted. For the preservation of his majorities in
Parliament the countenance of the new King was very necessary.

In the course of the peace negotiations of 1761 Pitt found
himself increasingly at variance with his colleagues, who thought
peace with Canada and something in the West Indies, together
with Clive's magnificent acquisitions in India, an eminently
satisfactory outcome. Pitt's insistence upon a monopoly of the
Newfoundland Fisheries, with the object of crippling French
naval power for ever, puzzled the Cabinet, who were apprehensive that to debase the enemy to the level of a secondary
power must invite a war of revenge. Although Choiseul had been
wooing a Spanish intervention before the negotiations began,
Pitt's obduracy made the Family Compact certain and here a

severe responsibility rested with him. Pitt's call for a pre-emptive strike at the treasure galleons savoured of piracy, though he was vindicated by the Spanish declaration of war which followed within weeks of his resignation. But that ill-considered act was fatal in ultimate consequence, for the country was deprived of his leadership and he of all influence over the negotiations, which Bute quietly resumed. Spain suffered humiliating blows at Havana and Manila whilst the French lost the Windward Islands. Pitt, out of office, saw the objectives of his *guerre à outrance* achieved. Meanwhile Newcastle was ousted by Bute, who became Prime Minister.

That the King should confidently accept the withdrawal of the most popular man in the kingdom proved the ineptitude of Pitt's judgement. Had Pitt used his popularity with finesse, he must have expected to succeed an ageing Newcastle at the Treasury. That claim to '*direct*', above King and Council, so totally at variance with established custom, took all obstacles from Bute's path. Pitt's apparently needless retirement bewildered the House of Commons, and his small personal following was embarrassed at his declared intent to lapse into privacy. The downfall of Newcastle, who had inherited the unquestioned loyalty of overwhelming majorities in both Houses of Parliament, represented no fundamental change in the system of government: the right of the King to choose his own Prime Minister had never been denied. But Newcastle and his friends certainly considered a revolution had been contrived, in that their presence in the councils of the realm, which they had always taken for granted, was dispensed with.

The Peace of Paris was Bute's achievement and, the Newfoundland Fisheries excepted, much the settlement to which Pitt would have consented in the negotiations of 1761. But by the autumn of 1762 the position had advanced substantially in Britain's favour, of which Pitt as minister would have taken a full advantage. The difference between Pitt and Bute involved the polity of Europe, the balance established by the Utrecht treaties. There the significant changes had been the annexation of Silesia by Frederick and the incursion for the first time of the Russian armies across the plains of eastern Europe. If France was permanently enfeebled, Frederick and Catherine the Great would have Poland and Turkey at their mercy, with Maria Theresa powerless either to intervene or secure her share of the spoils. The good sense of Parliament ratified the Peace which Pitt condemned as a betrayal of the nation. His mortification at finding himself deserted by so many one-time votaries was the inducement for his seeking to concert an opposition with Newcastle, despite his previous disclaimers.

The Peace concluded, Bute, who occupied one of the strongest positions ever enjoyed by a minister, abandoned ship. As the King was not prepared to consider Pitt, and Fox lacked the courage to take the helm, Grenville was the only possible leader. There followed a fascinating personal conflict. George III and Grenville had no differences of principles, but their mutual dislike was such that confidence was impossible. Grenville faithfully complied with the King's direction that Wilkes be prosecuted. The King saw no reason to obstruct Grenville's programme for rationalising the American establishment, of which the Stamp Act was intended only as an incidental part. King and minister thus joined in committing two of the greatest mistakes of the reign. None the less, Grenville had been in power only four months when the King authorised Bute to negotiate with Pitt and Newcastle the reconstruction of the great war ministry which he and the Favourite had encompassed to destroy. The plot would certainly have succeeded had not Pitt wrecked the game by his vindictive intent to oust everyone connected with the Peace. From that point Pitt shared with the King responsibility for the political uncertainties of the decade. The King had the excuse of inexperience, but Pitt during a succession of attempts to find a stable administration would show an unreasonable vanity and lack of accommodation towards practical considerations.

Initially the emergence of Wilkes as popular hero had a direct association with Pitt. The demagogue was Temple's protégé and had led the journalistic campaign against Bute's Peace. The mob that had called for Pitt the Great Commoner shouted 'Wilkes and Liberty'. Although Pitt sharply dissociated himself from Wilkes, he led the parliamentary opposition to the diminution of House of Commons privilege and the use of general warrants. This savage mode of procedure in cases of seditious libel had been developed since the Glorious Revolution and employed to defend successive Whig administrations. General warrants were finally abandoned in consequence of a series of court actions. To the public, Pitt had led the way as champion of constitutional liberties.

George III next attempted the construction of a ministry with Temple at the Treasury and Pitt as Secretary of State, without the Newcastle Whigs. Pitt did not, it would appear, fully consult Temple, who was not prepared to turn out his brother. Therefore the King resorted to the one opening remaining and commissioned Cumberland to form a pure Whig administration. From the outset the Rockingham administration lay in Pitt's shadow and slavishly adopted his policies. But news from America of resistance to the Stamp Act put the initial objectives of the ministry out of perspective. In the debates upon the Declaratory Act and the repeal of the Stamp Act Pitt and Grenville stole the show: the ministry put up a poor performance, apart from the advent of Edmund Burke.

Pitt applied to America the principle already accepted as a constitutional convention at home, that the means of government, namely taxation, be settled by the elected branch of the legislature. The axioms underlying representative government have never been more succinctly stated. As between Britain and America the difficulty was that the unquestioned right of Parliament to legislate for the colonies had in respect of the Stamp Act violated the control of the Assemblies over domestic taxation. The House of Commons were denying to complementary institutions of a like ancestry their own privileges. Pitt's attempt to find a *modus vivendi* met with a stubborn incomprehension. His distinction between taxation for revenue and taxation for the regulation of trade was never recognised and the Declaratory Act which he opposed remained sound law until the twentieth century. None the less, Pitt's doctrine that the power of Parliament to legislate for overseas possessions be limited to imperial affairs would be developed to provide the basis for relations between Great Britain and the Dominions of the latter day Empire.

Pitt coupled the defence of American liberty with an intimation that all was not well with parliamentary institutions at home. Dismissing with contempt the comfortable theory of virtual representation, he suggested a diminution of the pocket boroughs to the benefit of the county electorate, which must contract the influence of the House of Lords over the House of Commons. Pitt was the first major statesman since the Commonwealth to envisage the reform of Parliament. He looked for a development in representation in the light of changed social conditions over the century, within the sacred pattern of King, Lords and Commons. But to members accustomed to look upon the Constitution as perfect, his words were startling.

When in July 1766 the King dismissed Rockingham he had made certain this time that Pitt would form an administration, even without Temple. Pitt's seeking shelter in a peerage and the office of Lord Privy Seal was not intended as any indication of flaccidity of purpose. Criticism might more properly be directed against his appointments of Grafton to the Treasury, Charles Townshend to the Exchequer and Conway Leader of the House of Commons. But there was a singular dearth of men of experience and ability. Shelburne, Chatham's most consistent follower, could do nothing for him in the Commons.

At the beginning the administration looked like holding together. The discovery that no ambitious foreign policy was practicable need not have affected the conduct of domestic affairs. Chatham set out with every intention of guiding the ministry and regulating the minutiae of patronage as well. A persistence in this course, together with the King's ungrudging support, must have produced for him a growing parliamentary following, the foundation of a permanent system. Chatham put forward the principle that the rights of the East India Company must be placed solidly at the discretion of Parliament. He laid the foundations of a new understanding between the Protestant Irish landowners and Westminster. The relapse of Chatham's mind left all to ruin. The East India Company's Charter was renewed on traditional lines, which did not take into account the implications of the acquisition of Bengal. Under not unwelcome pressure from Grenville and the Whig opposition, Charles Townshend reopened the fatal issue of American taxation. Grafton, left to himself, made the error of allowing the House of Commons to put Luttrell in as member of Parliament for

Middlesex in place of Wilkes. Only in respect of Ireland were Chatham's ideas followed.

When in the summer of 1769 Chatham emerged from his seclusion, he sought to recover the initiative. His reconciliation with Temple and Grenville was a first attempt to rally a party, but too late. Chatham's 'resurrection' precipitated the fall of the Grafton ministry but not to his advantage. His parliamentary following was as limited and personal in character as at the time of his resignation in October 1761. The King found in North a man well able to manage the House of Commons, and too a friend. North opened his ministry by avoiding war with France and Spain over the Falkland Islands on honourable terms. Though Chatham criticised him for pusillanimity, he had himself as minister indicated that the Falkland Islands were not a justifiable *causus belli*. Chatham and Rockingham considered a concerted opposition, but mutual confidence was altogether lacking. Burke suspected Chatham's object was merely to use Rockingham's following to engineer his own return to power.

The Junius trials reopened the issue of seditious libels, over which Chatham championed the rights of juries to determine the case. The sole practical upshot was to divide him and Rockingham. Grenville's Elections Act was a creditable achievement, but over Wilkes and Middlesex Chatham was powerless to alter the mind of Parliament. Chatham's revival of the long-forgotten call for triennial in place of seven-year Parliaments deepened his breach with Rockingham and at that moment attracted little sympathy.

His opponents routed in the House of Commons, North step by step consolidated his position. The unhappy twists and turns which had characterised the first decade of the reign became a bad dream of the past and North appeared as secure as Pelham in his heyday. The American troubles subsided and seemed likely to be forgotten. Chatham's attempt to forward the rights of the rational dissenters led by Price and Priestley, the friends of Franklin, found acceptance in the House of Commons but stood no chance against administration and the Bishops in the Upper House. Essentially the popular cause had lost momentum. In the East India Regulating Act North encompassed a great chapter of legislation, designed to give Bengal sound and humane government. North's Quebec Act gave Canada a well-ordered and acceptable constitution for fifteen years and he has won acclaim for his singular justice to the French population. Chatham's criticisms were in part founded upon the just expectation that the boundary conditions especially must cause apprehension in New England. But his points of opposition to the strictly domestic provisions were disproved by the successful working of the Act.

Then North stumbled into the disaster of the American war. Chatham never deigned to notice any argument that the removal of the French menace by the conquest of Canada had stimulated the impulse to freedom in New England. To the contrary, he reiterated that the love of liberty was the proper birthright of the Thirteen Colonies. Though consistently adamant in his opposition to taxation for revenue, he was in no way prepared to envisage any shift in the ancient constitutional relationship. Although Chatham grasped fully the national consciousness of the Thirteen Colonies, he did not translate their aspirations in terms of freedom from imperial obligation, particularly in respect of trade. But he would never have countenanced the employment of British troops against their fellow subjects. Chatham died the greatest living Englishman, unheeded by King or country, a situation rendered inevitable by the failure of his ministry. Yet in six and a half years George III would appoint William Pitt the Younger Prime Minister, to rule Britain with that confidence and effectiveness which had eluded his father.

The posterity of the house of Pitt was not destined to outlive Chatham more than fifty years. The Younger Pitt secured the elevation of Chatham's nephew Thomas Pitt III of Boconnoc as Lord Camelford and of the 3rd Earl Temple as Marquis of Buckingham. The partnership of Pitt and Grenville reached the apogee when George Grenville's third son, William Wyndham, served as Foreign Secretary alongside the Younger Pitt in the struggle against revolutionary France and Napoleon. The head of the Pitt family of those days, the 2nd Lord Camelford of 'a turbulent, rakehelly' disposition, died in consequence of a duel in his late twenties. The 2nd Earl of Chatham was cruelly fated to resemble his father but be afflicted with a mind disconcertingly inert. Gluttony and the bottle further depressed his temper and gambling his estate. Because of his father's memory and his brother William, Lord Chatham was a General, a Knight of the Garter and entrusted with great offices of state. But the laughable fiasco of the Walcheren expedition of 1809 forfeited him all esteem. On his death on 3 October 1835 the Chatham title and the male line of Governor Thomas Pitt became extinct. Only two years later the proud house of Grenville, which had in 1822 achieved the summit of nobility with the Dukedom of Buckingham and Chandos, tumbled to dust with the bankruptcy of the 2nd Duke for two millions.

The Prime Minister historian Lord Rosebery considered a biography of Chatham unattainable, and a conspectus of his standing as domestic and imperial statesman defies clear delineation. To win the Seven Years War was Chatham's great and only concrete achievement. The conquest of Bengal, an event of comparable decision, was not of his making. The Peace deviated fundamentally from Chatham's concept of honour. Unlike almost every great statesman since the Glorious Revolution, Chatham was never responsible for a budget. Dexterity in the national finances has been the bond with Parliament to recommend most Prime Ministers, but not with Chatham. Indeed he professed a contempt for the financial aspects of government, a temper Walpole, Pelham and North and his son William would never have contemplated, let alone publicity declare. The Great Commoner never sat for a popular constituency, such as Middlesex or Westminster: the thirty burgesses of Bath were his closest propinquity to a democratic process. No encompassing essay in legislation, no beneficial reform or imperial statute stand his memorial.

Chatham's dominance of Parliament was personal, from the persuasion of his oratory, his clear integrity and his achievement in beating the French, the most popular thing any English gentleman could do. But he never manipulated either House of Parliament after the manner of the great Prime Ministers, though when in 1766 he formed his ministry he gave considerable indication of that aim. Indistinct were the sinews of Chatham's power, yet his primacy among men was acknowledged even by his enemies, who at the least paid him the respect born of fear. The bulk of his countrymen especially, it must be conceded, they who never experienced the shock of direct encounter, worshipped him with unstinted admiration. Even his faults, his childish ostentation, his great column at Burton Pynsent, his multitude of liveried retainers, appeared but a fitting keystone to his stature.

Chatham had been the saviour of the national pride in the face of France. In the cases of general warrants and parliamentary privilege he had served popular liberties. As upholder of the rights of the Middlesex electors he was defender of the Constitution. In the cause of America he identified political and religious freedom at home with the constitutional and natural rights of the English-speaking peoples overseas, and, the vindication too, of the national dignity against the House of Bourbon. On each count, Chatham led the sure way, to the example of posterity.

The British Empire which Chatham sought so nobly to extend and preserve, and the Younger Pitt presided over with such distinction, is no more. But the example of parliamentary democracy served and enriched by father and son remains largely the practice, and certainly the ideal, of the free world.

NOTES

Chapter 1: Pitt's Early Life

1 Lord Macaulay, *Sir William Temple: Historical Essays.*
2 Royal Hist. MSS. Comm. *Fortescue*, i. 18.
3 Royal Hist. MSS. Comm. *Fortescue*, i. 39.
4 Romney Sedgwick, *The History of Parliament, The House of Commons 1715–1754* (London, 1970), ii. 351–3. (Hence cited as H.O.P. 1715–1754.)
5 Geoffrey Holmes, *Politics in the Reign of Queen Anne* (London, 1967), 331.
6 Royal Hist. MSS. Comm. *Fortescue*, i. 51–2.
7 H.O.P. 1715–1754, ii. 350–3.
8 J. H. Plumb, *Sir Robert Walpole, The Makings of a Statesman* (London, 1956), 334–7.
9 Lord Edmond Fitzmaurice, *The Life of William, Earl of Shelburne* (London, 1912), i. 56.
10 G.E.C., The Complete Peerage, xii. 233 fn. e.
11 H.O.P. 1715–1754, i. 208, 227–8.
12 Royal Hist. MSS. Comm. *Fortescue*, i. 76–91.
13 H.O.P. 1715–1754, ii. 285–6.
14 H.O.P. 1715–1754, i. 208, 227–8, ii. 350–3.
15 *The Correspondence of Alexander Pope* ed. George Sherburn (Oxford, 1956), ii. 257, 302, 310, 314, 388, iii. 244, 375, iv. 404.
16 B.M. Add. MSS. 47097/8.
17 H.O.P. 1715–1754, i. 208, 227–8, ii. 114, 290–1, 350–5.

Chapter 2: Member for Old Sarum

1 William Hazlitt, *The Eloquence of the British Senate; The Complete Works of William Hazlitt*, ed. P. P. Howe (London, 1930–4), vii. 157.
2 The Earl of Ilchester, *Henry Fox, First Lord Holland* (London, 1920), i. Chapters II, III; H.O.P. 1715–1754, i. 227–8, 237–8, 350–1, ii. 48–50, 232–3, 349–56.
3 O. A. Sherrard, *Lord Chatham, A Minister in the Making* (London, 1952), 48–50.
4 *Lord Hervey's Memoirs* ed. Romney Sedgwick (London, 1952), 175.
5 B.M. Add. MSS. 22, 626, f. 11.
6 Basil Williams, *The Life of William Pitt, Earl of Chatham* (London, 1915), i. 67.
7 There is only one reference to Pitt in the entire Pope correspondence. A

casual postcript in Lyttleton's letter to Pope of 25 October 1738 refers to the presence of him and Chesterfield at Bath; *Pope Corr.* iv. 138–9.

8 Philip C. Yorke, *The Life and Correspondence of Philip Yorke, Earl of Hardwicke, Lord High Chancellor of Great Britain* (Cambridge, 1913), i. 156, 161–6.

9 *Memoirs and Correspondence of George, Lord Lyttleton*, ed. Robert Phillimore (London, 1845), 74–81.

10 Chatsworth MSS. 182. 11.

11 Williams, *Life of Pitt*, i. 68–75.

12 *Pope Corr.* iv. 142–4.

13 Yorke, *Life of Hardwicke*, i. 190–1.

14 Chatsworth MSS. 249.4; 182.13.

15 Williams, *Life of Pitt*, i. 80.

16 Chatsworth MSS. 114.15.

17 Yorke, *Life of Hardwicke*, i. 248–9.

18 Williams, *Life of Pitt*, i. 82–5.

19 John B. Owen, *The Rise of the Pelhams* (London, 1957), 1–9.

20 H.O.P. 1715–1754, i. 82–4, 290–1, 353–6.

21 P.R.O. 30/8/6 ff. 28–33.

22 *The Letters of Lord Chesterfield*, ed. Bonamy Dobrée (London, 1932), No. 356.

23 John Lord Campbell, LL.D., F.R.S.E., *Lives of the Lord Chancellors and Keepers of the Great Seal of England* (London, 1857), Vol. VI, 355.

Chapter 3: Pitt, Carteret and the Pelhams

1 *Boswell's Journey of a Tour to the Hebrides with Samuel Johnson LL.D. 1773*, ed. Frederick A. Pottle and Charles R. Bennett (London, 1963), 340.

2 Chatsworth MSS. 114.19.

3 Owen, *Rise of the Pelhams*, 87–101.

4 Williams, *Life of Pitt*, i. 90.

5 Owen, *Rise of the Pelhams*, 106–21, 133.

6 *The Grenville Papers*, ed. William James Smith (London, 1852), i. 1–16.

7 Owen, *Rise of the Pelhams*, 142–3; *Grenville Papers*, i. 16–17.

8 *Grenville Papers*, i. 18–20; Chatsworth MSS. 249.10; Owen, *Rise of the Pelhams*, 149–50.

9 Williams, *Life of Pitt*, 105–6; Owen, *Rise of the Pelhams*, 151–6.

10 M. Dorothy George, *English Political Caricature to 1792* (Oxford, 1959), 94.

11 Chatsworth MSS. 182.23.

12 Chatsworth MSS. 249.13–14; 259.2; 260.25, 27, 36; 290.7–9; Owen, *Rise of the Pelhams*, 197–208.

13 *Grenville Papers*, i. 29–35.

14 Althorp MSS. Sarah Duchess of Marlborough II, IV; A True Copy of the last Will and Testament of Her Grace Sarah, late Duchess Dowager of Marlborough (London, 1750), 68.

15 Owen, *Rise of the Pelhams*, 239–49, 250–67; George, *English Political Caricature to 1792*, 94.

16 *Grenville Papers*, i. 33–5.

17 Betty Kemp, *Sir Francis Dashwood* (Macmillan, 1967), 23–5; Chatsworth MSS. 260.50.

18 Chatsworth MSS. 260.51, 2; Owen, *Rise of the Pelhams*, 278–86.

19 *Marchmont Papers*, ed. Sir G. H. Rose (London, 1831), i. 143–7; Chatsworth MSS. 260.53.

20 Chatsworth MSS. 182.32; 249.26–7, 32; 260.55; 309.2–3; 330 A, B; Chesterfield, *Letters*, Nos. 890, 906–7; Owen, *Rise of the Pelhams*, 287–303.

21 *Correspondence of John, Fourth Duke of Bedford*, ed. Lord John Russell (London, 1842), i. 72–7, 82–3; *Grenville Papers*, i. 424.

22 Yorke, *Life of Hardwicke*, iii. 64–5.

23 George, *English Political Caricature to 1792*, 94.

24 Owen, *Rise of the Pelhams*, 306 f. 2.

25 Bedford Corr., i. 91–3; H.O.P. 1715–1754, ii. 83, 207.

Chapter 4: Paymaster-General

1 Chesterfield, *Letters*, No. 1758.

2 Plumb, *Sir Robert Walpole*, i. 203.

3 *Grenville Papers*, i. 424–5.

4 Yorke, *Life of Hardwicke*, i. 628–9.

5 *Bedford Corr.*, i. 132, 180–1, 187–90, 194–6, 199–202.

6 B.M. Add. MSS. 32, 713, f. 517, 32, 714, f. 79; *Grenville Papers*, i. 54–7.

7 H.O.P. 1715–1754, i. 56–7; *Bedford Corr.*, i. 321–3.

8 B.M. Add. MSS. 32, 714, f. 552; H.O.P. 1715–1754, i. 227–8, 237–8, 335, 350–1, 365–6, 369–70, 370–1; ii. 58, 83–4, 119, 350, 353–6; *Grenville Papers*, i. 54–7.

9 Owen, *Rise of the Pelhams*, 312–18; H.O.P. 1715–1754, ii. 204, 302–3, 339, 362–3; Sir Lewis Namier and John Brooke, *Charles Townshend* (London, 1964), 20.

10 Yorke, *Life of Hardwicke*, ii. 12–13; *Bedford Corr.*, i. 161–4.

11 *Grenville Papers*, i. 94–5, 426–7.

12 *Grenville Papers*, i. 80, 91.

13 B.M. Add. MSS. 32, 720, ff. 141, 180–7, 32, 721, ff. 129, 192, 242–8, 451.

14 *The Political Journal of George Bubb Dodington*, ed. John Carswell and Lewis Arnold Dralle (Oxford, 1965), 104–34, 178–80.

15 H.O.P. 1715–1754, ii. 353–4.

16 Horace Walpole, Earl of Orford, *Memoires of the Last Ten Years of the Reign of King George the Second* (London, 1822), i. 210–23.

17 Dodington, *Diary*, 187–94; Walpole, *Memoires of George II*, i. 247–8, 252–5.

18 *Grenville Papers*, i. 101; Chesterfield, *Letters*, No. 1882.

19 Dodington, *Diary*, 211.

20 Williams, *Life of Pitt*, i. 199; Walpole, *Memoires of George II*, i. 283–305.

21 Yorke, *Life of Hardwicke*, ii. 54–8, 72; Walpole, *Memoires of George II*, i. 310–15.

22 *Grenville Papers*, i. 102–5.

23 *Grenville Papers*, i. 105–6; Hartington to Devonshire, 5th and 6th March 1754; Chatsworth MSS. 260. 114–15.

24 Walpole, *Memoires of George II*, i. 321–2.

25 *Grenville Papers*, i. 105–11.

26 Chatsworth MSS. 257.19; 390.0; Yorke, *Life of Hardwicke*, ii. 192–5, 205–6; Ilchester, *Henry Fox*, i. 198–202; Sir Lewis Namier, *England in the Age of the American Revolution* (London, 1962), 117.

27 Phillimore, *Memoirs of Lyttleton*, 449–55; *Grenville Papers*, i. 112–13.

28 Yorke, *Life of Hardwicke*, ii. 188–91, 206.

29 Chatsworth MSS. 330.17–18.

30 *Grenville Papers*, ii. 4–15; Phillimore, *Memoirs of Lyttleton*, 460–1.

31 Chatsworth MSS. 253.6; H.O.P. 1715–1754, iii. 388–9; *Bedford Corr.*, i. 476–81; Dodington, *Diary*, 178–9, 256–61.

32 *Grenville Papers*, i. 115–18; Phillimore, *Memoirs of Lyttleton*, 461–2.

33 *Correspondence of William Pitt, Earl of Chatham*, ed. The Executors of his son John, Earl of Chatham (London, 1838), i. 89–107.

34 Sir Lewis Namier and John Brooke, *The History of Parliament: The House of Commons 1754–1790* (London, 1964), i. 57–63, 432, 454; ii. 480–1; iii. 290. (Hence cited as H.O.P. 1754–1790); *Grenville Papers*, i. 119–21, 127, 9, 131–2.

35 *Chatham Corr.*, i. 85–8.

36 Ilchester, *Henry Fox*, i. 219–20; Chatsworth MSS. 330.19–21; 260.116; 330.25; 260.122; 330.26.

37 Ilchester, *Henry Fox*, i. 217–18.

38 Ilchester, *Henry Fox*, i. 223–6.

39 Williams, *Life of Pitt*, i. 255; *Grenville Papers*, i. 131; Phillimore, *Memoirs of Lyttleton*, 477–81.

40 Chatsworth MSS. 180.21–2, 25–7; 186.1; 330.27; 335.1; 33.28.

41 Ilchester, *Henry Fox*, i. 231–42; *Chatham Corr.*, i. 124–38; James Earl Waldegrave, *Memoirs from 1754 to 1758* (London, 1821), 33–4; Yorke, *Life of Hardwicke*, ii. 221–2.

Chapter 5: Pitt and Fox Rivals

1 Waldegrave, *Memoirs*, 24–5.

2 The Hon. George F. S. Elliot, *The Border Elliots and the Family of Minto* (Edinburgh, 1897), 337–41.

3 *Letters from George III to Lord Bute*, ed. Romney Sedgwick (London, 1939), xlv–xlviii.

4 *Correspondence of Thomas Gray*, ed. Paget Toynbee and Leonard Whibley (Oxford, 1971), No, 296.

5 Dodington, *Diary*, 295–302.

6 Romney Sedgwick, *Letters from William Pitt to Lord Bute: Essays Presented to Sir Lewis Namier*, ed. Richard Pares and A. J. P. Taylor (London, 1956), No. 1.

7 Williams, *Life of Pitt*, i. 163; Yorke, *Life of Hardwicke*, ii. 196, 228–9.

8 Sedgwick, *Letters from Pitt to Bute*, Nos 2–3.

9 Yorke, *Life of Hardwicke*, ii. 229–33.
10 *Bedford Corr.*, ii. 165–7.
11 Sedgwick, *Letters from Pitt to Bute*, No. 5.
12 *Grenville Papers*, i. 433–4.
13 Yorke, *Life of Hardwicke*, ii. 236–7; Dodington, *Diary*, 321–4.
14 Sedgwick, *Letters from Pitt to Bute*, No. 6.
15 Yorke, *Life of Hardwicke*, ii. 237–44.
16 Dodington, *Diary*, 324–7.
17 Sedgwick, *Letters from Pitt to Bute*, No. 7.
18 Yorke, *Life of Hardwicke*, ii. 249.
19 H.O.P. 1754–1790, i. 55, 653–4; ii. 366–7; *Bedford Corr.*, ii. 170–1; Yorke, *Life of Hardwicke*, ii. 252–3.
20 Alan Valentine, *Lord George Germain* (Oxford, 1962), 30; H.O.P. 1754–1790, iii. 390.
21 Namier and Brooke, *Charles Townshend*, 41–2.
22 Elliot, *The Border Elliots*, 352.
23 Williams, *Life of Pitt*, i. 270.
24 Williams, *Life of Pitt*, i. 276; Sedgwick, *Letters from Pitt to Bute*, No. 10.
25 Phillimore, *Memoirs of Lyttleton*, 489–91; H.O.P. 1754–1790, ii. 327–8, iii. 74–5; Williams, *Life of Pitt*, i. 272–3.
26 J. R. Western, *The English Militia in the Eighteenth Century* (London, 1965), 127–8.
27 H.O.P. 1754–1790, ii. 327, 601.
28 Williams, *Life of Pitt*, i. 273; H.O.P. 1754–1790, iii. 219.
29 Yorke, *Life of Hardwicke*, ii. 254.
30 Ruddock F. Mackay, *Admiral Hawke* (Oxford, 1965), 116; Yorke, *Life of Hardwicke*, ii. 268.
31 Parl. Hist. XV. 699–703.
32 Western, *The English Militia*, 128–33.
33 Yorke, *Life of Hardwicke*, ii. 289–90 and f.n. 1.
34 Sedgwick, *Letters from George III to Bute*, No. 3.
35 Yorke, *Life of Hardwicke*, ii. 317.
36 *Grenville Papers*, i. 172–3.
37 H.O.P. 1754–1790, ii. 463.
38 P.R.O. 30/8/53 ff. 46–54; Sedgwick, *Letters from Pitt to Bute*, No. 12.
39 H.O.P. 1754–1790, ii. 189.
40 Sedgwick, *Letters from Pitt to Bute*, Nos 14–15.
41 P.R.O. 30/8/53 ff. 55–6.
42 H.O.P. 1754–1790, ii. 463.

Chapter 6: The Pitt and Devonshire Ministry

1 Waldegrave, *Memoirs*, 23.
2 *Grenville Papers*, i. 177–8.
3 Yorke, *Life of Hardwicke*, ii. 276–7, 326–9.
4 Williams, *Life of Pitt*, i. 283–4; *Grenville Papers*, i. 178–9.
5 H.O.P. 1754–1790, iii. 267; Walpole, *Memoires of George II*, ii. 95–6.

6 Ilchester, *Henry Fox*, ii. 2–4.
7 Devonshire Diary; Chatsworth MSS. 260.257.
8 *Bedford Corr.*, ii. 206–9.
9 Elliot, *The Border Elliots*, 353.
10 *Bedford Corr.*, i. 205.
11 Ilchester, *Henry Fox*, ii. 6–7.
12 *Bedford Corr.*, i. 205.
13 Chatsworth MSS. 463.0–1.
14 Ilchester, *Henry Fox*, ii. 7–10; *Bedford Corr.*, ii. 209–11.
15 Williams, *Life of Pitt*, i. 291 and f.n. 6; H.O.P. 1754–1790, ii. 388.
16 Ilchester, *Henry Fox*, ii. 11–12; *Bedford Corr.*, ii. 209–11.
17 P.R.O. 30/8/53 ff. 59–60; *Grenville Papers*, i. 436–9.
18 Namier and Brooke, *Charles Townshend*, 45–6.
19 P.R.O. 30/8/53 ff. 59–60 P.S.
20 Namier, *England in the Age of the American Revolution*, 112.
21 Chatsworth MSS. 463.11, 13.
22 Yorke, *Life of Hardwicke*, ii. 338.
23 Chatsworth MSS. 463.3.
24 Yorke, *Life of Hardwicke*, ii. 373–4; Sedgwick, *Letters from Pitt to Bute*, No. 16.
25 Sedgwick, *Letters from Pitt to Bute*, Nos 16–17; *Grenville Papers*, i. 182–4.
26 H.O.P. 1754–1790, iii. 290.
27 Yorke, *Life of Hardwicke*, ii. 375–8.
28 Namier, *England in the Age of the American Revolution*, 113.
29 Chatsworth MSS. 463.7.
30 *Bedford Corr.*, ii. 222–7.
31 Sedgwick, *Letters from Pitt to Bute*, No. 18.
32 *Correspondence of William Pitt when Secretary of State with Colonial Governors and Naval Commissioners in America* ed. Gertrude Selwyn Kimball (London, 1906), i. 1–29. (Hence cited as Pitt, *North American Corr.*); Pargellis, *Loudoun in America*, 231–3.
33 Chatsworth MSS. 463.8–9, 12; Sedgwick, *Letters from Pitt to Bute*, Nos 19–20.
34 H.O.P. 1754–1790, ii. 7; Namier and Brooke, *Charles Townshend*, 49; Williams, *Life of Pitt*, i. 308–9; Yorke, *Life of Hardwicke*, Chapter XXIV.
35 Waldegrave, *Memoirs*, 94–6.
36 Devonshire Diary; Chatsworth MSS. 260.257; Namier, *England in the Age of the American Revolution*, 112; H.O.P. 1754–1790, i. 314; iii. 537.
37 Sedgwick, *Letters from George III to Bute*, No. 4; Sedgwick, *Letters from Pitt to Bute*, No. 22.
38 Waldegrave, *Memoirs*, 100–2; Ilchester, Henry Fox, i. 38–41; Namier and Brooke, *Charles Townshend*, 49–50; Devonshire Diary; Chatsworth MSS. 260.257.
39 *Grenville Papers*, i. 191–4; Sedgwick, *Letters from Pitt to Bute*, No. 23; Namier and Brooke, *Charles Townshend*, 50–1.
40 Lucy S. Sutherland, The City of London and the Devonshire and Pitt Administration. Proceedings of the British Academy 1960.

41 Western, *The English Militia*, 134–40.

42 Walpole, *Memoires of George II*, ii. 202.

43 H.O.P. 1754–1790, iii. 391; Sedgwick, *Letters from George III to Bute*, No. 6.

44 Devonshire Diary; Chatsworth MSS. 260.257.

45 Yorke, *Life of Hardwicke*, ii. 367; Chesterfield, *Letters*, No. 2008; Waldegrave, *Memoirs*, 110–11.

46 H.O.P. 1754–1790, iii. 30.

47 Waldegrave, *Memoirs*, 108–10; Devonshire Diary; Chatsworth MSS. 260.257.

48 Yorke, *Life of Hardwicke*, ii. 398–9; Devonshire Diary; Chatsworth MSS. 260.257; Waldegrave, *Memoirs*, 115–30.

Chapter 7: The Pitt and Newcastle Ministry: Klosterseven and Rochefort

1 *An Eighteenth-Century Correspondence* ed. Lillian Dickens and Mary Stanton (London, 1910), 367.

2 Yorke, *Life of Hardwicke*, ii. 402; *Chatham Corr.*, i. 227–30.

3 Sedgwick, *Letters from Pitt to Bute*, No. 32.

4 H.O.P. 1754–1790, iii. 391.

5 Yorke, *Life of Hardwicke*, ii. 371–2, 409–11; Campbell, *Lives of the Chancellors*, vi. 313–15; *Chatham Corr.*, i. 232–7.

6 H.O.P. 1754–1790, ii. 538.

7 R. Hist. MSS. Comm. *Townshend*, 393.

8 Sedgwick, *Letters from Pitt to Bute*, No. 33.

9 H.O.P. 1754–1790, i. 366–7; ii. 605; iii. 43, 290.

10 Yorke, *Life of Hardwicke*, iii. 116 f.n. 1.

11 Pitt, *North American Corr.*, i. 84–9.

12 Sedgwick, *Letters from Pitt to Bute*, No. 39.

13 Pitt, *North American Corr.*, i. 106–10.

14 Valentine, *Lord George Germain*, 38.

15 Sedgwick, *Letters from Pitt to Bute*, No. 38.

16 Sedgwick, *Letters from Pitt to Bute*, No. 39.

17 Yorke, *Life of Hardwicke*, iii. 123 f.n. 6.

18 Mackay, *Hawke*, 164.

19 Yorke, *Life of Hardwicke*, ii. 117–19.

20 Sedgwick, *Letters from Pitt to Bute*, Nos 41, 42.

21 *Bedford Corr.*, ii. 267–70; Yorke, *Life of Hardwicke*, iii. 37.

22 Pitt, *North American Corr.*, i. 110–11.

23 Sedgwick, *Letters from Pitt to Bute*, Nos 44, 45.

24 *Grenville Papers*, i. 213–14; Mackay, *Hawke*, 167–80.

25 *Bedford Corr.*, ii. 275–81.

26 Sedgwick, *Letters from Pitt to Bute*, No. 47; Rex Whitworth, *Field Marshal Ligonier* (Oxford, 1958), 225–8.

27 Yorke, *Life of Hardwicke*, iii. 38–40.

28 Sedgwick, *Letters from Pitt to Bute*, No. 49.

29 Pitt, *North American Corr.*, i. 133–55.

30 Sedgwick, *Letters from Pitt to Bute*, No. 57; Whitworth, *Ligonier*, 236–7, 241–2.
31 Pitt, *North American Corr.*, i. 160–7; P.R.O. 30/8/96 ff. 82–91.

Chapter 8: Pitt's War: 1758

1 William Makepeace Thackeray, *The Virginians*.
2 Pitt, *North American Corr.*, i. 157–60, 167–9, 171–2, 176, 180, 183–97.
3 P.R.O. 30/8/96 f. 11.
4 *Bedford Corr.*, ii. 285–303.
5 Yorke, *Life of Hardwicke*, iii. 1–6, 42–5.
6 Williams, *Life of Pitt*, ii. 355–6.
7 Yorke, *Life of Hardwicke*, iii. 6–20, 46–50.
8 Pitt, *North American Corr.*, i. 256, 271–5.
9 Pitt, *North American Corr.*, i. 281–4, 291–3, 302–7.
10 P.R.O. 30/8/96 ff. 96–100.
11 Pitt, *North American Corr.*, i. 297–302.
12 Pitt, *North American Corr.*, i. 294–7.
13 Lieut-General Sir Reginald Savory K.C.I.E., C.B., D.S.O., M.C., *His Britannic Majesty's Army in Germany during the Seven Years War* (Oxford, 1966), 73.
14 *Grenville Papers*, i. 248–9.
15 Pitt, *North American Corr.*, i. 266–9.
16 Valentine, *Lord George Germain*, 39–41.
17 Sedgwick, *Letters of Pitt to Bute*, No. 81; *Grenville Papers*, i. 244–6.
18 Sedgwick, *Letters of George III to Bute*, No. 14.
19 Valentine, *Lord George Germain*, 42–4.
20 Whitworth, *Ligonier*, 257.
21 Pitt, *North American Corr.*, i. 309.
22 Whitworth, *Ligonier*, 260–2.
23 Sedgwick, *Letters of Pitt to Bute*, Appendix II; *Grenville Papers*, i. 261–3; Williams, *Life of Pitt*, i. 371–8.
24 Sedgwick, *Letters of Pitt to Bute*, Appendix II.
25 Whitworth, *Ligonier*, 269–71.
26 Pitt, *North American Corr.*, i. 352–5, 370–5, 406–10.
27 Valentine, *Lord George Germain*, 44–6.
28 Pitt, *North American Corr.*, i. 367–70, 386–7, 411.
29 Pitt, *North American Corr.*, i. 432–42.
30 H.O.P. 1754–1790, iii. 551; Williams, *Life of Pitt*, i. 397.
31 H.O.P. 1754–1790, ii. 557.
32 Sedgwick, *Letters of George III to Bute*, Nos 23–4.
33 *Grenville Papers*, i. 267–8, 272–3.

Chapter 9: Pitt's War: Annus Mirabilis and the Death of the King

1 David Garrick.
2 Pitt, *North American Corr.*, ii. 3–18; P.R.O. 30/8/96 f. 11.

3 Pitt, *North American Corr.*, ii. 20–6, 45–50, 52–3.

4 Pitt, *North American Corr.*, ii. 37–8.

5 Pitt, *North American Corr.*, ii. 54–6, 59–68, 78–80.

6 Savory, *His Britannic Majesty's Army*, 125–39; Valentine, *Lord George Germain*, 48.

7 Julian S. Corbett, *England in the Seven Years War* (London, 1907), i. 413.

8 Pitt, *North American Corr.*, ii. 92–118, 120–9, 135–8.

9 *Grenville Papers*, i. 301, 307–8.

10 H.O.P. 1754–1790, iii. 311–12.

11 Pitt, *North American Corr.*, ii. 115–20.

12 *Grenville Papers*, i. 310–12.

13 Sedgwick, *Letters from George III to Bute*, Nos 34–5.

14 Savory, *His Britannic Majesty's Army*, Chapter VI.

15 Valentine, *Lord George Germain*, 49–56.

16 Valentine, *Lord George Germain*, 49–56; Sedgwick, *Letters from George III to Bute*, No. 37.

17 H.O.P. 1754–1790, iii. 392.

18 Pitt, *North American Corr.*, ii. 143–4, 172–3.

19 R. Hist. MSS. Comm. *Townshend*, 308–9.

20 Pitt, *North American Corr.*, ii. 149–58.

21 Christopher Hibbert, *Wolfe at Quebec* (London, 1959), 152.

22 R. Hist. MSS. Comm. *Townshend*, 322–6.

23 Namier, *England in the Age of the American Revolution*, 66.

24 Devonshire Diary; Chatsworth MSS. 260.260.

25 P.R.O. 30/8/17 ff. 108, 117; B.M. Add. MSS. Eg. 1955, f. 16.

26 Devonshire Diary; Chatsworth MSS. 260.261.

27 *Gray Corr.*, No. 306.

28 R. Hist. MSS. Comm. *Rutland*, ii. 202.

29 H.O.P. 1754–1790, ii. 557.

30 Mackay, *Hawke*, Chapter 14; Whitworth, *Ligonier*, 312.

31 B.M. Add. MSS. 32, 88, f. 151.

32 Namier, *England in the Age of the American Revolution*, 79, f.n. 1.

33 Devonshire Diary; Chatsworth MSS. 260.261.

34 Williams, *Life of Pitt*, ii. 78–82.

35 Namier, *England in the Age of the American Revolution*, 66.

36 B.M. Add. MSS. 32, 926, ff. 20, 265.

37 B.M. Add. MSS. 32, 928, ff. 146, 296.

38 Williams, *Life of Pitt*, ii. 179.

39 Pitt, *North American Corr.*, ii. 237–43, 247–52, 260–4.

40 Chatsworth MSS. 260.262, 263.265; Sedgwick, *Letters from George III to Bute*, No. 58; *Grenville Papers*, i. 338–40.

41 Valentine, *Lord George Germain*, 57–70; H.O.P. 1754–1790, iii. 391.

42 Sedgwick, *Letters from George III to Bute*, No. 55.

43 Sedgwick, *Letters from George III to Bute*, No. 57.

44 Elliot, *The Border Elliots*, 362–4.

45 R. Hist. MSS. Comm. *Rutland*, ii. 205–18.

46 Pitt, *North American Corr.*, ii. 287–97.

47 Pitt, *North American Corr.*, ii. 303–5.
48 *Grenville Papers*, i. 344–6.
49 Pitt, *North American Corr.*, ii. 305–9, 324–33.
50 Namier, *England in the Age of the American Revolution*, 116–17.
51 Mackay, *Hawke*, 266–7.
52 Sedgwick, *Letters from George III to Bute*, No. 60.
53 *Grenville Papers*, i. 355.
54 Mackay, *Hawke*, 268–70.
55 Pitt, *North American Corr.*, ii. 344–7.
56 Mackay, *Hawke*, 271–3.
57 Sedgwick, *Letters from George III to Bute*, Nos 61–2.

Chapter 10: The New Reign: Lord Bute the Favourite

1 Dodington, *Diary*, 407.
2 John Brooke, *King George III* (London, 1972), 73–6.
3 Elliot, *The Border Elliots*, 362–5.
4 Devonshire Diary; Chatsworth MSS. 260.277–8.
5 Devonshire Diary; Chatsworth MSS. 260.275, 283.
6 Namier, *England in the Age of the American Revolution*, 119.
7 Devonshire Diary; Chatsworth MSS. 260.276–8; H.O.P. 1754–1790, iii. 392.
8 Devonshire Diary; Chatsworth MSS. 260.281–3, 285.
9 Devonshire Diary; Chatsworth MSS. 260.285.
10 Sedgwick, *Letters from George III to Bute*, No. 67.
11 Devonshire Diary; Chatsworth MSS. 286.288–90.
12 *Bedford Corr.*, ii. 421–9.
13 Devonshire Diary; Chatsworth MSS. 260.273, 297–310.
14 Pitt, *North American Corr.*, ii. 367–70.
15 Devonshire Diary; Chatsworth MSS. 260.273, 297.
16 Pitt, *North American Corr.*, ii. 365–9, 384–7.
17 H.O.P. 1754–1790, ii. 56, 301, 328, 557, 675, iii. 31, 542.

Chapter 11: Pitt Resigns Office

1 P.R.O. 30/8/17 f. 174.
2 Pitt, *North American Corr.*, ii. 389–90, 407–8.
3 Devonshire Diary; Chatsworth MSS. 260.311.
4 Namier, *England in the Age of the American Revolution*, 273–82.
5 Devonshire Diary; Chatsworth MSS. 260.312, 314, 316; *Bedford Corr.*, iii. 6–8.
6 *Catham Corr.*, ii. 116–18; H.O.P. 1754–1790, iii. 468–9; *Bedford Corr.*, iii. 11–12.
7 Pitt, *North American Corr.*, ii. 425–6, 444–6.
8 *Bedford Corr.*, iii. 14–17.
9 Devonshire Diary; Chatsworth MSS. 260.325.

10 *Bedford Corr.*, iii. 21–9.
11 Devonshire Diary; Chatsworth MSS. 260.322; *Bedford Corr.*, iii. 21–9.
12 Devonshire Diary; Chatsworth MSS. 260.324.
13 Namier, *England in the Age of the American Revolution*, 284–8.
14 Pitt, *North American Corr.*, ii. 440–2, 454–5.
15 Williams, *Life of Pitt*, ii. 95.
16 B.M. Add. MSS. 6819 ff. 125–9, 142–6.
17 Namier, *England in the Age of the American Revolution*, 292; *Bedford Corr.*, iii. 35–6; *Grenville Papers*, i. 385.
18 *Gray Corr.*, No. 331.
19 P.R.O. 30/8/17 f. 174.
20 H.O.P. 1754–1790, ii. 675, iii. 56.
21 Devonshire Diary; Chatsworth MSS. 260.341.
22 Namier, *England in the Age of the American Revolution*, 293.
23 *Bedford Corr.*, iii. 43–6.
24 Devonshire Diary; Chatsworth MSS. 260.341; Namier, *England in the Age of the American Revolution*, 291–2.
25 Devonshire Diary; Chatsworth MSS. 260.344.
26 Sedgwick, *Letters from George III to Bute*, No. 87.
27 Devonshire Diary; Chatsworth MSS. 260.343; Pitt, *North American Corr.*, ii. 469.
28 Devonshire Diary; Chatsworth MSS. 260.343.
29 Corbett, *Seven Years War*, ii. 203.
30 *Grenville Papers*, i. 388–93.
31 Sedgwick, *Letters from George III to Bute*, No. 90.
32 Devonshire Diary; Chatsworth MSS. 260.347; Williams, *Life of Pitt*, ii. 111–14.
33 *Bedford Corr.*, iii. 46–7.
34 *Grenville Papers*, i. 388–90, 409–11.
35 Pitt, *North American Corr.*, ii. 475.
36 Elliot, *The Border Elliots*, 367–8.
37 P.R.O. 30/8/18 ff. 211–12.
38 Elliot, *The Border Elliots*, 366–7, 368–70.
39 *Chatham Corr.*, ii, 146–53.
40 Williams, *Life of Pitt*, ii.
41 Sedgwick, *Letters from George III to Bute*, No. 91; *Bedford Corr.*, iii. 48–50; *Grenville Papers*, i. 395–6.
42 Namier, *England in the Age of the American Revolution*, 295–7; *Grenville Papers*, i. 412–14.
43 *Bedford Corr.*, iii. 56–9.
44 Namier, *England in the Age of the American Revolution*, 305.

Chapter 12: The Peace of Paris

1 *Boswell's London Journal 1762–1763* ed. Frederick A. Pottle (London, 1950), 74–5.
2 Namier, *England in the Age of the American Revolution*, 306–7.

3 Devonshire Diary; Chatsworth MSS. 260.349.
4 *Bedford Corr.*, iii. 59–65.
5 Devonshire Diary; Chatsworth MSS. 260.355.
6 Namier, *England in the Age of the American Revolution*, 299–302.
7 Sedgwick, *Letters from George III to Bute*, No. 93.
8 Williams, *Life of Pitt*, ii.
9 Devonshire Diary; Chatsworth MSS. 260.355.
10 Namier and Brooke, *Charles Townshend*, 69–70.
11 H.O.P. 1754–1790, iii. 392.
12 Peter Brown, *The Chathamites* (Macmillan, 1967), 190–5.
13 Yorke, *Life of Hardwicke*, ii. 574, iii. 293, 366.
14 Corbett, *Seven Years War*, ii. 304.
15 Devonshire Diary; Chatsworth MSS. 260.358; Namier, *England in the Age of the American Revolution*, 309.
16 Corbett, *Seven Years War*, ii. 329–31, 333–8.
17 Devonshire Diary; Chatsworth MSS. 260.358; *Bedford Corr.*, iii. 72–4; Namier, *England in the Age of the American Revolution*, 310–11.
18 Devonshire Diary; Chatsworth MSS. 260.361; Namier, *England in the Age of the American Revolution*, 311–12.
19 P.R.O. 30/8/53 f. 3.
20 Devonshire Diary; Chatsworth MSS. 260.362.
21 B.M. Add. MSS. 1955, f. 23.
22 Devonshire Diary; Chatsworth MSS. 260.367, 370; Namier, *England in the Age of the American Revolution*, 313.
23 Devonshire Diary; Chatsworth MSS. 260.378; Namier, *England in the Age of the American Revolution*, 316–18; Sedgwick, *Letters from George III to Bute*, Nos 127, 129.
24 H.O.P. 1754–1790, i. 301.
25 *Bedford Corr.*, iii. 75–8; Namier, *England in the Age of the American Revolution*, 318–23; Sedgwick, *Letters from George III to Bute*, Nos 136–7, 142.
26 Namier, *England in the Age of the American Revolution*, 324–6.
27 *Bedford Corr.*, iii. 118–19.
28 Namier, *England in the Age of the American Revolution*, 326.
29 Ilchester, *Henry Fox*, ii. 187–99.
30 Sedgwick, *Letters from George III to Bute*, No. 180.
31 B.M. Add. MSS. 32, 945, ff. 1–2.
32 Sedgwick, *Letters from George III to Bute*, Nos 233–4.
33 Ilchester, *Henry Fox*, ii. 207–9.
34 Namier and Brooke, *Charles Townshend*, 81.
35 *Grenville Papers*, ii. 3–8.
36 Namier and Brooke, *Charles Townshend*, 82.
37 Parl. Hist. xii. 1259–73.
38 *Bedford Corr.*, iii. 169–71.
39 Namier and Brooke, *Charles Townshend*, 82.
40 Parl. Hist. xii. 1274.
41 *Grenville Papers*, ii. 21–2.
42 B.M. Add. MSS. 26, 889 ff. 19, 36, 67, 74–8.

43 Namier, *England in the Age of the American Revolution*, 404–5.
44 *Bedford Corr.*, iii. 185–8.
45 H.O.P. 1754–1790, iii. 554; Yorke, *Life of Hardwicke*, iii. 447–8.
46 Sedgwick, *Letters from George III to Bute*, No. 267.
47 Williams, *Life of Pitt*.
48 Yorke, *Life of Hardwicke*, iii. 455–6.
49 Kemp, *Sir Francis Dashwood*, 54–62.
50 Sedgwick, *Letters from George III to Bute*, Nos 276, 280–1, 284–6, 287, 289, 291; *Grenville Papers*, ii. 32–40; Fitzmaurice, *Life of Shelburne*, i. 169; Namier and Brooke, *Charles Townshend*, 93–8.
51 Chatsworth MSS. 463.32; Sedgwick, *Letters from George III to Bute*, No. 298; Yorke, *Life of Hardwicke*, iii. 385.

Chapter 13: Pitt and the Grenville Administration

1 D.N.B., xxiii. 116.
2 *Bedford Corr.*, iii. 227–30.
3 Sedgwick, *Letters from George III to Bute*, No. 327.
4 *Grenville Papers*, ii. 55.
5 Yorke, *Life of Hardwicke*, iii. 472–3, 495–509.
6 *Grenville Papers*, ii. 93.
7 *Bedford Corr.*, iii. 236–7; *Grenville Papers*, ii. 88–90.
8 *Chatham Corr.*, ii. 235–6; *Grenville Papers*, ii. 95–7; Chatsworth MSS. 463.63.
9 Elliot, *The Border Elliots*, 376–81; *Grenville Papers*, ii. 97–8, 101.
10 H.O.P. 1754–1790, ii. 173.
11 *Chatham Corr.*, ii. 241–3.
12 *The Autobiography of Augustus Henry Third Duke of Grafton K.G.* ed. Sir William R. Anson Bart., D.C.L. (London, 1897), 29–30.
13 *Chatham Corr.*, ii. 253–8.
14 *Bedford Corr.*, iii. 238–40.
15 Chatsworth MSS. 363.34–6; Yorke, *Life of Hardwicke*, iii. 474–7.
16 Parl. Hist. xv. 1371.
17 Fitzmaurice, *Life of Shelburne*, i. 59.
18 Chatsworth MSS. 436.39.
19 P.R.O. 30/8/17. ff. 179.
20 George Thomas, Earl of Albemarle, *Memoirs of the Marquis of Rockingham and his Circle* (London, 1852), i. 180–2.
21 *Grenville Papers*, ii. 6–7, 115–25.
22 Albemarle, *Memoirs of Rockingham*, i. 178–84.
23 Albemarle, *Memoirs of Rockingham*, i. 185–203.
24 *Grenville Papers*, iii. 170–1.
25 Albemarle, *Memoirs of Rockingham*, i. 204–11.
26 Sedgwick, *Letters from George III to Bute*, No. 336.
27 *Grenville Papers*, iii. 191.
28 Paul Langford, *The Rockingham Administration* (Oxford, 1973), 12.
29 Albemarle, *Memoirs of Rockingham*, i. 212–13.

30 *Grenville Papers*, iii. 194–7.
31 Langford, *Rockingham Administration*, 14.
32 *Grenville Papers*, iii. 197–202.
33 Albemarle, *Memoirs of Rockingham*, i. 213–14.
34 *The Correspondence of Edmund Burke Volume I April 1744–June 1768* ed. Thomas W. Copeland (Cambridge, 1958), 206–8.
35 *Grenville Papers*, iii. 202–4; Albemarle, *Memoirs of Rockingham*, i. 217.

Chapter 14: Pitt and the Rockingham Administration

1 D.N.B., lx. 50; Horace Walpole, *Memoirs of the Reign of King George the Third* ed. G. F. Russell Barker (London, 1894), ii. 129–30.
2 Langford, *Rockingham Administration*, 16–36.
3 *Grenville Papers*, iii. 211–16.
4 Langford, *Rockingham Administration*, 39.
5 *Burke Corr.*, i. 206–8.
6 Langford, *Rockingham Administration*, 48–50.
7 Fitzmaurice, *Life of Shelburne*, i. 233–4.
8 Langford, *Rockingham Administration*, 105.
9 H.O.P. 1754–1790, iii. 393; *Chatham Corr.*, ii. 353–61.
10 *Bedford Corr.*, iii. 323–4.
11 Langford, *Rockingham Administration*, 117.
12 Langford, *Rockingham Administration*, 125–31.
13 Albemarle, *Memoirs of Rockingham*, i. 264–7; The Hon. Sir John Fortescue LL.D., D.Litt., *The Correspondence of George the Third from 1760 to December 1783* (London, 1927), No. 180; Sedgwick, *Letters from George III to Bute*, No. 337.
14 *Chatham Corr.*, ii. 368.
15 Langford, *Rockingham Administration*, 139.
16 *Burke Corr.*, i. 231–3.
17 Williams, *Life of Pitt*, ii. 189–97.
18 Langford, *Rockingham Administration*, 143–4.
19 *The Letters of Samuel Johnson* ed. R. W. Chapman (Oxford, 1952), No. 182.
20 Langford, *Rockingham Administration*, 145–66.
21 *Burke Corr.*, i. 237.
22 *Chatham Corr.*, ii. 397–400.
23 *Burke Corr.*, i. 239–41.
24 Langford, *Rockingham Administration*, 232–4.
25 *Burke Corr.*, i. 244–5, 248–9.
26 Grafton, *Autobiography*, 73–4.
27 Sedgwick, *Letters from George III to Bute*, No. 338.
28 Langford, *Rockingham Administration*, 239–40.
29 *Chatham Corr.*, ii. 484–5.

Chapter 15: The Chatham Administration

1 *Gray Corr.*, No. 423.

2 *Chatham Corr.*, ii. 438.
3 R. J. White, *The Age of George III* (London, 1968), 115.
4 Sedgwick, *Letters from George III to Bute*, No. 339.
5 *Chatham Corr.*, iii. 12–13.
6 *Grenville Papers*, iii. 263–6.
7 *Chatham Corr.*, ii. 443–4.
8 *Grenville Papers*, iii. 267–8.
9 *Chatham Corr.*, ii. 448.
10 John Ehrman, *The Younger Pitt The Years of Acclaim* (London, 1969), 5.
11 *Grenville Papers*, iii. 267–8.
12 Grafton, *Autobiography*, 92.
13 Namier and Brooke, *Charles Townshend*, 147–54.
14 *Grenville Papers*, iii. 279–80, 289.
15 P.R.O. 30/8/18 f. 217.
16 Vincent Harlow, *The Founding of the Second British Empire 1763–1793* (London, 1952), i. 20–9.
17 *Chatham Corr.*, iii. 15–19, 29–32.
18 *Chatham Corr.*, iii. 121.
19 George, *English Caricature in the Eighteenth Century*, 138.
20 Langford, *Rockingham Administration*, 271.
21 P.R.O. 30/8/56 ff. 54–5.
22 Fitzmaurice, *Life of Shelburne*, i. 60.
23 H.O.P. 1754–1790, ii. 398.
24 Sedgwick, *Letters from George III to Bute*, Appendix I.
25 H.O.P. 1754–1790, iii. 104, 342–4; Whitworth, *Ligonier*, 386.
26 *Bedford Corr.*, iii. 342–4.
27 H.O.P. 1754–1790, iii. 405.
28 P.R.O. 30/8/56, ff. 52; H.O.P. 1754–90, iii. 305, 405.
29 *Chatham Corr.*, iii. 55–6.
30 H.O.P. 1754–1790, ii. 627, iii. 206.
31 Fitzmaurice, *Life of Shelburne*, i. 59.
32 Langford, *Rockingham Administration*, 265.
33 Namier and Brooke, *Charles Townshend*, 155.
34 Langford, *Rockingham Administration*, 268.
35 *Chatham Corr.*, iii. 67–71.
36 Langford, *Rockingham Administration*, 269.
37 Namier and Brooke, *Charles Townshend*, 156.
38 G.E.C. *Complete Peerage*, vii. 573–5, viii. 110–17, 143–4.
39 *Chatham Corr.*, iii. 93 f.n. 1.
40 *Bedford Corr.*, iii. 348–54.
41 *Chatham Corr.*, iii. 125 f.n. 1.
42 Albemarle, *Memoirs of Rockingham*, ii. 17–26.
43 H.O.P. 1754–1790, ii. 77.
44 Namier and Brooke, *Charles Townshend*, 104–7.
45 *Bedford Corr.*, iii. 355–60.
46 Namier and Brooke, *Charles Townshend*, 160–1.
47 *Chatham Corr.*, iii. 147–9.

48 Namier and Brooke, *Charles Townshend*, 161–3; *Chatham Corr.*, iii. 147–9.
49 John Brooke, *The Chatham Administration 1766–1768* (London, 1956), 87–92.
50 *Chatham Corr.*, iii. 182–90.
51 *Chatham Corr.*, iii. 181.
52 *Chatham Corr.*, iii. 192–200; Brooke, *Chatham Administration*, 93.
53 Brooke, *Chatham Administration*, 105–8.
54 *Chatham Corr.*, iii. 226–7.
55 Namier and Brooke, *Charles Townshend*, 167.
56 *Chatham Corr.*, iii. 232–5.
57 Namier and Brooke, *Charles Townshend*, 179–80.
58 P.R.O. 30/8/56, ff. 86–91.
59 *Chatham Corr.*, iii. 252–3.
60 Namier and Brooke, *Charles Townshend*, 174.
61 Walpole, *Memoirs of George III*, iii. 17.
62 Namier and Brooke, *Charles Townshend*, 178–9.
63 Lucy S. Sutherland, *The East India Company in Eighteenth-Century Politics* (Oxford, 1952), Chapter VI.
64 *Chatham Corr.*, iii. 255–68.
65 Grafton, *Autobiography*, 136–7.
66 *Chatham Corr.*, iii. 265–81.
67 *Chatham Corr.*, iii. 282–3.
68 Harlow, *Second British Empire*, i. 512–17.
69 Namier and Brooke, *Charles Townshend*, 184.
70 Grafton, *Autobiography*, 166–8.

Chapter 16: Chatham and the Whig Opposition

1 *Memorials and Correspondence of Charles James Fox*, ed. Lord John Russell (London, 1857) i. 60.
2 *Bedford Corr.*, iii. 399 f.n.; Grafton, *Autobiography*, 172–3, 183.
3 Brooke, *Chatham Administration*, 328–31.
4 H.O.P. 1754–1790, iii. 640; Steven Watson, *The Reign of George III* (Oxford, 1960), 100–1.
5 P.R.O. 30/8/18 f. 223.
6 Walpole, *Memoirs of George III*, iii. 168.
7 H.O.P. 1754–1790, ii. 77–8.
8 Brooke, *King George III*, 271.
9 *The Correspondence of Edmund Burke Volume II July 1768–June 1774* ed. Lucy S. Sutherland (Cambridge, 1960), 43–6.
10 P.R.O. 30/8/18 f. 227.
11 *Burke Corr.*, ii. 50–3.
12 *Burke Corr.*, ii. 55–6.
13 *Chatham Corr.*, iii. 368–74.
14 Williams, *Life of Pitt*, ii. 269.
15 Alison Olson, *The Radical Duke* (Oxford, 1961), 140–1.
16 H.O.P. 1754–1790, ii. 77–8.

17 Brown, *The Chathamites*, 62, 318, 488.
18 Brown, *The Chathamites*, 205–6.
19 *Chatham Corr.*, iv. 1–18.
20 Harlow, *Second British Empire*, i. 29–32.
21 P.R.O. 30/8/6, ff. 17–18.
22 P.R.O. 30/8/53, ff. 206–22; Brown, *The Chathamites*, 107, 141–7, 185, 329–30.

Chapter 17 : Chatham and America

1 Hazlitt, *Works*, vii. 302–3.
2 Fitzmaurice, *Life of Shelburne*, i. 455–60.
3 *Chatham Corr.*, iv. 334–48; Brown, *The Chathamites*, 77.
4 *Chatham Corr.*, iv. 351–3.
5 *The Correspondence of Edmund Burke Volume III July 1774–June 1778* ed. George H. Guttridge (Cambridge, 1961), 28–36.
6 *Chatham Corr.*, iv. 357–60, 366–8.
7 *Burke Corr.*, iii. 87–90.
8 *Burke Corr.*, iii. 90–3.
9 *Chatham Corr.*, iv. 369–80.
10 *Burke Corr.*, iii. 101–3.
11 *Chatham Corr.*, iv. 380–90.
12 *Chatham Corr.*, iv. 407–13.
13 Shute Barrington, Bishop of Durham, *The Political Life of William Wildman, Viscount Barrington* (London, 1814), 140–50, 161–72.
14 *Chatham Corr.*, iv. 423–4.
15 *Chatham Corr.*, iv. 432; *Burke Corr.*, iii. 342–3.
16 *Chatham Corr.*, iv. 432–7.
17 *Chatham Corr.*, iv. 410–19.
18 *Chatham Corr.*, iv. 460–83.
19 Keith Feiling, *The Second Tory Party* (Oxford, 1938), 129–31.
20 Fortescue, *Letters of George III*, No. 2221.
21 *Chatham Corr.*, iv. 513–18.
22 *Chatham Corr.*, iv. 518–23.
23 *Burke Corr.*, iii. 427.

BIBLIOGRAPHY

Adolphus, John, *The History of England from the Accession of George III* (London, 1840).

Albemarle, George Thomas, Earl of, *Memoirs of the Marquis of Rockingham and his contemporaries* (London, 1852).

Alden, John Richard, *The American Revolution 1775–1783* (1954).

Almon, John, *The History of the Late Minority* (London, 1766).

A Review of Mr. Pitt's Administration (5th edn London, 1766).

Life of John Wilkes (London, 1805).

Anecdotes of the Life of the Rt. Hon. William Pitt, Earl of Chatham (London, 1810).

Ashton, T. S., *An Economic History of England: The 18th Century* (London, 1859).

Barrington, Shute, Bishop of Durham, *The Political Life of William Wildman, Viscount Barrington* (London, 1814).

Bedford, *The Correspondence of John, Fourth Duke of* ed. Lord John Russell (London, 1842).

Belsham, W., *Memoirs of the Reign of George III to the Session of Parliament ending A.D. 1792* (London, 1795).

Bleakley, Horace, *The Life of John Wilkes* (London, 1917).

Boswell, James, *Life of Johnson*, ed. G. B. Hill and L. F. Powell (Oxford, 1934).

Boswell's London Journal 1762–1763, ed. Frederick A. Pottle (London, 1950).

Boswell's Journal of a Tour to the Hebrides with Samuel Johnson LL.D., ed. Frederick A. Pottle and Clarke R. Bennett (London, 1963).

Brooke, John, *The Chatham Administration* (London, 1956). *The Reign of George III* (London, 1972).

Brougham and Vaux, Henry, Lord, *Historical Sketches of Statesmen who flourished in the Reign of George III* (London, 1839).

Brown, Peter, *The Chathamites* (London, 1967).

Burke, Edmund, *The Correspondence of*, ed. Earl Fitzwilliam and Sir F. Bourke, K.C.B. (London, 1844).

The Works of (Bohn's Standard Library, 1893).

The Correspondence of: vol. i April 1744–June 1768 ed. Thomas W. Copeland; vol. ii July 1768–June 1774 ed. Lucy S. Sutherland; vol. iii July 1774–June 1778 ed. George H. Guttridge.

Campbell, John, Lord, *Lives of the Lord Chancellors and Keepers of the Great Seal of England* (London, 1857).

Cartwright, F. D., *The Life and Correspondence of Major Cartwright* (London, 1826).

Chatham, *The Correspondence of William Pitt, Earl of*, ed. the executors of his son, John, Earl of Chatham (London, 1838).

Chesterfield, Lord, *Letters of*, ed. Bonamy Dobrée (London, 1932).

Christie, I. R., *Myth and Reality in Late Eighteenth-Century Politics* (London, 1970).

Cobban, Alfred, *Edmund Burke and the Revolt against the Eighteenth Century* (London, 1960).

Corbett, Julian S., *England in the Seven Years War* (London, 1907).

Costin, W. C. and Watson, J. Steven, *The Law and Working of the Constitution: documents 1660 to 1914* (London, 1961).

Coxe, Archdeacon W., *Memoirs of the Life and Administration of Sir Robert Walpole* (London, 1798).

Memoirs of the Administration of the Right Honourable Henry Pelham (London, 1829).

Dictionary of National Biography.

Dickinson, H. T., *Bolingbroke* (London, 1970).

Robert Walpole and the Whig Supremacy (London, 1973).

Dickson, P. G. M., *The Financial Revolution in England* (London, 1967).

Dodington, George Bubb, *The Political Journal of*, ed. John Carsell and Lewis Arnold Dralle (Oxford, 1965).

Donogue, Bernard, *British Politics and the American Revolution* (London, 1964).

Ehrman, John, *The Younger Pitt the Years of Acclaim* (London, 1969).

Elliot, The Hon. George F. S., *The Border Elliots and the Family of Minto* (Edinburgh, 1897).

Encyclopaedia Brittanica.

English Historical Documents 1714–1783 ed. D. B. Horn and Mary Ransome (Oxford, 1957).

Feiling, Keith, *The Second Tory Party 1714–1832* (Oxford, 1932).

Feiling, Sir Keith, *Essays in British History presented to*, ed. H. R. Trevor-Roper (London, 1964).

Fitzmaurice, Lord Edmond, *The Life of William Petty, Earl of Shelburne, afterwards Marquess of Lansdowne* (London, 1912).

Foord, Archibald S., *His Majesty's Opposition 1714–1830* (Oxford, 1964).

Fortescue, The Hon. Sir John, *The Correspondence of George III from 1760 to December 1783* (London, 1927).

George, M. Dorothy, *English Political Caricature to 1792* (Oxford, 1959).

Grafton, Augustus Henry, K.G., 3rd Duke of, *The Autobiographical and Political Correspondence of*, ed. Sir William R. Anson, Bart (London, 1892).

Gray, Thomas, *The Correspondence of*, ed. Paget Toynbee and Leonard Whibley (Oxford, 1971).

Grenville Papers, ed. William James Smith (London, 1852).

Guttridge, G. H., *English Whiggism and the American Revolution* (Berkeley, 1963).

Harlow, Vincent T., *The Founding of the Second British Empire 1763–1793*, vols. i and ii (Oxford, 1952 and 1964).

Hazlitt, W., *Complete Works*, ed. P. P. Howe (London, 1930).

Hervey, Lord, *Memoirs*, ed. Romney Sedgwick (London, 1952).

Hibbert, Christopher, *Wolfe at Quebec* (London, 1959).

Hollis, T., *Memoirs* (London, 1780).

Holmes, Geoffrey, *Politics in the Reign of Queen Anne* (London, 1967).

Horn, D. B., *The British Diplomatic Service 1689–1789* (Oxford, 1961).

Ilchester, The Earl of, *Henry Fox First Lord Holland* (London, 1920).

Jennings, Sir Ivor, and Young, C. M., *Constitutional Laws of the British Commonwealth* (Oxford, 1952).

Johnson, Samuel, *The Letters of Samuel Johnson*, ed. R. W. Chapman (Oxford, 1952).

Johnstone, Edith M., *Great Britain and Ireland 1760–1800* (St Andrews, 1963).

Junius, *The Letters of*, ed. C. W. Everett (London, 1927).

Kemp, Betty, *King and Commons 1660–1832* (London, 1959).

    Sir Francis Dashwood (London, 1967).

Kimball, Gertrude Selwyn, ed. *Correspondence of William Pitt when Secretary of State with Colonial Governors and Naval Commissioners in America* (New York, 1900).

Knollenberg, Bernhard, *Origin of the American Revolution: 1759–1766* (New York, 1960).

Langford, Paul, *The Rockingham Administration* (Oxford, 1973).

Lincoln, Anthony, *Some Political and Social Ideas of Dissent 1763–1800* (Cambridge, 1938).

Maccoby, S., *English Radicalism 1763–1786* (London, 1939).

Mackay, Ruddock F., *Admiral Hawke* (Oxford, 1965).

Mackesy, Piers, *The War for America 1775–1783* (London, 1964).

Mahon, H. T., *The Influence of Sea Power upon History 1660–1783* (London, 1889).

Marchmont Papers, ed. Sir G. H. Rose (London, 1831).

Miller, John C., *Origins of the American Revolution* (London, 1945).

Miller, Sanderson, *An Eighteenth-Century Correspondence* ed. L. Dickens and M. Stanton (London, 1910).

Namier, Lewis, *The Structure of Politics at the Accession of George III* (London, 1939).

    England in the Age of the American Revolution (London, 1962).

    Essays presented to, ed. Richard Pares and A. J. P. Taylor (London, 1956).

Namier, Sir Lewis, and Brooke, John, *The History of Parliament. The House of Commons 1754–1790*, 3 vols (London, 1964).

    Charles Townshend (London, 1964).

Nevins, Allan, *The American States during and after the Revolution 1775–1789* (New York, 1927).

Olson, Alison, *The Radical Duke, The Career and Correspondence of Charles Lennox, third Duke of Richmond* (Oxford, 1961).

Owen, John B., *The Rise of the Pelhams* (London, 1957).

Palmer, R. R., *The Age of the Democratic Revolution* (Princeton and Oxford, 1959).

Pares, Richard, *King George III and the Politicians* (Oxford, 1953).

Pargellis, Stanley McRory, *Lord Loudoun in North America* (Yale, 1933).

Pargellis, Stanley, and Medley, D. J. (eds.) *Bibliography of British History 1714–1789* (Oxford, 1951).

Plumb, J. H., *Sir Robert Walpole* (London, 1956 and 1960). *Chatham* (London, 1953).

Pope, Alexander, *The Correspondence of*, ed. George Sherburn (Oxford, 1956).

Postgate, Raymond, *That Devil Wilkes* (London, 1956).

Riker, T. W., *Henry Fox, First Lord Holland* (Oxford, 1911).

Ritcheson, Charles R., *British Politics and the American Revolution* (Oklahoma, 1954).

Roberts, M., *Splendid Isolation* (Reading, 1969).

Rosebery, Lord, Chatham, His Early Life and Connections (London, 1910).

Rudé, George, *Wilkes and Liberty* (Oxford, 1962).

Ruville, A. von, *William Pitt, Earl of Chatham*, tr. H. J. Chaytor (London, 1907).

Savory, Lieut-General Sir Reginald, K.C.I.E., C.B., D.S.O., M.C., *His Britannic Majesty's Army in Germany during the Seven Years War* (Oxford, 1956).

Sedgwick, Romney, *Letters from George III to Lord Bute* (London, 1939).
  The History of Parliament The House of Commons 1715–1754 (London, 1970).

Sherrard, O. A., *A Life of John Wilkes* (London, 1930).
  Lord Chatham, 3 vols. (London, 1952–8).

Shipley, The Rt Rev. Jonathan, Lord Bishop of St Asaph, *The Works of* (London, 1792).

Stromberg, Ronald N., *Religious Liberalism in Eighteenth-Century England* (Oxford, 1954).

Sutherland, Lucy S., *The East India Company in Eighteenth-Century England* (Oxford, 1952).

Sykes, Rev. Norman, *Church and State in England in the XVIIIth Century* (Cambridge, 1934).

Thomas, Roland, *Richard Price, Philosopher and Apostle of Liberty* (Oxford, 1924).

Tunstall, Brian, *William Pitt, Earl of Chatham* (London, 1938).

Valentine, Alan, *Lord George Germain* (Oxford, 1962).

Veitch, G. S., *The Genesis of Parliamentary Reform* (London, 1923).

Waddington, Richard, *La Guerre de Sept Ans*, 4 vols (Paris, 1899).
  Louis XV et Le Renversement des Alliances (Paris, 1896).

Waldegrave, James, Earl, *Memoirs 1754–1758* (London, 1821).

Walpole, Horace, *Memoires of the last ten years of the Reign of George The Second*, 2 vols (London, 1822).
  Memoirs of the Reign of George III, ed. G. F. Russell Barker (London, 1894).
  The Last Memoirs of Horace Walpole during the Reign of George III, ed. D. Doran and A. F. Stewart (London, 1910).
  The Correspondence of, ed. W. S. Lewis (Oxford and Yale, 1937–).

Watson, J. Steven, *The Reign of George III, 1760–1820* (Oxford, 1960).

Western, J. R., *The English Militia in the Eighteenth Century* (London, 1965).

White, R. J., *The Age of George III* (London, 1968).

Whitworth, Rex, *Field Marshal Ligonier* (Oxford, 1958).

Wilkes, John W., *A Whig in Power, a Biography of Henry Pelham* (Northeastern University Press, 1964).

Williams, Basil, *The Life of William Pitt, Earl of Chatham* (London, 1915).

Winstanley, D. A., *Lord Chatham and the Whig Opposition* (London, 1966).

Yorke, Philip C., *The Life and Correspondence of Philip Yorke, Earl of Hardwicke* (Cambridge, 1913).

INDEX

Abercrombie, James, Agent for Virginia 139

Abercromby, General James, C-in-C. N. America 161, 164–6; defeat at Ticonderoga 170–2, 176; superseded 178, 182, 403

Abreu, Count d' 200–3

Aché, Admiral Count d' 144, 152, 166, 177, 206, 224, 262

Addington, Dr Anthony 345, 350, 371, 384

Aiguillon, Duchess of 202

Aix-la-Chapelle, Peace of 84

Albemarle, 3rd Earl of 178; capture of Havana 262, 268; 286, 289, 295, 302, 331

Algarotti, Francis Count d', relations with Pitt 276

Allen, Ralph, relations with Pitt 45, 135, 181

Almon, John 362

Amelia, Princess 213, 296, 326

Amherst, General Jefferey, 1st Baron: Louisbourg campaign 162, 165, 170, 172, 177, 179, 181; C-in-C. N. America 180–2, 184–5, 187, 193, 197, 202–3, 207–9, 211, 224, 229, 235, 248, 386, 403; relations with Pitt 174, 231, 240, 293, 403

Amherst, Captain William 176

Anhalt-Zerbst, Princess of 199

Anne, Queen of Great Britain 255, 396–7

Anson, Admiral George, 1st Baron: circumnavigation 48, 173, 245, 268, 330, 396; Battle of Cape Finisterre 81; First Lord of the Admiralty 87, 120–2, 132, 149, 154–5, 210–12, 218, 245–6; capture of Havana 260, 268–9; 81, 84, 141, 403; death 169

Argyll, 2nd Duke of 51, 57

Argyll, 3rd Duke of 240

Asiento 17, 19

Augusta, Princess of Saxe-Gotha, see Wales, Princess of

Baker, Sir William 233, 304

Barré, Colonel Isaac: at Quebec 180, 195; bearer of Amherst's despatches to Pitt 209, 211, 258; attacks Pitt in House of Commons 258–9; supporter of Pitt 288, 290, 292–. 307, 318, 362–3, 367, 372, 387–8, 393

Barrington, General John 178, 184, 187

Barrington, 2nd Viscount 75–6; Secretary at War 116, 134, 138, 140, 149, 178, 355, 383; Chancellor of the Exchequer 230, 265; Treasurer of the Navy 266; relations with Pitt 249, 274, 329, 355, 357, 403

Bath 45, 66–7, 81, 90–1, 93, 98, 178, 309, 312, 336, 338–9, 341; Pitt, Freeman of 45; Pitt, M.P. for 151, 188, 410

Bath, 1st Earl of, see Pulteney

Bauffrémont, Admiral Chevalier de 143, 152

Beauchamp, Viscount 337

Beauséjour, capture of 115

Beckford, Alderman William 133, 168, 181, 197, 250, 253, 272, 275, 311; East India Company enquiry 338–9, 341–4; Lord Mayor 357, 360–1; relations with Pitt 133, 286–7, 360; death 361

Bedford, Gertrude, Duchess of 131, 311, 326

Bedford, 4th Duke of 51, 57, 90, 117, 188, 326, 359; First Lord of the Admiralty 68, 72–3, 75, 77, 80–1, 245; Secretary of State 84–6; opposition to Pelham and Newcastle 89–90, 111–13, 115–16; Lord Lieutenant of Ireland 133, 140, 149, 167, 222–3; Cabinet councillor 234–7, 241–2, 245, 251–3, 256; Lord Privy Seal